Accounting and Finance for Managers

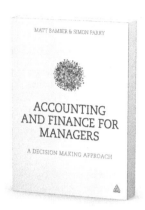

Accounting and Finance for Managers

Matt Bamber and
Simon Parry

KoganPage

LONDON   PHILADELPHIA   NEW DELHI

First published in Great Britain and the United States in 2014 by Kogan Page Limited

2nd Floor, 45 Gee Street	1518 Walnut Street, Suite 1100	4737/23 Ansari Road
London EC1V 3RS	Philadelphia PA 19102	Daryaganj
United Kingdom	USA	New Delhi 110002
www.koganpage.com		India

© Matt Bamber and Simon Parry, 2014

ISBN   978 0 7494 6913 9
E-ISBN   978 0 7494 6914 6

British Library Cataloguing-in-Publication Data

A CIP record for this book is available from the British Library.

CIP data is available.
Library of Congress Control Number: 2014004436

Typeset by Graphicraft Limited, Hong Kong
Print production managed by Jellyfish
Printed and bound by CPI Group (UK) Ltd, Croydon CR0 4YY

CONTENTS

Introduction 1

01 Introduction to accounting 5

Objective 5
Learning outcomes 5
Key topics covered 5
Management issues 6
Introduction 6
Who and what is an accountant? 7
The two forms of accounting: financial accounting and management
    accounting 11
The financial accountant 12
Who are the users of financial accounting information? 15
The regulatory and conceptual framework 16
The qualitative characteristics of useful financial information 17
The regulatory framework 20
The standard-setting process 23
Types of business entity 23
The annual report and financial statements 26
The elements of financial statements 28
The articulation of the financial statements 37
A brief guide to some key problems and issues with financial statements 37
Comprehension questions 38
Exercises 39
Answers to comprehension questions 41
Answers to exercises 44

02 Accounting concepts and systems 50

Objective 50
Learning outcomes 50
Key topics covered 50
Management issues 51
Introduction 51
What is the purpose of the financial statements? 51
Statement of comprehensive income (income statement) 51
The statement of financial position (balance sheet) 54
The statement of cash flows 55

Preparing a set of financial statements   57
The income statement: cost of sales working   62
Underlying concepts: measurement rules and fundamental accounting concepts   65
Three further property, plant and equipment issues   76
Recording accounting information   79
Comprehension questions   85
Exercises   85
Answers to comprehension questions   89
Answers to exercises   90

03   Financial analysis: Part I   96

Objective   96
Learning outcomes   96
Key topics covered   96
Management issues   97
Introduction   97
Financial statement analysis for investment purposes   98
Other users and their needs   99
Horizontal analysis and trend analysis   101
Vertical analysis   104
Ratio analysis   107
Key ratios   108
Weaknesses and limitations   145
Conclusion   146
Comprehension questions   147
Exercises   148
Answers to comprehension questions   151
Answers to exercises   154

04   Financial analysis: Part II   159

Objective   159
Learning outcomes   159
Key topics covered   159
Management issues   160
Introduction   160
The drive for information   161
Stakeholder management   162
Corporate social responsibility reporting   165
Earnings announcements, conference calls and investor presentations   166
Media relations: press releases and newspaper coverage   167
Social media and internet bulletins   170
Conclusion   171
Comprehension questions   171
Answers to comprehension questions   172

05   Business planning 175

Objective 175
Learning outcomes 175
Key topics covered 175
Management issues 175
Introduction 176
Why budget? 176
Business planning and control: the role of budgets 176
The budget-setting process 178
Practical budget-setting 180
The basic steps of preparing a budget 185
Budgeting in different types of organization 192
Limitations and problems with budgeting 194
Improving business planning and budgeting 198
Conclusion 201
Comprehension questions 201
Exercises 202
Answers to comprehension questions 203
Answers to exercises 205

06   Budgets and performance management 209

Objective 209
Learning outcomes 209
Key topics covered 209
Management issues 210
Introduction 210
Responsibility centres 211
The controllability principle 212
Profit-related performance measurement 212
Standard costing 216
Standard costing and variance analysis 218
Variance analysis 220
Performance management in investment centres 224
Which is the best measure: ROI or EVA? 226
Non-financial performance indicators 226
The balanced scorecard 227
Performance measurement in not-for-profit organizations 230
Value for money (VFM) as a public-sector objective 232
NPO performance measurement: an example 232
Behavioural aspects of performance management: gaming and creative
    accounting 235
External influences on performance 236
Performance management in modern business systems 237
Conclusion 239
Comprehension questions 239

Exercises 239
Answers to comprehension questions 242
Answers to exercises 244

07   Cash flow 247

Objective 247
Learning outcomes 247
Key topics covered 247
Management issues 247
Introduction 248
Why does a business need cash? 248
What is cash flow? 248
How much cash does a business need? 250
Methods of establishing cash balances 254
Cash forecasting: the cash budget 259
Cash management: strategies for improving cash flow 263
Interpreting and analysing a cash-flow forecast 279
Conclusion 284
Comprehension questions 284
Exercises 285
Answers to comprehension questions 286
Answers to exercises 288

08   Pricing decisions 292

Objective 292
Learning outcomes 292
Key topics covered 292
Management issues 292
Introduction 293
The accountant's perspective – costing and pricing 294
Absorption costing and full-cost-plus pricing 294
Problems with full-cost-plus pricing 298
Marginal-cost-plus pricing 299
Activity-based costing (ABC) pricing 300
Life-cycle costing and pricing 302
Conclusions: costing for pricing 304
The economist's perspective 304
The marketer's perspective 311
Combining the three perspectives: establishing an appropriate pricing
    strategy 314
Pricing strategies 315
Target pricing and target costing 320
Value engineering 321
Kaizen 321

Conclusion   321
Comprehension questions   322
Exercises   322
Answers to comprehension questions   323
Answers to exercises   325

09   Investment decisions   327

Objective   327
Learning outcomes   327
Key topics covered   328
Management issues   328
Introduction   328
Investment appraisal – the basics   329
Traditional evaluation techniques   330
Incorporating real-world complexities into investment appraisal   346
Investment appraisal within context   356
Taking a broader strategic view   361
Conclusion   362
Comprehension questions   363
Exercises   363
Answers to comprehension questions   366
Answers to exercises   368

10   Operational decisions   373

Objective   373
Learning outcomes   373
Key topics covered   373
Management issues   373
Introduction   374
Operational decision making   374
Cost–volume–profit analysis (CVP)   375
Relevant costing   388
Conclusion   400
Comprehension questions   401
Exercises   401
Answers to comprehension questions   403
Answers to exercises   405

Appendix A   An introduction to double-entry bookkeeping   409
*Appendix B   International Accounting/Financial Reporting Standards
                (as at 02.04.2013)*   429
Appendix C   Example earnings announcements   432
Appendix D   Discount tables   463
Appendix E   Annuity factors   465

References   467

Index   471

Introduction

In this book we hope to show you that, despite some imperfections and limitations, accounting information can help you make better-informed decisions as individuals and as managers. Though we talk about accountants and accounting, we hope that you will begin to understand and appreciate that this group of people do not produce all the accounting information. More importantly, the information they produce needs to be interpreted at an operational, tactical and strategic level by employees from across the organization regardless of background. You might think that certain professions are naturally exempted from the push and pull of accounting, but this is not true. Just ask any marketing director, for example, how he or she feels about this year's budget, or sales team managers what they think of their 'on-target earnings' bonus!

Despite the broad reach of the subject matter, accounting and finance as a discipline is often viewed with unease as students commonly have a pre-existing belief that it requires a strong grounding in mathematics, that it comprises a set of impossibly convoluted and complicated rules, or that it is simply boring! But these presuppositions are unfounded and ultimately untrue. What *is* true is that much of accounting and finance is a 'building-block' exercise ie one issue sets the foundation upon which the next can be built. Therefore, we have provided exercises throughout the text. Some of these are follow-my-lead 'worked-through exercises', while others give you the opportunity to practise for yourselves. We urge you to attempt these. They provide an opportunity to reflect on what you've learnt and question the underlying purpose of the process and/or result. We have also given a number of real-life examples and illustrations to help you get a better grasp of the material. We try to take you beyond the mechanics of generating 'an answer' and towards an understanding of why that 'answer' might be important.

To make the book as accessible as possible we have divided it into two broad sections: financial accounting (Chapters 1 to 4); and management accounting (Chapters 5 to 10). These are the two major sub-disciplines of accounting and finance in professional and academic life. The chapters vary quite considerably in length and to a certain degree this can be interpreted as a reflection of our view of their relative importance to a subject novice. Throughout each topic, the following advice pervades: the more you put in, the more you will get out. Only the tip of the iceberg is revealed during each chapter and therefore we urge you to pursue other sources as far and as wide as you can. That might be in the form of media releases, academic and trade journals, discussion forums, and so forth. The deeper you engage, the more you will understand and the greater the likelihood that you will ultimately be able to make better-informed decisions.

You might already be familiar with some of the more common terms such as 'annual report', 'financial statements', 'accountant' and 'auditor', but you might not know what they mean. That is fine. The financial accounting section expands on these and other related topics. The management accounting section introduces some practical and useful tools, methods and techniques to help you deliver solutions and suggestions to some major business problems.

The financial accounting section presents some common business vehicles, ie sole traders, partnerships, limited liability companies and public limited companies. The advantages and disadvantages of each are subsequently explained and explored. Though the first few chapters focus on *corporate* reporting practices (as it is simpler to extrapolate these to simpler forms of accounting than the other way round), much of the information and advice provided within both the financial accounting and management accounting chapters can also be mapped to other organizations, including those within the not-for-profit sector.

How to approach the content

Our objective has been to include key (or core) information in the body of the text. Alongside this, we have also included a number of examples and exercises. If you follow the primary exercise on the first run through, that is excellent and you might like to simply move on. Many, however, won't and if you fall into this camp there is no harm in following it through in more detail in your own time. We have also provided some supporting examples which run alongside the main text. These secondary and supplementary examples are different enough to stop even the most advanced students from becoming bored. It has always seemed strange to us that accounting and finance are portrayed as subjects which are passively learnt, on a surface level, facilitated by a teacher-led approach. We do not concur. You should see these examples the same way as you might learn to catch a ball, take a penalty, undertake an experiment, choose the right chemical etc. The examples help you to grow in experience and guide your future decision-making behaviour. Indeed, we have an advantage over other academic disciplines as our examples are interesting because they are real! You can see them in your everyday life, often panning out before your eyes. Once you begin to understand the subject, you will never see the world in the same way again.

We have also included notes which we have called '*expert view*'. The idea behind these is to encourage you to think more broadly and present you with further issues and questions that you could consider pursuing. Though these are non-essential, they bridge the gap between this introductory text and other, more advanced syllabuses. Solutions in accounting are not binary as many uninitiated believe. There is plenty of scope for discretion in practice and behaviour (normally legal but occasionally illegal!). Even at this first step into the discipline, we hope to show you some interesting arguments, conflicting viewpoints and how they (have) arise(n).

A note on terminology

We feel it is worth making clear at this early stage that this is a textbook designed for an international audience. Throughout, therefore, we have adopted International Financial Reporting Standards (IFRS) terminology. Occasionally we have referenced the relevant document produced by the International Accounting Standards Board (IASB), eg an International Financial Reporting Standard (IFRS), an International Accounting Standard (IAS) or the Conceptual Framework (F). Though we don't recommend *beginners* to pursue these references, there are some who might want to.

If you are interested, a site which is well worth a visit and which we strongly recommend is IASplus.com. This site is maintained by one of the *Big Four*[1] accounting firms – Deloitte. It is generally recognized as the go-to site for international financial reporting updates.

Proposed course outline

We fully expect lecturers who adopt this text to adopt different approaches to the content and the method of delivery. The book is designed to aid a standard 'lecture series followed by tutorial' approach, but the material and exercises have also been trialled in workshops and smaller seminar groups and found suitable for all sizes and formats.

University course lengths differ by institution and jurisdiction. Some standard course outlines are provided below.

Twenty-hour course (10 weeks * 2-hour lectures)

Week 1	Chapter 1
Week 2	Chapter 2
Week 3	Chapter 3
Week 4	Chapter 4
Week 5	Chapter 5
Week 6	Chapter 6
Week 7	Chapter 7
Week 8	Chapter 8
Week 9	Chapter 9
Week 10	Chapter 10

Sixteen-hour course (8 weeks * 2-hour lectures)

Week 1	Chapter 1
Week 2	Chapter 2
Week 3	Chapter 3
Week 4	Chapter 4
Week 5	Chapters 5 & 10
Week 6	Chapters 6 & 7
Week 7	Chapter 8
Week 8	Chapter 9

*Twenty-four-hour course (24 weeks * 1 hour lecture; or 12 * 2-hour lectures)*

Week 1	Chapter 1
Week 2	Chapter 1
Week 3	Chapter 2
Week 4	Chapter 2
Week 5	Subsidiary bookkeeping appendix
Week 6	Subsidiary bookkeeping appendix
Week 7	Chapter 3
Week 8	Chapter 3
Week 9	Chapter 4
Week 10	Chapter 4
Week 11	Chapter 5
Week 12	Chapter 5
Week 13	Chapter 6
Week 14	Chapter 6
Week 15	Chapter 7
Week 16	Chapter 7
Week 17	Chapter 7
Week 18	Chapter 8
Week 19	Chapter 8
Week 20	Chapter 9
Week 21	Chapter 9
Week 22	Chapter 9
Week 23	Chapter 10
Week 24	Chapter 10

Note

1 Deloitte, PricewaterhouseCoopers, Ernst & Young (EY), KPMG.

Introduction to accounting

OBJECTIVE

To provide an overview of the conceptual and regulatory framework that underpins financial accounting and an understanding of the content and structure of the financial statements.

LEARNING OUTCOMES

After studying this chapter, the reader will be able to:

- Discuss the role of the financial accountant and the information which they prepare.
- Describe the relationship between the statement of financial position, income statement and statement of cash flows.
- Understand the elements and structure of the annual report and primary financial statements.
- Describe the conceptual and regulatory framework of accounting.
- Evaluate what information the financial statements cannot provide.

KEY TOPICS COVERED

- Why do businesses need financial accountants and financial statements?
- The type of information financial accounts record.
- The concepts of assets and liabilities, income and expenditure.
- Introduction to the three primary financial statements: the statement of financial position, income statement and the statement of cash flows.
- Introduction to the accounting regulatory system and the way it has shaped the informational content of financial statements.
- Discussion of some key problems and issues with financial statements.

MANAGEMENT ISSUES

Managers need the skills to be able to 'read' rather than prepare financial statements. Equally importantly, they need an understanding of what financial statements can and cannot tell them about a business.

Introduction

Though it is incredible to us, there are always a minority of newcomers to accounting and finance who believe that our discipline is dull! Yet nothing could be further from the truth. Our job is perennially fascinating because it is dynamic. The role is constantly being redefined by innovation. The information you are about to learn has the ability to guide individual and corporate decision making fundamentally at every level. If you (choose to) work in an accounting firm or in industry, then rest assured that these places are almost always vibrant, energetic and intellectually stimulating.

Chapters 1–4 of this book discuss the role of the financial accountant alongside the purpose and usefulness of the information they produce. We outline some basic preparation rules, propose several analysis and interpretation methods, and introduce some broader questions about financial accounting and its role. Chapters 5–10 are concerned with management accounting and the sub-discipline financial management.

In this chapter we open by addressing some of the questions most frequently asked by those who are new to the world of accounting and finance, namely: What is an accountant? What is the accountant's role? What is the broad purpose of this function in an organization? We introduce the key elements of the conceptual and regulatory frameworks and follow this by identifying the most common types of business vehicle. This chapter therefore outlines who the preparers and users of financial information are. In addition, we introduce the standard-setters and describe their role in the accounting community. We conclude this chapter by providing an overview of some of the commonly perceived key problems associated with the main information product output of the financial accountant: the annual report and financial statements.

Having taught this for many years, we are well aware that there are learners who presume this material is both turgid and irrelevant. This combination is fatal to engagement. We have therefore tried to make this as interesting as possible by breaking up the delivery of 'hard facts' by bringing in other issues, such as who uses the information and why it might be important (necessary?) for there to be a legitimate and credible standard-setting body. A further problem is that this material can feel disjointed. This is because there is a minimum amount that you need to know and, sadly, there isn't enough space in an introductory textbook to consider some of the more interesting issues that underlie its development, refinement, purpose and importance. In an introductory text it seems excessively cruel to put forward these questions where there are no right or wrong answers. We would, however, like to take this opportunity to ask you to consider them as you make your way through the material. For example: Do you think a global financial reporting system is desirable? Do you think it is right that accountants should be allowed to be self-governing? Do you think domestic governments should intervene to make rules *fairer* to their jurisdiction? Do you think accounting systems should comprise a set of restrictive rules or do you think they should be based on principles? Why is there a vibrant accounting and finance academic community? Additionally, given the rapid pace of change in practice (in real life), how can the relatively slow-moving research community help the profession?

Who and what is an accountant?

One thing that has remained unchanged for millennia is that every day, in our private and work lives, we rely on accountants and accounting information to make better-informed decisions. To put this in context, some examples of decisions you might face include whether to: buy an asset, rent it, or make it; price a product higher or lower than your competitors; outsource a product, project, department or operation; take on a new contract; acquire a competing business. Needless to say, there are many more!

The Oxford dictionary defines accounting (noun) as 'the process or work of keeping financial accounts' while an accountant (noun) is 'a person whose job is to keep or inspect financial accounts'. This definition, however, is overly simplistic. For a long time, accounting was considered a process of collecting, analysing and communicating financial information to allow users to make better-informed decisions. This work remains at the forefront of the role but more recently accountants have been asked to expand their remit into new areas. For example, accountants are now deeply involved in the preparation of non-financial information, including corporate social responsibility reporting. The image of the staid, conservative, grey-suited drone is outdated. The job has changed. We now need to be communicators as well as doers. We need to be client facing rather than just hit buttons on a calculator. There is a new breed of accountant and whether you believe this is a change for the better or worse, it seems to be a change that is here to stay.

The good news is that accounting is largely a refinement of common sense. Among other factors, relative levels of reliance on financial information, increased regulation and professionalization have driven increased sophistication of presentation and methods, but at the heart of all accounting is the idea that financial data should be converted into useful information for decision making. If either the process or the output were to become overly complex or burdensome, the profession might risk damaging this core objective.

> ### Expert view 1.1: Seeking definitions – what is an accountant?
>
> The subtleties and complexities of the definition problem are illustrated by the recently drafted consultation paper produced by the International Federation of Accountants (IFAC) in 2011, entitled 'A proposed definition of "professional accountant"'. This work drew attention to a number of important problems exacerbated by a lack of specificity in the term 'professional accountant'.
> IFAC organized their definition into three descriptive levels:
>
> 1 Initially, the term 'professional accountant' is defined by emphasizing some form of official accounting qualification (eg formal education, certification, or chartering).
>
> 2 IFAC then state what a professional accountant *does* by outlining the core responsibilities that imply the application of skills in the context of society's expectations. Thus, their definition recognizes the public-interest responsibilities of accountants and their profession.
>
> 3 Finally (which is optional and contingent upon the characteristics of each jurisdiction), the definition states that professional accountants can be differentiated from one another by certain factors, such as types of responsibilities (eg public-sector accounting, auditing role) and the level of formal training or education generally.

A simple way to understand the role of an accountant is through an illustration. As you work through the paragraph, try to picture yourself as the protagonist. You will see *how* and *why* the simplest forms of accounting developed.

ILLUSTRATION 1.1   Climb On!

For a long time, you have been wondering how to convert your passion for rock climbing into a business opportunity. During a recent climbing trip you met Chris, a climbing-gear designer. He agreed to give you 100 chalk bags and 100 climb-oriented t-shirts for $4 and $5 each, respectively. You came to an agreement with him that you'd make payments on an ad-hoc basis as the goods were sold. As soon as you arrived home you listed the first 30 chalk bags and 50 t-shirts on an internet-based auction site. These sold within three days of their listing for $8 and $10 respectively. Half of these customers paid immediately. You offered 20-day credit terms on the sales and your past experiences tell you that customers tend to take full advantage of this policy.

You are keen to work out your *financial position* before you proceed any further.

TABLE 1.1   Solution to Illustration 1.1

What do you own?		What do you owe?	
70 chalk bags which you bought for $4 each	$280	You owe Chris money for the 100 chalk bags at $4 each	$400
50 t-shirts which you bought for $5 each	$250	You owe Chris money for the 100 t-shirts at $5 each	$500
You received $8 per chalk bag, and collected 15 units worth of sales immediately	$120		
You are owed for (the remaining) 15 chalk bags sold at $8 per unit	$120		
You received $10 per t-shirt, and collected 25 t-shirts worth of sales immediately	$250		
You are owed for (the remaining) 25 t-shirts sold at $10 per unit	$250		

Through the medium of this example, we have introduced many of the basic tenets of accounting. Your mind should be racing with the same questions as business owners and their stakeholders have been asking for millennia. From an *internal* perspective, you were simply interested in your financial position:

- How much more (or less) wealthy am I?
- Who do I owe money to?
- How much do I owe?
- Who owes me?
- How much do they owe me?
- How much cash have I got?
- How much are my inventories (unsold goods) worth?

However, given this analysis your interest might have been piqued and you are now pondering other associated questions about your performance, future position and cash flows, plus any constraints and opportunities which you might face. These might include:

- Have I excluded any costs?
- Have I made a profit?
- Am I charging a sensible price?
- Will all my customers pay?
- How long will Chris be willing to wait for his payment?
- Will Chris allow me to buy more inventories?
- Can I negotiate the purchase price down?
- Will the goods Chris sells me be manufactured to the same quality?
- ... and so forth.

Extract 1.1: Perspectives from accounting research

Many people who first start studying accounting and finance cannot believe that there is a large, thriving, active research community. The problem is that more often than not, all that people know of accountants comes through the media who like to portray us, and the information we produce, in binary terms. They lead casual audiences to believe that it is 'right' or 'wrong', 'black' or 'white'. What they don't tell you is that the discipline is a sea of grey (not grey suits) and rarely are decisions so clear cut.

Maintaining and cultivating the link between practice (ie the accounting profession) and academia is important. There needs to be a vibrant academic community in the same way that the academic community needs a strong, credible and socially responsible accounting profession. There are those who argue that the gap has never been wider, while others argue that it's never been narrower. Kaplan (2011) has a more balanced view and suggests in his paper, 'Accounting scholarship that advances professional knowledge and practice', that though research (academic scholarship) has helped craft the direction of professional decision making and contributed to professional knowledge, there are many areas where the community could do more. He states:

As accounting scholars have focused on understanding how markets and users process accounting data, they have distanced themselves from the accounting process itself. Accounting scholarship has failed to address important measurement and valuation issues that have arisen in the past 40 years of practice. This gap is illustrated with missed opportunities in risk measurement and management and the estimation of the fair value of complex financial securities.

Kaplan (2011)

Let's not be too disheartened, though, for when a community recognizes a performance gap and there is a positive attitude towards change, this is normally the first tentative step on the pathway to finding solutions.

The two forms of accounting: financial accounting and management accounting

Broadly speaking, accounting divides into two forms: financial accounting and management accounting. The principal differences can best be summarized into four categories as shown in Table 1.2.

TABLE 1.2   Differences between financial accounting and management accounting

Key differences	Financial accounting	Management accounting
Users	External, principally owners of the business eg shareholders	Internal management of the company
Format	Governed by region-specific law, exchange-specific regulation and accounting standards	Can take any form depending upon the purpose of the information
Frequency	Normally annually. Large listed entities sometimes report quarterly or half-yearly dependent upon regulation	As required. Some information is produced and some exercises are performed, as a matter of course, daily, weekly, monthly, quarterly and annually. Other information is required on an *ad-hoc* basis
Content	Dominated by historic information based on past transactions	Forward-looking perspective. Detailed analysis of past results and incorporation of known changes, in order to plan for the future

Exercises: now attempt Exercise 1.1 on page 39

Expert view 1.2: The origins of accounting

Bookkeeping, as we know it, was first documented by Luca Pacioli (often referred to as the 'Father of Accounting') in his text *Summa de arithmetica, geometria, proportioni et proportionalita* (Venice, 1497). Within this mathematics textbook was a section describing the method of double-entry bookkeeping employed by Venetian merchants. Pacioli described a system of journals and ledgers which accounted for assets, liabilities, gains and losses. However, systems of recording assets and liabilities, income and expenditure have existed for millennia. For example, clay tablets which appear to record financial transactions have been found in Egypt and Mesopotamia dating to before 2000 BC. Indeed, Jones (2011) dates the first accounting scandal to the same period.

The financial accountant

So, we know there are fundamental differences between financial accounting and management accounting. Let's now look more closely at where one would find financial accountants and what they are responsible for producing and preparing. It is common for financial accountants to work within accounting practices that provide external services and advice to entities about their financial reporting and related matters, eg audit and accounting services. They can also be found within organizations, preparing in-house accounting records and associated information.

Expert view 1.3: Professional accounting qualifications

To the uninitiated, it might be natural to presume that when people refer to themselves as 'an accountant', they mean 'Chartered Accountant'. However, to be able to call oneself a Chartered Accountant it is necessary to be a member of the Institute of Chartered Accountants in England and Wales (ICAEW), Scotland (ICAS), Ireland (CAI), Australia (ICAA), Zimbabwe (ICAZ), New Zealand (ICANZ), The Canadian Institute of Chartered Accountants (CICA) or The South African Institute of Chartered Accountants (SAICA).

Job adverts in the UK commonly specify 'CCAB qualified accountant required'. The Consultative Committee of Accountancy Bodies (CCAB) is an umbrella group and has five member bodies: Association of Chartered Certified Accountants (ACCA); Chartered Institute of Public Finance and Accountancy (CIPFA); ICAEW; CAI; and ICAS.

NOTE: The Chartered Institute of Management Accountants (CIMA) gave notice to withdraw from this group in March 2011.

It is common for financial accountants to be trained by, and work within, accounting partnerships. These range from sole practitioners working in isolation to global organizations generating tens of billions of dollars in revenue per annum. There are a number of so-called *elite* professional accounting firms which have become household names. Collectively they are known as the Big Four, essentially because there are four of them: PricewaterhouseCoopers; Deloitte; KPMG; and Ernst and Young (now known as EY).

There are fears about the long-term viability of this dominance and most in the profession expect changes in the not too distant future (see Extract 1.2). However, the accounting services marketplace is competitive. There are hundreds of accounting firms outside of these Big Four. Organizations regularly put work out for tender as they are not obliged to stay with one firm. Indeed, from a commercial perspective, there is no better way of being offered a lower fee from your current auditor than by asking others to bid competitively against them!

Extract 1.2: Big Four dominance

UK Competition Commission Says Big Four Audit Dominance Not Best for Investors

March 4, 2013
Accountingweb
By Frank Byrt

The United Kingdom's Competition Commission (UKCC) says that the nation's audit market is dominated by the Big Four accounting firms, which has stanched competition for audit work from public companies to the detriment of their shareholders. The UKCC, in its 'Statutory Audit Services Market Investigation' report released on 22 February 2013, suggested that among the possible remedies is mandatory rotation of audit firms.

UKCC's report is a major milestone in a 16-month probe that was set in motion by a critical report from the House of Lords Economic Affairs Committee in 2011. The UKCC's inquiry focused on Big Four firms KPMG, Deloitte, Ernst & Young (EY) and PricewaterhouseCoopers (PwC).

'Essentially, we identified two clusters of issues,' UKCC Audit Investigation Group Chair Laura Carstensen told AccountingWEB UK. 'The first was "stickiness" and propensity of companies not to switch auditors and adverse issues that can result. And the second was to make sure auditors are more squarely aligned with what shareholders want.'

UKCC Recommendations

- Mandatory tendering.
- Mandatory rotation of audit firms.
- Expanded remit and/or more frequent audit quality reviews.
- Prohibit 'Big Four only' clauses in loan documentation.
- Strengthen accountability to the audit committee.
- Better shareholder–auditor engagement.
- Extended reporting requirements.

The UKCC concluded that Big Four firms hold most of the big company audits and that those organizations rarely change auditors, which hurts the competition for public company audit work and results in higher prices, lower quality, and less innovation and differentiation than would be the case in a more open market.

The lack of competition creates a risk of auditors being insufficiently independent from executives and insufficiently sceptical of their attempts to present the accounts in the best possible light, the report said.

How can this be interpreted and why is it relevant to you?

The existence of a Big Four has benefits but there are also drawbacks. Extract 1.2 identifies two potential issues: *stickiness*; and a threat to goal congruence. There is some debate about whether audit firms should be forced to rotate after a fixed term has been served, ie the job should be mandatorily put out to tender every five years, maybe with the incumbent firm not being allowed to engage in the process. The former has recently been proposed in the UK by the Competition Commission in a series of measures to limit the dominance of these élite firms and increase competition in the market. It is clear, however, that though this will solve one set of problems, it creates another: eg set-up costs, learning curve effects, a risk that sector/industry audit specialism won't be developed. There is no doubt that an audit firm who 'is in the pocket' of the senior executive (or vice versa) is an unhealthy situation, but none of the proposed solutions is perfect.

Ultimately, the central function of the financial accountant is to prepare (review or audit) the annual report and financial statements. Traditionally this document acts as a summary of the organization's performance and position. More recently it has become a repository for other information, and this point will be discussed in more detail later.

Alongside providing accounting support, the range of services provided by financial accountants (an accounting firm) can be summarized as follows:

- *assurance services*, including auditing and regulatory compliance;
- *taxation services*, including taxation planning, developing taxation strategies and taxation compliance work;
- *transaction work*, including advice to help businesses grow, prosper or reinvent themselves on issues such as obtaining funding, or mergers and acquisitions;
- *advisory services*, including internal audit, risk management advice and corporate recovery (insolvency).

Who are the users of financial accounting information?

If financial accountants are responsible for the preparation of the annual report and financial statements, it is worth asking the follow-on questions: 'who uses this information?' and 'what do they use this information for?' (Figure 1.1).

The Conceptual Framework for Financial Reporting (Conceptual Framework or 'F') identifies the primary users of general-purpose financial reporting as present and potential investors, lenders and other creditors. They use this information to make decisions about buying, selling or holding equity or debt instruments and providing or settling loans or other forms of credit [F, objective {OB} 2]. The information is intended to allow these stakeholders to assess an entity's performance and position as well as gauge future cash-flow prospects. These users will probably be keen to

FIGURE 1.1   Users of financial reporting information

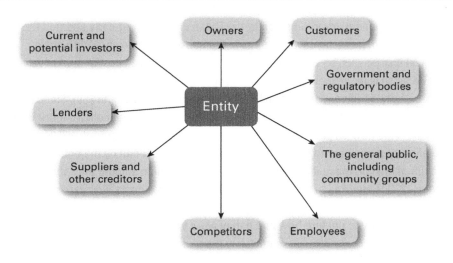

assess how well management have discharged their responsibilities in the use of the entity's resources [F, OB4].

The Conceptual Framework notes that there are also other stakeholders who might find general-purpose financial reports useful. Among these are regulators, the public, the government, customers, employees and competitors. The IASB notes that interested parties should not limit themselves to the financial report; there is other information available which would be useful when undertaking a full assessment of an entity's position and performance.

Exercises: now attempt Exercise 1.2 on page 39

The regulatory and conceptual framework

There are a limited number of professions that can claim to be self-governing, but accounting is one of them. The government has ceded responsibility to a group of experts whom they have deemed to be credible, reliable and socially responsible. In many ways, this is a great benefit. It does mean, however, that the central coordinating body (or bodies) need to be able to respond to any problems quickly and efficiently and with the requisite levels of ability and skill when challenged by economic, political, social and technological complexities.

The profession needs a strong, robust and fair conceptual and regulatory framework. The following paragraphs aim to introduce the main players in the environment as well as outline some of the processes.

Expert view 1.4: A current problem for the accounting standard-setters

A recent example of the type of problem faced by the profession is the case of financial instruments reporting standards. These are being regularly updated to take account of financial developments in the use and complexity of derivative financial instruments, eg what value should these be shown at: cost or market value? This decision is made more difficult when you know that the cost of these commonly economically significant assets/liabilities is normally $nil (or close to $nil). Standard-setters need to ask themselves: 'How do you value an instrument where there is no market?' 'And how do you create a rule that would be fit for all purposes?' 'How do you allow management to explain to the reader the risks faced by the entity as a result of holding these instruments?' 'Is there a minimum amount they should disclose?' It is amazing to think that a decade or so ago, companies were able to hold massive amounts of highly volatile derivative financial instruments without it being mandatory to declare how much they were worth. Though the rules we have now may not be perfect, they are certainly more useful than what we had before.

Principles-based versus rules-based standards

The IASB, in their role as standard-setter, aspire to create principles-driven requirements rather than rules-driven regulations. This is thought to alleviate some of the problems created by hard rules (eg de jure compliance, or 'work around the rules') and allow organizations to be able to meet requirements even when faced with a situation not previously encountered. This does, however, mean that organizations frequently need to make judgements because the reporting code is not completely rigid and immovable.

The Conceptual Framework

In addition to the way the regulations are written, it is also important to note that there is a document outlining the Conceptual Framework for accounting. This provides supplementary guidance when there are no specific reporting requirements or regulations governing the reporting area. That means that this document can be used to guide preparers when there isn't a standard that tells them what to do. The Conceptual Framework is a frame of reference which has two purposes: first, it is used by companies to aid their financial reporting decision making; and second, it is used by the IASB to help them to develop new accounting standards and revise old ones.

The Conceptual Framework deals with the following key issues:

a the objective of financial reporting;

b the qualitative characteristics of useful financial information;

c the definition, recognition and measurement of the elements from which financial statements are constructed; and

d concepts of capital and capital maintenance.

The objective of general-purpose financial reporting is to provide financial information about the reporting entity that is useful to key stakeholders. The concept of usefulness is subject to great debate. Accounting and finance research has attempted to define and refine the notion of financial reporting quality. The key problem, however, is that *quality* is a nebulous term and thus the integrity and robustness of any definition is questionable.

The qualitative characteristics of useful financial information

Defining a nebulous concept such as 'quality' has proved to be difficult for everyone who has ever approached the subject. For example, how easy is it to say what makes Shakespeare's *Hamlet* such a wonderful play? What contributes to its quality? Can those characteristics be mapped to other texts? Accountants and their representative bodies have had the same problem. What characteristics ensure that information is of sufficient quality; or useful for decision making? In response, the IASB state that for financial information to be useful, first and foremost it must be relevant and faithfully represent what it purports to represent. There are then four further enhancing characteristics: comparability, verifiability, timeliness and understand-ability. These are summarized in Figure 1.2 and some definitions of these characteristics follow.

It is almost impossible to define quality, but it is also reasonably difficult to define these other terms. We thought it would be useful to set out how the standard-setters have chosen to define them (F, Qualitative Characteristics {QC} 6–20):

The fundamental characteristics

- **Relevant** financial information is capable of making a difference in the decisions made by users. Information may be capable of making a difference in a decision even if some users choose not to take advantage of it or are already aware of it from other sources. Financial information is capable of making a difference in decisions if it has predictive value, confirmatory value or both.

- Financial reports represent economic phenomena in words and numbers. To be useful, financial information must not only represent relevant phenomena, but it must also **faithfully represent** the phenomena that it purports to represent. To be a perfectly faithful representation, a depiction would have three characteristics. It would be complete, neutral and free from error.

The enhancing characteristics

- Users' decisions involve choosing between alternatives, for example, selling or holding an investment, or investing in one reporting entity or another. Consequently, information about a reporting entity is more useful if it can be compared with similar information about other entities and with similar information about the same entity for another period or another date. **Comparability** is the qualitative characteristic that enables users to identify and understand similarities in, and differences among, items.

- **Verifiability** helps assure users that information faithfully represents the economic phenomena it purports to represent. Verifiability means that different knowledgeable and independent observers could reach consensus, although not necessarily complete agreement, that a particular depiction is a faithful representation. Quantified information need not be a single-point estimate to be verifiable. A range of possible amounts and the related probabilities can also be verified.

- **Timeliness** means having information available to decision-makers in time to be capable of influencing their decisions. Generally, the older the information is the less useful it is. However, some information may continue to be timely long after the end of a reporting period because, for example, some users may need to identify and assess trends.

- Financial reports are prepared for users who have a reasonable knowledge of business and economic activities and who review and analyse the information diligently. Classifying, characterizing and presenting information clearly and concisely make it **understandable**.

FIGURE 1.2 The qualitative characteristics

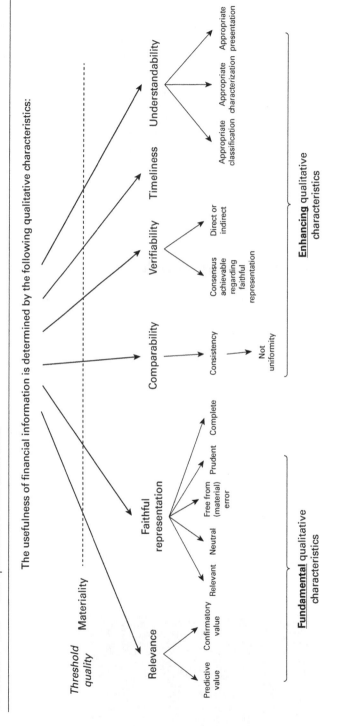

The usefulness of financial information is determined by the following qualitative characteristics:

Materiality

You will often hear accountants refer to the separate notion of **materiality**. This concept is critical to an understanding of the aims and objectives of financial reporting and auditing. An item is deemed material if its omission or misstatement could influence decisions that users make on the basis of financial information about a specific reporting entity.

Materiality therefore is an entity-specific variable. It is based on the nature or magnitude (or both) of the item(s) to which the information relates in the context of an individual entity's position. Consequently, there is no single specified measure or quantitative threshold for materiality. Each item must be reviewed on its own merits and in the broader context.

> Exercises: now attempt Exercise 1.3 on page 40

The regulatory framework

We have briefly introduced the Conceptual Framework and therefore it is now time to turn to the regulatory framework. It is not essential at this level of study for you to know the intricacies of the accounting standard-setting process or the wider regulatory framework. However, an outline of the structure of the major bodies and processes form both interesting and worthwhile knowledge. An outline of the structure of the IFRS Foundation is shown in Figure 1.3. Figure 1.4 provides a brief overview of the phases of the standard-setting due process.

FIGURE 1.3   The structure of the IFRS Foundation (**www.IFRS.org**)

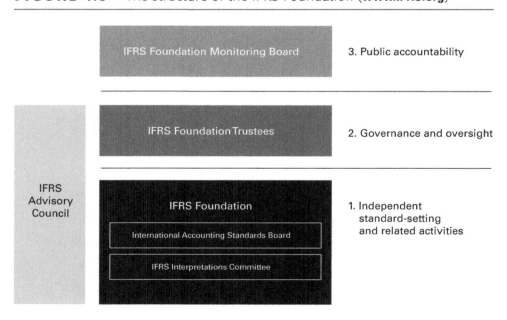

The IFRS Foundation

The IFRS Foundation is an independent, not-for-profit private-sector organization. The IFRS Foundation sets at its core the notion of public interest which is mirrored by the definition of accountants and their work (eg IFAC, 2011). The principal objectives of the IFRS Foundation are as follows:

- to develop a single set of high-quality, understandable, enforceable and globally accepted International Financial Reporting Standards (IFRSs) through its standard-setting body, the IASB;
- to promote the use and rigorous application of those standards;
- to take account of the financial reporting needs of emerging economies and small and medium-sized entities (SMEs); and
- to promote and facilitate adoption of IFRSs, being the standards and interpretations issued by the IASB, through the convergence of national accounting standards and IFRSs.

Source: **www.IFRS.org**

The IASB

The IASB acts as an independent standard-setting body on behalf of the IFRS Foundation. The IASB currently has 15 full-time members who are responsible for the development and publication of IFRSs. Interestingly, all meetings of the IASB are held in public and are webcast. The IASB and the IFRS Foundation heavily stress the notions of comparability, inclusiveness and consultation. They actively engage with stakeholders from around the world, including investors, analysts, regulators, business leaders, other accounting standard-setters and the accountancy profession.

The IFRS Interpretations Committee

The 14 members of the IFRS Interpretations Committee are responsible for reviewing, on a timely basis, widespread accounting issues that have arisen within the context of current IFRSs and to provide authoritative guidance (IFRICs) on those issues. The members are drawn from different professions and countries.

Expert view 1.5: Is this an unfair or biased system?

Though there is research which finds limited evidence of varying levels of relative influence among stakeholder groups during the standard-setting process, the IASB have put in place a system which has the potential to be fair and rigorous (see Figure 1.4). There is a combination of observable and non-observable phases and though it has been argued that these 'dark' periods impair transparency, they also allow the Board to take, behind closed doors, valuable expert advice which otherwise might not be provided. In order to make the process more transparent, the Board has recently opened up Board meetings to the public, made minutes available and also webcasts them.

FIGURE 1.4 IASB standard-setting due process

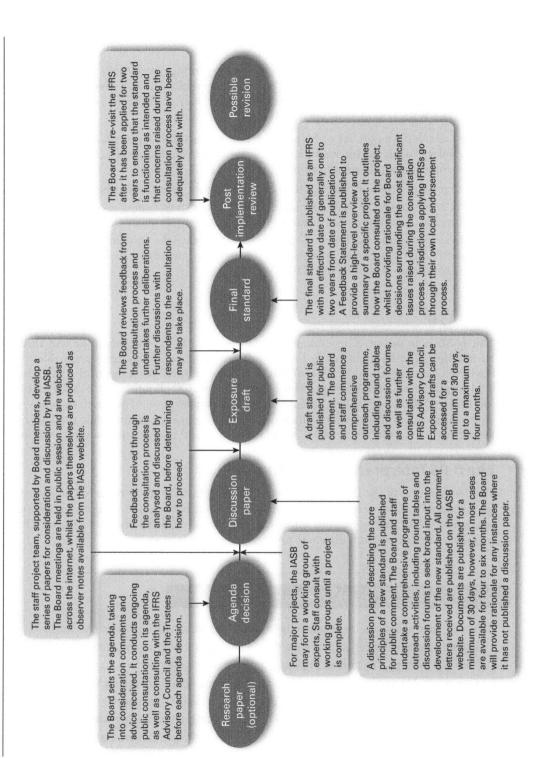

Exercises: now attempt Exercise 1.4 on page 40

The standard-setting process

Figure 1.4 outlines the standard-setting process in financial reporting. This is the template for accounting requirements' innovation and implementation. As you can see, the process is designed to be robust, involved and transparent as the outcome needs to be agreed among stakeholders. Agreement between constituents – including preparers, users, auditors, representative bodies and so forth – helps to ensure the continued legitimacy of the standard-setter. It should also mean that the requirements are likely to be met by preparers and their value understood by users.

Types of business entity

We are now at the crossroads between topics being covered in this chapter. The first part considered the role of the accountant and the systems and processes that have grown up around them. The conceptual and regulatory framework has been described. For accounting to exist, there must be something to account for. Therefore in terms of basic background information, we address two further questions: 'What is a business?' and 'What is the purpose of a business?'

The answer to both questions is far from straightforward. Indeed, they often overlap and intertwine.

What is a business?

One could argue that in its simplest sense a business should be defined by its legal form. Therefore, we shall briefly review the most common types of business entity that exist.

There are a wide range of business vehicles, or forms of business ownership, available. Each has their relative advantages and disadvantages. In the UK, the government has developed an excellent resource which explains the major differences between the various business vehicles available. The site also offers advice on how one might set up a business (**https://www.gov.uk/browse/business/setting-up**). There are three which are particularly useful to be aware of:

1 sole trader;

2 partnership;

3 limited company.

Sole trader

As the name suggests, a sole trader is someone opting to work for themselves. As seen in the example above – Climb On! – we put 'you' in the position of running your own business. The business is not incorporated, ie it is not a limited liability company. You do not share the ownership of the business with anyone else, ie you have no business partner(s). This doesn't mean that you cannot have any employees, it is just not common. Businesses of this type are normally quite small in terms of assets, liabilities, revenues and expenses. There are many everyday examples of people going into business on their own, such as plumbers, electricians, hairdressers, private tutors, artists, photographers and so forth.

The financial accounting information a sole trader is *required* to produce is limited. It is normally required to satisfy tax authorities' purposes. Occasionally financial institutions might request specific information, particularly for lending purposes.

Establishing oneself as a sole trader, therefore, is frequently the first step for many entrepreneurs. The main advantage of this business vehicle is the retention of control. The owner is solely responsible for all decision making. The other key advantage is the reduced accounting and legal regulatory burden. The major disadvantage is the unlimited liability! In other words, a sole trader is wholly responsible for all liabilities of the business.

Partnership

A partnership occurs when *two or more people* decide to run a business together. As with establishing a business as a sole trader, the regulatory burden is low, especially in comparison with limited companies. Partnerships range considerably in size. It is probably more common that they have low assets, liabilities, revenues and expenses; however, they can be huge global businesses. Examples again include hairdressers, plumbers, tutors and so forth. They also include businesses such as medical practices, legal practices and accounting practices.

The advantage of forming a partnership is that you can share responsibility and the burdens of ownership. It is also likely that the skill-set available will be more varied and expertise could be easier to channel towards specific projects. In an accounting partnership, for example, you might want the skills of both a financial accountant and a tax accountant; it is rare that one person is an expert in both. The disadvantages largely stem from behavioural issues. Sharing ownership often places significant burdens on pre-existing well-functioning relationships. Also, there are some people who simply like making all the decisions, not sharing this role!

Limited company

In the UK, a privately held business is referred to as a limited company; this is commonly abbreviated to 'Ltd'. The equivalent term used for a private company in Australia is Proprietary Limited Company (abbreviated to Pty. Ltd.). In India and Pakistan the designation Pvt. Ltd. (Private Limited) is used for all private limited companies. In South Africa the term Pty. Ltd. is used. In the United States, the expression 'corporation' is preferred to limited company and it is common to see the abbreviation 'Inc.' (short for 'Incorporated'), but in many states 'Ltd.' is also permitted.

The word 'limited' relates to the level of financial exposure. An entity can be incorporated as a limited liability company, at which point, in law, it becomes a separate legal entity. Therefore, while sole traders and partners are personally responsible for the amounts owed by their businesses, the shareholders of a limited liability company are only responsible for the amount to be paid for their shares. A limited liability company conducts all activities in the name of the entity, eg invoices are issued in the company's name, bank accounts need to be set up in the company's name (not directors' or managers' names). Note, however, that it is not uncommon for lenders and trading partners to ask the directors of companies for personal guarantees, which, of course, negates much of the advantage associated with incorporation.

As with partnerships, companies can range in size from small to huge. Most companies which are household names are public limited companies. There are several advantages and disadvantages to incorporating. Some of these are shown in Table 1.3.

TABLE 1.3   Advantages and disadvantages of incorporating

Advantages	Disadvantages
Limited liability reduces the personal investment risk.	The regulatory burden is far greater on limited liability companies than on sole traders and partnerships. A limited company has to publish annual financial statements. These are public statements of account, meaning, of course, that anyone (including competitors and employees) can see how well (or badly) the entity has done. As stated above, sole traders and partnerships do not have to publish their financial statements. *Note: the regulatory burden on public limited companies is far greater again!*
It is theoretically more straightforward to generate funds for a limited company because new shares can be sold when additional financing is required. With no cap on the number of different shareholders, investors could come from anywhere and everywhere. Indeed, most of the world's major companies are public limited companies (plc), which means their shares are publicly traded.	Limited companies accounts must comply with the relevant domestic or international financial reporting requirements.
The existence of a partnership or sole trader is dependent upon the owners. A limited liability company, on the other hand, has a separate legal identity from its shareholders which means that directors, management and owners can come and go but the company will continue to exist regardless.	It is a common requirement in domestic law that large companies' financial statements are audited. In other words, they are subject to an independent review to ensure that they are true and fair, and comply with all relevant legal requirements and accounting standards. This process can be both time-consuming and expensive.
There are potential tax advantages. A company pays corporate income tax whereas sole traders and partners pay personal income tax.	Though raising finance is listed as an advantage, note also that share issues are regulated by law and a public sale of shares on a stock exchange can be an extremely expensive affair (and sometimes an expensive failure). It is also quite difficult to reduce the level of share capital or to get rid of shareholders who are deemed to be standing in the way of management objectives.
Assuming liquid secondary markets, leaving your position as an owner of share capital in a limited liability company is far simpler than exiting your position as a partner.	

What is the purpose of a business?

The second question has no clear-cut response. It is commonly believed that a corporate entity's objective is 'to maximize shareholder wealth'. However, this financial objective should be balanced against a set of non-financial objectives.

Non-financial objectives are typically clustered under three broad sub-headings:

1 ethical;

2 social;

3 environmental.

A business can be a commercial organization, involved with manufacturing, designing, developing, selling and so forth. Shareholders will likely remain satisfied provided that the risk–return relationship continues within their accepted bounds. However, there are other stakeholders who must also be satisfied. It has been argued that 'the customer is king', ie the entity exists both 'for' and 'because of' its customers. The community which the entity serves might be a crucial factor in relation to performance. Thus, social and environmental policies could dictate relative levels of success (failure). Investment in plant, property, equipment, employees and so forth is a function of a business and these investments will, it is hoped, generate jobs and profits which, in turn, will yield tax revenues which are essential to the economy of the country of residence as a whole.

The annual report and financial statements

Every business should (and will) produce a summary of their position and performance for a period of account. There is a set of primary financial statements which is included in the annual report and financial statements. Their contents and a basic preparation guide will be slowly introduced to you over the coming pages and chapters.

The IASB reported in the Conceptual Framework for Financial Reporting 2010 (Conceptual Framework) that 'the objective of financial statements is to provide information about the **financial position**, **performance** and **changes in financial position** of an entity that is useful to a wide range of users in making economic decisions'. The Conceptual Framework requires any IFRS reporting entity to produce the following information about its economic resources, claims, and changes in resources and claims:

a Economic resources and claims

- Economic resources and claims are recorded in the entity's *statement of financial position*.
  - Chapter 2 includes a series of exercises and examples which are designed to show you how to prepare a basic set of financial statements which includes a statement of financial position and a statement of comprehensive income (income statement). Chapters 3 and 4 provide a summary of how these statements can be used as tools to interpret the performance and position of the entity.

- Economic resources and claims are the entity's assets and liabilities (see below for definitions). These can either be current or non-current in nature.
- Users need to be aware of the nature and value of an entity's economic resources and claims to aid an assessment of the financial strengths and weaknesses, liquidity and solvency position, and its need and ability to obtain financing [F, OB13].

b Changes in economic resources and claims
  - An entity should make users aware of, and allow them to distinguish between, any changes in economic resources and claims which result from either: i) the entity's performance; or ii) other events or transactions [F, OB15].
    - Changes in the entity's performance: economic resources might change, for example, as a result of an increase in production during the period of account. It is likely that at the end of the year the business will hold more non-current assets (to meet the production requirements), inventories (unsold units will increase because the size of order will have comparably increased), trade receivables (ie amounts owed by customers at the end of the period), trade payables (ie amounts owed to suppliers), and so forth.
    - Other events or transactions: a company might, for example, issue new share capital in order to fund the business. This is, by definition, not a performance-related event.
  - The changes in an entity's economic resources and claims resulting from performance are presented in the *statement of comprehensive income* [See International Accounting Standard 1 *Presentation of Financial Statements* {IAS 1}, paragraphs 81–105].
    - The preparation of financial statements is covered in Chapter 2 while interpretation of this financial information is considered in Chapters 3 and 4.
  - The changes in an entity's economic resources and claims resulting from other events and transactions are reported in the *statement of changes in equity* [See IAS 1,106–110].
  - Changes in economic resources and claims could impact on users' assessments of past performance and a company's ability to generate future cash flows.

c Financial performance reflected by past cash flows
  - The statements of financial position, comprehensive income and changes in equity are prepared on an accruals (accounting) basis. As results reported under accruals accounting and cash accounting are likely to be different, entities are also asked to prepare a statement of cash flows [See IAS 7 Statement of Cash Flows].
  - This statement details how the entity generates cash and spends it [F, OB20].

The elements of financial statements

As we know, the financial statements present information about an entity's economic resources, claims, and changes in resources and claims. However, these terms can be confusing because they are not in everyday use. Instead, it might be more helpful to rephrase these into the following more commonly known terms (extracted from the Conceptual Framework).

i) Financial position terminology

Asset – a resource controlled by an entity as a result of past events and from which *economic benefits* are expected to flow to the entity.

- On the face of the statement of financial position these are separated into current (due within one year) and non-current assets (due in more than one year).
- Examples of current assets include inventories, trade receivables and cash held at bank and in hand. Non-current assets include property, plant and equipment.

Liability – a present obligation of the entity arising from past events, the settlement of which is expected to result in an outflow from the entity of resources embodying *economic benefits*.

- On the face of the statement of financial position these are separated into current (falling due within one year) and non-current liabilities (falling due in more than one year).
- Examples of current liabilities include trade payables and a bank overdraft. Non-current liabilities include long-term debt (eg bank loans) and provisions for future costs.

The definitions of an asset and liability contain reference to *future economic benefits*. This is the potential to contribute, directly or indirectly, to the flow of cash and cash equivalents to the entity.

Equity – the residual interest in the assets of the entity after deducting all its liabilities.

Provision – a present obligation which satisfies the rest of the definition of a liability, even if the amount of the obligation has to be estimated.

ii) Income statement terminology

The IASB has adopted a balance sheet approach to accounting. This means that gains and losses are measured in terms of changes in assets and liabilities. In other words, an increase in an asset will give rise to a gain, while an increase in a liability will give rise to a loss. Equally, a decrease in assets equates to a loss and a decrease in a liability equates to a gain.

Gains – increases in economic benefits.

Losses – decreases in economic benefits.

ILLUSTRATION 1.2   Tesco plc

Tesco plc has recently stood out as one of the UK's most successful businesses and is one of the world's largest retailers. The company employs approximately 500,000 employees in over 6,200 stores and operates across 14 markets.

Expert view 1.6: Complex financial statements

The financial statements presented here are for illustration purposes. Presenting the financial statements of a fictional entity lacks integrity and risks masking some of the complexities. However, seeing the financial statements of one of the world's largest businesses creates issues as well. Do not concern yourself with jargon you do not recognize but rather embrace the fact that at this stage, you can draw out an elementary understanding. Once you have completed the financial accounting sections you might want to come back to this section to see how far your learning has progressed.

Let us work through the introductory pages of their annual report together. It is common for large listed entities such as Tesco plc to provide an initial summary which brings together the key indicators related to performance and position related to the current and prior years. Tesco plc have called this section 'Tesco at a glance 2011/12' (Figure 1.5).

If you wish to see this document in full and in colour, follow this link:

http://www.tescoplc.com/files/reports/ar2012/files/pdf/tesco_annual_report_2012.pdf

The annual report typically follows a standardized format which is presented within the first couple of pages (see Tesco's contents page in Figure 1.6). This allows you to navigate around what is a sizeable document quickly and easily. The advent of technology has been particularly useful to search these weighty documents. The annual report is designed for a variety of user groups and, as such, the portions that are relevant are dependent upon what you want to discover.

FIGURE 1.5   Tesco at a glance 2011/12

Tesco at a glance 2011/12

We are one of the world's largest retailers with operations in 14 countries,* employing almost 520,000 people and serving millions of customers every week.

£72.0bn
Group sales

+7.4%
Group sales growth

£3.8bn
Group profit before tax

+5.3%
Group profit before tax growth

+1.6%
Underlying profit before tax**

+2.1%
Underlying diluted earnings per share***†

14.76p
Full year dividend per share

UK		Asia		Europe
Revenue±	Trading profit	Revenue±	Trading profit	Revenue±
£42.8bn 66% of Group	£2,480m 66% of Group	£10.8bn 17% of Group	£737m 20% of Group	£9.9bn 15% of Group
Revenue growth± +5.0%	Trading profit growth (1.0)%	Revenue growth± +10.5%	Trading profit growth +21.8%	Revenue growth± +7.3%
Employees 300,373	Stores 2,979	Employees 117,015	Stores 1,719	Employees 94,409

UK		Asia		Europe	
Market position	1st	Market position	1st or 2nd in all except China	Market position	1st c
Multiple formats include	Hypermarkets, superstores, supermarkets, convenience	Multiple formats include	Hypermarkets, supermarkets, convenience	Multiple formats include	Dep supe hype
Loyalty scheme	Clubcard – around 16 million active members	Loyalty scheme	Clubcard in Malaysia and Thailand, Family Card in South Korea, Legou Tesco Membercard in China – over 20 million active members across Asia	Loyalty scheme	Club activ
dotcom	First grocery home shopping service 1997	dotcom	South Korea 2002, planned launches in at least one major city in each market in the next few years	dotcom	Repr 2011 2012 in ea

Fascia brands include:

TESCO extra   TESCO   TESCO Metro

TESCO express   one stop   Dobbies

Fascia brands include:

TESCO extra   Home plus   TESCO 乐购

TESCO Lotus   乐都汇   乐购 TESCO express

Home plus Express

Fascia brands include:

TESCO extra   T

TESCO kipa   TES

---

* In India, we have an exclusive franchise agreement with Trent, the retail arm of the Tata Group. We are supporting the development of their Star Bazaar format. Continuing operations exclude Japan which has been treated as discontinued following our decision to sell the business.

** See glossary for full accounting definitions.
† Calculated on a constant tax rate basis.

FIGURE 1.5 *continued*

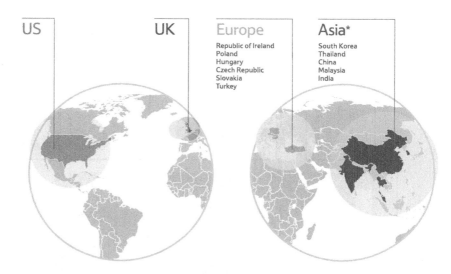

US	UK	Europe	Asia*
		Republic of Ireland	South Korea
		Poland	Thailand
		Hungary	China
		Czech Republic	Malaysia
		Slovakia	India
		Turkey	

Trading profit

£529m
14% of Group

Trading profit growth
+0.4%

Stores
1,351

2nd in all except Turkey
artment stores, hypermarkets,
ermarkets, compact
ermarkets, convenience
card in all markets – over 7 million
e members across Europe
ublic of Ireland 2000, Prague
l, planned launches in Warsaw
? and in at least one major city
ch market in the next few years

:SCO   TESCO *Supermarket*

:O *expres*   TESCO *express*

my

US

Revenue±

£0.6bn
1% of Group

Trading loss

£(153)m
(4)% of Group

Revenue growth±
+27.3%

Improvement in trading loss
+17.7%

Employees
5,056

Stores
185

Market position	A West Coast start-up business
Loyalty scheme	Friends of Fresh & Easy – two-thirds of a million active members

Fascia brand:

fresh & easy
neighborhood Market

Tesco Bank

Revenue±

£1.0bn
2% of Group

Trading profit

£168m
4% of Group

Revenue growth±
+13.6%

Trading profit growth
(36.4)%

Employees
2,818

Baseline profit growth
+29.3%

Insurance	Car, home, pet, travel, life, over 50s, health, dental, breakdown
Savings	Fixed rate, internet, instant access, retail bonds
Cash	Loans, credit cards, ATMs, travel money
Future launches	Mortgages, current accounts
Loyalty scheme	Clubcard

TESCO Bank

± Revenue excludes the accounting impact of IFRIC 13.

FIGURE 1.6 Tesco's contents list

Senior executives provide an analysis of the performance and position of the business. There is no prescribed format for these disclosures. Here, to accompany the executives' narrative, Tesco plc has chosen to include an update on their strategy and an explanation of their business model.

The financial statements and notes have become increasingly complex. In response and to shelter the user from the need to delve into the detail, the entity will often highlight certain key performance indicators and provide a financial review.

The annual report has also become a repository for certain regulatory disclosures, including those related to corporate governance issues and directors' remuneration.

OVERVIEW

1 Chairman's statement

STRATEGIC REVIEW

3 Chief Executive's review*
9 Strategy in action*
24 Business model*

PERFORMANCE REVIEW

29 Key performance indicators*
33 Financial review*

GOVERNANCE

38 Board of Directors
40 Principal risks and uncertainties*
48 General information*
50 Directors' report on corporate governance
64 Directors' remuneration report

FINANCIAL STATEMENTS

88 Statement of Directors' responsibilities
89 Independent auditors' report to the members of Tesco PLC
90 Group income statement
91 Group statement of comprehensive income
92 Group balance sheet
93 Group statement of changes in equity
94 Group cash flow statement
94 Reconciliation of net cash flow to movement in net debt note
95 Notes to the Group financial statements
142 Tesco PLC – Parent Company balance sheet
143 Notes to the Parent Company financial statements
151 Independent auditors' report to the members of Tesco PLC
152 Five year record
IBC Financial calendar
IBC Glossary

It is not uncommon for an entity's annual report to contain certain non-financial disclosures, including details of the ethical, social and environmental philosophy and actions within a corporate social responsibility (CSR) report.

Increasingly, large companies such as Tesco plc produce a stand-alone CSR report.

Most large listed entities conclude their annual report with a summary of the last five years' performance, a calendar of their financial year (including reporting dates) and a glossary.

Unlike the front-end of the annual report, which is not subject to rigorous auditing, the financial statements and notes to the financial statements are.

A statement of directors' responsibilities is followed by the auditors' report.

Following this are the primary financial statements and the notes to the financial statements.

As Tesco plc reports on a consolidated basis (ie all results from entities within the group are brought together in this single report), the parent company's financial statements are also presented here. Separate financial statements will be prepared independently for all the entities in the group, often for tax purposes as well as compliance.

The income statement

FIGURE 1.7   Tesco's income statement

Year ended 25 February 2012	notes	52 weeks 2012 £m	52 weeks 2011* £m
Continuing operations			
Revenue	2	**64,539**	60,455
Cost of sales		**(59,278)**	(55,330)
Gross profit		**5,261**	5,125
Administrative expenses		**(1,652)**	(1,640)
Profits/losses arising on property-related items		**376**	432
Operating profit		**3,985**	3,917
Share of post-tax profits of joint ventures and associates	13	**91**	57
Finance income	5	**176**	150
Finance costs	5	**(417)**	(483)
Profit before tax	3	**3,835**	3,641
Taxation	6	**(879)**	(864)
Profit for the year from continuing operations		**2,956**	2,777
Discontinued operations			
Loss for the year from discontinued operations	7	**(142)**	(106)
Profit for the year		**2,814**	2,671
Attributable to:			
Owners of the parent		**2,806**	2,655
Non-controlling interests		**8**	16
		2,814	2,671
Earnings per share from continuing and discontinued operations			
Basic	9	**34.98p**	33.10p
Diluted	9	**34.88p**	32.94p
Earnings per share from continuing operations			
Basic	9	**36.75p**	34.43p
Diluted	9	**36.64p**	34.25p

Notes

- The income statement follows a standard pro-forma.

- It is designed to allow a user to assess the performance of the entity over the period of account.

- It is only a relatively recent phenomenon that companies are forced to disclose more than their revenue and profit before tax.

- Key line items include: revenue, gross profit, operating profit (otherwise known as profit before interest and tax [PBIT]) and profit for the year (otherwise known as retained profit).

The statement of financial position

FIGURE 1.8   Tesco's statement of financial position

	notes	25 February 2012 £m	26 February 2011* £m
Non-current assets			
Goodwill and other intangible assets	10	4,618	4,338
Property, plant and equipment	11	25,710	24,398
Investment property	12	1,991	1,863
Investments in joint ventures and associates	13	423	316
Other investments	14	1,526	938
Loans and advances to customers	17	1,901	2,127
Derivative financial instruments	21	1,726	1,139
Deferred tax assets	6	23	48
		37,918	35,167
Current assets			
Inventories	15	3,598	3,162
Trade and other receivables	16	2,657	2,330
Loans and advances to customers	17	2,502	2,514
Derivative financial instruments	21	41	148
Current tax assets		7	4
Short-term investments		1,243	1,022
Cash and cash equivalents	18	2,305	2,428
		12,353	11,608
Assets of the disposal group and non-current assets classified as held for sale	7	510	431
		12,863	12,039
Current liabilities			
Trade and other payables	19	(11,234)	(10,484)
Financial liabilities:			
Borrowings	20	(1,838)	(1,386)
Derivative financial instruments and other liabilities	21	(128)	(255)
Customer deposits and deposits by banks	23	(5,465)	(5,110)
Current tax liabilities		(416)	(432)
Provisions	24	(99)	(64)
		(19,180)	(17,731)
Liabilities of the disposal group classified as held for sale	7	(69)	–
Net current liabilities		(6,386)	(5,692)
Non-current liabilities			
Financial liabilities:			
Borrowings	20	(9,911)	(9,689)
Derivative financial instruments and other liabilities	21	(688)	(600)
Post-employment benefit obligations	26	(1,872)	(1,356)
Deferred tax liabilities	6	(1,160)	(1,094)
Provisions	24	(100)	(113)
		(13,731)	(12,852)
Net assets		17,801	16,623
Equity			
Share capital	27	402	402
Share premium		4,964	4,896
Other reserves		40	40
Retained earnings		12,369	11,197
Equity attributable to owners of the parent		17,775	16,535
Non-controlling interests		26	88
Total equity		17,801	16,623

Notes

- The statement of financial position is commonly referred to by its previous title, the balance sheet. You will notice that this balance sheet balances: net assets are £17,801 million and the total equity is also £17,801 million. There is simply a happy coincidence in the terminology however. The balance sheet was named thus because it is a rephrasing of the expression 'list of balances'.

- It has been said that the statement of financial position is akin to a financial photograph. It is a snapshot of an entity's position at a certain point in time capturing summarized details of assets and liabilities.

- Though there are several formats permitted under financial reporting regulations, the above format is the most common in the UK.

- The statement is structured in order of liquidity, ie how quickly the asset or liability will be translated into cash.

The statement of cash flows

See Figure 1.9 on the following page.

Expert view 1.7: The financial year-end

Organizations can set their year-end to whatever date they prefer. There are many determinants, including: when the financial director/controller is least busy (for example, a toy manufacturer would look to avoid the busiest times of the year, eg Christmas), when asset values are maximized (eg inversely it is possible that a toy manufacturer might call their year-end around traditional gift-giving periods when their inventories are most valuable, eg Christmas), at a time when it is most convenient for your external accountant (possibly reducing your bill slightly).

Exercises: now attempt Exercise 1.5 on page 40

FIGURE 1.9   Tesco's statement of cash flows

Year ended 25 February 2012	notes	52 weeks 2012 £m	52 weeks 2011* £m
Cash flows from operating activities			
Cash generated from operations	29	5,688	5,613
Interest paid		(531)	(614)
Corporation tax paid		(749)	(760)
Net cash generated from operating activities		4,408	4,239
Cash flows from investing activities			
Acquisition of subsidiaries, net of cash acquired		(65)	(89)
Proceeds from sale of property, plant and equipment, investment property and non-current assets classified as held for sale		1,141	1,906
Purchase of property, plant and equipment and investment property		(3,374)	(3,178)
Proceeds from sale of intangible assets		–	(3)
Purchase of intangible assets		(334)	(373)
Net decrease/(increase) in loans to joint ventures		(122)	(194)
Investments in joint ventures and associates		(49)	(174)
Investments in short-term and other investments		(1,972)	(683)
Proceeds from sale of short-term and other investments		1,205	719
Dividends received from joint ventures and associates		40	62
Interest received		103	128
Net cash used in investing activities		(3,183)	(1,873)
Cash flows from financing activities			
Proceeds from issue of ordinary share capital		69	98
Increase in borrowings		2,905	2,217
Repayment of borrowings		(2,720)	(4,153)
Repayment of obligations under finance leases		(45)	(42)
Purchase of non-controlling interests		(89)	–
Dividends paid to equity owners		(1,180)	(1,081)
Dividends paid to non-controlling interests		(3)	(2)
Own shares purchased		(303)	(31)
Net cash used in financing activities		(1,366)	(2,994)
Net decrease in cash and cash equivalents		(141)	(628)
Cash and cash equivalents at beginning of the year		2,428	3,102
Effect of foreign exchange rate changes		24	(46)
Cash and cash equivalents including cash held in disposal group at the end of the year		2,311	2,428
Cash held in disposal group		(6)	–
Cash and cash equivalents at the end of the year	18	2,305	2,428

Notes

- The format of the statement of cash flows is governed by its own financial reporting standard – International Accounting Standard 7: Statement of Cash Flows (IAS 7).

- Cash generated/spent is categorized into one of three sections: operating activities; investing activities; and financing activities.

The articulation of the financial statements

Though this might seem a little confusing to get your head around at first, the following illustration shows how the financial statements fit together. Feel free to refer back to this as you're working through some of the exercises in Chapters 2, 3 and 4.

FIGURE 1.10   How the financial statements fit together

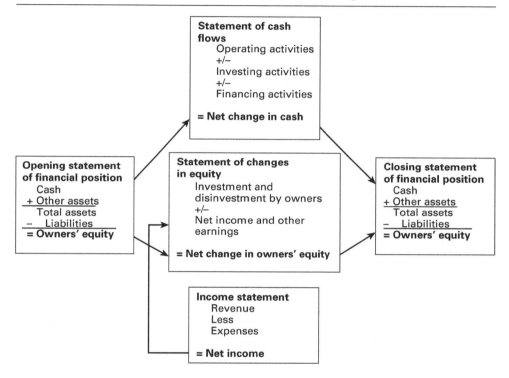

A brief guide to some key problems and issues with financial statements

We do not want to finish this chapter on a negative note, but it seems timely to consider some of the problems with financial statements. You might think that some of these are more important than others and you'd be right. We will reflect on some of these over the next few chapters but, for the time being, a summary is sufficient:

● Trade-offs between the qualitative characteristics, especially between the enhancing characteristics. A position might be inherently complex, therefore making it less verifiable, comparable and understandable.

● Owing to the nature of the financial reporting and auditing process, financial statements generally suffer from not providing timely information. The information contained therein is based on past transactions and when it is published, it will relate to a period that has already passed. This is why many argue that the annual report is simply a regulatory document which carries confirmatory value rather than a positive economic one.

- The cost–benefit issue. In other words, at what stage do the reporting requirements become overly complex and burdensome? Is there a point where the costs of preparation outweigh the benefits of the information produced?

- There is a wide range of users and the potential for conflict between them is vast. The IASB has promoted the idea that current and potential investors are the primary user group; however, the annual report and financial statements has not significantly altered to reflect this. It has been found that the participation of investors in the standard-setting due process has been extremely limited. Therefore, if an annual report's first audience is supposed to be the investor community, then why do they not get more involved?

- The conflict between accounting firms' varied interests means that their participation in the standard-setting process and in the audit, preparation and presentation of financial statements leads to potentially schizophrenic behaviour. They must often feel divided between representing their own self-interest, the public interest, client interests and the institutional interest.

- Standard-setting is a complex process and full agreement is unlikely to be reached given the conflicting and competing interests of the varied stakeholder groups.

- Despite the benefits inherent in the notion, is international accounting an aspiration rather than an achievable reality?

- Selecting appropriate recognition and measurement methods will vary dependent upon the class of asset (liability) and the information available. For example, derivative financial instruments (eg forward exchange contracts, options, swaps) cost little to purchase but have the potential to expose entities to material obligations. Which is a preferable measurement method? Mark-to-market or historic cost?

Exercises: now attempt Exercise 1.6 on page 41

COMPREHENSION QUESTIONS

1 What are the two main forms of accounting? List the principal differences between the types of information that practitioners of each discipline produce.

2 What is meant by the terms trade receivables and trade payables?

3 Potential and current investors are the primary users of financial statements but there are others. List four different users aside from investors and explain their information needs.

4 List the two fundamental qualitative characteristics of financial reporting and provide a brief description of both.

5 List the four enhancing qualitative characteristics of financial reporting and provide a brief description of each.

6 Who are the IASB and what is their role within the IFRS Foundation and standard-setting framework?

7 There are several advantages to incorporating your business, but can you list some of the commonly perceived disadvantages?

8 Define the three terms: asset; liability; and equity.

Answers on pages 41–44

Exercises

(Answers on pages 44–49)

Exercise 1.1: A comparison between financial and management accounting

Reflect on the supplementary questions raised in Illustration 1.1. Do you think it is straightforward to ascertain accurate and reliable answers? Try to write in jargon-free terms an example of the information that might be prepared by a financial accountant versus a management accountant.

Exercise 1.2: Identifying the users of financial reports

Using the information presented in Figure 1.1, list THREE key user groups for each of the following organizations and briefly explain what each group might hope to ascertain from the publicly available financial information prepared by the entity:

(a) Compartmentalized Inc is a company that specializes in making self-fold boxes for storage and transportation purposes. The entity was founded in 1923. It has grown in a slow but structured and organic fashion from a family-run business with four staff to an international organization generating revenues of $85 million with a workforce of over 400 people. The company has no debt and is still family owned.

(b) Gronk plc is a ferry company boasting Europe's second-largest fleet. The company provides services to almost every major port on the continent. During the last five years, the company has acquired four competitors who were in financial distress and facing bankruptcy. This has led to high levels of borrowing.

(c) Worldwide Water is a not-for-profit charitable organization. Their objective is to provide safe drinking water across Zambia.

Exercise 1.3

Can you provide a suggestion for each of the following, briefly explaining your rationale:

(i)   A balance which could be material owing to its magnitude?

(ii) A balance which could be material owing to its nature?

(iii) A balance which could be material owing to its context?

Exercise 1.4

The internationalization of financial reporting has attracted significant attention. There are many in favour and, equally, many opposed. The United States (US), for example, has continued to use US Generally Accepted Accounting Principles (GAAP) as opposed to adopting international standards.

(a) Briefly list the key advantages of international financial reporting harmonization.

(b) Briefly outline what you think the key barriers to international reporting adoption might be.

Exercise 1.5

This is a simple exercise to familiarize you with the kind of information that is presented in the financial statements. Examine the three primary statements presented above to discover the following information:

(a) What is the value of Tesco plc's property, plant and equipment for the year ended 25 February 2012?

(b) What is the value of their loans and advances to customers for the year ended 25 February 2011?

(c) How much cash and cash equivalents did Tesco plc hold at the end of the most recent financial year?

(d) How much revenue did Tesco plc generate during the year to 25 February 2012?

(e) What was the operating profit for Tesco plc during the years to 25 February 2011 and 2012?

(f) What was the sum of current assets at 25 February 2012? And, as far as possible, can you provide a breakdown of this balance?

(g) How much cash did Tesco plc generate through financing activities during 25 February 2012?

Exercise 1.6

The IASB acknowledges within the Conceptual Framework that general-purpose financial reports cannot provide all the information that users may need to make economic decisions. They suggest that users will need to consider pertinent information from other sources as well.

(a) Briefly outline what you feel the financial statements cannot tell an external user.

(b) List examples of further information (ie beyond the annual report and financial statements) which a potential investor would require before making an investment (or disinvestment) decision.

Answers to comprehension questions

1 The two forms of accounting are commonly referred to as financial accounting and management accounting. The differences can be classified into four categories as follows:

TABLE 1.4

Key differences	Financial accounting	Management accounting
Users	External	Internal
Format	Regulated	Any
Frequency	Normally annual	As required
Content	Dominated by historic information based on past transactions	Forward-looking

2 Trade receivables arise when a sale has been made on credit but the money that relates to that invoice has not been collected at the end of the period. This is recorded as a current asset in the statement of financial position because it is an amount owed to you at the period end.

Trade payables arise when a purchase has been made, the materials/goods received but the payment has not been made. This needs to be recorded as a current liability in the statement of financial position as it is an amount owed by you at the period end.

3 Users and their information needs:

Lenders – they have loaned funds to the business under some formal agreement. They require information as reassurance that the obligations arising as a result of their debt provision will be met.

Suppliers – similar to lenders. They also require some information in order to decide whether to continue to trade with the business.

Employees – without human capital a business would struggle to survive. Employees are concerned about the ongoing stability of the firm and the profitability thereof. They might also be interested in remuneration, especially if bonuses are linked to profitability or financial position.

The public – Businesses have a direct impact on the environment around them, socially, ethically and environmentally. Therefore, in all these regards, the public might want information regarding a business's performance and future prospects.

Government – need information for tax purposes, regulatory purposes, employment prospects, statistics compilation.

Customers – often have a long-term involvement with the business and they need reassurance regarding the long-term future. There may be warranty arrangements.

4 The fundamental characteristics:

- Relevant financial information is capable of making a difference in the decisions made by users. Information may be capable of making a difference in a decision even if some users choose not to take advantage of it or are already aware of it from other sources. Financial information is capable of making a difference in decisions if it has predictive value, confirmatory value or both.

- Financial reports represent economic phenomena in words and numbers. To be useful, financial information must not only represent relevant phenomena, but it must also faithfully represent the phenomena that it purports to represent. To be a perfectly faithful representation, a depiction would have three characteristics. It would be complete, neutral and free from error.

5 The enhancing characteristics:

- Users' decisions involve choosing between alternatives, for example selling or holding an investment, or investing in one reporting entity or another. Consequently, information about a reporting entity is more useful if it can be compared with similar information about other entities and with similar information about the same entity for another period or another date. Comparability is the qualitative characteristic that enables users to identify and understand similarities in, and differences among, items.

- Verifiability helps assure users that information faithfully represents the economic phenomena it purports to represent. Verifiability means that different knowledgeable and independent observers could reach consensus, although not necessarily complete agreement, that a particular depiction is a faithful representation. Quantified information need not be a single-point estimate to be verifiable. A range of possible amounts and the related probabilities can also be verified.

- Timeliness means having information available to decision-makers in time to be capable of influencing their decisions. Generally, the older the information is the less useful it is. However, some information may continue to be timely long after the end of a reporting period because, for example, some users may need to identify and assess trends.

- Financial reports are prepared for users who have a reasonable knowledge of business and economic activities and who review and analyse the information diligently. Classifying, characterizing and presenting information clearly and concisely make it understandable.

6 The International Accounting Standards Board – or IASB – acts as an independent standard-setting body on behalf of the IFRS Foundation. The IASB currently has 15 full-time members who are responsible for the development and publication of IFRSs. They actively engage with stakeholders from around the world, including investors, analysts, regulators, business leaders, other accounting standard-setters and the accountancy profession. Their principal objective is to develop a single set of high-quality, understandable, enforceable and globally accepted international financial reporting standards (IFRSs).

7 The disadvantages of incorporation include the following:

(a) The regulatory burden is far greater on limited liability companies than on sole traders and partnerships. A limited company has to publish annual financial statements. These are public statement of account, meaning, of course, that anyone (including competitors and employees) can see how well (or badly) the entity has done. As stated above, sole traders and partnerships do not have to publish their financial statements. *Note: the regulatory burden on public limited companies is far greater again!*

(b) Limited companies accounts must comply with the relevant domestic or international financial reporting requirements.

(c) It is a common requirement in domestic law that large companies' financial statements are audited. In other words, they are subject to an independent review to ensure that they are true and fair, and comply with all relevant legal requirements and accounting standards. This process can be both time-consuming and expensive.

(d) Though raising finance is listed as an advantage, note also that share issues are regulated by law and a public sale of shares on a stock exchange can be an extremely expensive affair (and sometimes an expensive failure). It is also quite difficult to reduce the level of share capital or to get rid of shareholders who are deemed to be standing in the way of management objectives.

8 Definitions of some key financial terms:

(a) asset – a resource controlled by an entity as a result of past events and from which economic benefits are expected to flow to the entity;

(b) liability – a present obligation of the entity arising from past events, the settlement of which is expected to result in an outflow from the entity of resources embodying economic benefits;

(c) equity – the residual interest in the assets of the entity after deducting all its liabilities.

Answers to exercises

Exercise 1.1 A comparison between financial and management accounting

The preparation of the annual report and financial statements – statement of financial position, statement of comprehensive income, statement of cash flows – is the domain of the financial accountant. Though the information is relevant to the senior management team and board of directors, one would hope that this annual exercise was an opportunity to review and bring together rather than learn. It is principally driven by an external demand and therefore is largely externally focused. The financial statements are prepared according to rules and regulations. They are prepared at certain points in time, normally annually. They are prepared using historic information, are based upon records of past transactions and therefore have the tendency to be backwards-looking.

The management accountant would be concerned with fundamental problems such as setting prices and determining costs. From this, the management accountant would seek to provide information that would help the senior management team. For example, through setting budgets, evaluating the working capital position (current assets versus current liabilities), appraising investment opportunities and guiding strategic decisions.

Exercise 1.2 Identifying the users of financial reports

(a) Compartmentalized Inc:

Owners: This is a family-run company and therefore the key information users will be the family themselves. The business is now a large organization and therefore accurate record-keeping is essential as a management discipline. Often the preparation of financial statements is in itself a worthwhile venture as it ensures that at least once a year, the various parts of the business are brought together, accounts are reconciled and balances examined. They might use the information to guide their decision making. If they prepare segmental information then it might be an opportunity to focus on relative levels of profitability between business areas.

Employees: The financial statements often add some level of transparency to employees. If the business has performed satisfactorily then any pre-existing feelings of instability, insecurity or unrest might be quelled. If staff bonuses are linked to performance or position then the financial statements might shed some light on the level of remuneration afforded.

Competitors: Competitors could use Compartmentalized Inc's financial information to reflect on their own performance and position. This could be used for many decisions, including pricing, product cost, outsourcing and financial strategy.

(b) Gronk plc

Current and potential shareholders: Gronk is a listed company and therefore the management has stewardship responsibilities to their current shareholders. Their position and performance will influence their current investors' view on whether to retain their level of investment, increase it or reduce it. Potential investors will also be advised whether to buy stock in Gronk. Normally this advice will be provided by investment analysts and the instructions will be conveyed through institutional investors. Information contained within the annual report is used to inform this advice and to prepare valuation estimates.

Lenders: Gronk plc has significant borrowings. The lenders will consult the financial information to ensure there have been no loan covenant breaches. They might also use the information to gauge the level of risk of current and future lending.

Customers: Customers will often book their holidays months in advance of their departure date. If appropriate (insurance) cover is not taken then customers leave themselves exposed to entity-specific risk. Assuming the financial information released is positive, then customer doubts and fears could be assuaged.

(c) Worldwide Water

Public – charitable donors: Funds are accumulated through the goodwill of the public who make donations. The public, therefore, would be interested to see how effectively and efficiently the charity is using their financial resource. They might be looking to reappraise their charitable giving and therefore they could attempt to perform a reconciliation of the amount of 'good' done for every dollar spent.

Public – charitable donation beneficiaries and their advocates: It is possible that the beneficiaries, and those who act on their behalf, will also want to see how effectively the resources of the charity have been managed.

The government and her regulatory bodies: Though taxation is not a concern as Worldwide Water is a not-for-profit entity, the government might provide financial (and non-financial) support. It is likely, therefore, that the charity will have some form of financial accountability and associated regulation. Often the government will supply charities with non-financial targets which might drive financial rewards.

Exercise 1.3

There are many possible alternatives. The following are among them:

(i) A balance which could be material owing to its magnitude? The problem with identifying balances according to their magnitude (or size) is that the value will differ by entity. There are some rules of thumb that can be employed. Some organizations use 5 per cent of profit before interest and tax to determine what is material from what is not. However, for an entity whose worth is high but profits are low, this can cause significant frictions and drive an inappropriate level of focusing on detail which is not relevant to a user's understanding of the performance or position of the entity (ie immaterial). Some organizations use a combination of income statement measure and financial position measure, eg 1 per cent of net assets + 1 per cent of turnover.

Balances which are material by their magnitude will also differ dependent upon the industry and financial strategy of the entity. For example, a manufacturing firm is likely to have high inventories and therefore these will probably be material owing to their magnitude. An airline, however, which is likely to have low inventories – they will stock on-board food, drinks and small amounts of product for in-flight duty-free sales which will be a fraction of the value of the aeroplanes and corresponding liabilities – is unlikely to need to focus their energy on their inventories balance.

Misstatements within individual balances might be material owing to their context (see iii).

(ii) A balance which could be material owing to its nature? There are several examples of balances which are material simply because of their nature. For example, any misstatement of an entity's issued share capital is likely to be deemed material. Equally, there are some balances which are deemed material because they are sensitive, for example directors' remuneration.

(iii) A balance which could be material owing to its context? An error of $20,000 in a revenue balance of $1 million is unlikely to be material. However, if a customer files for bankruptcy owing you $20,000 and your total trade receivables are $100,000 then this sum would be considered to be material in context.

Exercise 1.4

The key advantages of international financial reporting harmonization include the following:

- comparability;
- information access;
- aids internal communication;
- makes the appraisal of foreign entities more straightforward;
- benefits to global accounting firms and their accounting staff;
- ease of transfer of staff.

And so on...

The key barriers to international reporting adoption:

- different purposes for preparing financial information;
- different legal systems;
- different user groups;
- nationalism.

And so on...

Exercise 1.5

(a) £25,710 million

(b) Non-current portion: £2,514 million; current portion: £2,657 million; total: £5,171 million. (Note: prior-year figures are provided alongside current year balances.)

(c) £2,305 million. (Note: you can extract this balance from either the statement of financial position or the statement of cash flows; by default they *must* agree.)

(d) £64,539 million.

(e) 2011: £3,917 million; 2012: £3,985 million.

(f) £12,863 million, broken down as shown in Table 1.5.

TABLE 1.5   Exercise 1.5(f)

	£m
Inventories	3,598
Trade and other receivables	2,657
Loans and advances to customers	2,502
Derivative financial instruments	41
Current tax assets	7
Short-term investments	1,243
Cash and cash equivalents	2,305
Assets of the disposal group and non-current assets classified as held for sale	510
Total	12,863

(g) £(1,366) million. (Note: the figure is negative, ie cash outflow. This is largely because the group paid out £1,180 of dividends to equity owners.)

Exercise 1.6

(a) Brief outline of what the financial statements cannot tell an external user:

Internally, one would hope that all relevant financial information related to the entity would be freely available between the senior management team. However, external users do not get to see the same level of detail related to account balances. Issues such as individual customer accounts and exposure to creditworthiness are not freely disclosed. A company might show certain assets at an over- or under-value owing to an accounting policy choice, but as an externality you would not be aware of such things. The information being passed around internally is up to date and often forecasted ahead, taking into account project-specific risks. The information an external user has available often lacks this timeliness and any adjustment for risk tends to be based upon assumptions rather than facts.

The financial statements are audited but the front end of the annual report is simply checked for consistency. This might mean that narrative and graphical representations can lead to differing external interpretations, and sometimes misinterpretations. Not only does the potential for impression management exist within the textual and graphical narratives, there is also the opportunity for the entity to engage in earnings management (sometimes referred to as smoothing) practices. Indeed, the preparation of financial statements often requires managers use their judgement because of choices in accounting policy. Among some accountants, the employment of managerial judgement is both welcomed and supported because it can lead to more meaningful – and hence useful – information.

(b) Examples of further information required before making an investment (or disinvestment) decision:

There was a time when the release of the annual report and financial statements was the most important moment in the financial calendar for followers of a firm. Though it is still significant, the acceleration in sophistication of communication networks and the media has meant that this level of importance has diminished. There are many examples of information not contained within the annual report. The role of investment analysts is now ultra-competitive and the relative ability to gather public and private information from disparate and far-ranging sources might make the difference to one's career.

Retail analysts, for example, can go to absurd lengths. It is not a simple case of reading the broadsheet newspaper headlines or following the entity's press releases. They could investigate potential next opportunities for new markets by reading trade journals, visiting possible sites, speaking to local people, attending council meetings and so forth. The new constraints on analysts are time and resource, rather than lack of timely information or sophistication in interpretation.

Accounting concepts and systems

OBJECTIVE

We use this chapter to introduce the types of financial accounting information you will encounter in your daily managerial lives. We provide a basic guide to bookkeeping and outline how to prepare a straightforward set of financial statements. Some measurement rules and accounting concepts are also explained.

LEARNING OUTCOMES

After studying this chapter, the reader will be able to:

- Describe the key elements of an accounting system.
- Identify the different types of accounting adjustment.
- Assess the impact of accounting adjustments on reported results.
- Prepare basic primary financial statements.

KEY TOPICS COVERED

- What accounting systems record and how.
- Cash-based accounting, accruals and other accounting adjustments.
- The impact of accounting adjustments on the statement of financial position and on profit.
- Practical issues of adjustment, for example dealing with tangible non-current assets.

> **MANAGEMENT ISSUES**
>
> This chapter will deal specifically with the management skills of understanding and assessing the impact of accounting adjustments on the reported results.

Introduction

During this chapter we try to show you why financial statements are important, describe their contents and show you how to prepare a straightforward set. Appendix A deals with double-entry bookkeeping and works through the same examples using this method.

Even though this material represents only the tip of the iceberg in terms of depth and breadth, it is extremely helpful to know how information emerges out of data. In turn, the series of exercises contained herein should show you that the quality, complexity and context are crucial to grasp before you go on to try to form an assessment and appraisal of an entity's position and performance.

This chapter also introduces some key accounting concepts and conventions. These should reveal that interpreting – and to an extent, preparing – financial statements is an art, not a science. This also highlights how accounting procedures and policies can impact on reported results. As managers, you need to be aware that accounting is not a system of rigid or fixed rules where output is predefined. Rather, there is flexibility within the regulations which allow scope for presentational, recognition, measurement and disclosure differences.

What is the purpose of the financial statements?

This question is the most obvious starting point for this chapter. Towards the end of the previous chapter we showed you Tesco's financial statements. We hope that you have also gone away and looked up a couple of companies' annual reports in which you have a special interest. For Tesco, we showed you three primary financial statements: the statement of comprehensive income (income statement); the statement of financial position; and the statement of cash flows. This chapter will focus on these and walk you through the accounting for some basic transactions.

Statement of comprehensive income (income statement)

The income statement shows how much profit the business has made during a specific period of time. We told you that the 'period of account' is normally a year, but large organizations are often required to produce interim statements, eg quarterly.

The layout of the income statement will depend on the entity, but there are a selection of headings which are typical, including:

- **Gross profit**: A company generates revenue by undertaking its normal operating activity, eg selling goods and/or services. The costs that *directly* relate to selling these goods ('cost of goods sold'; or more usually, 'cost of sales') is deducted from the revenue. This generates the gross profit figure.

  The gross profit is stated before the deduction of *indirect* expenses – such as operating expenses, finance costs or tax – and before adding any 'other' income generated, not arising from the normal operating activity – such as finance income.

- **Operating profit**: Business expenses which are not directly incurred in relation to the generation of revenue are deducted after the gross profit line. These indirect costs might include items such as rental costs, business rates, heating and lighting costs, administrative expenses, wages and salaries, depreciation and so forth.

  Finance income and/or costs (which include interest receivable/payable) and taxation are deducted from the operating profit, which is why the operating profit is sometimes referred to as profit before interest and tax (PBIT) or earnings before interest and tax (EBIT).

- **Profit for the year (period)**: The profit for the year is arrived at by deducting all other expenses from the operating profit. This total is transferred to the statement of financial position on a rolling basis each year. The balance on this account accumulates under the heading 'Retained earnings'.

Figure 2.1 shows an income statement for a fictional entity – Malambo Inc. – for illustration purposes.

Expert view 2.1: Comprehensive income

The statement of comprehensive income is actually subdivided into two parts. The top part is the 'income statement' and the bottom part is the section that captures the 'comprehensive income'. As a basic rule of thumb, the income statement shows an entity's realized gains and losses whereas the statement of comprehensive income as a whole identifies those which are both realized and unrealized. Examples of unrealized balances could include gains and losses arising from issues such as revaluing property to its open market value, cash-flow hedging gains and losses, and foreign exchange translation gains and losses.

Online content

Listed companies such as Tesco plc have higher levels of reporting requirements and are subject to greater levels of scrutiny and regulation. We have provided a couple of examples (available online) which show that there is still freedom to present information differently.

FIGURE 2.1 Malambo Inc

Malambo Inc. is a fictional entity. The example exists simply to illustrate the various components of an income statement. You will note that the company generates revenue of $900,000, gross profit of $600,000, operating profit (PBIT) of $366,000 and profit for the year of $267,000. The statement includes the organization's name, the statement's title and the period covered.

Malambo Inc.
Income statement
For the year ended 30 September 2014

	$
Revenue	900,000
Cost of sales	300,000
Gross profit	600,000
Operating expenses:	
Heat and light	25,000
Rent and rates	50,000
Motor running costs	8,000
Wages and salaries	100,000
Insurances	40,000
Postage, packaging and stationery	4,000
Depreciation	6,000
Amortization	1,000
Operating profit	366,000
Finance income	5,000
Finance costs	14,000
Profit before taxation	357,000
Taxation	90,000
Profit for the year	267,000

We recommend that you search on the internet for your 'most (least) favoured brand' or 'most (least) favoured company'. Sometimes, a personal involvement or an ability to contextualize makes a subject more meaningful.

The statement of financial position (balance sheet)

The statement of financial position (commonly referred to as the balance sheet) is akin to a financial photograph: a snapshot of the current worth of an organization at one moment in time.

Financial statements are prepared according to one golden rule, as follows:

- Every **debit** entry in the ledger accounts must be matched by a corresponding **credit** entry.

And nowhere is this rule more visible or understandable than in the statement of financial position. The **accounting equation** is as follows:

- Assets – Liabilities = Capital (shareholders' funds).

Both assets and liabilities are categorized as either current (due within one year) or non-current (due in more than one year). Below is a brief description of each category and a few examples:

- **Non-current assets** are bought with the intention to use them to generate revenue over the course of a number of years. There are two forms of non-current assets – tangible and intangible. The former are those which it is possible to touch, see and feel. Intangible assets are assets that have a realizable market value despite not having a physical presence. The rules governing the capitalization (ie bringing onto the statement of financial position as an asset) of intangible assets are quite strict. Analysts typically reassess the value of an entity's intangible assets, as they are commonly a key driver of the difference between market value (ie the share price) and book value (ie the notion of net worth shown at the foot of the statement of financial position).
  - Examples of tangible non-current assets include: property (land and buildings), plant, equipment, fixtures, fittings, motor vehicles and so forth.
  - Examples of intangible non-current assets include: (purchased) goodwill, patents, royalties, computer software and so forth.
- **Current assets** are expected to be sold or converted into another form within one year.
  - Examples include: inventories, trade receivables, cash held in hand or at bank, cash equivalents, prepayments.
- **Non-current liabilities** are amounts owed by the business which it is not obligated to repay within the next 12 months.
  - Examples include: bank loans, mortgages, debentures, loan stock, provisions and so forth.
- **Current liabilities** are obligations which need to be settled within the next 12 months.
  - Examples include: bank overdraft, short-term borrowings, trade payables, taxation and so forth.

Online content

We have provided a couple of examples (available online at: **www.koganpage.com/accountingfm**) which show some complex entities' statements of financial position to mirror the income statements provided. As before, we recommend that you search for brands and companies you are acquainted with and have a look at their annual reports.

The statement of cash flows

The statement of cash flows shows whether we have earned or spent cash (and cash equivalents) during the year. The focus of the statement of cash flows is, as the name suggests, cash inflows versus cash outflows. The statement is divided between three activities: operating; investing; and financing.

Expert view 2.2: Preparing a statement of cash flows

Students of financial accounting commonly find this the most difficult of the three primary statements to prepare. This is surprising because you often know the answer before you start – if you know the opening and closing cash position and (available from the statement of financial position or from your books and records), then preparing the statement of cash flows is simply a reconciliation exercise where you organize movements in balances in to appropriate categories (ie decide whether they are operating, investing or financing).

Note that the income statement and balance sheet are prepared on an **accruals basis** whereas this statement is prepared on a **cash basis**. This is important because organizations can be profitable (or loss-making) but be losing (or gaining) cash. We will explain this in more detail later. Ultimately, the accounting profits and the cash profits will reconcile, but the chances of them being identical year to year are negligible.

The key differences between profits on an accruals basis versus those measured on a cash basis relate to:

- **Timing differences**. For example, goods might be sold to an entity, delivered immediately and an invoice for payment raised at the same time. However, if you grant a credit period then you should expect your customers to take advantage of it (after all, this is essentially an interest-free loan for them). Therefore, the revenue can be booked to the income statement as the transaction took place during the period, but if the cash has not been received by the end of the period then it will show as a balance being owed to you. In other words, the cash follows the sale.

- **Accounting estimates**. It is necessary for accountants to make accounting estimates during the preparation of the financial statements. One example is the accounting for depreciation against tangible non-current assets. Depreciation acts as a proxy for the costs related to wear and tear of an asset over time, so assets classified as non-current must be written off to the income statement as their revenue-generating potential is consumed (more on this later). In cash terms, however, the payment will often occur up-front.

- **Accounting transactions that bypass the income statement**. For example, capital expenditure, sale of share capital, repayments of loans and so forth.

- **Changes in the working capital position**. For example, an increase in inventories means that an entity has invested cash in inventories, which it hopes to translate back into cash through the sale of these goods. Figure 2.2 shows the working capital cycle and reveals how the process of investment and re-investment in working capital makes the management of short-term resources crucial. It also shows the importance to a business of focusing on the cash cycle.

Expert view 2.3: Financial reporting regulation

Financial reporting is governed by many regulations, foremost of which are the International Financial Reporting Standards (IFRS). The predecessor to the IASB was called the International Accounting Standards Committee (IASC). This body released International Accounting Standards (IAS). Though IAS' are in a process of being developed and refined, it is intended that they will all be replaced by IFRS'. This exercise is far from being complete and many still exist. Therefore, you will commonly see references to IAS as well as IFRS. For a full list see Appendix B.

We will come back to this idea again in later chapters but, for the time being, it is worth noting that the concept of cash is important in both financial and management accounting. Cash is often described as the 'lifeblood' of the business because without cash, a business cannot expect to survive for long.

FIGURE 2.2   Working capital cycle

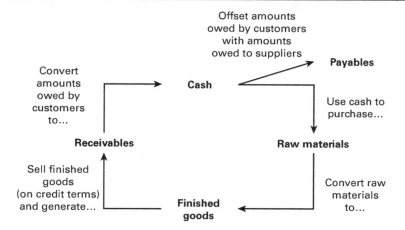

Figure 2.2 illustrates how a traditional manufacturing business operates while also serving to highlight the importance of cash to the process. While a company holds inventories or they are owed money, the cash balance is reduced. This can be offset by owing others money (payables), but if management extend their credit terms too far, beware the consequences. This is, of course, an over-simplification but it does highlight the importance of efficiency.

When preparing a statement of cash flows, you will notice that an increase in a current asset (eg inventories) will lead to a decrease in cash. We hope that Figure 2.2 makes it obvious to see why.

Exercises: now attempt Exercise 2.1 on page 85

Preparing a set of financial statements

Even though it may never be necessary for you to be called upon to prepare a full and detailed set of financial statements, an understanding of the basics is essential to any interpretative study of financial information. During this section, our aim is to cover only the basic, but most valuable, tenets.

Double-entry bookkeeping: an introduction

Double-entry bookkeeping is a system of recording financial transactions. The underpinning principle is that every debit entry must have an equal and opposite credit entry. Recognizing amounts in a timely and structured manner has helped owners and managers organize their day-to-day business for millennia. Today, there are many computerized bookkeeping packages which are extremely useful in assisting accounting staff to produce key reports. These accounting packages, however, do not teach you accounting *per se*; they just simplify the process of data entry.

Expert view 2.4: Mastering the basics of financial accounting

Financial accounting should be seen as a building-block exercise. You should strive to master the skills and knowledge gathered at each stage before moving on to the next. There is one caveat, and this relates to double-entry bookkeeping. Many accountants talk of a 'eureka' or a 'light bulb' moment. What they mean is that one day they woke up and found that double-entry bookkeeping simply makes sense! Thinking logically always helps. Every time you engage in a financial transaction, imagine the double-entry bookkeeping system at work. For example, you buy a newspaper from the shop. You have exchanged your money for an asset of (deemed) equivalent worth.

WORKED EXERCISE 2.1   Mobius (1)

Let us suppose that you wish to start your own business, Mobius Inc. The following transactions shown in examples Mobius (1) to Mobius (3) represent the first week of trading for the entity.

On day 1, you opt to put financial distance between you and the trading entity and transfer $1,000 from your personal bank account to a bank account you hold in the name of the new enterprise – Mobius Inc.

Assuming that the new business is a separate legal entity, how does this affect the accounting equation?

Assets	–	Liabilities	=	Shareholder's funds (ie your injection of capital)
$1,000	–	$0	=	$1,000

NOTE: As you can see, the accounting equation captures both sides of the transaction and only by making the entry twice does the equation (and, by extension, the statement of financial position) balance.

Continuing this exercise...

On day 2, you borrow $500 from a friend to provide further financial help to your business. How does this impact on the accounting equation?

Assets	–	Liabilities	=	Capital
1,500	–	$500	=	$1,000

NOTE: The effect of the financial transaction is to increase assets by $500 as the amount borrowed from your friend would be deposited in the current account of the business. The liabilities would increase by $500. This represents the new loan the business has taken on. The capital that you invested has neither increased nor diminished in the process of this transaction and therefore remains at $1,000. This, of course, means that your accounting equation continues to balance.

The transactions above illustrate that if an adjustment is made to one side of the equation, you **must** make an identical adjustment **either** to the other side of the equation **or** to the same side.

Exercise 2.2: Accounting equation adjustments

Continuing the worked exercise above, make the necessary adjustments for the following transactions:

(a) On day 3, Mobius Inc invests $500 of cash by acquiring a new computer.

(b) On day 4, Mobius Inc buys some raw materials worth $400 and holds them as inventories. The cash required to settle the invoices related to these purchases does not need to be found for 10 days as these are the credit terms offered.

The transactions above relate exclusively to the statement of financial position. They require making changes to assets, liabilities and equity with no profit implications. This is overly simplistic, therefore these next worked exercises of individual transactions provide the opportunity to see how the accounting equation changes when an entity trades.

WORKED EXERCISE 2.2   Mobius (2) – trading activities

On day 5, Mobius Inc uses the raw materials purchased the previous day to produce 30 units of finished goods stock.

On day 6, half of these are sold for $50 per unit. Cash is received immediately for five of those sold. The remainder were sold to customers on 10-day credit terms.

Solution

The transfer between raw materials and finished goods inventories has no impact on the accounting equation (in reality it is difficult to imagine that no value is added to the product [eg extra materials, direct labour], but for simplicity's sake, let us assume that this is the case). We would simply transfer $400 from one category of current assets to another – raw materials inventory to finished goods inventory. Therefore, at this stage, the accounting equation remains unchanged, as follows:

$$\text{Assets} \quad - \quad \text{Liabilities} \quad = \quad \text{Shareholder's funds}$$
$$\$1900 \quad - \quad \$900 \quad = \quad \$1,000$$

However, the sale of the product does generate a change in the entity's net worth. Ultimately, most organizations hold as their corporate objective the maximization of shareholder wealth and it is unsurprising that goods are bought and subsequently every effort is made to sell them for a profit. In this case, the goods cost $400 and were transformed into 30 saleable units of inventory, of which half were sold for $50 per unit. Five were paid for immediately while 10 have been sold under 10-day credit terms. Therefore, the changes to the accounting equation that we will record are as follows (see Table 2.1):

(i)   Revenue generated: 15 units * $50 = $750

(ii)   Of which, cash collected was 5 * $50 = $250 and amounts owed from customers was 10 units * $50 = $500

(iii) Amount of inventory used to generate these sales was $200.

TABLE 2.1

Assets	$	Liabilities	$	Capital	$
Opening balance	1,900	Opening balance	900	Opening balance	1,000
				i) Revenue	750
ii) Cash collected	250				
ii) Owed by customers	500				
iii) Inventories consumed	(200)			iii) Cost of goods sold	(200)
Closing balance	**2,450**		**900**		**1,550**

The effect on assets and liabilities is straightforward. Assets increase due to the extra amount of cash held and the amount of money owed by customers. Liabilities remain unchanged.

Why has the level of shareholder's funds changed? The business has managed to generate $550 of profit ($750 of revenue less $200 of inventories consumed). These retained profits are added to the shareholder's funds and remain there until spent or distributed.

WORKED EXERCISE 2.3   Mobius (3) – the financial statements [week 1]

Preparing complex financial statements at this stage of your accounting learning is not necessary. However, it is possible to translate the information we have into a basic set of summarized financial statements:

Mobius Inc **Summarized Statement of Financial Position** **As at the end of week 1**	$
Assets **Non-current assets** Computer (500 [3])	500
Current assets Cash at bank (1,000 [1] + 500 [2] – 500 [3] + 250 [5c])	1,250
Inventories	
Raw materials (400 [4] – 400 [5a])	0
Finished goods (400 [5a] – 200 [5b])	200
Trade receivables – amounts owed by customers (500 [5c])	500
Liabilities Loan from friend (500 [2])	(500)
Trade payables – amounts owed to supplier (400 [4])	(400)
Net assets	**1,550**
Shareholder's funds (capital and reserves) Capital (1,000 [1])	1,000
Retained profits (550 [transferred from income statement])	550
Shareholder's funds	**1,550**

Mobius Inc **Summarized Income Statement** **For the period ended DD/MM/YYYY (week 1)**	$
Revenue (750 [5c])	750
Cost of sales (200 [5b])	(200)
Profit	**550***

* Transfer to statement of financial position at the end of the period of account

NOTE: transaction numbers are shown in square brackets to help identify the matching accounting entry. You will notice that after each transaction is entered, the statement of financial position could be closed off and would balance, ie the top half would equal the bottom half.

> ### Expert view 2.5: Revenue and expenses
>
> The IASB would prefer we thought of gains and losses arising as a result of assets and liabilities increasing and decreasing. However, it is probably more common for non-accountants to think of profits as being generated when revenue exceeds expenses.
>
> **Revenue** typically relates to the income an organization generates by selling goods and services.
>
> **Expenses** (costs) are incurred in the process of generating revenue.

At the end of the period of account, an income statement is reset to zero because this statement reports '**for the period ended**', whereas the statement of financial position shows the position of the entity '**as at the period ended**'.

Therefore, let us assume that the above transactions represent Mobius Inc's position as at the end of the first week of trading and the business is about to begin the second week. The income statement balances would be reset to zero and the profit of $550 taken to the statement of financial position where it will be retained until it is used (consumed by losses or distributed).

The income statement: cost of sales working

The cost of sales working in the statement of financial position applies the accruals concept to match the expense to the period in which it is incurred. The cost of sales is sometimes referred to as 'the cost of goods sold'. In other words, we are matching the units of product sold to the direct cost of purchasing (producing) those units. The basic working is as follows:

Cost of sales	
Opening inventories	X
Purchases	X
(Closing inventories)	(x)
	X

> Exercises: now attempt Exercise 2.3 on page 86

WORKED EXERCISE 2.4   Mobius (4) – the financial statements continued

Now that we have a statement of financial position as at the end of week 1, we can adjust straight to the face of the statements and thus monitor how the business's net worth and profitability levels change during the second week of trading, as shown in Table 2.2.

Remember: bookkeeping is a dual-aspect method and you will need to post every transaction twice for the statement of financial position to balance.

TABLE 2.2

Day of trading	
8	• The business acquired raw materials valued at $800. • Invoices need to be paid within 10 days.
9	• All the raw materials were converted into 60 units of finished goods inventories.
10	• The company received a utilities bill for $200 which it paid immediately out of cash. *Note: assume this charge relates exclusively to this period of account.*
11	• Mobius Inc. sold 35 units of inventories for $60 per unit. Cash was received for 20 of these units and the remainder were offered to customers on 10-day credit terms.
12	• Mobius Inc. bought a printer/scanner for $100. • Mobius Inc. bought some stationery including paper and envelopes for $50.
13	• Mobius Inc. received $500 from customers who had bought goods on credit terms.
14	• Amounts invoiced by suppliers during week 1 of $400 were paid. • Mobius Inc. paid a web designer $750 to develop an online presence for the business.

Solution

The exercise has been completed in order of appearance in the text above. All transactions have been accurately and appropriately double-entered and can be traced through by reference to square brackets. The opening balances from week 1 have simply been brought forward and therefore have no transaction number.

Mobius Inc
Summarized Statement of Financial Position
As at the end of week 2

Assets	
Non-current assets	
Computer (500)	500.00
Printer/scanner (100 [5])	100.00
Current assets	
Cash at bank (1,250 – 200 [3] + 1,200 [4] – 100 [5] – 50 [6] + 500 [7] – 400 [8] – 750 [9])	1,450.00
Inventories	
Raw materials (0 + 800 [1] – 800 [2])	0.00
Finished goods (200 + 800 [2] – 466.67 [4])	533.33
Trade receivables – amounts owed by customers (500 + 900 [4] – 500 [7])	900.00
Liabilities	
Loan from friend (500)	(500.00)
Trade payables – amounts owed to suppliers (400 + 800 [1] – 400 [8])	(800.00)
Net assets	2,183.33
Shareholder's funds (capital and reserves)	
Capital (1,000)	1,000.00
Retained profits	
Brought forward	550.00
Profit generated during week 2	633.33
Shareholder's funds	2,183.33

Mobius Inc
Summarized Income Statement
For the period ended DD/MM/YYYY (week 2)

Revenue (2,100 [4])	2,100.00
Cost of sales (466.67 [4])	(466.67)
Gross profit	1,633.33
Expenses:	
Utilities (200 [3])	(200.00)
Printing, postage and stationery (50 [6])	(50.00)
Web development costs (750 [9])	(750.00)
Profit	633.33

Exercises: now attempt Exercise 2.4 on page 87

Underlying concepts: measurement rules and fundamental accounting concepts

Let's take a short break from these preparation exercises and turn our attention to some measurement rules and underlying concepts. You'll appreciate that not everything is as easy to account for as, say, exchanging cash for a newspaper. Indeed, the above exercises portray a series of simple transactions during which we have deliberately minimized your exposure to recognition, measurement and presentation problems. The following section outlines some of the potential complexities and the guidelines accountants have developed to deal with them.

Following this, we will pick up the case of Mobius Inc again and work through some more preparation exercises to illustrate how these concepts are articulated through numbers rather than text.

Measurement rules

There are some basic measurement rules which are applied in financial accounting. These rules explain *how* balances are recorded in the financial statements. Owing to the importance of the measurement basis used for the values recorded in the financial statements, it is unsurprising that few areas have attracted so much academic and professional commentary. The following are considered to be key:

- historical cost accounting;
- current cost accounting;
- mixed measurement model;
- money measurement concept;
- business entity concept.

Online content

More information is provided about these measurement rules online at:
www.koganpage.com/accountingfm

Fundamental accounting concepts

There are a number of fundamental accounting concepts which are enforced either through regulation or legislation. The following concepts are relevant:

- accruals concept;
- going concern;
- prudence;
- disaggregation;
- materiality.

A brief review of each follows.

Accruals concept

The accruals concept is often referred to as the matching concept or matching rule. Indeed, the reference to 'matching' is a simpler way to envisage its operation (even if it does not strictly hold in some domestic GAAP). The accruals concept states that revenues, profits and the associated costs should be matched to the same period's income statement.

There are many everyday instances where a transaction would be recorded in different accounting periods dependent upon whether you employed an accruals accounting system or a cash accounting one. For example, electricity bills are commonly issued and paid in arrears. Imagine that you have 11 monthly invoices related to your electricity costs for the year ending 31 December and are awaiting the 12th and final invoice. You will need to accrue for the expense because the electricity was being consumed during the period of account. You will have to bring the cost into this period's income statement and provide for it by setting up a corresponding liability in the statement of financial position.

Extending this example, it is possible that you might need to estimate the level of consumption for the 12th month because the electricity company hasn't issued their invoice before your accounts finalization date. It is easy to see how accruals accounting can lead to increased subjectivity because sometimes it is necessary to estimate the value of future transactions.

Expert view 2.6 Do not confuse accruals and the accruals concept

Though the terms are clearly related, you should be careful not to define an accrual in the same way as you define the accruals concept. An entity would need to accrue for the electricity cost (ie bring the cost into this period's income statement) by setting up an accrual (ie set up a current liability in the statement of financial position) because of the accruals concept (ie matching concept). The accruals concept is also responsible for giving rise to assets (ie prepayments) and associated gains.

Going concern

Entities are required to prepare accounts on the basis that they are a going concern. This means that the business is commercially viable, able to pay its obligations as they fall due, and whose owners (or other controllers) intend it to continue in operation for the foreseeable future. In particular, when an entity provides assurances over its going concern status, one should be able to assume that the entity will not go into liquidation or scale down its operations in a material way within a period of 12 months or more.

Despite standard-setters and professional bodies assuring investors that they should not panic if an entity records a statement declaring that they are not a going concern, one should note that it is extremely difficult to find an annual report containing this statement. Providing a statement that an entity is not a going concern, some might argue, should be interpreted as a signal of transparency and openness. Instead of presenting an explicit negative statement about their going concern status, companies facing an uncertain future tend to refer to *doubts* over their foreseeable future.

The key financial accounting complication of not maintaining a going concern status is that the assets and liabilities should be valued and shown at their 'break-up' value ie the amount they would sell for if they were sold off piecemeal and the business were broken up. For example, non-current assets would need to be presented as current assets. Their previously recorded value (ie cost less accumulated depreciation) would need to be adjusted to their 'forced sale' value.

Expert view 2.7: Going concern (extracts of going concern disclosures)

Though there are some jurisdictions (eg the United States) where a statement of an entity's going concern status is not expressly required, the directors of most companies include some reference to the likelihood of continuing to trade as normal into the foreseeable future. Indeed, such a statement is roundly encouraged by stakeholders even where not required (as shown by Gallagher and Paul, 2012). Examples from two companies follow: first, Whitbread plc, a major retail brand conglomerate; and second, Oxford Instruments plc, a leading provider of high-technology tools and systems for research and industry.

i) Whitbread plc

Annual report and accounts 2011/12 (p 27)

Available from Whitbread plc's download centre: **www.whitbread.co.uk/global/ download-centre/reports-and-presentations.html**.

Going concern

A combination of the strong operating cash flows generated by the business and the significant headroom on its credit facilities support the directors' view that the Group has sufficient funds available for it to meet its foreseeable working capital requirements. The directors have concluded that the going concern basis remains appropriate.

ii) Oxford Instruments plc

Annual report and financial statements 2012 (p 21)

Available from Oxford Instrument plc's download centre: **www.oxford-instruments.com/investors**.

Going concern

The Group's business activities, together with the factors likely to affect its future development, performance and position, are set out in the chief executive's statement. The financial position of the Group, its cash flows, liquidity position and borrowing facilities are described in this financial review.

The diverse nature of the Group combined with its current financial strength provides a solid foundation for a sustainable business. The directors have reviewed the Group's forecasts and considered a number of potential scenarios relating to changes in trading performance. The directors believe that the Group will be able to operate within its existing debt facility which expires in December 2014. This review also considered hedging arrangements in place. As a consequence, the directors believe that the Group is well placed to manage its business risks successfully.

The financial statements have been prepared on a going concern basis, based on the directors' opinion, after making reasonable enquiries, that the Group has adequate resources to continue in operational existence for the foreseeable future.

Neutrality (and/or) prudence

Accounting transactions and other events are sometimes uncertain and yet, in order for the information to be useful for decision making and fulfil the fundamental qualitative characteristics, these uncertain transactions and events still have to be reported in a timely manner (to correspond to the appropriate period of account). Thus, it is necessary for management to make estimates that counteract the uncertainty. Historically, it has been preferable to err towards prudence. This is not to say that accuracy is not important to accountants and the information which they produce.

The European Financial Reporting Advisory Group (EFRAG), alongside the national standard-setting bodies of France, Germany, Italy and the UK, published a joint bulletin in April 2013 outlining their position on the prudence convention. Within this bulletin they drew attention to the history of prudence and its usefulness. The Fourth EU Directive on Company Law of 1978 requires that 'valuation must be made on a prudent basis' and that, in particular, only profits made at the balance sheet date may be included, whereas account must be taken of all losses related to the financial year or to a previous one. The origins of prudence, however, date much further back.

Accounting regulators have preferred to write requirements that drive a conservative approach to recording transactions, ie in simple terms, a 'plan for the worst' approach. The tendency has been for losses to be recognized at the point at which management are aware of their probable realization, whereas gains are recognized only when they are certain to be received. While some see prudence as the opposite of imprudence – a clearly undesirable feature of any financial reporting system – others see prudence as introducing bias into the financial statements.

There appears to have been a shift in attitudes during recent years. The idea that prudence should be the dominant desirable attribute has passed and in its place the IASB have woven the concept of *neutrality*. It is not entirely certain what this means though. Certainly, the deletion of the term prudence from the chapter on qualitative characteristics was seen by some as a turning point. At the same time, the previously fundamental qualitative characteristic 'reliability' was replaced by 'faithful representation'. The Conceptual Framework's basis for conclusions states that faithful representation 'encompasses the main characteristics that the previous frameworks included as aspects of reliability'. The section continues by stating that 'substance over form, prudence (conservatism) and verifiability, which were aspects of reliability in the previous framework are not considered aspects of faithful representation'.

The IASB have been careful to design their Conceptual Framework to distinguish between the following:

i   the deliberate understatement of assets and profits, or overstatement of liabilities and expenses; and

ii   the adoption of a cautious approach in making the judgements necessitated by uncertainty so that assets and income are not overstated and liabilities and expenses are not understated.

See supporting online content **www.koganpage.com/accountingfm** for a brief article which draws attention to various practical drawbacks of (over-)prudence.

Expert view 2.8: Conditional versus unconditional conservatism

Academic literature also distinguishes conditional conservatism that results in asymmetric timeliness in the recognition of good and bad news (the latter recognized earlier) and unconditional conservatism, which results in systematic understatement of net assets. According to some academic literature, users find early recognition of losses useful, as they are less frequently anticipated by the market than gains. There is a general agreement on the usefulness of conditional conservatism, while unconditional conservatism is more contentious.

Disaggregation

To disaggregate means to separate into component parts. This principle is applied in accounting whereby material assets and liabilities should normally be disclosed separately at their gross amounts, rather than being netted off against each other. For example, netting off short-term borrowings from a positive cash balance is not permitted.

Materiality

We have already discussed this concept, which might in its own way reinforce how fundamental it is to financial accounting and accounting more generally. We introduced materiality as the threshold quality. In other words, information is deemed to be material – by size or nature – where its exclusion would impair an assessment of an entity's position or performance. This rule is advantageous in many ways, not least because it allows accountants to focus their attention on the balances which are significant and, by default, to avoid absurd situations where immaterial balances are being investigated at great cost by companies' accountants.

WORKED EXERCISE 2.5   Mobius Inc (5)

Until this point, everything has been straightforward. You're now ready to move to the next level, and the following worked exercise shows how tangible non-current assets are accounted for. Though there are many standards, IAS 16 *Property, Plant and Equipment* is a good vehicle to allow us to discuss in more detail the prudence and accruals conventions.

The previous exercise concluded at the end of week 2. Let us pick up the exercise at the start of week 3. The closing position looked like this (ie opening statement of financial position as of first day of week 3):

Mobius Inc **Summarized Statement of Financial Position** **As at the start of week 3**	
Assets	
Non-current assets	
Computer	500.00
Printer/scanner	100.00
Current assets	
Cash at bank	1,450.00
Inventories	
Raw materials	0.00
Finished goods	533.33
Trade receivables – amounts owed by customers	900.00
Liabilities	
Loan from friend	(500.00)
Trade payables – amounts owed to suppliers	(800.00)
Net assets	2,183.33

Shareholder's funds (capital and reserves)	
Capital	1,000.00
Retained profits (weeks 1 & 2)	1,183.33
Shareholder's funds	**2,183.33**

The following information is relevant to weeks 3 and 4:

Tangible non-current assets

(a) By the end of week 4, which marks the conclusion to your first full month's trading, you have noticed signs of wear and tear appearing on both of your tangible non-current assets – the printer/scanner and the computer. You believe that the printer will continue effectively for 20 months, at which point it will be scrapped. The computer is unlikely to be usable for business purposes after 40 months but you know a friend will buy it off you at that time for $100.

(b) On the first day of week 3 you decide to buy a new motor vehicle which will be used exclusively for business purposes. The useful economic life of the motor vehicle is estimated to be five years, at which stage the terminal value would be $0. The invoice from the supplier showed the following costs:

	$
Motor vehicle	19,500
Delivery charge	500
Additional extras:	
Non-standard black matt paint job	1,000
Convertible roof function	2,000
Tank of petrol	150
Road tax (for the year)	200
Total	23,350

You take out a loan with a coupon rate of 10 per cent for the full amount from your bank to finance the purchase. The interest is paid quarterly in arrears. The principal (ie capital amount borrowed) is due to be repaid in full in five years' time.

Solution and explanation

The depreciation expense which appeared in Figure 2.1 now deserves separate attention.

Depreciation is an accounting estimate. The cash to acquire these assets has been paid on the day of acquisition. We know that assets devalue over time and therefore it would be inappropriate (according to the *prudence concept*) to hold them on the face of our statement of financial position at their purchase price until the day they are sold or disposed of. Instead we spread the cost over the useful economic life of the asset (according to the *accruals convention*). Depreciation is the measure of wearing out, consumption or other reduction in the useful economic life of a non-current asset whether arising from use, effluxion of time or obsolescence through technical or market changes.

Printer/scanner

You have estimated that the economic life of the printer/scanner is 20 months. Therefore, at the end of the month, you should show the asset as being reduced by one-twentieth of its value ie $100 / 20 years = $5 depreciation.

This depreciation charge gets netted off the carrying value (purchase price) of the non-current asset (ie $100 – $5 = $95) while the cost is taken to the income statement as an expense (reducing profit by $5). The amount which is shown on the face of the statement of financial position is called the net book value (NBV).

This process would continue each month until the asset reaches the end of its useful economic life. In other words, in each of the next 20 months you would charge $5 per month against the asset until all $100 had been consumed (Table 2.3).

TABLE 2.3

	Cost	Depreciation	Accumulated depreciation	Net book value
Month 1	100	5	5	95
Month 2	100	5	10	90
Month 3	100	5	15	85
Month 4	100	5	20	80
Month 5	100	5	25	75
Month 6	100	5	30	70
Month 7	100	5	35	65
Month 8	100	5	40	60
Month 9	100	5	45	55
Month 10	100	5	50	50
Month 11	100	5	55	45
Month 12	100	5	60	40
Month 13	100	5	65	35
Month 14	100	5	70	30
Month 15	100	5	75	25
Month 16	100	5	80	20
Month 17	100	5	85	15
Month 18	100	5	90	10
Month 19	100	5	95	5
Month 20	100	5	100	0

The depreciation charge shown in Table 2.3 is taken to the income statement every month. The NBV (the final column) appears on the face of the statement of financial position.

Computer

The treatment of the computer is similar. The only difference is that the asset has an estimated terminal (residual) value.

You have estimated that the computer will last for 40 months, at which point it will be sold for $100. Therefore, now we need only depreciate the asset down to its expected terminal value, as follows:

$$\frac{\text{Cost} - \text{residual value}}{\text{Useful life}} = \text{Depreciation charge}$$

$$\frac{\$500 - \$100}{40 \text{ months}} = \$10 \text{ per month}$$

Therefore, at the end of the first month, the computer would be worth $490 ($500 – $10) and the depreciation charge for this month (and every month until the end of the asset's useful life) would be $10.

Acquisition of motor vehicle

IAS 16 Property Plant and Equipment states that the cost of an asset will include all costs in bringing the asset to its required location and condition. As you can see, this is a subjective exercise. Is the convertible-roof function a necessary improvement or adjustment to the asset to ensure it is suitable for the purpose?

Remember that the capitalized balance goes to the statement of financial position and will be written off over the useful economic life of the asset. Any costs which you deem to be inappropriate to capitalize should be taken straight to the income statement. We suggest the following treatment:

	Capital $	Expense $
Motor vehicle	19,500	
Delivery charge	500	
Additional extras:		
Non-standard black matt paint job	~~1,000~~	1,000
Convertible roof function	~~2,000~~	2,000
Tank of petrol	~~150~~	150
Road tax (for the year)	~~200~~	200
Total	20,000	3,350

The carrying value of the asset would be recorded in the statement of financial position at a cost of $20,000 and would be depreciated over five years. There is no terminal (residual) value. However, if depreciation is calculated on a pro-rata basis, remember that you have owned this asset for only two weeks. Therefore:

Cost		20,000
Depreciation	20,000 / 5 years	
	= $4,000 per year	
	= $333.33 per month	
	= approx. $77 per week assuming 52 weeks a year	(154)
Net book value		19,846

Bank loan to finance the purchase of the vehicle

The total loan required was $23,350. The loan is repayable in full in approximately five years' time and therefore would be classified as a **non-current liability**.

The interest payments (at 10 per cent per annum) are due quarterly in arrears. The annual interest charge would be $2,335 ($23,350 * 10%). The quarterly charge would be $583.75. As we are accounting for only two weeks' worth of unpaid interest, the amount we need to accrue is $90 (calculated as: $2,335 / 52 weeks = (approx.) $45 per week).

As we owe the interest at the end of the first month of trading, it needs to be classified as a liability. Whereas the loan balance is repayable in several years' time, the interest is due within the next few months. Therefore this balance should be classified as a current liability. A corresponding charge against profit needs to be made for the period to ensure that we have matched the appropriate expense to the period.

The accounting entries would be as follows:

- Increase the cost of tangible non-current assets in the statement of financial position by $20,000.

- Charge $3,350 immediately to the income statement for the 'additional extras'.

- Increase the level of non-current liabilities by the same amount, ie $23,350. *Remember, you needed a loan to pay the motor vehicle supplier!*

- Charge $154 to the income statement related to the depreciation charge. The other side of the double entry needs to be posted to the accumulated depreciation account. The net effect of this entry is to reduce profit by $154 and reduce the carrying value of the motor vehicle by $154.

- Finally, you need to accrue for the interest which is unpaid at the month end. $90 needs to be charged against profit for the year and a current liability for unpaid interest needs to be shown in the statement of financial position.

Extracts from statement of financial position and income statement for the period ended week 4 (month 1)

NOTE: these are extracts, ie the statements are summarized and incomplete. We have simply highlighted the balances that have changed as a result of the above transactions.

Mobius Inc.
Extract from the Statement of Financial Position
As at the end of week 4

	Opening balance $	Adjustment $	Note:	Closing balance
Assets				
Non-current assets				
Computer	500	(10)	2	490
Printer / scanner	100	(5)	1	95
Motor vehicle ($20,000 [cost] – $154 [accumulated depreciation])		19,846	3, 4	19,846
Current liabilities				
Loan interest accrual		(90)	5	(90)
Non-current liabilities				
Bank loan (10%; repayable in 5 years' time)		(23,350)	3	(23,350)
Shareholder's funds (capital and reserves)				
Loss		(3,609)	6	(3,609)

Mobius Inc.
Extract from the Income Statement
For the period ended DD/MM/YYYY (week 4)

Expenses				
Depreciation – printer/scanner		(5)	1	(5)
Depreciation – computer		(10)	2	(10)
Motor vehicle costs (additional extras)		(3,350)	3	(3,350)
Depreciation – motor vehicle		(154)	4	(154)
Finance costs		(90)	5	(90)
Profit/(loss)	0	(3,609)	6	(3,609)

Notes:

1 Depreciation charge on printer/scanner for the period of account.

2 Depreciation charge on computer for the period of account.

3 Motor vehicle 'additional extras' acquisition costs.

4 Depreciation charge on motor vehicle for period of account.

5 Interest paid on loan.

6 Transfer profit (loss) to statement of financial position (this transfer has been made purely for illustration purposes and assumes that no other transactions took place during the period and we are closing off our ledgers).

Three further property, plant and equipment issues

Let us take this opportunity to discuss briefly three further issues which you should be aware of when accounting for tangible non-current assets:

- recognition and subsequent measurement;
- disposal of non-current assets;
- alternative depreciation methods.

Recognition and subsequent re-measurement

We have simplified the example by assuming that all non-current assets are tangible and that the assets are included at cost. The reality is that some non-current assets are intangible – thus making the carrying value more difficult to quantify – and an entity has the choice whether to revalue assets to their open market value (fair value) at the end of each accounting period. If management choose to adopt a revaluation policy then this must be maintained and certain assets should not be cherry-picked because of their value over other assets. In other words, if you have some property that you believe has increased in value and other property that hasn't, you cannot choose to revalue only those assets which you believe it would be beneficial to revalue from a financial position perspective.

Disposal of non-current assets

We have dealt with the acquisition of non-current assets but this is only a part of the story. These assets can be disposed of or sold. If we take the example of the computer in the example above, we are depreciating the asset down to a value of \$100 over 40 months. That means that at the end of the second (complete) year the asset would be held in the statement of financial position at an NBV of \$260 (ie \$500 – \$10*24 months). If you decide to sell the asset and find someone willing to pay you $300, you would make a profit of $40. If you sell the asset for $100, you would make a loss of $160.

At the point of disposal, the asset and its accumulated depreciation is completely written off (leaving no trace of the asset in your statement of financial position) and the gain (loss) on the difference between the sales proceeds and the NBV is credited (debited) to the income statement.

In a perfect world, there would be no difference between the sales proceeds and the NBV. This would mean that your depreciation estimations were accurate. However, it is unusual not to see gains or losses on disposal. These are simply a reflection of the level of under- or over-depreciation over the ownership period. In other words, a gain means that you were overly prudent in your estimation of the devaluation of the asset; a loss means that you were not prudent enough. The final entry to reconcile proceeds and the NBV is a correcting entry.

Alternative depreciation methods

There are many commonly accepted methods for calculating depreciation. The reason that the rules are flexible is because depreciation is an accounting estimate. Subjectivity is permitted but the underlying ethos is that balances should be a true and fair reflection and that the costs of ownership should be matched against the economic benefits which the asset provides. Organizations should record their assets and liabilities, gains and losses as appropriately and accurately as possible. Given that management are presumed to know more than other stakeholders, it is only right that they should be responsible for choosing the depreciation policy.

In the case of depreciation we are deriving a measure to establish the level of wear and tear on an asset, ie the consumption or other reduction in the useful economic life of a non-current asset whether arising from use, effluxion of time or obsolescence through technical or market changes. Therefore, it is easy to see why different methods of depreciation have evolved.

The two most commonly used methods to calculate depreciation are straight-line basis; and reducing-balance basis. It is simplest to illustrate the differences between these methods through a worked exercise.

WORKED EXERCISE 2.6   Depreciation methods

You purchase an asset for $500 and expect the residual value to be $0. In the first instance, you depreciate the asset on a straight-line basis and in the second, you depreciate the asset on a reducing-balance basis:

1   The **straight-line basis** seeks to depreciate assets evenly over a period of time.
    You believe that the tangible non-current asset has a five-year useful economic life.
    Therefore, each year you will charge $100 depreciation against the asset ($500 / 5 years).
    Figure 2.3 shows the NBV of the asset over the time period.

FIGURE 2.3   An illustration of the impact of straight-line basis depreciation

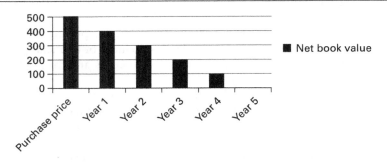

2   The **reducing-balance basis** is commonly used for assets which lose value early in their economic lives and less later. Examples of assets which you might choose to depreciate on a reducing-balance basis are motor vehicles, high-tech goods and so forth.

To calculate the reducing-balance basis depreciation charge you need to know an appropriate percentage to apply. Let us presume that the asset needs to be depreciated at 20 per cent on a reducing-balance basis (note: the above example shows the asset being depreciated at 20 per cent on a straight-line basis). In the first year, the depreciation charge is the same as under the previous depreciation basis because it is simply 20 per cent of the purchase price. However, the second year, and all subsequent years, calculates depreciation based upon the net book value (ie year 2 depreciation is $400 [NBV] * 20% = $80). The workings below and Figure 2.4 illustrate the difference.

	$	NBV $
Purchase price	500.00	
Year 1 depreciation charge (20%)	(100.00)	
Net book value at end of year 1		400.00
Year 2 depreciation charge (20%)	(80.00)	
Net book value at end of year 2		320.00
Year 3 depreciation charge (20%)	(64.00)	
Net book value at end of year 3		256.00
Year 4 depreciation charge (20%)	(51.20)	
Net book value at end of year 4		204.80
Year 5 depreciation charge (20%)	(40.96)	
Net book value at end of year 5		163.84
Year 6 depreciation charge (20%)	(32.77)	
Net book value at end of year 6		131.07
... And so forth		

FIGURE 2.4 An illustration of the impact of reducing-balance basis depreciation

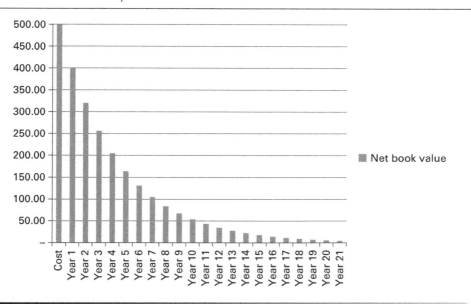

Recording accounting information

As we draw towards the conclusion of this chapter, you might like to have a visual representation of the way accounting books and records are maintained. We have simplified the record-keeping process as far as possible mainly because the advent of computerized bookkeeping packages means that many of these processes happen behind the scenes. At the press of a button these systems allow one to print exception reports, a trial balance at a certain date, draft financial statements and so forth. Systems also allow you to drill down to customer or supplier accounts, locating single invoices if required; this would have been a long and exhaustive process not so long ago! Of course, manual systems allow you to do the same; it is just that it is more time-consuming. The flow chart in Figure 2.5 shows how information is collated and transferred between ledgers, how it is subsequently summarized into a trial balance and then rephrased into a set of financial statements.

FIGURE 2.5   Accounting books and records

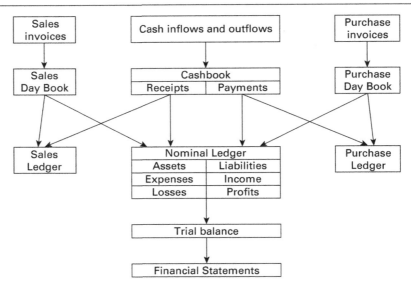

Exercises: now attempt Exercise 2.5 on page 87

WORKED EXERCISE 2.7   Mobius (6)

Period-end adjustments

At the end of every accounting period, it is highly likely that a company will need to make a series of period-end adjustments. The depreciation of non-current assets is an example of one of these. Frequently the adjustments are correcting entries, accounting for estimates or adjusting the figures to an accruals basis. Let us once again consider the statements of financial position and income for Mobius Inc as at the end of week 4.

The following information is relevant:

(i)   Mobius Inc had a telephone line installed along with a broadband connection during the third week of trading. The phone company invoices quarterly in arrears and you have not yet received your first invoice. This transaction has not been recorded in your accounting records and therefore is not included within the financial statements above. You have estimated that the usage during this first period of account will cost approximately $100.

(ii) On the last day of week 4, you found a suitable location to base the business. The monthly rental cost is $1,000 and the landlord required you to pay in advance. You paid in cash.

(iii) Mobius Inc sold $20,000 of product on credit terms. The total amount owed by customers (from all transactions) at the end of the period was $4,900.

(iv) Mobius Inc bought a further $9,000 of raw materials on credit during weeks 3 and 4 of trading. Exactly $8,000 worth was converted into finished goods, of which three-quarters were sold. The remainder were held as inventories at the end of the period. These were the only goods held at the end of the period as those finished goods brought forward from weeks 1 and 2 were sold during week 3. Suppliers were owed $2,000 in total at the end of the accounting period.

Solutions

(i) Mobius Inc reports on an accruals basis (not a cash basis). This convention asks that revenues, profits and the associated costs incurred while earning them should be matched to the same period's income statement. Therefore, we need to charge the relevant proportion of the telephone cost against this period's profit or loss. To operationalize this accounting entry, we need a corresponding entry in the statement of financial position. In other words, we need to charge the $100 telephone expense to the income statement and set up a current liability for the same amount in the statement of financial position.

(ii) The $1,000 rental expense needs to be carried forward to the next period as this is the period in which it is incurred. Let us break down this transaction into two parts. The first part is the cash transaction. When the cash leaves the bank account, the corresponding entry would be to set up the rental expense in the income statement. However, as we know, the expense should be carried forward to the next period of account and therefore we have a charge of $1,000 against profit which should not be there. We need a period-end correcting entry as the second part of the accounting transaction.

As the cash has been physically paid out, the 'cash at bank' balance cannot, and should not, be adjusted. Instead, we need to include a current asset of a different type; in this case, a prepayment. By increasing assets by $1,000 this leaves us with the other side of the entry to post to the income statement. All we need do is set this off against the $1,000 charge which we had included as part of the cash transaction. This reduces the rental cost in the income statement to $0 and sets off the prepayment gain against the cash loss, leaving the current asset position at a net $0 position.

NOTE: The third part of the transaction is not dealt with here because it relates to the release of the prepayment. At the end of the next accounting period, the rental cost will need to be charged against profits and the prepayment removed from the statement of financial position (and possibly another set up in its place).

(iii) Revenue should be increased by $20,000. Trade receivables should be moved to $4,900. The cash balance should be corrected appropriately to reflect the amounts received from these sales and the amounts invoiced but not collected from prior periods.

(iv) The company has purchased $9,000 of raw materials, of which $8,000 was converted into finished goods stock and three-quarters sold. Therefore, there are inventories left over at the end of the period. The closing balance of raw materials should be shown as a current asset worth $1,000 and the closing finished goods inventories should be included at $2,000.

Closing trade payables (current liabilities) should be shown in the statement of financial position at $2,000. We must assume that all other balances have been paid.

The closing financial statements for the first four weeks of trading would be as follows:

Mobius Inc Summarized Statement of Financial Position As at the end of week 4	$	$
Assets		
Non-current assets		
Computer		490
Printer / scanner		95
Motor vehicle		19,846
		20,431
Current assets		
Cash at bank (1,450 [b/fwd] – 1,000 [2a] +	8,650	
16,000 [3b] – 800 [4a] – 7,000 [4e])		
Inventories		
Raw materials (1,000 [4d])	1,000	
Finished goods (533.33 [b/fwd] – 533.33 [4b] + 2,000 [4d])	2,000	
Trade receivables – amounts owed by customers	4,900	
(900 + 20,000 [3a] – 16,000 [3b])		
Prepayments (1,000 [2b])	1,000	
	17,550	
Current liabilities		
Trade payables – amounts owed to suppliers	(2,000)	
(800 [b/fwd] – 800 [4a] + 9,000 [4c] – 7,000 [4e])		
Loan interest accrual	(90)	
Accruals (100 [1])	(100)	
	(2,190)	
Net current assets		15,360
Non-current liabilities		
Loan from friend		(500)
Bank loan		(23,350)
Net assets (liabilities)		11,941
Shareholder's funds (capital and reserves)		
Capital		1,000
Retained earnings (weeks 1–4)		10,941
Shareholder's funds		11,941

Mobius Inc Summarized Income Statement For the period ended DD/MM/YYYY (week 4)	$	$
Revenue (2,850 [b/fwd] + 20,000 [3a])		22,850
Cost of sales		
Opening inventories	0	
Purchases (666.67 [b/fwd] + 533.33 [4b] + 9,000 [4c])	10,200	
Closing inventories (1,000 [4d] + 2,000 [4d])	(3,000)	
		(7,200)
Gross profit		15,650
Expenses:		
Utilities		(200)
Printing, postage and stationery		(50)
Web development costs		(750)
Depreciation (5+10+154)		(169)
Motor vehicle costs		(3,350)
Telephone services (100 [1])		(100)
Rental costs (+1,000 [2a] – 1,000 [2b])		0
Profit before interest and tax		11,031
Finance costs		(90)
Profit		10,941

WORKED EXERCISE 2.8   Mobius (7)

Statement of cash flows

Mobius Inc is a simple business with no complex transactions and therefore converting the accruals-based financial information to reveal the cash flows is quick and straightforward. Of course, being at the end of the first period of trading also simplifies the preparation process. Note the format, in particular the categorization into three distinct sections: operating activities; investing activities; and financing activities. This is designed to facilitate the interpretation and analysis of the cash position.

Mobius Inc	
Statement of Cash Flows	
For the period ended DD/MM/YYYY (month 1)	$
Cash generated from operating activities:	
Cash generated from operations **(note 1)**	4,490
Interest paid (include either here or financing below)	(90)
Dividends paid (include either here or under financing below)	0
Net cash flow from operating activities	4,400
Cash flows from investing activities:	
Assets purchased	(20,600)
Assets sold	0
Net cash flow from investing activities	(20,600)
Cash flow from financing activities:	
Issue of shares	1,000
Receipt of loan	23,850
Repayment of loan	0
Net cash flows from financing activities	24,850
Net cash inflow/(outflow) from activities	8,650
Opening net cash	0
Closing net cash	8,650

Note 1: Reconciliation of net cash from operating activities

Cash generated from operations	
Profit for period	10,941
Interest paid	90
Depreciation	169
Increase in trade receivables (including prepayments)	(5,900)
Increase in trade payables (including accruals)	2,190
Increase in inventories	(3,000)
	4,490

Exercises: now attempt Exercise 2.6 on page 88

Expert view 2.9: Statement of cash flows

The advantage of being asked to prepare a statement of cash flows (over the preparation of the other financial statements) is that you are given the balancing figure – the closing balance of cash and cash equivalents. Sometimes this might be a combination of balances (eg petty cash, bank overdraft, short-term cash and cash equivalents) but ultimately, this makes the exercise easier to complete.

Interestingly, you might like to note that when completing this exercise in real life, computerized bookkeeping packages often struggle to produce an accurate statement of cash flows unless the person responsible for inputting the data clearly labels items 'cash' and 'not cash'.

COMPREHENSION QUESTIONS

1 Outline the content and purpose of the statement of financial position.

2 Outline the content and purpose of the statement of comprehensive income.

3 Outline the content and purpose of the statement of cash flows.

4 What is the accruals concept? Provide one example to show you understand this.

5 If an entity's accounts are prepared on a break-up basis, what does this mean?

6 List and describe two methods of depreciation. For each, provide an example of an asset where it might be appropriate to use that method.

Answers on page 89

Exercises

Answers on pages 90–95

Exercise 2.1: The components of financial statements

(a) The income statement shows:

Income – Expenditure = Profit

Can you provide examples for each of these categories?

Examples of income	Examples of expenditure

(b) The statement of financial position shows:

Assets – Liabilities = Shareholders' funds (net worth)

Can you provide examples of both assets and liabilities?

Examples of assets	Examples of liabilities

Exercise 2.2 can be found on page 59

Exercise 2.3: Climb On!

Illustration 1.1 in Chapter 1 provided the following information:

For a long time, you have been wondering how to convert your passion for rock climbing into a business opportunity. During a recent climbing trip you met Chris, a climbing-gear designer. He agreed to give you 100 chalk bags and 100 climb-oriented t-shirts for $4 and $5 respectively. You came to an agreement with him that you'd make payments on an ad-hoc basis as the goods were sold. As soon as you arrived home you listed the first 30 chalk bags and 50 t-shirts on an internet-based auction site. These sold within 3 days of listing them for $8 and $10 respectively. Half of these customers paid immediately. You offered 20 day terms on the sales and your past experiences tell you that customers tend to take full advantage of this policy.

Required:
Based on this information, prepare a statement of financial position and an income statement.

Exercise 2.4 Goblin Combe plc

State which of the following items could appear as an asset on the statement of financial position of Goblin Combe plc, a leading premium drinks business:

- $150,000 of product sold during the year to Troillus Direct Inc under 40-day credit terms. The amount remained outstanding at the end of the year and management believe that the amount will never be paid.

- Goblin Combe plc holds $22 million of finished goods inventories as at the year-end. Of this amount, $500,000 relates to a product which was banned from sale during the year. The directors have ascertained that this particular product is highly effective as paint remover. A buyer has been found for this and they are willing to pay $100,000 for the full quantity of this otherwise unsaleable stock.

- A competing company produced a popular whisky called 'Arbol'. Goblin Combe plc acquired the company (and by default the 'Arbol' brand) at the start of the year for $30 million. The fair value of the assets less liabilities, at that time, was estimated to be $10 million.

- Goblin Combe plc hired a new corporate communication team. It is confidently expected that their services will lead to an increase in profits by over $12 million per annum.

- A product was developed by a rival company, Old Down Quarry Inc. The directors of Goblin Combe plc decided to buy the exclusive rights to manufacture and distribute this product for the next four years at a cost of $2 million. The new drink has already proved successful and sales have exceeded expectations.

Exercise 2.5 Climb On! (continued)

Trading continues apace for your new business Climb On! The products have proved to be popular and, seeing this as your opportunity to seize the day, you decided to expand and grow the business.

Here follows a summary of your **cash book**, ie all cash transactions during the year to 31 December 2013:

Cash In Description	$	Cash Out Description	$
Cash sales	32,000	Payments to suppliers	49,000
Receipts in respect of credit sales	106,000	Purchase of machinery	55,000
Capital invested (transfer from private bank account)	30,000	Rent and rates	7,800
Bank loan	45,000	Utilities	3,500
Interest received	200	Insurance	1,200
Sale of machinery	2,500	Telephone	300
		Postage and packaging	200
		Website development costs	1,500
		Travel/climbing trips	10,500
		General expenses	6,300
		Wages (staff)	12,000
		Drawings (your remuneration)	8,000
		Interest paid	2,300
		Balance carried forward	58,100
	215,700		215,700

The following information is also available:

(a) The machinery was purchased on 1 April 2013. The estimated useful economic life of these assets is four years. The residual value is estimated to be $nil. You may assume a full year's depreciation in the year of purchase but none in the year of sale.

(b) Some of the machinery quickly proved to be unnecessary and was sold during the year for $2,500. The original cost was $5,000.

(c) Utilities bills of £400 were still owed as at 31 December 2013.

(d) Closing inventories as at 31 December 2013 were $14,000.

(e) Trade receivables as at 31 December 2013 were $10,500.

(f) Trade payables as at 31 December 2013 were $18,000.

(g) You need to provide for $1,500 of accounting fees as at 31 December 2013.

Exercise 2.6 Climb On! (continued)

Based upon your solution to Exercise 2.5, prepare a statement of cash flows for Climb On! for the period ended 31 December 2013.

Answers to comprehension questions

1 Statement of financial position (commonly referred to as the balance sheet), as the name suggests, is a record of a company's financial position as at a certain point in time. For this reason people think of it as a financial photograph: a snapshot of the current worth of an organization.

2 Statement of comprehensive income shows how much profit the business has made during a specific period of time. We told you that the 'period of account' is normally a year but large organizations are often required to produce interim statements, ie bi-annually or quarterly.

3 Statement of cash flows shows whether a business has earned or spent cash (and cash equivalents) during the year. The focus of the statement of cash flows is, as the name suggests, cash inflows versus cash outflows. The statement is divided between three activities: operating; investing; and financing.

4 The accruals concept (often referred to as the matching concept or matching rule) states that revenues, profits and the associated costs incurred while earning them should be matched to the same period's income statement. There are many everyday instances where a transaction would be recorded in different accounting periods dependent upon whether you employed an accruals accounting system or a cash accounting one. It is common for rent to be paid in advance, for example. In this instance, as at the year-end you will have overpaid or *prepaid* the rental expense.

5 When an entity prepares accounts on a break-up basis it means that the management do not believe the business will continue into the foreseeable future and that it has ceased to be a going concern. If this is the case, all assets and liabilities are presented as though they were current.

6 There are several ways to account for depreciation of a non-current asset and it is the business's responsibility to choose that which is most fair and appropriate. The two most commonly used methods are straight-line depreciation and reducing-balance basis. Straight-line depreciation reduces the value of the asset in equal annual increments until the asset reaches its terminal residual value or is sold. The reducing-balance basis uses the net book value of the asset and reduces this incrementally each year. The former is used for assets such as fixed-term leases while the latter can be used for items such as motor vehicles that tend to lose value early in their life cycle but hold value later.

Exercise 2.1 The component of financial statements

INCOME – EXAMPLES	**EXPENDITURE – EXAMPLES**
• Income from product sales • Rental income from property (owned and being leased to a third party) • Dividends received from investments held • Interest received from borrowings made • Gains on financial instruments held for trading purposes **And so forth…**	• Purchases of raw materials used in the production of products • Utilities bills, eg electricity, gas, oil, water, telephone • Rents paid • Business rates • Taxation • Interest paid on loans and other credit arrangements • Fuel **And so forth…**

ASSETS – EXAMPLES	**LIABILITIES – EXAMPLES**
Assets are typically clustered into two groups: long-term (non-current assets) and short-term (current assets). Examples include: Non-current assets • Tangible non-current assets, for example property, plant and equipment, motor vehicles, fixtures and fittings • Intangible non-current assets, including goodwill, royalties, patents, development expenditure, brand name and so forth Current assets • Such as inventories, bank and cash, trade receivables, prepayments and so forth	Liabilities are also typically clustered into long-term (non-current) and short-term (current). Examples include: Non-current liabilities • Non-current liabilities such as long-term debt (eg loans, mortgages, debentures and so forth), provisions for liabilities due in more than one year (eg provisions against environmental costs or deferred taxation) and so forth • Current liabilities such as trade payables, bank overdraft, short-term borrowings, accrued expenses and so forth It is also worth noting that the balance sheet equation is sometimes restructured to read: Assets = liabilities + shareholders' funds This is because shareholders' funds are the accumulated capital of the business and thus might be seen to represent the final liability of the firm.

Exercise 2.2: Accounting equation adjustments

The starting position was as follows:

Assets	– Liabilities	= Capital
$1,500	– $500	= $1,000

Adjustments would be required as follows:

(a)

Assets	– Liabilities	= Capital
($1,500 – $500 + $500)	– $500	= $1,000
ie		
$1,500	– $500	= $1,000

(b)

($1,500 + $400)	– ($500+$400)	= $1,000
ie		
$1900	– $900	= $1,000

Exercise 2.3: Climb On!

Climb On!
Statement of Financial Position

Current assets

Cash at bank (Revenue * 50%)	370.00
Trade receivables (Revenue * 50%)	370.00
Inventories ([70*$4]+[50*$5])	530.00

Liabilities

Trade payables ([100*$4]+[100*$5])	(900.00)

Net assets 370.00

Capital and reserves

Retained earnings	370.00

Climb On!
Income Statement

Revenue ([30*$8]+[50*$10])	740.00
Cost of sales ([30*$4]+[50*$5])	(370.00)

Profit 370.00

Exercise 2.4: Goblin Combe plc

Definition reminder: an asset is a resource controlled by an entity as a result of past events and from which economic benefits are expected to flow to the entity.

- Under normal circumstances, the $150,000 would have been included as an asset and shown as part of the trade receivables balance. However, it would appear that the amount is not recoverable (ie economic benefits are not expected to flow to the entity) and therefore should be written off and not appear as an asset at the year-end.

- Accounting tends towards prudence and inventories should be included at the lower of cost and net realizable value. Therefore, the final value of finished goods inventories in the statement of financial position will be $21.6 million, ie $22m − $0.5m + $0.1m.

- The assets acquired are worth $10 million but the cash being paid is $30 million. We know that cash will be reduced by $30 million and assets will increase by $10 million. Therefore an accounting entry is required for the difference between these two figures. Essentially the company is paying for the intangible value of the entity, so taking the cost to the income statement as an expense would be inappropriate.

  In accounting terminology this difference is referred to as goodwill. In accounting we tend towards prudence and therefore there are rules which determine whether an intangible asset can be included on the statement of financial position. In this instance, the difference between the consideration payable for a business and the aggregate fair value of its identifiable assets less liabilities can be classified as (purchased) goodwill and included on the statement of financial position as an intangible asset. At the end of each accounting period an impairment test will highlight whether this intangible asset is being included at an appropriate value.

- Human capital is an example of an asset class which cannot be capitalized. Though there has been a great deal of professional and academic debate about the 'rights' and 'wrongs' of this approach, ultimately employees are not capitalized. Amounts paid to employees should be taken directly to the income statement.

- This is an example of an intangible asset which can be capitalized. The acquisition cost should be matched against the expected life span. Annual impairment tests are required to ensure that that asset is being carried forward each year at an appropriate value.

Exercise 2.5: Climb On! (continued)

Climb On! **Statement of Financial Position** **As at 31 December 2013**	
	$
Assets	
Non-current assets	
Machinery (workings 1 & 2)	37,500
Current assets	
Inventories	14,000
Trade receivables	10,500
Cash at bank	58,100
Current liabilities	
Trade payables	(18,000)
Accruals (utilities)	(400)
Accruals (accounting fees)	(1,500)
Non-current liabilities	
Bank loan	(45,000)
Net assets (liabilities)	55,200
Shareholder's funds (capital and reserves)	
Capital	30,000
Drawings	(8,000)
Retained earnings	33,200
Shareholder's funds	55,200

Climb On!
Income Statement
For the period ended 31 December 2013

	$	$
Revenue (32,000+106,000+10,500)		148,500
Cost of sales		
Opening inventories	0	
Purchases (49,000+18,000)	67,000	
Closing inventories	(14,000)	
		(53,000)
Gross profit		95,500
Expenses:		
Rent and rates		(7,800)
Utilities (3,500 + 400)		(3,900)
Insurance		(1,200)
Telephone		(300)
Postage and packaging		(200)
Website development costs		(1,500)
Travel/climbing trips		(10,500)
General expenses		(6,300)
Wages (staff)		(12,000)
Depreciation		(12,500)
Loss on disposal of machinery		(2,500)
Accounting fees		(1,500)
Profit before interest and tax		35,300
Finance income		200
Finance costs		(2,300)
Profit		33,200

Working 1: Disposal	
Disposal proceeds	2,500
Net book value (no depreciation during year of sale;	
therefore cost)	(5,000)
Loss on disposal	(2,500)

Working 2: Non-current assets	
Machinery acquired	55,000
Machinery sold during the year	(5,000)
Depreciable amount	50,000
Depreciation charge (depreciate over 4 years)	(12,500)
Net book value as at 31 December 2013	37,500

Exercise 2.6: Climb On! (continued)

Climb On!
Statement of Cash Flows
For the period ended 31 December 2013

Cash generated from operating activities:		$
Cash generated from operations **(note 1)**		45,700
Interest paid (include either here or financing below)		(2,100)
Net cash flow from operating activities		43,600
Cash flows from investing activities:		
Assets purchased	(55,000)	
Assets sold	2,500	
Net cash flow from investing activities		(52,500)
Cash flow from financing activities:		
Capital paid in	30,000	
Drawings	(8,000)	
Receipt of loan	45,000	
Net cash flows from financing activities		67,000
Net cash inflow/(outflow) from activities		58,100
Opening net cash		0
Closing net cash		**58,100**

Note 1: Reconciliation of net cash from operating activities

Cash generated from operations	
Profit for period	33,200
Interest paid	2,100
Depreciation	12,500
Loss on disposal	2,500
Increase in trade receivables (including prepayments)	(10,500)
Increase in trade payables (including accruals)	19,900
Increase in inventories	(14,000)
	45,700

Financial analysis: Part I

OBJECTIVE

The objective of this chapter is to facilitate the development of financial information analysis and interpretation skills. The emphasis of this first financial analysis chapter will be on undertaking appropriate forms of analysis, including calculating key management ratios. This chapter will show how the results of the various techniques described can be employed to help assess the position and performance of an entity.

LEARNING OUTCOMES

After studying this chapter, the reader will be able to:

- Identify the main aspects of performance which can be evaluated through financial statements.
- Apply horizontal, trend, vertical and ratio analysis to the financial statements contained within an organization's annual report.
- Evaluate a company from the viewpoint of current and potential investors as well as other stakeholders.

KEY TOPICS COVERED

- Aspects of financial analysis: profitability, liquidity, efficiency, solvency and investors' returns.
- The use of ratios and other techniques to analyse and appraise full sets of company accounts.
- This chapter will contain mini case study exercises in which students must evaluate a company from varying viewpoints.

MANAGEMENT ISSUES

Although it is useful that managers be able to compute ratios, it is more important that they are able to develop the analytical skills through interpretation and analysis of financial statements.

Introduction

This chapter considers various forms of financial statement analysis, including:

- horizontal analysis;
- trend analysis;
- vertical analysis;
- ratio analysis.

We will combine these approaches in the chapter that follows. We will assume that undertaking these forms of analysis is (relatively) new to you. When used appropriately, ratio analysis can be a highly effective way of manipulating data into meaningful information. The key to undertaking ratio analysis is to focus on the audience and their question(s). A current (or potential) investor, for example, might want to know about the position, performance and financial strategy of the organization. A lender might want to gauge the short-term liquidity – to gauge whether the firm can make their obligatory interest payments – and the long-term solvency – to identify whether there could be problems meeting repayment plans. On the other end of the continuum, an environmental campaigner would probably have very different motivations for investigating the annual report and financial statements. When calculating and interpreting key ratios they are likely to be judging the firm from a social, environmental or ethical perspective. Therefore, the ability to calculate a long series of financial ratios is good knowledge to have but a more useful skill-set to develop is being able to identify the most appropriate ratios and then have the capacity to interpret them.

The usefulness of financial ratios has long been established. Chen and Shimerda (1981) in their paper 'An empirical analysis of useful financial ratios' have this to say:

> Financial ratios have played an important part in evaluating the performance and financial condition of an entity. Over the years, empirical studies have repeatedly demonstrated the usefulness of financial ratios. For example, financially-distressed firms can be separated from the non-failed firms in the year before the declaration of bankruptcy at an accuracy rate of better than 90% by examining financial ratios. In determining bond ratings, when financial ratios were the only variables used, the resulting ratings were virtually identical with institutional ratings. There is one recurring question with the use of financial ratios: which ratios, among the hundreds that can be computed easily from the available financial data, should be analysed to obtain the information for the task at hand? (pp 51–60).

During this chapter we provide a list of financial ratios which we believe are the most useful for you to know. Alongside each ratio we show how it can be calculated and a guide to help you develop your analysis and interpretation skills. In an attempt to make this more real to you and to bring the content alive, we have worked through the ratios of an airline.

We subdivide the chapter into five broad categories:

- profitability;
- liquidity;
- efficiency;
- solvency; and
- investors' returns.

Financial statement analysis for investment purposes

Investment-led financial statement analysis – buy, hold or sell – is predicated on the assumption that investors are rational, risk averse and seek to maximize their returns in terms of the present value of future cash flows. In other words, we presume that investors have an efficient frontier where returns are traded off against risks, and investments will be rejected where the rewards are not appropriate.

However, before an investment should be made in an entity, there are two fundamental assumptions:

1 Buying shares on a stock exchange is not just an investment on paper, it is an investment in a business.

2 Before you invest in a business, you should know the business.

Therefore, do not limit your assessment of position and performance to a numeric exercise. If you are going to undertake an analysis exercise for a business in which you are either an investor or considering making an investment, it is essential that you understand the industry and the firm's position in it. Among the issues which you should consider are:

- the objectives of the organization;
- the business strategy;
- knowledge of the products sold/services offered;
- knowledge of the products being developed;
- your level of trust in the senior management team, and their vision;
- the competitiveness of the industry and the position of the business within it;
- the reputational capital of the business;
- the political, legal, regulatory, social and ethical environment in which the business operates;
- the technology required to bring the product to market;

- the reliance on skilled and unskilled employees and the competitiveness of the job markets;
- and so on...

Other users and their needs

As stated earlier, investors are not the only user group who have financial information needs. They are also not the only group who are interested in an entity's financial statements. Table 3.1 sets out some broad motivations that these various user groups might have, alongside the type of information that would satisfy their needs.

TABLE 3.1 User groups' information needs

User group	Potential motivations to consult the annual report	Example financial information requirements
Investors	Concerned with the stewardship of the entity. The key issues are growth (historic and potential), performance (past, present and future), position, risk and returns.	What is the return on the investment (dividend and capital growth) versus the level of risk taken?
Employees	Employees would want to know whether the firm was stable and solvent.	Is the company financially stable and will it continue into the foreseeable future? Levels of borrowing and maturity would be useful information. How profitable is the business and the segment I work in?
Customers	Might be a motivation to investigate based upon fairness of prices, or maybe an over-reliance on one supplier.	Is the company profitable? If so, is there an issue of over-profitability? How do prices compare to competitors? Is the company (who is your supplier) solvent or should you be looking for an alternative?
Lenders	Is the firm solvent and does it have the short-term resources to meet interest payments?	Consider issues such as interest cover ratios, return on capital employed, debt to equity ratios.

TABLE 3.1   *continued*

User group	Potential motivations to consult the annual report	Example financial information requirements
Suppliers and other creditors	Suppliers would be primarily concerned with whether they will be paid what they are owed. They might also have dependency issues, ie whether the company who is their customer will continue to operate into the foreseeable future or whether they should be looking for new customers.	Consider issues such as liquidity (short-term financial position), working capital position and requirements, and solvency issues (medium- to long-term financial position).
Public	Is the firm operating in a manner that is environmentally, socially and ethically responsible?	For large entities, the annual report either includes or is accompanied by a corporate social responsibility report. This is, of course, highly useful to decision making about non-financial matters. The public, particularly communities within which big businesses operate, will also be concerned with community matters, eg how do the company treat employees in terms of remuneration; will the company continue to exist and invest in the local community; is it growing or contracting? Therefore, standard measures of profitability and performance will also be important to this user group.
Government and their agencies	The government and their agencies will be concerned with a range of issues such as taxation, directors' remuneration, employment details, governance and so forth. The annual report is often the nominated repository for such disclosure requirements.	The questions being asked will depend upon the nature of the enquiry. Levels of revenue are important to sales tax (value added tax [VAT]) concerns. Levels of operating profit will be relevant to corporation tax. The solvency of the entity might be interesting when establishing the broader macroeconomic environment.

Horizontal analysis and trend analysis

Technique outline

Horizontal analysis invites you to make horizontal comparisons on a line-by-line basis. The objective is to gauge relative levels of performance (or position) for a firm over a given period of time. It is possible, of course, to undertake this analysis on raw numbers (horizontal analysis), but more often than not, it is better to use the first period of account as your base position and set to '100' (trend analysis). You would then analyse future periods' percentage growth against this base position. Therefore, if revenue moved from $100 million in year 1 to $110 million in year 2, revenue growth could be expressed as either $10 million (horizontal analysis) or 1.1 (or 110 per cent of base; trend analysis) (ie $110m – $100m / $100m). Alternatively, if revenue fell during year 2 to $75 million, this would be recorded as 0.75 (or 75 per cent of base), indicating a 25 per cent decrease from the opening position.

Though carrying out this exercise can be time-consuming, it can also be rewarding in terms of its ability to reveal patterns and trends, as well as irregularities and anomalies. It is not uncommon for this analysis to be the first step for audit firms when they receive a new set of annual financial information. It is a straightforward analytical review. Comparing figures on a line-by-line basis can form the basis of discussions with the financial controller about the performance for the period. This technique also has the capacity to immediately highlight any exceptional movements in balances from previous years' accounts, and thus those balances that are higher risk (because of the possibility of misstatement). This can help to focus audit work on areas of potential material error or misstatement.

When forecasting, this technique is often employed as a believability check and it is not uncommon for people to talk about the hockey-curve effect, ie a graph depicting revenues increasing in the shape of a hockey stick are likely to be 'too good to be true'.

We have chosen to adopt Ryanair Holdings plc (hereafter, 'Ryanair') as a case study to showcase these techniques. Over the past decade they have become a household name across Europe and earned a reputation as a successful low-cost airline. By way of introduction, their corporate website states the following:

> Ryanair is the world's favourite airline operating over 1,500 flights per day from 53 bases on 1,500 low fare routes across 28 countries, connecting over 168 destinations. Ryanair operates a fleet of over 290 new Boeing 737-800 aircraft with firm orders for a further 13 new aircraft (before taking account of planned disposals), which will be delivered over the next year. Ryanair has a team of more than 8,500 people and expects to carry over 80 million passengers in the current fiscal year.
>
> (**www.ryanair.com** [April 2013])

Worked exercise 3.1 provides a decade's worth of selected financial information – 2003 through to 2012. Horizontal analysis reveals a strong growth profile.

WORKED EXERCISE 3.1   Horizontal analysis and trend analysis for Ryanair Holdings plc

TABLE 3.2

	2003 $	2004 $	2005 $	2006 $	2007 $	2008 $	2009 $	2010 $	2011 $	2012 $
Sales	842,508	1,074,224	1,319,037	1,692,530	2,236,985	2,713,822	2,941,965	2,988,100	3,629,500	4,390,200
Operating profit	294,837	272,836	369,080	413,265	471,745	537,080	92,631	402,100	488,200	683,200
Profit after tax	239,398	206,611	280,043	306,712	62,983	390,708	(169,200)	305,300	374,600	560,400
Dividends	–	–	–	–	–	–	–	–	500,000	–
Share repurchase	–	–	–	–	–	–	–	–	–	124,600
Interest payable	30,886	47,564	57,629	73,958	82,876	97,088	130,544	72,100	93,900	109,200
Shareholders' equity	1,241,728	1,455,288	1,734,503	1,991,985	2,539,773	2,502,194	2,425,061	2,848,600	2,953,900	3,306,700
Non-current liabilities	847,440	996,884	1,434,348	1,796,362	2,033,742	2,268,207	2,583,610	3,165,200	3,804,900	3,879,300
Capital employed	2,089,168	2,452,172	3,168,851	3,788,347	4,573,515	4,770,401	5,008,671	6,013,800	6,758,800	7,186,000
Current assets	1,114,346	1,317,973	1,653,421	2,053,627	2,354,276	2,387,122	2,543,077	3,063,400	3,477,600	3,876,000
Current liabilities	377,539	486,826	649,302	845,872	1,117,730	1,557,150	1,379,191	1,549,600	1,837,200	1,815,000
Trade receivables	14,970	14,932	20,644	29,909	23,412	34,178	41,791	44,300	50,600	51,500
Trade payables	61,604	67,936	92,118	79,283	54,801	129,289	132,671	154,000	150,800	181,200
Inventories	22,788	26,440	2,460	3,422	2,420	1,997	2,075	2,500	2,700	2,800
Basic EPS	31.71	27.20	35.10	20.00	28.20	25.84	(11.44)	20.68	25.21	38.03

TABLE 3.2 continued

	2003 $ Base (100)	2004 $ 2004	2005 $ 2005	2006 $ 2006	2007 $ 2007	2008 $ 2008	2009 $ 2009	2010 $ 2010	2011 $ 2011	2012 $ 2012
Sales	842,508	128	157	201	266	322	349	355	431	521
Operating profit	294,837	93	125	140	160	182	31	136	166	232
Profit after tax	239,398	86	117	128	26	163	(71)	128	156	234
Interest payable	30,886	154	187	239	268	314	423	233	304	354
Shareholders' equity	1,241,728	117	140	160	205	202	195	229	238	266
Non-current liabilities	847,440	118	169	212	240	268	305	374	449	458
Capital employed	2,089,168	117	152	181	219	228	240	288	324	344
Current assets	1,114,346	118	148	184	211	214	228	275	312	348
Current liabilities	377,539	129	172	224	296	412	365	410	487	481
Trade receivables	14,970	100	138	200	156	228	279	296	338	344
Trade payables	61,604	110	150	129	89	210	215	250	245	294
Inventories	22,788	116	11	15	11	9	9	11	12	12
Basic EPS	32	86	111	63	89	81	(36)	65	80	120

Issues

The major issues with this kind of analysis are:

- Presuming that balances are comparable between years:
  - There are likely to have been changes in accounting policies, accounting requirements, financial strategy and so forth that make direct like-for-like comparisons impossible.
- Deciding which period to set as the baseline year:
  - For example, setting 2009 as Ryanair's baseline year would generate significantly less useful results.

A note on financial analysis exercises

Remember that the simplest aspect of these exercises is completing the data collection exercise and performing the mechanical calculations. The focus of any financial analysis should fall on the '*analysis*'. Ensure that you do not simply ask yourself questions such as 'how much' or 'how little' has balance X changed, but also 'why' and 'so what'. Some preliminary questions you might like to ask yourself are:

- What does this information tell me about the company's performance?
- Has the company done well compared with other financial periods?
- Has the company exceeded its own targets?
- How does it compare with other companies in the same industry?
- What are the future prospects of: i) the firm; ii) the local economy; iii) the global economy; iv) customers and suppliers; v) political reform; vi) social, environmental and ethical circumstances etc?

Vertical analysis

What is vertical analysis?

While horizontal analysis identifies trends across time periods setting a specific year as the base, vertical analysis seeks patterns in the data on a year-by-year basis. In an income statement, the revenue should be restated as '100' and all subsequent figures are measured according to this baseline. In the statement of financial position, use your (net) assets figure as the baseline. This will mean, of course, you have two totals both adding up to '100'. This exercise will highlight those balances which are significant (in terms of size) from those which are less so. Again, auditors use this technique to identify material balances and areas of higher than average potential risk.

Worked exercise 3.2 shows Ryanair's statement of financial position as at 31 March 2012 and income statement for the year ended 31 March 2012 plus one comparative period.

WORKED EXERCISE 3.2   Vertical analysis for Ryanair Holdings plc

TABLE 3.3

Income statements For the year ended 31 March	2012		2011	
	$	%	$	%
Revenue	4,390.2	100.0%	3,629.5	100.0%
Operating expenses:				
Staff costs	(415.0)	−9.5%	(376.1)	−10.4%
Depreciation	(309.2)	−7.0%	(277.7)	−7.7%
Fuel and oil	(1,593.6)	−36.3%	(1,227.0)	−33.8%
Maintenance, materials and repairs	(104.0)	−2.4%	(93.9)	−2.6%
Aircraft rentals	(90.7)	−2.1%	(97.2)	−2.7%
Route charges	(460.5)	−10.5%	(410.6)	−11.3%
Airport and handling charges	(554.0)	−12.6%	(491.8)	−13.6%
Marketing, distribution and other	(180.0)	−4.1%	(154.6)	−4.3%
Icelandic volcanic ash related cost	0.0	0.0%	(12.4)	−0.3%
Operating profit	683.2		488.2	
Other income/(expense):				
Finance income	44.3	1.0%	27.2	0.7%
Finance expense	(109.2)	−2.5%	(93.9)	−2.6%
Foreign exchange gain/(loss)	4.3	0.1%	(0.6)	0.0%
Gain on disposal of property, plant and equipment	10.4	0.2%	0.0	0.0%
Profit before tax	633.0		420.9	
Tax expense on profit on ordinary activities	(72.6)	−1.7%	(46.3)	−1.3%
Profit for the year	560.4		374.6	

Expert view 3.1: Reflections of other stakeholders

This is not a criticism of the firm, but while current and potential investors might be pleased to see profits rise, how do you think employees will feel about these figures? Do you think environmentalists will be happy to see increased numbers of passengers and an airline achieving higher levels of profitability?

TABLE 3.4

Statements of financial position As at year ended 31 March	2012		2011	
	$	%	$	%
Non-current assets				
Property, plant and equipment	4,925.2	54.7%	4,933.7	57.4%
Intangible assets	46.8	0.5%	46.8	0.5%
Other non-current assets	153.0	1.7%	137.9	1.6%
Total non-current assets	5,125.0	56.9%	5,118.4	59.5%
Current assets				
Inventories	2.8	0.0%	2.7	0.0%
Other assets	64.9	0.7%	99.4	1.2%
Current tax	9.3	0.1%	0.5	0.0%
Trade receivables	51.5	0.6%	50.6	0.6%
Derivative financial instruments	231.9	2.6%	383.8	4.5%
Restricted cash	35.1	0.4%	42.9	0.5%
Financial assets: cash > 3 months	772.2	8.6%	869.4	10.1%
Cash and cash equivalents	2,708.3	30.1%	2,028.3	23.6%
Total current assets	3,876.0	43.1%	3,477.6	40.5%
Total assets	9,001.0	100.0%	8,596.0	100.0%
Current liabilities				
Trade payables	181.2	2.0%	150.8	1.8%
Accrued expenses and other liabilities	1,237.2	13.7%	1,224.3	14.2%
Current maturities of debt	368.4	4.1%	336.7	3.9%
Derivative financial instruments	28.2	0.3%	125.4	1.5%
Total current liabilities	1,815.0	20.2%	1,837.2	21.4%
Non-current liabilities				
Provisions	103.2	1.1%	89.6	1.0%
Derivative financial instruments	53.6	0.6%	8.3	0.1%
Deferred tax	319.4	3.5%	267.7	3.1%
Other creditors	146.3	1.6%	126.6	1.5%
Non-current maturities of debt	3,256.8	36.2%	3,312.7	38.5%
Total non-current liabilities	3,879.3	43.1%	3,804.9	44.3%
Equity and reserves				
Issued share capital	9.3	0.1%	9.5	0.1%
Share premium account	666.4	7.4%	659.3	7.7%
Capital redemption reserve	0.7	0.0%	0.5	0.0%
Retained earnings	2,400.1	26.7%	1,967.6	22.9%
Other reserves	230.2	2.6%	317.0	3.7%
Equity and reserves	3,306.7	36.7%	2,953.9	34.4%
	9,001.0	100.0%	8,596.0	100.0%

Interpreting vertical analysis information

It should be straightforward to appreciate why this mode of analysis is both appealing and informative. An analyst's focus will be immediately drawn to the most significant balances. By comparing with prior years' vertical analysis, it can also be used as a form of horizontal analysis. In the case of Ryanair, the key drivers of profitability are revenue, staff costs, depreciation, fuel and oil, route charges, and airport and handling costs. Fuel and oil costs equate to more than one-third of total revenue (2012: 36.5 per cent; 2011: 33.8 per cent) and are therefore of prime importance to the end result. Thus, changes in the wholesale price of fuel – which has become an increasingly volatile commodity – or a shift in the way the cost of fuel and oil is managed (hedging programme) can have far-reaching (positive or negative) consequences for an airline such as Ryanair.

The asset balances which stand out from the face of the statement of financial position are the non-current assets (ie the aeroplanes) and the level of cash and cash equivalents. The horizontal analysis reveals that Ryanair does not maintain an annual dividend payment policy and therefore cash is accumulated or used to generate returns unless spent. The company requires a cash buffer to protect itself during lean periods. The airline industry is particularly volatile and there are, unfortunately, many instances over the past decade of entities which have not survived. The dividend payment in 2009, however, probably highlights that the management believed that the cash resources being held were far larger than were required and they had two options available: either the cash needed to be reinvested in the business; or the shareholders needed to be rewarded. The latter option was taken. The liability that is most prominent relates to long-term debt which is required to purchase the non-current assets.

Please note that there are many other useful and insightful observations one could make based upon the vertical analysis above. This is a method, however, which should be used in conjunction with other techniques as it simply allows an analyst to undertake a quick appraisal of key figures. The strength of the technique lies in its simplicity to perform and draw swift conclusions. Its weaknesses stem from the same roots.

Ratio analysis

Introduction to ratio analysis

Ratio analysis, at least in theory, is a straightforward process. One simply needs to carefully select a relevant numerator and divide it by an equally relevant denominator to produce a calculation that has the potential to provide new insights. Once the result has been found, an interpretation and further analysis should follow where applicable. Your calculation might provide a ratio, a percentage, a number of times or a number of days, dependent upon the relationship you have chosen to examine.

You should note at this stage the important consideration that attempting to interpret one ratio in isolation is almost completely redundant. The purpose of the exercise is to draw an opinion about relative levels of position and performance.

The question we should be asking is, 'relative to whom or what'? In short, ratio analysis is most commonly used in order to:

- evaluate current year performance and position;
- compare performance and position across time periods;
- assess whether target ratios have been met;
- review firm-specific performance against the industry as a whole.

Expert view 3.2: Ratio analysis interpretation skills development

Practise, practise and practise! Read, read and read!

We are surrounded by financial information and news. Though we can set out ratios to learn and give you some hints and advice on how to interpret the results, nobody is able to develop interpretation skills without practice and without reading what others have written:

> Ratios are tools, and their value is limited when used alone. The more tools used, the better the analysis. For example, you can't use the same golf club for every shot and expect to be a good golfer. The more you practise with each club, however, the better able you will be to gauge which club to use on one shot. So too, we need to be skilled with the financial tools we use.
> (Diane Morrison, CEO REC Inc)

As a word of caution and advice, we have found that it is common for students to learn a long list of ratios without genuinely engaging with the material which they are being asked to examine. This is perfectly understandable, especially for those who have not been required to perform this type of analysis before. It is also a problem for those who are not actively engaging on a daily basis with current affairs, particularly the business news. We strongly advocate that you pursue a broader contextual understanding. This will facilitate a more rewarding experience and will allow you to analyse the figures in a more precise and discerning manner.

Key ratios

Profitability ratios

Profitability ratios are intended to measure the performance of the entity. Less sophisticated observers might focus exclusively on the bottom line, ie profit for the year and compare with the previous year. Indeed, as Extract 3.1 shows, profitability is a *headline grabber*. Equally, however, Extract 3.1 shows that the business reporter has dug deeper into the information to understand why the levels of profitability have changed. Thus, though year-on-year profits are important, relying on them as an assessment of annual (or ongoing) performance is somewhat naive. Also, comparing actual profits between entities is not an especially useful measure given the importance of relative size to levels of return. We present the three core profitability ratios below alongside interpretation hints. These are:

- return on capital employed;
- gross profit margin; and
- net profit margin.

Of course, we strongly advise that you drill down into the results and undertake further analysis where appropriate. This can be done using other financial and non-financial performance-related information as well as by employing other analysis techniques, eg horizontal analysis, trend analysis or vertical analysis.

Extract 3.1: Profitability as a headline grabber

a) Profits rise

Google profits rise despite trend to cheaper mobile ads

Daily Telegraph (19 April 2013)
By Martin Strydom

Google profits rose 16 per cent to $3.35bn in the first three months of the year as revenue increased despite a trend toward cheaper ads on smartphones and tablets.

Larry Page, the Google co-founder and chief executive, said: 'We had a very strong start to 2013, with $14bn in revenue, up 31 per cent year-on-year.' The profits beat Wall Street's expectation and Google shares, which ended the official Nasdaq trading day slightly down, regained ground in after-hours trades to $777.

The number of paid clicks on ads posted at Google pages was 20pc greater than those seen in the first quarter last year and up three per cent from the final quarter of 2012. Meanwhile, in a closely watched figure, the cost per click for advertisers dropped four per cent, indicating a trend toward less expensive mobile ads. Google executives highlighted the 'big bets' being taken by the company, ranging from Android mobile gadget software to self-driving cars and Internet-linked glasses.

b) Profit warning

Mulberry pins third profit warning on thrifty tourists

Chief executive says Somerset-based luxury label needs to focus on tactical international advertising

The Guardian, Friday 22 March 2013
By Josephine Moulds and Simon Neville

Mulberry shares have plunged by nearly a fifth after the fashion and handbags business issued a third profit warning in a year, blaming a fall in profits on lower spending by tourists in London after Christmas. The Somerset-based luxury label, famous for its trademark Bayswater and Alexa bags – which start at £800 and go up to £4,500 for versions in ostrich leather – said full-year profits would not meet market expectations due to 'disappointing' trading over the past 10 weeks. However, Mulberry's chief executive, Bruno Guillon, who joined a year ago, defended the performance and said the latest warning would not affect his international expansion plans. He said: 'We are still very confident with the strategy and will not be changing it. We need to focus on increasing our international presence, particularly with tactical advertising, so that tourists coming to London and Paris from China know about the brand.'

In October, bosses issued a 'severe' profit warning after lower than expected international retail sales and a shortfall in wholesale revenue. Mulberry investors suffered losses of 22 per cent in June when the company warned of a sales slowdown. Guillon said: 'Sales in London have been particularly bad, with tourists not spending in our stores.' However, according to the Office for National Statistics most recent data, tourist spending in the UK increased 11% in January to £1.24bn, although the number of foreign tourists fell 1 per cent.

It is the latest in a series of disappointments for the brand, which has seen an incredible rise in recent years, with shares hitting £23.90 in April last year. They closed at £10.26 on Friday. Mulberry is now targeting pre-tax profits of £26m for the year to March, compared with expectations of £30.7m. Revenues are expected to come in at £165m, against analyst forecasts of £175m. Wholesale revenues for the year are expected to be down by about 15 per cent on last year, as a result of slimming down its operations and lower than expected ordering during the season. It was the wholesale business that caused the October profit warning, after the company focused on supplying department stores it felt were more in keeping with the brand's premium position.

Despite increasing focus on the international market, Guillon said the business would keep its UK identity and is opening a new factory in Bridgwater, Somerset, creating 300 jobs. However, the 20 stores opening this year will all be overseas. Mulberry expects retail like-for-like sales to grow by 6 per cent this year. The company insisted the order book for autumn/winter 2013 was building 'satisfactorily'.

(a) Return on capital employed (ROCE)

It is common for investors to view the return on capital employed (ROCE) as the most important measure of performance. Unfortunately, there are over 30 possible variations to the calculation of this ratio, which can make comparisons problematic. We present the most commonly used version, but when you are provided with this information, always maintain an enquiring mind. There are also many closely related ratios, for example return on investment (ROI), return on shareholders' funds (ROSF) and accounting rate of return (ARR).

ROCE is calculated as:

$$\frac{\text{Profit}}{\text{Capital}} \times 100\% \quad \text{Or, more precisely:} \quad \frac{\text{Profit before interest and tax}}{\text{Capital employed}} \times 100\%$$

What does this ratio reveal?

The ROCE weighs up the level of return generated during a period of account relative to the amount of capital that has been provided. Sometimes the ROCE is used as a threshold measure by management when deciding whether to accept or reject future proposed projects. It is also commonly used when appraising historic performance. In other words, looking at this relationship through the eyes of the capital provider, investors are attempting to gauge how well their money has been spent and how well the resources have been managed. In extreme cases, one could argue that an entity that returns less than the risk-free rate of return might be better off liquidating the assets and investing the cash proceeds in 10-year US government treasury bonds.

It is not a truism to suggest that the higher the ROCE the better. This oversimplifies the problem by ignoring context. A high ROCE does not necessarily mean that an entity is a *good* investment. Remember that investors weigh up returns against risk. For example, an entity with an average ROCE of, say, 10 per cent in the oil and gas extraction industry would be seen as a relatively poor performer, whereas the same ROCE achieved by a property trust company, for instance, would be seen as a healthy investment.

One could rightly suggest, however, that if the ROCE fell below the company's investors' expected weighted required rates of return, the investment would be deemed a poor one. Corporate entities are looking to invest in projects that generate wealth. If the ROCE falls below these required rates of return, the projects which are being undertaken are destroying wealth. Occasionally the decision to take on lower-yielding projects is necessary, but to do so on a regular and long-term basis increases the risk of capital extraction which would be detrimental to the position of the firm.

Drilling down to interpret the changes in the ratio

A ratio provides a result about which one can make broad, descriptive and somewhat meaningless statements. For example, as Worked exercise 3.3 shows, the ROCE has increased from 7.2 per cent in 2011 to 9.5 per cent in 2012. An interpretation of this ratio should not be limited to statements such as: 'This change points towards a good year for Ryanair in terms of returns to investors and their performance.'

Apart from anything, we don't know whether this does actually indicate a good year for the company. Before we could make this assessment we would need to ask a number of follow-up questions, for example:

- Were the results in line with targets?
- How do the results compare to those from previous years?
- Does this ROCE meet or beat market expectations?
- How did competitors perform during the same period of account?
- How has this percentage increase been achieved?
- Is this ROCE sustainable?

If all you have to work with is the financial information itself, your analysis will be limited. Nevertheless, you will be able to make some strides towards identifying trends, patterns, strengths, weaknesses and potential areas of upside and downside risk. For accounting non-specialists it can be difficult to see how the balances in the primary statements interlink, but it is extremely helpful if you are able to engage with this idea. This is partly why we went through the exercises in Chapters 1 and 2, to help you to see the interrelationship between assets and liabilities, gains and losses.

There are two variables that determine an entity's ROCE: profit; and capital employed. For the ratio to move upwards like this (from 7.2 per cent to 9.5 per cent), one of the following must have occurred:

- Profit has increased and capital employed has decreased.
- Profit has increased proportionately more than capital employed.
- Capital employed has decreased proportionately more than profit.
- Profit has stayed the same and capital employed decreased.
- Capital employed has stayed the same and profit has increased.

In this example, profit has risen by almost 40 per cent while capital employed has risen by 6 per cent. The weight in the formula is leant to the denominator (because of the volume of capital employed). Nevertheless, these movements upwards are all significant. Further analysis shows that a 21 per cent increase in revenue is matched to only an 18 per cent rise in costs. These changes during the year have given rise to a sizeable movement in operating profit. The increase in the amount of capital employed has arisen almost entirely because of the increase in retained earnings, ie the amount of accumulated profit taken to retained earnings in the statement of financial position as a result of a successful year's trading. It is unsurprising that the chief executive's report on the period starts with the sentence: 'Our results for the past year underline the enduring strength of Ryanair's ultra low fare airline model here in Europe' (Ryanair annual report, 2012, p 5).

If things had been different and capital employed had increased, we would need to drill down into other balances. For example, it might be that non-current liabilities could have increased, in which case you might want to see whether this was the result of borrowing to fund the acquisition of new long-term assets. If it was used to buy aeroplanes or other revenue-generating property, plant and equipment (PPE), we would expect to see an increase in non-current assets in the statement of financial position as well. This would then impact on ratios such as asset turnover. More importantly, we would expect to see increases in revenue as a result of asset purchases, assuming the assets were put to use. Note, however, that there may be a lag given that it is unlikely that these assets could be brought into immediate use. (It is not uncommon for airlines to buy planes from other failed or failing airlines because they can get bargains through financial distress gains but then ground them for a time until they find a suitable route.) Given this information, you should now have a whole host of further questions which you would want to investigate, for example:

- How did the company manage to increase revenue by 20 per cent without seeing any rise in non-current liabilities?
- Were the planes previously underutilized?
- Did customer demand drop off last year and pick up this year?
- Were planes bought in previous years which have been brought into operational usage this year?
- Were planes acquired through non-debt-financed contracts, eg through operating leases?
- Were there price rises this year?
- And so forth...

Complications in the calculation

i) How should profit be defined?

When we refer to profit in the calculation of ROCE, it is usual to consider *operating profit* as the most useful indicator of performance rather than the profit for the year or retained profits. This is also referred to as profit before interest and tax (or 'PBIT'). The rationale for using this figure over others is that it provides a clearer message about current performance, and just as importantly, current stewardship. Using this figure also aids greater comparability between entities which are often subject to different financing requirements and taxation regimes.

Why exclude taxation costs?

Assuming that taxation regimes are fair (ie higher profits = higher tax charge), then relatively high taxation costs should be interpreted as a reflection of better performance and, by extension, all things being equal, good stewardship. Therefore judging performance based upon profits after tax risks levelling out the playing field by inappropriately recognizing those companies with lower tax bills based upon lower pre-tax profits. Of course, we acknowledge that tax is controllable to a certain degree and sound financial planning alongside flexible accounting policies and practices can reduce the annual tax-cost burden. If you choose to invest in a business it would be unusual and unwise to invest in the management's ability to manage tax costs rather than their ability to generate operating profits.

Why exclude finance costs?

Interest expenditure normally dominates the finance costs category (although other costs are included, eg gains and losses on derivative financial instruments held for trading). Loans are normally matched to the term over which the assets are held. For example, an aeroplane is thought to continue to generate revenues for approximately 23 years and loans are negotiated on this basis. If the senior management team turnover rate is, say, one every five years or so, we must ask whether it is fair and appropriate to judge new management against old loans.

There is also some debate over whether profit before interest and tax actually means profit before interest *payable* and tax. Indeed, it is common for finance income to be added to the operating profit number while finance costs are excluded from operating profit.

ii) What does capital employed mean?

Those responsible for providing capital to a corporate entity have the expectation that the management will select and undertake value-generating activities which adequately and appropriately reward the risks which they have chosen to bear. Capital provision, or project financing, is considered to arise from one or both of these sources: equity and/or debt.

- Equity can be provided through internal financing, such as accumulated reserves or shortening the working capital cycle. However, it is far more common that the term equity is used in reference to the raising of funds through the sale of share capital.

- Debt is a term which is used to refer to all forms of borrowing – of which there are many. Companies might, for example, apply for loans from banks or other lenders, take out mortgages to help them buy land and buildings, long-term hire purchase agreements to acquire plant, vehicles and machinery, sell loan stock to finance an expansion plan, and so forth.
  - Note that we have drawn your attention only to long-term debt financing, thereby ignoring other forms of short-term debt such as a bank overdraft. In short, there are no rules for inclusion or exclusion of short-term borrowings. We suggest that if a bank overdraft is used as a long-term financing option, it should be included as debt under capital provided.

Capital provided can therefore be summarized as:

Equity + Debt

In relation to the statement of financial position, we suggest you use as a proxy for these two categories:

Shareholders' funds + Non-current liabilities

Occasionally you will see businesses average out the capital employed. We suggest that this is practical when appraising single one-off investments (as the opening and closing capital required will be easily to hand), but when your focus is on calculating the ROCE for the entity as a whole, it is simpler to extract the closing (period-end) positions and use these.

Dairy firm Graham's sees sales and profits surge

Graham's said the increased cost of raw milk, cream and fuel were 'still proving challenging'

BBC online (28 October 2013)

New contract wins and significant brand investment have helped to lift sales and profits for Graham's The Family Dairy.

The Stirlingshire-based company report that sales climbed by 21 per cent to £68m in the year to the end of March. Annual pre-tax profits more than doubled to just over £1m.

However, the company warned it still faced tough trading conditions, with continuing volatility in milk prices and a squeeze on margins. Managing director Robert Graham said: 'A focus on the Graham's brand and understanding the value of our brand has brought great success during this period, however as a business we continue to face tough trading conditions.' The increased costs of raw milk, cream and fuel are still proving challenging. 'New contract wins and improved internal cost management have led to strong sales growth.'

He added: 'However our commitment to invest for the long-term in operations, plant and machinery in challenging market conditions means that we are not currently seeing a true return on capital employed.'

Expansion drive

The company has been investing heavily in its brand name, including spending a six-figure sum on a TV advertising campaign. In recent years it has expanded its product range to include butter, cream and ice cream. The Bridge of Allan-based firm is planning further expansion after being granted a total of £630,000 earlier this year through the Scottish government's Food Processing, Marketing and Co-operation (FPMC) Award. The cash will help the business to buy a site and install a yoghurt and cottage cheese line in Bridge of Allan and build new lines for semi-skimmed milk processing and low fat spreads in Nairn.

Anglo American boss says profits 'unacceptably poor'

Mark Cutifani is looking to shake up Anglo American

BBC online (26 July, 2013)

The boss of Anglo American, Mark Cutifani, has described his company's profits as 'unacceptably poor'.

The mining giant reported a 68 per cent drop in first-half profits, after it was hit by falling commodity prices, as the global economic picture remained weak. Profits after tax fell to $403m (£262m) for the six months to the end of June, compared with

$1.254bn in 2012. Mr Cutifani promised to cut spending and halve the number of pipeline projects. He also said the company would boost production at underperforming mines. 'Our performance at the operating level, compared to our budgets, has been unacceptably poor,' Mr Cutifani said.

'Over the last eight (quarters) only 11 per cent of operations are delivering consistently against their targets – we have to up that,' he added. He also said he wanted a 'more disciplined approach to planning, to execution and delivery'.

Mr Cutifani was appointed chief executive back in April, when he took over from Cynthia Carroll. However, Anglo American did see some benefit from improvements in certain areas of production and a fall in the currencies of the countries where it operates. As such, the company's underlying operating profit only fell 15 per cent to $3.262bn during the first half.

Tough times

Anglo American is the smallest of the big international mining companies and its shares have not kept pace with the likes of Rio Tinto and BHP Billiton in recent years. Anglo has had some big issues to deal with, most recently labour unrest at its operations in South Africa and multi-billion-dollar cost overruns at its Minas Rio iron ore project in Brazil. By slashing costs and pipeline projects, simplifying the company's management structure and improving the performance of its assets, Mr Cutifani is hoping to improve cashflow by $1.3bn within three years.

He also intends to raise the return on capital employed (ROCE) to 15 per cent, from its current 11 per cent. ROCE is a crucial figure mining companies use to measure the value of the assets they own.

(b) Gross profit margin

The gross profit margin is a key ratio which enables the analyst to assess trading performance before deducting operating expenses. Or, in other words, the direct profit earned in relation to the sales made. The ratio is calculated as:

$$\frac{\text{Gross profit}}{\text{Revenue}} \times 100\%$$

It is rare that there are definitional problems like those shown in the calculation of the ROCE above. The gross profit is calculated as:

$$\text{Revenue}$$
$$\text{Minus} \quad \text{Cost of sales}$$

We introduced cost of sales as being:

	Opening inventories
Plus	Purchases
Minus	Closing inventories

And, in many cases, this simple method is employed. However, the cost of sales is more appropriately referred to as the cost of goods sold. The revised inference is that you are expected to include the direct costs of production in this figure. The cost of goods sold includes not only direct materials purchase costs, but direct labour costs and similar. Inclusion or exclusion of costs 'above the line' (ie within cost of sales or above the gross profit line) between entities can create difficulties when performing analysis. If you are undertaking sector (or industry) analysis and you identify significant differences from one company to the next, we suggest you calculate the net profit margin and ensure that this isn't the result of an expense classification difference.

Most companies will disclose their gross profit figure. Airlines, however, cluster all of their costs into operating expenses. This is unusual. It does mean that we are not able to calculate a gross profit margin for Ryanair. Nevertheless, when analysing a change in this ratio, your first challenge will be to work out why. There are only two variables:

- Has revenue increased, decreased or stayed the same?
- Has the cost of sales increased, decreased or stayed the same?

To help target your investigations, you might consider the following possible explanations as to why the variation could have arisen:

- Changes in the sales mix, eg:
  - Were new products launched during the year?
  - Were old products withdrawn from sale?
  - Were high-margin/low-margin products more/less popular this year than in prior years?
- Changes in sales price.
- An increase/decrease in discounts offered to customers.
- A change in inventories sourcing procedures or/and supplier(s).
- Changes to the products and the associated raw materials requirements.
- An increase/decrease in production process efficiency.
- An increase/decrease in discounts being offered by suppliers.
- Changes to cost classifications, from or to operating expenses.
- An increase/decrease in inventory value write-offs due to obsolescence or other factors.
- And so forth...

(c) Net profit margin

The net profit margin is a key ratio which enables the analyst to assess trading performance after the deduction of operating expenses. It is a measure of operating profit in relation to revenue and provides a guide as to how well the company has performed during the year. The ratio is calculated as:

$$\frac{\text{Operating profit}}{\text{Revenue}} \times 100\%$$

As discussed above (in relation to the ROCE), the calculation of the net profit margin can also be adapted to take different measures of profitability. Most commonly, the net profit margin uses operating profit (PBIT). This facilitates comparability and takes into account the costs which are controllable by management.

Levels of profitability are inherently difficult to compare between entities and between years, let alone between companies operating in different industries. Results will be dependent upon managerial stewardship and firm performance, but will also relate to external events such as the prevailing economic conditions and the degree of competition.

Ryanair's net profit margin has increased from 13.5 per cent in 2011 to 15.6 per cent in 2012. As with previous ratios, this observation requires further analysis and explanation. A naive observer would be keen to make the point that this is an improvement on the prior year and indeed, it might be. However, this statement is not verifiable without reference to other information. You might like to consider the following questions:

- What does your horizontal, trend and vertical analysis show you about the cost structure and year-on-year line item comparisons?
- Have costs risen in line with, above or below inflation?
- To what extent is the movement in the profit margin a reflection of commodity price movements which are less (or sometimes even un-)controllable, eg fuel costs?
- How have other companies responded to the economic climate and have their costs moved comparably to the entity under review?
- Have there been any recognition or measurement accounting policy changes, eg changes to depreciation rates?

Though each entity's cost structure and strategy will be different, the level of change in certain costs is generally worthy of separate enquiry when you are undertaking this form of analysis:

- research and development;
- depreciation and amortization;
- pension costs;
- employee costs, including staff training and development spend (if separately disclosed);
- directors' remuneration;
- government grants.

WORKED EXERCISE 3.3   Ryanair's profitability ratios

Return On Capital Employed:

$$\frac{\text{Profit}}{\text{Capital}} \times 100\%$$

	2012 €m	2011 €m
Operating profit (PBIT) (excluding finance income and costs)	683.2	488.2
Shareholders' funds	3,306.7	2,953.9
+	+	+
Non-current liabilities (including *all* non-current liabilities)	3,879.3	3,804.9

$$\frac{683.2}{7,186.0} \times 100\% \qquad \frac{488.2}{6,758.8} \times 100\%$$

$$=9.5\% \qquad\qquad =7.2\%$$

Gross profit margin:

$$\frac{\text{Gross profit}}{\text{Revenue}} \times 100\%$$

Gross profit	N/A	N/A
Revenue	4,390.2	3,629.5

$$=N/A \qquad\qquad =N/A$$

Net profit margin:

$$\frac{\text{Operating profit (PBIT)}}{\text{Revenue}} \times 100\%$$

Operating profit (PBIT) (excluding finance income and costs)	683.2	488.2
Revenue	4,390.2	3,629.5

$$\frac{683.2}{4,390.2} \times 100\% \qquad \frac{488.2}{3,629.5} \times 100\%$$

$$=15.6\% \qquad\qquad =13.5\%$$

Extract 3.3: Ryanair Holdings plc: Chairman's report, 2012

CHAIRMAN'S REPORT

Dear Shareholders,
I am very pleased to report a 25 per cent increase in profit after tax to a new record of €503 million. This was a strong performance despite a €367 million rise in fuel costs which we managed to offset by a 16 per cent rise in average fares. During the year Ryanair delivered a number of significant milestones:

- We grew our traffic by 5 per cent to 76 million passengers.

- We took delivery of 25 (net) new aircraft and we had a year-end fleet of 294 Boeing 737-800s.

- We opened 6 new bases and 330 new routes bringing the total number of routes operated to over 1,500.

- We improved our industry leading passenger service with better punctuality, fewer lost bags and less cancellations.

- We completed a share buyback of €125 million in fiscal 2012 and €68 million in April 2012, and the board have proposed a dividend of €0.34 per share amounting to approximately €489 million subject to shareholder approval at the annual general meeting. The combination of the second special dividend (subject to shareholder approval) and previous share buybacks and dividends will mean that Ryanair has returned an industry leading €1.53 billion to shareholders over the past 5 years.

Fuel costs as a proportion of our total operating costs have risen to 43 per cent in fiscal 2012. We are 90 per cent hedged for fiscal 2013, at just over $100 per barrel and we are faced with a further €320 million increase in our fuel bill, a total increase in 2 years of €687 million. Oil price rises and higher winter airport charges at certain government owned airports will make it commercially sound to ground up to 80 aircraft rather than suffer losses operating these aircraft during the winter when yields are significantly lower. Nevertheless, we still expect passenger volumes in fiscal 2013 to grow by approximately 5 per cent to 79 million passengers.

In the airline industry, we yet again face another challenging year with significantly higher fuel prices and with European government fiscal deficits resulting in austerity measures and leading to falling European consumer confidence. As recessionary pressures continue we believe more carriers will exit the industry and we intend to take advantage of those developments, as we have this year, when we opened a new base in Budapest following the closure of Malev, and significantly expanded our operations at Barcelona and Madrid following the closure of Spanair. We believe that the winners will be those airlines with strong balance sheets (we currently have over €3.8 billion in cash), the lowest costs and a strong sustainable business model...

Notwithstanding the issues we face, the outstanding people at Ryanair continue to work hard on behalf of shareholders to reduce our costs while at the same time delivering the lowest fares in Europe to our 79 million passengers. As a result, we still expect to generate significant profits in fiscal 2013 although these are likely to be lower than we enjoyed in fiscal 2012.

Yours sincerely,
David Bonderman
Chairman

Expert view 3.3: Financial analysis provided by the senior management team

One of the benefits of modern corporate reporting is the provision of a large amount of self-analysis and reflection from the senior management team. Extract 3.3 shows how Ryanair's Chairman interprets the 2012 results. Of course, this text might be intended for self-promotion purposes and there are signs of impression management. Nevertheless, what is written by these company representatives needs to be consistent with the financial information which is reported elsewhere in the annual report. It is a fantastic learning tool for those who are new to corporate reporting and financial analysis.

Liquidity ratios

Liquidity ratios are intended to provide users with an understanding of the short-term position of an entity, where short-term means the next 12 months. A change in levels of short-term assets and liabilities can also provide some assurances over solvency and the sustainability of current levels of performance. Excessively high levels of current liabilities would be a red-flag issue for investors. However, excessively high levels of current assets would be interpreted as a poor use of resources. Achieving the correct working capital position balance (ratio of current assets versus current liabilities) is as much an art as a science. Note that these measures can be manipulated by window dressing, ie creating or holding assets, which you otherwise would not have, at the end of an accounting period.

There are many liquidity ratios which could be produced; however two key ratios which you should start with are the current ratio and the acid test ratio (otherwise known as the quick ratio).

(a) Current ratio

The current ratio is calculated as follows:

$$\frac{\text{Current assets}}{\text{Current liabilities}}$$

The result is expressed as a ratio, but can also be seen as a level of coverage. You might see references to target ratios. More specifically, in the past a current ratio of $2:1$ and a quick ratio of $1:1$ were seen as being ideal. The presumption is that an entity can remain liquid if it has the ability to cover its immediate bills two times over if called upon to do so. Times, however, have changed and the perceptions of over/under-resourcing have also shifted. Management are frequently appraised on their ability to extract the maximum value out of their short-term liquid resources.

Commentators who hold to the belief that there is an optimum ratio of current assets to current liabilities often neglect to mention the pay-off between liquidity and profitability. If one has finite inventory production capabilities and makes the conscious decision during a period of account to stockpile inventories, then (assuming all other things are equal) the following would occur:

- current assets will be higher at the end of the period;
- thus, the current and quick ratios will increase;
- but the amount of inventory sold will be lower;
- and therefore profits will be lower.

As Worked exercise 3.4 shows, the proportion of current assets held versus current liabilities in 2012 by Ryanair was 2.14; or, current liabilities were covered by current assets 2.14 times. It is common for an increase in the ratio to be interpreted as an indicator of a *better* position. As with the profitability ratios, however, liquidity ratios cannot be appropriately or accurately commented upon without taking into account the drivers of the change and the broader context in which the change has occurred.

In the case of Ryanair, the increase has been driven mainly by a net increase in cash and cash equivalents. The fair value of short-term derivatives holdings has dropped (assets and liabilities). Though this could potentially have a material impact on fuel costs and other hedged expenses, the impact on the liquidity ratios is not significant. The company was holding over €3 billion in cash at the end of 2012. Generating this amount of cash must be viewed as positive. However, not being able to spend it on operations might be seen as a weakness hence why the company has returned approximately $1.53 billion to shareholders over the past five years and the promise that further investments in aircraft are likely to follow in 2014/15. Also, in a broader context, one should not forget that this increase in cash and rise in profitability has occurred during a period of economic uncertainty, turmoil and recession. Therefore, an important point which we are neglecting to mention is the relative performance of the firm during this period in comparison to other airlines, and more specifically, other low-cost airlines.

(b) Acid test (quick) ratio

The acid test ratio is similar to the current ratio. The denominator remains the same (ie current liabilities) but the numerator, current assets, is adjusted for inventories. The acid test ratio is calculated as follows:

$$\frac{\text{Current assets minus inventories}}{\text{Current liabilities}}$$

The rationale for removing inventories from current assets is that they are the least liquid of assets within the class. When businesses are faced with an immediate need for cash and face genuine bankruptcy risk, their inventories are worth very little. When an entity sells inventories as a going concern, they are almost always worth more than their cost. When an entity is being wound up, the inventories held are normally worth significantly less than cost as buyers perceive the opportunity to buy at a bargain price, plus they are aware that continued spare-parts production will likely cease and maintenance will not be as readily available if the company does not survive. This phenomenon has been shown to affect companies across a wide range of industries and size does not mean you get treated differently, for example MG Rover (motor vehicles) and Lehman Brothers (financial services).

Inventories held for airlines are typically low, especially airlines like Ryanair which specialize in low-cost short-haul journeys. Ryanair carry a small amount of on-board food and duty-free goods which are intended to be sold in-flight. Therefore the impact on their liquidity position is immaterial. It might be interesting to note that when airlines are faced with bankruptcy concerns, it is more common for competitors or new entrants to attempt to take advantage of their position by buying the struggling firm's non-current assets – planes and landing slots – at heavily discounted prices (rather than their inventories).

WORKED EXERCISE 3.4   Ryanair's liquidity ratios

Current ratio:
$$\frac{\text{Current assets}}{\text{Current liabilities}}$$

	2012 €m	2011 €m
Current assets	3,876.0	3,477.6
Current liabilities	1,815.0	1,837.2
	$\frac{3,876.0}{1,815.0}$	$\frac{3,477.6}{1,837.2}$
	=2.14 : 1 (or 2.14 times)	=1.89 : 1 (or 1.89 times)

Current ratio:

Current assets – inventories
Current liabilities

	2012 €m	2011 €m
Current assets	3,876.0	3,477.6
Less	–	–
Inventories	2.8	2.7
Current liabilities	1,815.0	1,837.2

	$\dfrac{3,873.2}{1,815.0}$	$\dfrac{3,474.9}{1,837.2}$
	=2.13 : 1 (or 2.13 times)	=1.89 : 1 (or 1.89 times)

Efficiency ratios

Efficiency ratios are calculated to provide analysts with information about the utilization of (short-term) resources. This broad definition means that there are many ratios which could be calculated and many relationships which might be worthy of detailed attention. We would urge you to start with three basic working capital ratios and investigate further if required. These are as follows:

- trade receivables collection period;
- inventories holding period;
- trade payables payment period.

The aim of the exercise is to gauge whether the entity under consideration has managed their resources more or less efficiently than i) in previous years and ii) their competitors As with other ratio categories, however, the interpretation of the results will depend upon context, eg:

- the industry the firm operates in;
- the working capital management strategy (aggressive or defensive) adopted by the entity;
- the state of the economy;
- competitors' approaches to working capital management;
- credit rating and availability of short-term credit;
- and so forth...

The application of the prudence concept in financial accounting means that results remain broadly comparable year on year. The inventories are valued at the lower of cost and net realizable value, the trade receivables figure is shown net of balances owed but which are not likely to be received, while trade payables includes amounts owed to suppliers which are obligated liabilities of the entity.

Other ratios you might consider that could be used to explore efficiency include:

- inventory turnover ratio (Cost of Sales / (Closing) Inventories);
- average inventories turnover ratio (Cost of Sales / Average Inventories [opening inventories plus closing inventories divided by 2]);
- non-current assets turnover ratio (Revenue / Non-current assets);
- revenue per employee (or any other non-financial cost driver);
- revenue per aeroplane (or any other major asset class).

Extract 3.4: A profitable company with poor liquidity – what's the worst that can happen?

Wet 'N' Wild waterpark enters administration

BBC (online) 17 October, 2013

Wet 'N' Wild was opened in North Shields in 1993

A waterpark in North Tyneside has gone into administration, putting nearly 70 jobs at risk.

Wet 'N' Wild in North Shields went into administration on Monday despite being profitable 'for much of the year'.

The indoor waterpark opened in 1993 and employs 69 people, the majority of whom will be made redundant, administrators PwC said.

A spokesman for PwC claimed it had 'no alternative' but to close the park and was seeking interested buyers.

The company has been working with North Tyneside Council to pay off tens of thousands of pounds worth of business rates and other liabilities, the BBC understands.

The council has not been involved in the administration process.

Toby Underwood, joint administrator and partner at PwC, said: 'Despite operating profitably for much of the year the business faced liquidity issues over the forthcoming months.

'Unfortunately, with the quieter winter trading period upon us we have had no alternative but to close the waterpark with immediate effect and make the majority of employees redundant.

'We will continue to maintain the waterpark while seeking a sale.'

(a) Trade receivables collection period

The trade receivables collection period is calculated as follows:

$$\frac{\text{Trade receivables}}{\text{Credit sales}} \times 365 \text{ days}$$

A note on the calculation of trade receivables collection period

Note that the credit sales figure is rarely disclosed in an annual report. The headline figure, revenue, however, is almost always shown separately and can be used as a proxy for credit sales. Sometimes this is disaggregated into categories, which might be helpful for your analysis (for example, BMW Group plc divide revenue between motor vehicle sales and financial services revenue [interest received on loans offered to purchase BMWs by BMW Group plc]). You should be aware that substituting revenue for credit sales might distort your analysis. Though the majority of companies trade exclusively through short-term credit agreements (eg invoices demanding payment is received within 28 days), this is not always the case. If you are investigating the ratios of a supermarket, for example, the majority of customers pay in cash at the checkout/till. These businesses permit only a handful of customers to buy 'on account'. If, in this case, you use revenue to calculate the trade receivables collection period, the result produced will drastically shorten the *real* collection period.

Some argue that it is more appropriate to use average trade receivables than closing trade receivables. They suggest that this tells you how long the average customer takes to pay. Both closing and averaging have weaknesses. If it is obvious that they produce significantly different results, a reconciliation alongside an explanation would be required.

Interpreting the trade receivables collection period

Though there are benefits to both buyer and seller, analysts tend to view trade receivables as short-term interest-free loans to customers. The longer you allow your customers to pay, the longer your working capital cycle. In turn, the greater the period of time is that you must spend without cash. In this regard, there is an opportunity cost attached to trade receivables, ie an entity could be doing something more valuable with their cash, for example investing it profitably in operations.

In short, the trade receivables collection period is designed to indicate the length of time (in days) it takes for credit customers to pay for the products or services they purchased. Commonly a shorter collection period compared to prior years and industry averages is better. This means that you are recycling your cash quicker. Assuming that the entity is profitable, this also means that you are contributing to the generation of cash more effectively. In other words, you are using your resources more efficiently. A shorter(-ening) trade receivables collection period could indicate improved credit collection management, eg careful selection of creditworthy customers, chasing late payments more vigorously, and so forth.

There are, however, several problems with this naive interpretation:

- The nature of the calculation means that weight is added to larger customers. Thus, if one large customer pays faster (slower), it will skew the result.

- If several smaller customers are not paying, it would be difficult to pick up from this simple ratio calculation; and yet this might be information important to your analysis and to the business more generally.
- One might be suspicious of the policies and processes of a company with a shorter than average trade receivables collection period.
  - A business that maintains a demanding (pushy?!) cash collection department/strategy runs the risk of alienating customers, especially if the operational area is competitive and customers could go elsewhere for similar products or services.
  - Offering large discounts might speed up collection but there would be an offsetting impact on profitability.
- A shorter than average number of collection days might be due to an underlying weakness in the calculation, eg the inclusion of cash sales in the revenue figure.

Unfortunately, Ryanair's trade receivables collection period provides an almost meaningless result (see Worked exercise 3.5). On the face of it, the calculation shows that the number of outstanding days is low (around four days). This would ordinarily be interpreted as an extremely efficient use of short-term resources. When this is analysed in context, however, this conclusion lacks robustness. The majority of Ryanair's customers are not offered a credit settlement period. Instead, customers pay when they book their flights, ie by cash in advance. As we do not have the disaggregated revenue figure, it is impossible to say how long customers who are allowed credit take to settle their obligations. Providing some reassurance that the risk of default should not be a material concern for investors, the company does separately disclose that 'no individual customer accounted for more than 10% of [their] accounts receivable at March 31, 2012, March 31, 2011 or at March 31, 2010' (Ryanair Holdings plc, Annual Report 2012, p 155) and only 0.2 per cent of this balance was deemed to be impaired, or irrecoverable.

(b) Inventories holding period

The inventories holding period is calculated as follows:

$$\frac{\text{Inventories}}{\text{Cost of sales}} \times 365 \text{ days}$$

Inventories are frequently a significant asset class for businesses and represent a large amount of short-term resource being tied up. The inventories holding period tells the analyst how many days the business is keeping their average item of stock. Given that any holding of inventories represents tied-up cash – and by extension the lost opportunity to use that cash for value-creating activities – then the shorter the inventories holding period, the better.

Interpreting yearly differences should be straightforward. The following might explain movements:

- a variation in sales mix;
- a change in products or services offered;
- commodity price movements;

- supply chain changes;
- a growth (decline) in demand;
- improved (worsened) inventories control management;
- high (low) levels of obsolete stock;
- a change in buying strategy, eg bulk purchasing (to take advantage of discounts), or more cautious buying policies;
- a period of firm-specific growth;
- and so forth.

There are two issues that prevent comparability between entities:

1 There are different inventory demands between industries and this will lead to large differences in the result of the inventories holding period calculation. For example, supermarkets stock short-life products by and large and therefore their inventory days will be relatively low, whereas house-building companies might have long inventory days given the nature of their business.

2 Not all business inventory management strategies are alike, either within or between industries. Some companies will adopt sophisticated inventory management practices while others will lag behind. Every entity will weigh up the costs versus the benefits of introducing advanced inventory control systems innovations and make their choice accordingly. For example, just-in-time (JIT) systems are popular in the motor vehicle production industry. This involves having high-quality raw materials delivered by the supplier, as the name suggests, *just in time* for production! Note that this system is not for everybody, though, as there are many potential problems that could arise, for example a breakdown in the relationship with supplier(s), unexpected production discrepancies, quality issues, late changes to orders, priority orders and so forth.

If we look more closely at Ryanair's inventory holding period, the first thing to note is the oddity in the calculation. Most companies disclose their cost of sales, but airlines classify all expenses as operating expenses. We have therefore been forced to find a substitute. There is a strong temptation to use only maintenance, materials and repairs, but a more balanced view might be to use operating expenses as a whole. Both calculations are shown below. The differences are sizeable but whichever way we look at them, inventories holding is not a material risk for Ryanair. The numerator, ie the inventories balance, represents less than a third of 1 per cent of the entity's total assets and less than half of 1 per cent of profit after tax.

This was not always the case, however. Inventories held by the company were reduced significantly during 2005. The inventory holding period at that time moved from over 12 days in 2004 to below one day in 2005. The company now only holds essentials in stock, for example a limited amount of food available for on-board snacks and a small selection of duty-free products which are intended to be sold mid-flight. As Extract 3.5 shows, on-board food is not a trivial matter for airlines. Bean counting is an oft-used derogatory term for accountants, but this article brings the expression to life as well as the importance of the function to a successful business. The report highlights one airline, Delta, who saved $210,000 per annum simply by cutting one strawberry from their salads.

Beyond Mile-High Grub: Can Airline Food Be Tasty?

Published March 10, 2012 in *The New York Times*
By Jad Mouawad

Last year, Delta hired Michael Chiarello, a celebrity chef from Napa Valley, to come up with new menus for business-class passengers flying on transcontinental routes – New York to Los Angeles and New York to San Francisco. It was not the first time that Delta had worked with a renowned chef. The airline has served meals created by Michelle Bernstein, a Miami chef, since 2006 in its international business class.

'Our chefs are like portrait painters,' Mr Wilander says. 'They can get pretty creative. But we need to translate that into painting by numbers.' That process began last May, when Mr Chiarello met with executives and catering chefs from Delta at a boxy industrial kitchen on the edge of the San Francisco airport to demonstrate some of his recipes. Among the dozens of dishes he tried were an artichoke and white-bean spread, short ribs with polenta, and a small lasagna of eggplant and goat cheese.

'I am known for making good food, and airlines generally are not,' says Mr Chiarello, who is also the author of a half-dozen cookbooks, the host for a show on the Food Network, and a former contestant on 'Top Chef Masters' and 'The Next Iron Chef.' 'I probably have a lot more to lose than to gain doing this.'

Huddled around him, white-toqued chefs from Delta and its catering partners weighed each ingredient on a small electronic scale, took scrupulous notes and pictures and tried to calculate how much it would cost to recreate each dish a thousand times a day.

It took Mr Chiarello six months to come up with the menu. He tested recipes, picked seasonal ingredients, considered textures and colors and looked at ways to present his meals on a small airline tray. Then Delta's corporate chefs had to learn his way of cooking and serving. Bean counters – the financial kind – priced each item. Executives and frequent fliers were drafted to taste his creations.

There were a lot of questions. How should cherry tomatoes be sliced? (The answer: Leave them whole.) What side should a chicken fillet be grilled on? (Skin first.) How many slices of prosciutto can be used as appetizers? (Two large ones, rather than three, struck the balance between taste and price.)

For airlines like Delta, these are not trivial matters. A decision a few years ago to shave one ounce from its steaks, for example, saved the airline $250,000 a year. And every step of kitchen labor increases costs when so many meals are prepared daily. An entrée accounts for about 60 per cent of a meal's cost, according to Delta, while appetizers account for 17 per cent, salads 10 per cent and desserts 7 per cent.

Delta also calculated that by removing a single strawberry from salads served in first class on domestic routes, it would save $210,000 a year. The company hands out 61 million bags of peanuts every year, and about the same number of pretzels. A one-cent increase in peanut prices increases Delta's costs by $610,000 a year.

Others are catching on. United Airlines said in February that it would upgrade its service to first- and business-class passengers and would change the way it prepares meals 'to improve the quality and taste.' It also said it would start offering a new ice cream sundae option with a choice of six toppings on international flights. On domestic flights, premium passengers will get new snacks, including warm cookies.

(c) Trade payables payment period

The trade payables payment period is calculated as follows:

$$\frac{\text{Trade payables}}{\text{Credit purchases}} \times 365 \text{ days}$$

A note on the calculation of trade payables payment period

The trade receivables collection period, as discussed above, demands that revenue is divided by credit sales and multiplied by 365 days. However, the credit sales figure is rarely provided and therefore we need to find a substitute. Though revenue is not a perfect replacement, it is normally a satisfactory proxy. The same problem exists for credit purchases. This figure is rarely publicly disclosed. Therefore we need to find a substitute. Commonly, one would use the cost of sales figure. This is because in its simplified state, the cost of sales is: (i) the product of opening inventories plus purchases minus closing inventories; and (ii) it is unusual for a large business not to make purchases on credit terms.

The complications for analysing Ryanair's efficiency ratios (see Worked exercise 3.5) are that: firstly, expenses are classified as operating expenses; and secondly, trade payables could relate to any of these operating expenses presented. Therefore, we have used operating expenses as a substitute for cost of sales. Note that this is unusual.

Interpreting the trade payables payment period results

If one views holdings of current assets, such as trade receivables and inventories, as reducing an entity's cash resource, then current liabilities such as trade payables can be seen as an offset to these effects. While trade receivables are essentially an entity making interest-free loans to customers, trade payables are the reverse, ie suppliers granting interest-free loans to the business. Therefore, it is common to believe that a higher trade payables payment period is preferable.

However, when the number of days a company takes to pay their suppliers increases beyond a certain level, significant additional risks could arise, mainly resulting from behavioural issues and the loss of supplier goodwill. A relationship breakdown could bring serious problems; for example, a supplier who is made to wait disproportionately long before payment could penalize the slow-paying entity by providing poor-quality product. In a worst-case scenario, they might simply stop supplying products or services at all and poison the market against the slow payer.

In the case of Ryanair (see Worked exercise 3.5), the trade payables payment period has remained fairly constant at around 17 to 18 days. Note that in 2003 this was as high as 41 days. As with the other working capital ratios, it is difficult to interpret what this actually means. Also, though the balance is material (€181 million: 2012), it is not at the level which would cause an investor grave concern. The movement of €30 million seems like a large shift but in the grand scheme of the business, this is insignificant.

WORKED EXERCISE 3.5 Ryanair's efficiency ratios

Trade receivables collection period:

$$\frac{\text{Trade receivables}}{\text{Credit sales}^a} \times 365 \text{ days}$$

[a] We have had to substitute revenue for credit sales.

	2012 €m	2011 €m
Trade receivables	51.5	50.6
Revenue	4,390.2	3,629.5

$$\frac{51.5}{4,390.2} \times 365 \qquad\qquad \frac{50.6}{3,629.5} \times 365$$

$$= 4.3 \text{ days} \qquad\qquad\qquad = 5.1 \text{ days}$$

Inventory holding period:

$$\frac{\text{Inventories}}{\text{Cost of sales}^b} \times 365 \text{ days}$$

[b] We have had to find an appropriate substitute for cost of sales given that airlines do not classify items as direct costs, rather only as operating expenses. A possible expense relating to inventories is 'maintenance, materials and repairs', but we have calculated the inventory holding period based on this figure and the total operating expenses figure. Note therefore that these calculations are for illustration purposes only.

	2012 €m	2011 €m
Inventories	2.8	2.7
Maintenance, materials and repairs	(i) 104.0	(i) 93.9
Operating expenses (see note above; substituted for cost of sales)	(ii) 3,707.0	(ii) 3,141.3

$$\text{(i)} \ \frac{2.8}{104.0} \times 365 \qquad\qquad \text{(i)} \ \frac{2.7}{93.9} \times 365$$

$$= 9.9 \text{ days} \qquad\qquad\qquad = 10.5 \text{ days}$$

$$\text{(ii)} \ \frac{2.8}{3,707.0} \times 365 \qquad\qquad \text{(ii)} \ \frac{2.7}{3,141.3} \times 365$$

$$= 0.3 \text{ days} \qquad\qquad\qquad = 0.3 \text{ days}$$

Trade payables payment period:

$$\frac{\text{Trade payables}}{\text{Credit purchases}^c} \times 365 \text{ days}$$

[c] In the same way as one would substitute revenue for credit sales in the calculation of the trade receivables collection period, one would normally substitute cost of sales for credit purchases in the calculation of the trade payables payment period. However, because airlines do not disclose a cost of sales, we need to find an appropriate substitute for this figure. As with the inventory holding period, we have opted to use operating expenses but stress again that this is for illustration purposes only.

	2012 €m	2011 €m
Trade payables	181.2	150.8
Operating expenses (see note above)	3,707.0	3,141.3

$$\frac{181.2}{3,707.0} \times 365 \qquad \frac{150.8}{3,141.3} \times 365$$

$$= 17.8 \text{ days} \qquad = 17.5 \text{ days}$$

Solvency ratios

We explained that liquidity ratios are intended to provide users with an understanding of the short-term position of an entity. Solvency ratios, on the other hand, allow users to evaluate how the entity is positioned for the medium and long term. Without some form of financing, it would be impossible for a company to invest in projects which generate value. Thus, their going concern status would be impaired. The investment cycle can be envisaged as shown in Figure 3.1.

FIGURE 3.1   Financing a new project

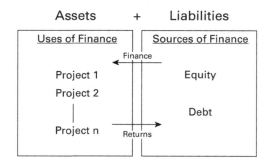

Expert view 3.4: Debt – the company's perspective versus the shareholders' perspective

From a company's perspective: Debt is a preferable financing option because, by and large, it is cheaper to service than equity and because of the tax relief allowed on interest payments but not allowed on dividend payments (if you wish to prove this to yourself, just think about the order of the income statement and note that the tax charge occurs *after* the interest charge).

From a shareholder's perspective: Debt financing increases the (perceived) risk as it normally has all, or some, of the following characteristics:

- Interest payments are an obligation. (Dividends are discretionary.)

- Debt is secured. For example, non-repayment of mortgage payments on a building can lead to the asset(s) being repossessed by the lender and sold to settle the liability. (Shares are rarely secured over assets.)

- Debt has a finite life, ie there is a redemption date. (Equity is a permanent investment.)

- Equity providers rank last in a winding up.

The primary solvency ratios consider relative levels of debt and equity as this ratio sheds light on the way the business is financed. It is argued that as an entity's levels of debt rise, equity providers (shareholders) require a greater return to offset this financing risk. The graph shown in Figure 3.2 highlights the relationship between the cost of debt and the cost of equity as financing risk (ie proportionately higher borrowings) is introduced into the business. The cost of debt is the weighted average required return of providers of debt finance. The cost of equity is the required return of investors with an equity stake in the business. Note that at extreme levels of financing risk, the required returns of both debt providers and equity providers increase drastically. This reaction builds in the compensation required for the exposure to bankruptcy risk.

Despite this knowledge, it is always difficult for an analyst to compare and interpret a company's level of financing. Generally speaking, we would state that a careful balance between debt and equity needs to be achieved. A *high* gearing ratio (the proportion of debt to equity) would suggest a greater exposure to solvency risk. However, the critical question is: 'what is high?' Also, a low gearing ratio would suggest that the comparative cost advantage that debt offers has not been appropriately taken advantage of. Again, this does not provide any insight into the question: 'what is low?' Compounding our interpretation issue is the problem that there will be inherent differences at the firm level, industry level and global level which will need to be explored and explained.

FIGURE 3.2 The costs of financing a new project

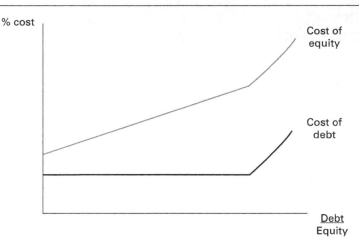

At the firm level, differences may arise because:

- Access to debt and equity markets vary.
- The availability of debt at a firm level will differ between entities and between time periods.
- The riskiness of the investment and proposed projects will need to be considered by providers of finance in context.
- There may be varying managerial preferences towards debt or equity and when management change, these preferences are likely to change also.
- And so forth.

At the industry level, differences may arise because:

- The types of projects being funded vary and therefore so do their financing requirements. For example, a company investing in large assets for continuing revenue generation (eg house building, large construction projects, aeroplanes etc) will have greater and more regular financing requirements. Both real and relative debt levels will normally be higher in these industries as a result.
- Market perceptions of the industry's capital requirements will vary.
- And so forth.

At the global level, differences may arise because:

- There will be varying levels of availability for different forms of financing owing to the economic scenario.
- Global market sentiment towards future investment and financing arrangements changes over time.
- There may be government or regulatory interventions. For example, legislation over financing levels (financial institutions being required to

maintain tier 1 capital ratios, for example) or restrictions on credit lines to small, medium or large businesses within certain geographies.

- Global and domestic money markets demand and supply levels will vary.
- It might be less beneficial given (expected) rates of inflation and the opportunity costs of other investments.
- And so forth.

There are three core ratios which are most frequently undertaken which shed light on an entity's exposure to financing risk:

1 capital gearing ratio;
2 interest cover;
3 dividend cover.

(a) Capital gearing ratio

There are several acceptable ways to calculate a company's level of gearing. All things being equal, we would like to use the following definition:

$$\frac{\text{Market value of Debt}}{\text{Market value of Equity}} \times 100\%$$

However, if we only have the financial statements available, a practical and straightforward alternative is:

$$\frac{\text{Non-current liabilities}}{\text{Shareholders' funds}} \times 100\%$$

Calculation difficulties

- Financing risk measures market value against market value rather than book value against book value. These figures will be markedly different, especially for a mature and profitable company. It would be extremely rare for a company which has traded for several years to continue to sell their shares at book value; investors will be asked to pay a premium. Applying book values will probably add weight to debt. Prudence might tell you, however, that this is not an altogether bad thing. Nevertheless, it is worth noting that the gearing ratio as calculated using this method will be for guidance purposes only.
- Non-current liabilities will contain balances which are not debt instruments, for example provisions. Ideally, the only non-current liabilities you would capture would be those which related directly to long-term debt obligations.
- Current liabilities may contain some liabilities which are being used to finance the business, and which therefore should be included in the calculation of gearing. For example, a bank overdraft or other short-term bank loans might be plugging a financing gap. Their short repayment terms might contribute to a clearer understanding of financing risk if included in the calculation.
- The problems associated with the definition of shareholders' funds were covered above in the description of ROCE. These issues also exist here.

Interpreting the gearing ratio

As stated above, the larger the gearing ratio the greater the financing risk. Ultimately, assuming that this stays within rational bounds, investors do not mind how high financing risk rises provided that they are adequately and appropriately compensated for it. Various prompts on how to interpret an increase (decrease) in the ratio are provided above.

In the case of Ryanair, the gearing ratio is 54 per cent (unadjusted) or 49.6 per cent (adjusted). This has decreased from last year, which, although being a good sign, does still prompt one to comment that there appears to be a heavy reliance on debt financing. We would, however, expect an airline to maintain a high gearing ratio given their operational strategies. They buy long-lived assets (over 20 years) and it would be poor financial management to finance these through short-term loan obligations. An airline which has a strong purchase and early replacement policy regarding their fleet of planes – as Ryanair appears to have – would have proportionately higher financing requirements than other businesses in the same sector. An analyst would be more concerned to see low levels of debt for an entity such as this.

Should an analyst be concerned about these debt levels? This is a much more difficult question! Levels of liquidity and the amount of cash retained as a buffer suggest that any short-term problems could be dealt with. The main problem when interpreting solvency ratios is that, by default, we are speculating about medium- to long-term performance, ie forecast profits/cash flows that will be generated by the business. Any interpretation that involves estimating future demand (or events) is subject to error.

As with other ratios, therefore, an analyst would search for additional information to support their evaluation. Not only do companies estimate future demand, but the airline industry as a whole has a regulatory body who regularly seek to appraise what will happen in the coming months and years. One would also like to know the gearing ratios of other companies in the same sector, as well as gearing ratios for other companies in other comparable sectors, ie those traditionally associated with high levels of borrowing.

Extract 3.6: The chicken or the egg: solvency problems versus liquidity?

'Lack of solvency created bank's problems'

Management at the Co-operative Bank 'took its eye off the ball' leading to significant internal management issues, a banking analyst has claimed.

By Kevin White | Published May 15, 2013 | FTadviser (Financial Times online)

Speaking after the mutual plunged into crisis last week, Ian Gordon, a banking analyst for Investec, said the Co-operative Bank's problems were rooted around a lack of solvency.

Last week ratings agency Moody's downgraded the bank's creditworthiness on concerns it could need a government bailout...The size of the hole in the balance sheet could be as high as £1.8bn, according to an analyst note from Barclays this week. The note said Co-op bond holders may be targeted, as the mutual cannot issue equity. The subsequent downgrade in its credit rating led to an almost immediate resignation of the bank's chief executive Barry Tootell, and the announcement of a strategic review of the entire business by new group chief executive Euan Sutherland.

Mr Gordon said: 'Unlike the liquidity problems faced by the likes of HBoS, Northern Rock, and Bradford & Bingley in 2008, the Co-operative Bank's problems lie in solvency, or a lack of it.' The bank had a £113,300 fine in January from the FSA over failure to handle 1629 PPI complaints correctly. It also wrote down £150m on Finacle IT project (to date). He added that the price action seen last Friday, which saw bond prices fall by 25 per cent, 'suggested that the market was pricing in the prospect of a default'. He added: 'The bank is less capitalized than some of its peers and as a mutual it has been allowed by the regulator to be run with less scrutiny. 'For the bank to be made as safe and secure as possible it needs a cash injection, but I don't think that will necessarily lead to a bailout. It's more likely the Co-operative Group itself will step in.'

When asked whether the bank had a lack of solvency, a spokesman for the Co-operative Bank said: 'We are aware of the solvency issues and the need to improve capital ratios.' When asked about Mr Gordon's comments that the bank had been run with less regulatory scrutiny, the spokesman added: 'It is true that the bank is not a plc but we regularly publish our accounts and engage with investors, the press and regulators, and are subject to considerable scrutiny.'

According to its results for 2012, the banking division contributed 17.6 per cent of revenue to the group, with its revenue of £2.21bn for 2012 dwarfed by the food retail division's revenue of £7.44bn. It repeated an overall operating loss of £280.5m for 2012 (compared to 2011 profit of £141.1m) and a loss before tax of £673.7m (compared to 2011 profit of £54.2m).

(b) Interest cover

The interest cover ratio shows the number of times a company (theoretically) could have paid their finance costs from their earnings. The ratio is calculated as follows:

$$\frac{\text{Operating profit}}{\text{Finance costs}}$$

This is therefore a guide to the solvency of the business. Again, as with other ratios, it is difficult to suggest that there is an optimum level of coverage. We would suggest, however, that if the interest cover ratio falls below 1, this is a strong signal that current debt levels are unaffordable, ie the company cannot afford to pay its obligations even once. If, in the following months or years, interest payments are not made, the lender might bring into effect claw-back clauses.

A high level of coverage is also not desirable. If a company could afford to pay its finance costs, say 10 times over, then investors might question whether the company is taking appropriate advantage of comparatively cheaper forms of financing, ie debt.

In the case of Ryanair, interest payments can be covered approximately six times. Though this appears on the high side, it is probably a reflection of the company's profitability rather than an inappropriate capital financing strategy. Indeed, these levels of affordability would almost certainly be interpreted as reassuring by an analyst, who could perceive the gearing levels as being high and future profits volatile (the airline industry is subject to periods of significant demand variability).

(c) Dividend cover

This is another useful measure, especially for a company where shareholders are regularly rewarded by dividends (and not just capital growth). The dividend cover ratio shows an analyst how many times the company could have paid the dividend out of available profits. It is calculated as:

$$\frac{\text{Profit after tax}}{\text{Dividends}}$$

As with the interest cover ratio, there is no optimum position. A ratio of less than 1 would indicate a lack of affordability and a reduced likelihood of the dividend remaining at that level. A high level of coverage might have shareholders questioning why the dividend payment wasn't larger, especially if there is no evidence that profits are being reinvested in profitable activities.

Ryanair rarely pays dividends. Instead, their shareholders are rewarded through capital growth (which can be captured by selling shares). However, cash levels grew as profits were retained and the management took the decision to make a one-off dividend payment in 2011. The coverage is 0.7 times. This is not particularly helpful to our analysis because of the one-off nature of this event. It is interesting, in many ways, that the one-off dividend could almost be covered out of one year's profits. This might spur investors to query whether future dividend payments are a reasonable request, especially if reserves continue to be retained rather than invested in operations.

WORKED EXERCISE 3.6   Ryanair's solvency ratios

Gearing ratio:

$$\frac{\text{Non-current liabilities}^a}{\text{Shareholders' funds}} \times 100\%$$

[a] We have presented two non-current liabilities figures. The first assumes that all non-current liabilities should be classified as debt, while the second assumes that only balances classified as 'non-current maturities of debt' are debt. In neither have we included 'current maturities of debt' obligations (2012: €368.4m; 2011: €336.7m).

	2012 €m	2011 €m
Non-current liabilities (unadjusted)	3,879.3	3,804.9
Non-current liabilities (adjusted)	*3,256.8*	*3,312.7*
Shareholders' funds (unadjusted)	7,186.0	6,758.8
Shareholders' funds (adjusted)	*6,563.5*	*6,266.6*

$$\frac{3,879.3}{7,186.0} \times 100\% \qquad \frac{3,804.9}{6,758.8} \times 100\%$$
$$= 54.0\% \qquad\qquad = 56.3\%$$

$$\frac{3,256.8}{6,563.5} \times 100\% \qquad \frac{3,312.7}{6,266.6} \times 100\%$$
$$= 49.6\% \qquad\qquad = 52.9\%$$

Interest cover:

$$\frac{\text{Operating profit}}{\text{Finance costs}}$$

	2012 €m	2011 €m
Operating profit	683.2	488.2
Finance costs	109.2	93.9

$$\frac{683.2}{109.2} \qquad\qquad \frac{488.2}{93.9}$$
$$= 6.3 \text{ times} \qquad = 5.2 \text{ times}$$

Dividend cover:

$$\frac{\text{Profit after tax}}{\text{Dividends}}$$

	2012 €m	2011 €m
Profit after tax	560.4	374.6
Dividends	N/A	500.0

$$\qquad\qquad\qquad\qquad \frac{374.6}{500.0}$$
$$= \text{N/A} \qquad\qquad = 0.7 \text{ times}$$

Investor ratios

Current and potential investors are the intended primary users of financial statements. The ratios set out above would carry some interest to all stakeholders whereas the set of ratios that follow are of the greatest value and interest to this primary user group. Again, there are many ratios an investor might calculate to appraise their stance in relation to the entity under consideration, but you will come across the following most regularly as they are also the most useful:

- investor returns: dividend yield and capital yield;
- earnings per share;
- price to earnings ratio.

(a) Investor returns: dividend yield and capital yield

The dividend cover ratio allows analysts to interpret an entity's dividend payment in book value terms, ie how many times a company could have paid the dividend from available annual accounting profits. Of more interest to shareholders is the yield on the investment they have made. There are two components to an annual return on equity: dividends and capital growth. These are calculated as:

$$\frac{\text{Dividend (per share)}}{\text{Market price (per share)}} \times 100\%$$

PLUS

$$\frac{\text{Capital growth (per share)}}{\text{Market price (per share)}} \times 100\%$$

The dividend yield ratio reveals to an investor the rate of (dividend) return on their investment. Worked exercise 3.7 illustrates how investors can measure their annual returns. Worked exercise 3.8 shows Ryanair's investor returns. The numbers might be slightly misleading as we are using naive unadjusted information to interpret complex positions. For example, even though Ryanair did not pay a dividend during 2012, there was a share buyback, which is a different way in which a company can reward shareholders (which isn't a dividend payment or capital growth). Also, the share price on 31 March 2010 was €3.68 but on 1 April 2010 it rose to €4.00. This is a significant change and leaves us unsure of which information to input as being more reliable and relevant. Nevertheless, a basic interpretation would be that buying shares in Ryanair (as with all airlines) could lead to highly volatile returns. During good times, the pay-off is large; in bad times, the returns are low. If you are investing for the long term, you would need to look further at average returns. In these periods, the dividend compensates for the negative capital growth in 2011, while the capital growth compensates for the lack of dividend in 2012.

WORKED EXERCISE 3.7

TABLE 3.5

	Share price at 1.1.X0	Share price at 31.12.X0	Dividend for the year
Mirage plc	160p	180p	12p
Lost Illusions plc	100p	105p	3p

The dividend yield for the two entities is as follows:

Mirage plc

$$\frac{12}{160} \times 100\% = 7.5\%$$

Lost Illusions plc

$$\frac{3}{100} \times 100\% = 3.0\%$$

Note, however, that there is also capital growth to factor into your returns analysis.

Mirage plc

$$\frac{20\,(180 - 160)}{160} \times 100\% = 12.5\%$$

Lost Illusions plc

$$\frac{5\,(105 - 100)}{100} \times 100\% = 5.0\%$$

Therefore, the total annual return on each of these two stocks can be measured as:

Mirage plc = 20.0% (7.5% + 12.5%)
Lost Illusions plc = 8.0% (3.0% + 5.0%)

(b) Earnings per share (EPS)

The EPS is normally shown on the face of the income statement, ie it is a publicly disclosed figure. To avoid manipulation of this figure, there are accounting regulations which govern the calculation of this figure (IAS 33 *Earnings Per Share*). In summary, the basic calculation is as follows:

$$\frac{\text{Profit attributable to shareholders}}{\text{Weighted average number of shares outstanding during the period}}$$

The standard interpretation of EPS is that as the figure increases, the better the position of the shareholder. Owing to the complexities of the underlying accounting and possible transactions, it is possible (although not straightforward) for management to play around with this ratio so that it tells investors what they want to hear. Note, however, that any accounting-led manipulation strategy can only work for a finite period of time before any gaming is unravelled!

Expert view 3.5: IAS 33 definition of basic EPS

The lengthier explanation as set out in IAS 33 is: basic EPS is calculated by dividing profit or loss attributable to ordinary equity holders of the parent entity (the numerator) by the weighted average number of ordinary shares outstanding (the denominator) during the period. [IAS 33.10] The earnings numerators (profit or loss from continuing operations and net profit or loss) used for the calculation should be after deducting all expenses, including taxes, minority interests and preference dividends. [IAS 33.12] The denominator (number of shares) is calculated by adjusting the shares in issue at the beginning of the period by the number of shares bought back or issued during the period, multiplied by a time-weighting factor. IAS 33 includes guidance on appropriate recognition dates for shares issued in various circumstances. [IAS 33.20–21]

Ryanair's EPS is increasing. The entity's average share capital outstanding has not moved significantly, therefore the key driver of this change must be increased earnings. Indeed, this is the case, as shown by the horizontal analysis as well as the profitability ratio calculations reported above.

(c) Price to earnings (P/E) ratio

The P/E ratio is a common ratio undertaken to appraise an investment through the eyes of the capital provider. Interpreting this ratio, however, is not straightforward. Applying an unsophisticated view, the underlying principle is that the result gives you a multiplier, ie how many times you would need to multiply current earnings before arriving at the price you would pay for the share on the open market. In turn, this allows you to appraise the value of your investment and any future investments the company intends to make, thus allowing you to price future projects and the entity as a whole. It also provides an indication of how quickly an investment in the stock of this entity might pay back. In other words, a P/E ratio of, say, 10 could be interpreted to mean that the current price is 10 times the value of current earnings; or it would take 10 consecutive earnings at that level to repay the investment at that price.

The P/E ratio should be calculated as follows:

$$\frac{\text{Market price (per share)}}{\text{Earnings (per share)}}$$

When investors see a profitable business carrying a high P/E ratio, the expectation is for future growth (in earnings) above inflation. The basic tenets of supply and demand intermixed with efficient markets presumptions lead rational investors to infer that a high P/E ratio driven by a change in the numerator, ie share price (market value per share), indicates stronger than average demand for the stock. Where there is demand, the share price rises and this precedes the realization of the amount paid by shareholders for this future growth. Demand is created by above average performance, or more commonly, the promise of future above average performance.

As you can imagine, the share price of a company can move for many reasons and accounting earnings might not be a genuine reflection of position and current or future performance. Therefore, not only would you need to undertake further investigation into the underlying data; ultimately, you would also need to appraise the P/E ratio in context. Comparing P/E ratios between companies in the same industry can be especially revealing (see online content at: **www.koganpage.com/accountingfm**).

Ryanair's P/E ratio appears high and is an indicator that the market believes that the company will continue to be profitable over and above costs and inflation. The decline in the 2012 P/E ratio needs to be investigated in more detail. Note that the EPS and the share price were significantly lower in 2011 than in 2012 but the net effect is that the P/E ratio was higher. This is because the current year (2012) EPS result did not rise as far as the current year share price.

WORKED EXERCISE 3.8   Ryanair investor ratios

Note: the share price at close 31.03.2012 was €4.48; 31.03.2011: €3.36; 31.03.2010: €3.68. Dividend yield:

$$\frac{\text{Dividend}}{\text{Market price}} \times 100\%$$

Capital growth:

$$\frac{\text{Capital growth}}{\text{Market price}} \times 100\%$$

	2012 €m	2011 €m
Dividend per share (dividend / number of shares)	N/A	€500 million / 1,455 million shares = €0.34 per share [rounded]

	2012 €m	2011 €m
Market price per share (at start of period)	3.36	3.68
	N/A	$\frac{0.34}{3.68} \times 100\%$
	N/A	$= 9.2\%$
Capital growth per share (Period end share price MINUS prior year share price)	1.12	(0.32)
Market price per share (at start of period)	3.36	3.68
	$\frac{1.12}{3.36} \times 100\%$	$\frac{(0.32)}{3.68} \times 100\%$
	$= 33.3\%$	$= (8.7)\%$
Return per share	$(0\% + 33.3\%) = 33.3\%$	$9.2\% - 8.7\% = 0.5\%$

Earnings Per Share:

$$\frac{\text{Profit attributable to shareholders}}{\text{Weighted average number of shares outstanding during the period}}$$

	2012 €	2011 €
	= 0.3803	= 0.2521

Price to Earnings ratio:

$$\frac{\text{Market price (per share)}}{\text{Earnings (per share)}}$$

	2012 €	2011 €
Market price (per share)	4.48	3.36
Earnings per share	0.3803	0.2521
	$\frac{4.48}{0.3803}$	$\frac{3.36}{0.2521}$
	$= 11.78$	$= 13.33$

Weaknesses and limitations

As we have progressed through this chapter, the major weaknesses and limitations of the various financial analysis techniques might have been obvious to you. Some of the questions you might have been asking yourself are the following.

1 Is true comparability possible?
Sub-questions include:

- What entities are we comparing, and why have we chosen to compare them?
- What are the differences between these entities strategically, economically, politically, culturally?
- Do these entities have similar accounting policies? In other words, do the financial statements capture comparable information?
    - Though accountants are required to choose policies that ensure financial information is presented in a representation that is 'true and fair', managerial judgement is still required. For example, the difference between two identical companies estimating the useful economic lives of identical assets differently can have a serious impact on profits. If one airline chooses to depreciate planes over 25 years while another believes they will last for only 10 years, this will have a significant impact on accounting profit from year to year, with the latter entity recognizing the costs earlier than the former.
    - Annual results can be manipulated without needing to employ accounting flexibility. For example, cutting back on certain items of expenditure – such as staff training and development costs, advertising and marketing expenses – during the year will produce an immediate improvement in profits. The medium- to long-term impact on profits, however, will inevitably be detrimental.
    - There are complex accounting transactions which can be hidden, often by posting the movement through equity and holding back the realization of gains/losses to future periods.
- Is comparability between time periods possible?
    - Have there been one-off events during the year which have impacted positively/negatively on the profitability of the entity?
    - If so, should we (can we) adjust for these in our analysis?
    - Is the broader economic/political/social/cultural climate comparable?

2 Financial statements are backwards-looking and are composed from historic information. The preparation and audit of the annual report is a lengthy exercise and for public listed companies, the filing deadline is three months after the year-end. Therefore, by the time you are able to analyse the financial statements for the year ended 31 March 2012, for example, the first quarter of the following year will be nearly complete. Regardless of business, industry, geography or any other externality, three months can be a long time!

3 The financial statements do not tell the whole story (see Chapter 4). During the past couple of decades we have witnessed an exponential growth in the means and methods a company is able to use to communicate with investors and other stakeholders. The hunger from the public for news has also made companies more proactive in their communication strategies. Though the annual report continues to be important, its previous status as the cornerstone to an investor's understanding of the entity's position and performance has been replaced. For analysts, working with live information at their fingertips, the annual report has taken on a more confirmatory role.

Conclusion

In this chapter, we have outlined four possible methods to analyse financial information:

- horizontal analysis;
- trend analysis;
- vertical analysis;
- ratio analysis (profitability; efficiency; liquidity; solvency; and investor ratios).

We have presented these in an accounting context and have applied each method to the annual report. We have argued that, to extract the greatest value from your analysis, you need to view the investment through the eyes of the interested party. For example, if you are undertaking analysis on behalf of a potential investor who is considering buying shares in a company, you need to understand that you are offering advice to someone who will be acquiring a stake in a business. This business is in competition with others and therefore they also need to be examined. The context – economic, social, political and technological – is also critically important as it will inform your analysis.

The mechanics of financial statement analysis are relatively simple. The subsequent interpretation of the results, however, is far more difficult. Let us presume that you are calculating the gross profit ratio and using this information to interpret performance; one approach you could take would be as follows:

- Perform calculations: period comparisons; inter-industry comparisons.
- Appraise relative performance in naive terms, ie:
  - Has the ratio increased or decreased; industry ratio increased or decreased?
  - State that an upward move would generally be considered positive, while downward would be negative.
  - State that a gross profit ratio higher than those of peers would be generally considered a positive sign.

- Try to explain why there has been a change:
  - Has anything changed related to the business or their accounting policies comparing this year to those previous OR between this entity and other entities in the industry OR between the current political/economic/social/technological climate and that of prior periods?
  - Use horizontal analysis, trend analysis and vertical analysis to make sense of the accounting numbers that underpin this change (ie revenue and cost of sales).
- Try to find other supporting evidence to substantiate your reasons, eg press releases.
- Answer the question 'so what?':
  - What are the implications and consequences of this change?
  - Do you believe it is sustainable (or will be sustained)?
  - What are the implications for the investment?
- What are the limitations in the analysis you have performed?
  - What further information would you need before you were satisfied that your recommendation was appropriate and accurate?

Financial analysis is subjective. There is a wealth of data available, both quantitative and qualitative. Part of the skill in undertaking these exercises is knowing when and where to stop. You will need to apply judgement and this is fine-tuned through practice and experience.

COMPREHENSION QUESTIONS

1 List THREE profitability ratios and show how they should be calculated.

2 Discuss THREE possible reasons why an entity's gross profit margin might increase from one year to the next.

3 What is meant by 'liquidity' and why might a supplier want to assess the liquidity position of one of their customer companies?

4 Describe the working capital cycle and calculate the length of this for a company of your choice.

5 Show how you might appraise the solvency of an entity and state what you feel might be some red-flag issues.

6 What are the limitations of ratio analysis as a form of financial analysis?

Answers on pages 151–153

Exercises

Answers on pages 154–158

Exercise 3.1

Hawk Limited (Hawk) manufacture and distribute washing machines. The board of directors (BoD) have been concerned for some time that their share of the market has been in decline, mainly as a result of industry-wide competition. They are also aware that to a certain extent the industry has become the victim of its own success as washing machines have become more reliable and durable and therefore do not need replacing as regularly. Therefore, the BoD are considering making an investment in Sparrow Limited (Sparrow).

Sparrow manufacture dishwashers. The BoD believe that the synergistic gains will include advantages over competitors from shared technologies, a greater distribution network, an increase in skilled employees and management, and a shared clerical and manufacturing headquarters.

Table 3.6 shows the recently issued (summarized) financial statements of Hawk and Sparrow for the year ended 31 October 2013.

TABLE 3.6

Statements of comprehensive income	Hawk		Sparrow	
	2013 £000s	2012 £000s	2013 £000s	2012 £000s
Revenue	12,000	13,000	9,500	7,800
Cost of sales	(8,000)	(8,200)	(4,100)	(2,600)
Gross profit	4,000	4,800	5,400	5,200
Operating expenses	(2,500)	(2,550)	(2,600)	(2,700)
Finance costs	(550)	(500)	(900)	(300)
Profit before tax	950	1,750	1,900	2,200
Income tax expense	(300)	(600)	(800)	(900)
Profit for the period	650	1,150	1,100	1,300
Statements of financial position				
Non-current assets	13,075	12,000	11,000	6,000
Current assets	2,600	2,800	1,500	1,400
Current liabilities	(3,200)	(3,000)	(2,500)	(1,500)
Non-current liabilities	(275)	(250)	(4,500)	(1,500)
	12,200	11,550	5,500	4,400

TABLE 3.6 *continued*

Statements of comprehensive income	Hawk		Sparrow	
	2013 £000s	2012 £000s	2013 £000s	2012 £000s
Equity and reserves	12,200	11,550	5,500	4,400
Current assets include:				
Inventories	800	900	700	400
Trade receivables	1,000	1,800	750	600
Bank	800	100	50	400
Current liabilities include:				
Trade payables	1,550	1,300	650	400
Other payables	1,200	1,200	1,000	200
Current tax payable	450	500	850	900

Required:

(a) The BoD of Hawk Limited have asked you to analyse the position and performance of Sparrow Limited.

(b) As part of this analysis, the BoD have also asked that you use the information above to compare and contrast the position and performance of Hawk Limited with Sparrow Limited. They have asked you to conclude your analysis by stating, with reasons, whether you feel Hawk Limited should make a bid to acquire Sparrow Limited.

Exercise 3.2

Extracts from the (summarized) financial statements of Barksdale plc, a retail group, for the year ended 31 December 2013 are shown in Table 3.7 together with an extract from the chief executive's report that accompanied their issue.

TABLE 3.7

Statement of comprehensive income	2013 £m	2012 £m
Revenue	9,062	9,022
Cost of sales	(5,690)	(5,535)
Gross profit	3,372	3,487
Operating expenses	(2,501)	(2,276)
Operating profit	871	1,211
Finance income	50	65
Finance costs	(215)	(147)
Profit on ordinary activities before taxation	706	1,129
Income tax expense	(199)	(308)
Profit for the year	507	821

Statement of financial position	2013 £m	2012 £m
Non-current assets	5,868	5,979
Current assets		
Inventories	1,020	850
Trade receivables	45	47
Cash and cash equivalents	5	100
Other current assets	320	185
	1,390	1,182
Total assets	**7,258**	**7,161**
Share capital and reserves	2,100	1,964
Non-current liabilities	2,851	3,208
Current liabilities		
Trade payables	1,410	1,250
Other current liabilities	897	739
	7,258	**7,161**

Extract from the chief executive's report:

The year at a glance
During the year we acted decisively to meet the challenges of the global
economic downturn, taking steps to manage costs tightly and respond quickly to
the changing needs of our customers. Our adjusted profits are down on last year
to £507m. This is due in part to conditions on the High Street as well as our

conscious decision to improve our value, without compromising our quality. We have built unrivalled trust in the Barksdale brand over the last 125 years, and will not sacrifice our core principles when times get tough. Though we have a strong emphasis on food, furniture and general merchandise, it is clothing that is our customers' biggest discretionary purchase and as the UK's leading clothing retailer, with the largest market share, it was inevitable that demand would ease off as customers reined in their spending. Although value market share is marginally down from 11.0 to 10.7 per cent, we have held our volume market share at 11.2 per cent. We believe this is evidence that our team are in tune with our customer base. We paid a dividend of £300 million during 2013 compared to £350 million which was paid out in 2012.

Required:
Based solely on the information provided above, you have been asked by a potential investor to analyse the position and performance of Barksdale plc.

Answers to comprehension questions

1 Three possible ratios include:

   (a) Gross profit margin

   $$\frac{\text{Gross profit}}{\text{Revenue}} \times 100\%$$

   (b) Net profit margin

   $$\frac{\text{Profit before interest and tax}}{\text{Revenue}} \times 100\%$$

   (c) Return on capital employed

   $$\frac{\text{Profit before interest and tax}}{\text{Capital employed}} \times 100\%$$

   But there are many others, including revenue per employee, costs per square foot of factory space and so forth.

2 There are, of course, many reasons why an entity's gross profit margin might increase. Simply speaking, a change in the gross profit margin relates to a positive change in one of two variables: revenue and cost of sales. For example, maybe revenue rose during the period proportionately quicker than cost of sales, or cost of sales decreased proportionately quicker than revenue.

Revenue could have increased as a result of:

(a) a change in sales mix;

(b) a change in product portfolio;

(c) a change in selling price.

Cost of sales might have decreased due to:

(a) a change in production mix;

(b) a change in product portfolio;

(c) a change in purchase price.

Note, however, that an increase in the gross profit margin might not always be a good outcome. The problem with percentages is that they deal with relative terms rather than actual. It is important also to consider further ratio analysis and performing horizontal, trend and vertical analysis.

3   In this case, liquidity refers to an entity's short-term financial position. In simple terms: can the company afford to continue operating to the same level for the foreseeable future?
    For a supplier this could be important, especially if the entity to whom they are supplying is a key customer and makes up a large proportion of their output uptake. If the entity could not afford to continue, their supply chain is under threat and they will have to start looking for other outlets. They will also consider the level of the customer's indebtedness and start calling in unpaid invoices. In extreme situations, they might stop supplying the customer until their liquidity position improves.

4   The working capital cycle is calculated as:

Trade receivables collection period

+

Inventories holding days

−

Trade payables payment period

Downloading the annual report and financial statements for any listed entity is straightforward. Think of a brand you like/buy from/are interested in and type their name into a web browser followed by the phrase 'annual report' or 'investors' and it is normally the first link you'll be offered. They normally come in pdf form but there is also an option with most companies to see an electronic copy online.

5 Solvency is often calculated using the gearing ratio, ie the level of debt to equity. There are several definitions of this formula but the most commonly used is total gearing, ie non-current liabilities divided by capital employed. The other common ratio used to work out whether a firm has over- (or under-)borrowed (leveraged) is the interest cover ratio.

Saying that a company is over-leveraged without inter-year and inter-firm comparisons is inappropriate. If a company had a gearing ratio in excess of the sector average or had a steeply accelerating gearing ratio year on year, we would be concerned.

If a company's interest cover ratio is less than 1, this could signify impending problems and solvency issues. If a company's interest cover ratio is greater than, say, 10, this would be a reasonable indicator that the firm could borrow more (obviously, caveats apply about annual performance, future capital investment, and sustainability of returns).

Maintaining an optimum level of gearing (debt to equity) is a complex process.

6 Limitations of ratio analysis: there are many limitations, including (but not restricted to) the following:

- Understanding/interpreting ratios

  - Is comparability possible?

  - What entities are we comparing, and why have we chosen to compare them?

  - What are the differences between these entities strategically, economically, politically, culturally?

  - Do these entities have similar accounting policies? In other words, do the financial statements capture comparable information?

  - Is comparability between time periods possible?

- Financial statements are backwards-looking and are composed from historic information.

- The financial statements do not tell the whole story (see Chapter 4).

Answers to exercises

Exercise 3.1

TABLE 3.8

	Hawk		Sparrow	
	2013	2012	2013	2012
Gross profit margin	33.3%	36.9%	56.8%	66.7%
Net profit margin	12.5%	17.3%	29.5%	32.1%
ROCE	12.0%	19.1%	28.0%	42.4%
Current ratio	0.81	0.93	0.60	0.93
Quick ratio	0.56	0.63	0.32	0.67
Trade receivables days	30.4	50.5	28.8	28.1
Inventory holding period	36.5	40.1	62.3	56.2
Trade payables days	70.7	57.9	57.9	56.2
Interest cover	2.7	4.5	3.1	8.3
Gearing	2.2%	2.1%	45.0%	25.4%

Discussion should be rewarded appropriately with a maximum of *two* marks being awarded for a well-developed point and *one* mark being awarded for a relevant interpretation. Answers that simply state movements in ratios will not be rewarded with any discussion marks.

Students who choose to answer the question using a SWOT (strengths, weaknesses, opportunities and threats) analysis should be rewarded appropriately, provided they evidence their discussions with relevant information.

Profitability

Sparrow's turnover has increased quite markedly but this has been matched by a downturn in profitability.

There are numerous suggestions that might account for this movement; however, it is most likely that Sparrow is aggressively chasing new business through either new markets or new products. We would not know for certain, however, without other evidence being made available, eg strategy documents, prior-year financial statements and so on.

Sparrow's ROCE has fallen. This will have a negative impact on the valuation of the firm and could knock on to the offer that is made by Hawk for a controlling stake in Sparrow. Again, we would need more information before we could fully interpret this movement in ROCE, such as prior-year financial statements.

A net profit margin of around 30 per cent appears high. This is true particularly as we note Hawk's net profit margin (NPM) of 12 per cent which operates in a similar trading environment.

Liquidity

Sparrow's position seems quite stable as evidenced by a current ratio of 0.93 in 2012 and 0.60 in 2013. Though textbooks would suggest this should be around 2:1, modern businesses rarely reach these levels owing to borrowing being relatively cheap and accessible. In light of the credit crunch this might change.

Sparrow is holding a large amount in inventory in 2013 compared to 2012. This reflects the increased level of trading being undertaken by the firm.

Sparrow's working capital cycle has increased by five days from 28 days to 33 days. This appears to be as a result of other short-term payables. One suspects that these arise as a result of new business and are most likely to be short-term warranty provisions. New products and/or new markets might give rise to new problems and the accountants may have preferred to take a prudent position against future losses on short-term warranties.

Solvency

Interest cover remains consistent and Sparrow appears to be financially stable and solvent for the time being.

Non-current liabilities have trebled, however. These have increased to pay for new PPE which might have been required to facilitate the expansion in trade evidenced by the increased turnover.

Comparison with Hawk

It would be appropriate for students to state that any conclusion about investment could not be purely based on the limited information available. Students should be rewarded for mentioning issues such as that accounting policies might differ, accounting practice might differ and so forth.

Profit margins appear to be lower in washing machines than in dishwashers. There is no suggestion why this might be; however, washing machines are more common household appliances than dishwashers and therefore dishwashers might attract a margin premium based on their luxury product orientation in the market.

The declines in margins and ROCE particularly highlight that the BoD are right to consider a change of strategy and, by engaging with a firm with higher margins, might be involving themselves in a bootstrapping exercise. It might be possible to lift their margins, reduce their cost of sales (COS) and increase their PE ratio by investing in an apparently less risky, higher-yield industry. The empirical proof of success for such strategies is mixed.

Hawk appears to be liquid and solvent, judging by the working capital position and the level of debt.

At a glance it would appear that Hawk could borrow significantly more than it is currently doing and thereby potentially adjust its financing risk and reduce its cost of capital. The gearing ratio is very low and this appears to be the quickest route to financing the investment in Sparrow. The issue therefore is not necessarily affordability but, instead, whether this is the right strategy.

Conclusion

The BoD are right to consider a diversification and it is logical that shareholders in a company that makes washing machines will not object too heavily to an investment in a company that makes dishwashers.

It would appear that this is a worthwhile investment; however, this conclusion is based only on the evidence presented. We would need to know a lot more about the quantitative and qualitative benefits of the synergistic gains and whether Sparrow's growth strategy will continue or whether 2013 (or 2012) was an anomaly year in terms of results.

Exercise 3.2

TABLE 3.9

	2013	2012
Gross profit margin	37.2%	38.6%
Net profit margin (using PBIT)	9.6%	13.4%
Dividend cover	1.7	2.3
Interest cover	4.3	8.7
Current ratio	0.60	0.59
Quick ratio	0.16	0.17
Trade receivables collection period in days	1.8	1.9
Inventories holding period	65.4	56.1
Trade payables days	90.4	82.4
Operating cycle in days	(23.2)	(24.5)
Gearing	57.6%	62.0%
Return on capital employed (before finance income)	17.6%	23.4%

Some comments about profitability

Margins have decreased, in particular the net profit margin. Though the chief executive claims that costs have been controlled, it is clear that profitability is affected by them. This makes one believe that there is a high proportion of fixed costs. This is likely given the nature of the business – ie high street retail. Rents will remain static, as will utilities and other operating expenses. It is possible to identify that there are two areas where cut-backs can be genuinely made: in production and the linked activities such as shipping etc (which seem unlikely given the increase in revenue) and in wages and salaries. Both of these cuts might knock on to quality (whether these be quality of service or quality of product) and this is something that Barksdale is trying to avoid.

The chief executive notes that the downturn has affected business. This is clear from the margins. The sales mix might have changed, which has led to a lower GP margin, but it seems more likely that goods have had to be discounted to sell.

What is strange, however, is that revenue has gone up. Even if we consider inflationary adjustments it seems that there is the indication that production has not been cut back. The chief executive remarks that people are buying less. Is this evidence that the sales mix has changed? Are fewer people buying more expensive goods? This is speculation but seems to be a likely answer.

It might be that there is a revenue recognition problem but it is impossible to tell from what has been provided.

The ROCE has decreased significantly. This will concern investors. The chief executive is right to try to explain away this drop. It is worth noting, however, that the ROCE appears high, especially given the economic downturn and the very low interest rates.

Investors will be kept 'happy', one suspects, with the dividend payment.

Some comments about liquidity

There are no significant changes to the current ratio or quick ratio but it is worth noting that they are both quite low. This is not unusual for a retail business which trades with very few trade receivables, looks to maintain a small amount of rolling stock (inventories) and will probably seek to maximize its trade payables days in terms of lengthening its working capital cycle. Given the nature of the business and the size and scale of operations, inventories are always likely to be reasonably high, which might put a strain on flexibility and adaptability in the immediate short term.

On the surface, if we were simply to consider the ratios we might think that there are problems; however, if we set these ratios in context it is less worrying.

What we might comment on is the low and diminishing cash balance and the high gearing ratio. Are more funds available when the cash runs out? If not, how will the firm maintain its working capital given that payables days have already been extended out to 90 days? If I were an investor I would probably have concerns over this.

Some comments about solvency

The gearing ratio is high at over 50 per cent. See comments above about future sources of finance.

It would be important to know the maturity profile of this debt and whether facilities need to be renewed imminently.

The interest cover figure does not suggest that this is a time for warning bells; however, it has halved in the last 12 months. This is definitely a figure to watch, and any further negative changes might portend future liquidity and solvency problems.

The SWOT analysis might include:

Strengths: diverse range of goods; size; economies of scale; revenue strong; well-managed operating cycle; market share.

Weaknesses: economic climate; commodities prices; market saturation/ competition.

Opportunities: overseas growth; brand regeneration; strong balance sheet for extra fundraising; consumer demand recovery in certain sectors.

Threats: exchange rates; high-street position costly; online competition; barriers to entry might mean that the firm is a potential takeover target.

Conclusion

On balance the company appears to have suffered owing to the economic climate and though there are possible concerns about quality and about adaptability, it seems that the business is in reasonable financial health and the position and performance do not raise any significant concerns.

Financial analysis: Part II

OBJECTIVE

The objective of this chapter is to further develop an understanding of financial analysis and interpretation skills. The first financial analysis chapter focused upon the interpretation of financial statements as presented in the annual report. This second chapter provides an overview of some other key forms of corporate financial communication and an introduction to some basic underlying theory.

LEARNING OUTCOMES

After studying this chapter, the reader will be:

- Able to understand that financial information is communicated through varying means and in different forms.

- Aware that corporate communication may be factually accurate but it might be presented, written or distributed in a way that sends out information signals.

KEY TOPICS COVERED

- Different forms of corporate communication.

- Examples and an overview of corporate communication use, misuse and abuse.

MANAGEMENT ISSUES

We continue to build on Chapter 3 which leads with the presumption that interpreting and analysing financial information is a key skill for managers and their decision making. We move away from the financial statements and look at other parts of the annual report as well as other forms of corporate communication.

Introduction

Despite owning the business, shareholders are not allowed access to a company's premises without agreed authorization, let alone being granted access to the underlying records. Instead investors, as with all stakeholders, rely on the company to provide them with information. The financial statements – contained within the annual report – were studied in the previous chapter and are one means of communicating financial information. These are not, however, by any means the only way that financial information is disclosed by an entity.

Within the annual report there are several sections which disclose information that could be important to your financial analysis. You might also like to consider reviewing the following when undertaking your analysis:

- reflections from members of the senior management team on position, performance and strategy;
- operating and financial review/management commentary/management discussion and analysis (title varies dependent upon jurisdiction);
- directors' remuneration report;
- corporate social responsibility report;
- corporate governance procedures, practices and policies;
- background information on company directors.

Indeed, the annual report is not even the only place where a company produces a set of financial statements. For large companies, interim reporting is required (quarterly or half-yearly). Companies also regularly release earnings statements which show the current performance and position; though these present adjusted numbers, they are driven by the IFRS-led financial statements. Whenever significant transactions or events occur – for example a sale of new shares, a proposed merger or acquisition – financial statements are released along with forecasts of future results. To view financial information simply in terms of financial statements is to adopt too narrow a perspective.

Several studies from the 1980s and 1990s show that the annual report is either the most important or second most important source of information for users of financial statements. A more recent study by Abraham, Marston and Darby (2012) investigating the sources of information perceived to be most useful for risk analysis is presented in the following table:

TABLE 4.1   Sources of information perceived to be most useful for risk analysis (Abraham *et al*, 2012)

Information source	Mean	Standard deviation
Meetings with management	4.5	0.7
Results announcements	4.2	0.9
Trading statements	4.1	0.8
Peer companies	4.0	0.5
Annual report & accounts	3.9	1.0
Industry experts	3.8	1.0
Analysts	3.6	1.1
Interim statements & quarterly reports	3.6	1.0
Interim reports and accounts	3.4	1.0
Market news	3.2	1.0
Newspapers	3.0	0.9
Financial news channels	2.8	0.9
Internet bulletins	2.3	1.1

Though it would be useful to discuss all of these forms of communication, there are constraints over time and syllabus. Therefore, we propose to cover those which we think are most interesting and thought provoking. We will look at:

- corporate social responsibility reporting;
- earnings announcements, conference calls and investor presentations;
- media relations: press releases and newspaper coverage;
- social media and internet bulletins.

The drive for information

Not only has there been a major expansion in the forms and means of corporate communication in recent times, but there has also been a huge upsurge in demand for information from investors and other stakeholders. This combination of increased supply and demand has created a beast that seemingly cannot be sated. It has been said that every day individuals are exposed to around 13,000 separate corporate messages. When situations are out of the ordinary, the messages and responses multiply.

A further effect of this new era for communication is that media outlets have adopted a more sensationalist approach. This has been driven partly by the availability of material but also by an economic pressure on news outlets brought about by increased competition.

If we take crisis events as extraordinary, it has been shown that the mass media's communication approaches, forms and strategies fundamentally differ from those which are adopted on an average news day. Often these will involve delivering greater volume, bolder immediacy and increasingly graphic portrayals of events; especially those moments of crisis or catastrophe. In turn, the response to crisis from the (perceived) responsible organization(s) has been shown to be moderated correspondingly. Crises elicit emotions from stakeholders and thus there is an attribution effect and responsibility needs to be either taken or denied.

It has been stated within crisis communication research that honesty, openness and candour are paramount, whilst the impact of poor, inappropriate or incomplete corporate communication contributes to negative perceptions and value destruction. In other words, we know that the messages coming out of companies can be deliberately – and sometimes appallingly – distorted in order to manage consumers' impressions. However, this approach to communication manipulation needs to be carefully considered to avoid erosion of reputational capital.

Stakeholder management

The primary purpose of corporate communication is managing relationships with stakeholders. These relationships are required to create, develop and foster reputational capital. It is necessary to acknowledge that many businesses have stepped back from the neo-classical economic theory of organization and accepted socio-economic theory in its stead. The word 'accounting' has as its root 'accountability'. Indeed, linguistically, these two words do not share a stem; they share meaning. Though we acknowledge that the primary corporate objective is the maximization of shareholder wealth, we also believe that businesses must also be accountable to stakeholders beyond this group.

Earlier we established that the users of financial information were varied. Their interests differ, their objectives are varied and the information they require from corporate disclosure might not always be the same. They are, however, important to the continuance of the organization as their acceptance sustains the reputational capital. Also related to this, it is necessary for organizations to open up to other stakeholder groups beyond current and potential investors because this develops checks and balances that help to protect the welfare of society. Though it might not be possible to correlate 'doing good' directly with returns, a combination of engagement, words and actions can foster intangible returns such as employee, customer and supplier goodwill.

Companies and their management teams are aware, however, that there are different grades of stakeholder, ie those that drive value and with whom it is essential the firm communicates fully and transparently in order to protect reputational capital,

FIGURE 4.1   Stakeholder typology: one, two or three attributes present. Source: Mitchell *et al*, 1997, p 874

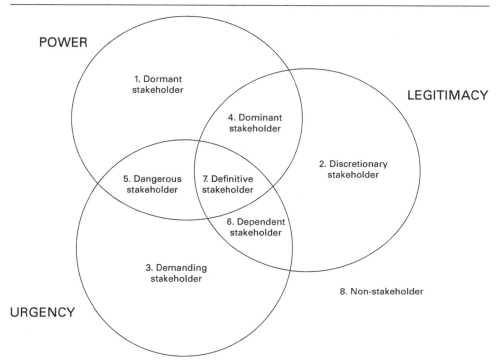

and those where it is simply desirable. Divisions have been made between stakeholders based upon their interests. A split between interests that are *economic* and *moral* in nature has been suggested. A more detailed stakeholder salience model has been developed which categorizes stakeholders according to their relative salience to the organization. This might seem irrelevant to you at first glance; however, you should note that it inevitably guides a company's communication strategy and therefore will also influence how you should approach the information that is presented.

Mitchell, Agle and Wood (1997) propose three underpinning attributes to salience:

- power (ability to levy power upon an organization);
- legitimacy (the legitimacy of the claim on the organization);
- urgency (the degree to which a stakeholder can call for immediate action).

The stakeholder's relative level(s) of power, legitimacy and urgency determines their level of prominence. It also defines the depth and breadth of stakeholder-targeted communication. The seven stakeholder categories (an eighth – non-stakeholder – is also recorded) are shown in Figure 4.1. These classifications are further analysed in Table 4.2.

TABLE 4.2   Stakeholder classifications

Latent stakeholders – possess one (of the three) attributes.
Owing to the limited time and resources available to managers, it is likely that they will
do very little about stakeholders whom they believe possess only one of the three
attributes. It is possible that their existence (ie the latent stakeholders) will not be
acknowledged. Note that this relationship cuts both ways, and these stakeholders are
unlikely to pay attention to the entity.

Category	Attribute(s)	Description
1. Dormant	Power	Possess power to impose their will on a firm, but by not having a legitimate relationship or an urgent claim, their power remains unused.
2. Discretionary	Legitimacy	Possess the attribute of legitimacy, but they have no power to influence the firm and no urgent claims.
3. Demanding	Urgency	Those with urgent claims but having neither power nor legitimacy are the 'mosquitoes buzzing in the ears' of managers: irksome but not dangerous, bothersome but not warranting more than passing management attention, if any at all.

Expectant stakeholders – possess two attributes.
Stakeholder salience will be moderate where two of the stakeholder attributes – power,
legitimacy, and urgency – are perceived by managers to be present.

4. Dominant	Power and legitimacy	In the situation where stakeholders are both powerful and legitimate, their influence in the firm is assured, since by possessing power with legitimacy, they form the 'dominant coalition' in the enterprise (Cyert & March, 1963). The expectations of any stakeholders perceived by managers to have power and legitimacy will 'matter' to managers.
5. Dangerous	Power and urgency	When a stakeholder lacks legitimacy but has urgency and power, that stakeholder will be coercive and possibly violent, making the stakeholder 'dangerous', literally, to the firm. 'Coercion' is suggested as a descriptor because the use of coercive power often accompanies illegitimate status.
6. Dependent	Legitimacy and urgency	Dependent stakeholders lack power but have urgent legitimate claims; they depend upon others (other stakeholders or the firm's managers) for the power necessary to carry out their will. Because power in this relationship is not reciprocal, its exercise is governed either through the advocacy or guardianship of other stakeholders, or through the guidance of internal management values.

TABLE 4.2 *continued*

> **Definitive stakeholders** – possess all three attributes.
> Stakeholder salience will be high where all three of the stakeholder attributes are perceived by managers to be present.
>
> | | | |
> |---|---|---|
> | 7. Definitive | Power, legitimacy and urgency | By definition, a stakeholder already exhibiting both power and legitimacy will be a member of a firm's dominant coalition. When such a stakeholder's claim is urgent, managers have a clear and immediate mandate to attend to and give priority to that stakeholder's claim. |

SOURCE: Adapted from Mitchell *et al*, 1997: 874–79.

It is unsurprising that the IASB has arrived at the verdict that the primary user group of the annual report is current and potential investors. Other users are deemed secondary. Those falling within this second group do not have the (immediate) power to demand actions, such as the removal of board members or the halting of certain projects. The primary group's interests are mainly economic in nature and therefore there is a constant dialogue with them. Most large businesses recognize the importance of reputational capital and therefore also have a communication programme to engage with the secondary users and their (mainly) moral concerns.

Corporate social responsibility reporting

Corporate social responsibility (CSR) reporting is an area which has developed rapidly in recent years. Reports that were once seen as a joke in the corridors of banks and large organizations are now state-of-the-art representations of the aims, goals, achievements and aspirations in the fields of ethical, social and environmental performance and position. The demand for organizations to behave responsibly has been consumer driven; ultimately, we all want to live in a better world. See, for example, the volume of 'fair-trade' products available on the shelves in the supermarkets or even the ethical banking alternatives now on hand.

Stakeholders whose salience was (and is) not high were asking companies to answer concerns of a moral nature. Their replies have become thorough. In turn, there has been a recent reported shift in perspective from definitive stakeholders – those with high salience – towards these disclosures, perceiving them to have economic as well as moral value.

During the past decade, there has been a dramatic growth in investment in funds with a social responsibility focus under professional management. This means that investors are deliberately choosing to buy stock in businesses that meet social responsibility targets. There has been commensurate demand for non-financial CSR information which cannot be obtained through the traditional path of analysing financial statements.

CSR reports place emphasis on issues such as:

- community matters;
- health and safety;
- diversity and human resources matters;
- environmental programmes.

Large organizations commonly release a CSR report alongside their traditional annual report. Therefore, though the disclosures are largely unregulated and voluntary, this has become part of their year-end reporting process, thus fuzzying the border between what is *voluntary* and that which is *mandatory*. The other primary route to disclosing CSR information is through the mass media via the corporate website and/or press releases.

CSR reporting research suggests that corporate disclosures of policies, practices and strategies are designed to achieve one of the following four, sometimes intertwined, objectives:

- reputation risk management;
- legitimacy;
- image restoration;
- impression management.

However, we do not want you to have the impression that CSR reporting is dominated by deliberate manipulation and distortion. Indeed, there are genuine grounds for hope and optimism. Researchers regularly highlight areas of good practice. It is the aim of the majority of those who work in this field: to encourage improvements to information and its communication; to promote fuller and more transparent disclosures; and to make suggestions to help bridge the information asymmetry gap between stakeholders and management. We simply urge the reader to be aware that all corporate communication is designed in a way that is intended to maximize shareholder value and bolster reputational capital. Therefore, we would argue that stakeholders should be alert for signs of information management, but praise the steps forward that have been made (and are being made) in this field over such a short period of time.

Earnings announcements, conference calls and investor presentations

The annual report has recently come to be regarded as a confirmatory (or regulatory) document, mainly because large companies have regular (normally quarterly) results/earnings announcements, sometimes referred to as press releases. These announcements provide summarized (adjusted) IFRS numbers for the period under consideration. These announcements also include a summary of the material movements during the period plus an analysis of the position and performance. These range in complexity and in content but also commonly provide an outline of the company strategy and the possible impact this might have on future performance.

There has been a great deal of work undertaken investigating the use of *promotional language* in these releases and the impact that has on the investor community. Though results are mixed, it would appear that longer reports tend to quell the negative impact of unexpected earnings (probably because they close the information asymmetry gap); tone affects investors' reactions; and framing can influence investors' perceptions. Appendix C contains two examples of earnings announcements documents: 1. IBM plc's 1st Quarter 2013 earnings announcement; 2. Aluminium Corporation of China Limited's (CHALCO) 1st Quarter 2013 earnings announcement.

Whereas CSR information is principally aimed at secondary stakeholders, this information is intended for a select audience of primary stakeholders: the definitive stakeholders in Mitchell *et al*'s (1997) framework. Both the earnings announcement documentation and the conference call or investor presentation that follow are publicly accessible (available through the corporate website and live broadcast over the internet), but the list of invitees is short. The communication is directed at sell-side analysts so that they can provide updates to their sales teams and clients.

These events occasionally – although rarely – coincide with the release of the annual report. Normally, however, the annual report follows between a couple of days and a couple of weeks after the earnings announcement. Given that we operate in markets which interpret information almost instantaneously, this time lag means that, in many cases, the annual report is out of date before it is even sent to the printers.

There are those who argue that the conference call/investor presentation does not provide incremental information over and above the accompanying earnings announcement. However, analysts' time is a key limiting resource and, therefore, others state that their attendance at these events proves by default that they have some worth. All agree that improved timeliness is a genuine benefit to this communication event. There is an argument that the company-enforced limiting of stakeholder participation creates a two-tier system. This occurs even amongst the definitive stakeholders themselves, as not all analysts and investors are invited to attend. We are convinced by the conclusions of the seminal study by Frankel, Johnson and Skinner (1999, p 149) which stated: 'we find that conference calls provide information to market participants over and above the information contained in the corresponding press release [earnings announcement], as evidenced by elevated return variances and trading volumes.' Therefore, we urge you to consider these events when undertaking your financial analysis.

Media relations: press releases and newspaper coverage

Communicating with, and through, the mass media has become central to organizations and the investor relations role. There is evidence that links a favourable representation in the media with improved performance. To achieve success, however, companies need to get their message out and have it interpreted in the way they would like. Newspapers and news organizations are vital to generating publicity. They are also important to preserving and enhancing reputational capital and transmitting information to stakeholders who might otherwise be hard to reach (or influence). The mass media therefore essentially acts as a conduit.

As stated above, the public are bombarded with daily corporate slogans and messages. It is also worth remembering, however, that journalists are also bombarded with events and press releases. How does one message get picked up by the press whilst others are left behind? There are certain techniques and strategies that can be employed but often it is simply down to fads, fashions, extraordinary events or luck.

In most mainstream newspapers, business news used to be limited to a single page buried towards the middle of their publication. In recent times, there has been an upsurge in the demand for this information and coverage has increased proportionately. The way that news outlets interpret events impacts on corporate reputation. Companies have a new awareness that the way the media interprets their financial information can have an impact far beyond their definitive stakeholders. Some financial information can even provoke latent and expectant stakeholders into action. See, for example, the reporting of the tax affairs of Starbucks, Amazon and Google (Extract 4.1).

Extract 4.1: Media relations

Google, Amazon, Starbucks: The rise of 'tax shaming'

By Vanessa Barford & Gerry Holt
BBC News Magazine (4 December 2012) (an extract from the news release: full story available at:
http://www.bbc.co.uk/news/magazine-20560359)

Global firms such as Starbucks, Google and Amazon have come under fire for avoiding paying tax on British profits. There seems to be a growing culture of naming and shaming companies. But what impact does it have?

Companies have long had complicated tax structures, but a recent spate of stories has highlighted a number of tax-avoiding firms that are not seen to be playing their part.

Starbucks, for example, had sales of £400m in the UK last year, but paid no corporation tax. It transferred some money to a Dutch sister company in royalty payments, bought coffee beans from Switzerland and paid high interest rates to borrow from other parts of the business. Amazon, which had sales in the UK of £3.35bn in 2011, only reported a 'tax expense' of £1.8m. And Google's UK unit paid just £6m to the Treasury in 2011 on UK turnover of £395m.

Everything these companies are doing is legal. It's avoidance and not evasion. But the tide of public opinion is visibly turning. Even 10 years ago news of a company minimizing its corporation tax would have been more likely to be inside the business pages than on the front page. What changed? And is 'shaming' of companies justifiable and effective?

Momentum has been growing for the last few years.

In September 2009, *The Observer* ran with the headline: 'Avoiding tax robs our public services, declares minister'. The paper reported that the government was planning to say tax is a 'moral issue' and that it was 'determined to end avoidance and evasion'.

October 2010 – and the Vodafone case – saw the *Daily Mail* report: 'Vodafone closes Oxford Street store at £6bn tax protest'.

...

Another impact of tax shaming is that some people, such as 45-year-old self-employed businessman Mike Buckhurst, from Manchester, boycott brands. 'I've uninstalled Google Chrome and changed my search engine on all my home computers. If I want a coffee I am now going to go to Costa, despite Starbucks being nearer to me, and even though I buy a lot of things online, I am not using Amazon. 'I'm sick of the "change the law" comments, I can vote with my feet. I feel very passionate about this because at one point in my life I was a top rate tax payer and I paid my tax in full,' he says.

Occasionally the BBC website opens up stories to comment and these are subsequently 'rated' by other users. There is some debate in the online community about the type of stories that are opened up and the parties concerned. Nevertheless, they provide a direct line into the minds of stakeholders. We note from the story cases of individuals opting out of products offered by these 'named and shamed' companies. One of the most interesting things about this story to the interested observer is the two most highly rated comments (see Extract 4.2). These individuals draw attention to another company which is also alleged to be involved in this form of tax management – Apple. Their comments suggest that there is media bias towards this organization.

Extract 4.2: Two most popular comments on the story: 'Google, Amazon, Starbucks: The rise of "tax shaming"'

Muesli3
4th December 2012–12:43

I am curious as to why in every single article it's the same three companies being mentioned. How is it that these companies are getting shamed much more than Apple with their 2% rate?!

production_malfunction
4th December 2012–13:07

I totally agree with the other comments on here regarding Apple. How these people are managing to get away with only paying 2%, while at the same time avoiding media scrutiny, is beyond me.

BBC put down your iPhones and do your job please.

It has been found that companies participate in the framing of news items. Companies write press releases in the hope that journalists will pick them up. Journalists rely on companies to write press releases because they cannot be everywhere at once. This sometimes creates a peculiar dialogue between unrelated – and sometimes conflictingly motivated – parties being reflected outwards. Often the original press release is simply paraphrased and disseminated. With this in mind, you will frequently find that press releases written by companies and made available to journalists are written in the third person to make things simpler for the journalists to adopt.

Press releases tend to carry predominantly good news, ie news intended to create value, for example the launch of a new product, undertaking a successful tender. Despite journalists being told to eschew a positive linguistic turn and focus on facts, corporate communication via press releases continues to be inherently optimistic in tone and therefore it is common for the related news release to be influenced towards this position. Some have suggested they tend towards the *propagandaic*. Interestingly, it has been found that the tone is hardened when the communication addresses economic or financial matters. Nevertheless, it is interesting to see that almost every study of corporate communication has picked up strong signals linked to attribution theory. In other words, companies tend to attribute successes to 'I' or 'we' and failures to an externality.

Behind the scenes, it is common for companies to communicate formally and informally with news outlets. They do not simply issue press releases and cross their fingers. They also brief face-to-face through press conferences and meetings/interviews with company personnel. In addition, companies actively monitor the effectiveness of their communication strategies.

In summary, the media is a perfectly acceptable way to substantiate your financial analysis and to triangulate findings. Newspapers need to sell copy and therefore you should expect a level of sensationalism, therefore in turn you should employ a healthy level of scepticism. However, this can only go so far. If the information is inaccurate and leads to a significant level of value destruction, it is likely that they will be held to account. Normally, newspapers will provide information which has come from a reputable source (often the company itself) which extends your analysis, lending weight to some arguments whilst rejecting the validity of others.

Social media and internet bulletins

As yet, nobody really knows how social media and internet bulletins will impact on corporate communication. In the meantime, we can only comment on what has happened. The majority of the world's corporate household names maintain social media accounts, such as *Facebook*, *YouTube* and *Twitter*. Their audiences are different, not just in terms of the demographic but also the information needs. There are all sorts of other internet-based means that allow companies to transmit information in a more accessible way to stakeholders, eg blogs, bulletin boards and so forth.

We have observed three major changes as a result of this new media technology (although there are bound to be many more): the immediacy of information availability; the reach of this information; and the ability for users to comment on content.

The advantages are that companies can be first to *frame* an event and set the news agenda. However, the immediacy means that an inappropriate lead, a lack of thoughtfulness in the communiqué or an inaccurate reflection of the events can have serious effects.

As the technology and the behaviour of the actors develop, it will be possible to work out if this new media is fad or fashion and here to stay. At the same time, an ethical framework will surely emerge to govern the authors and the audience. This is essential for the long-term sustainability of this form of communication. In the meantime, the digital landscape is a potential goldmine of untapped information that will bolster your financial analysis with previously hard-to-reach evidence. Equally, note that this might also be a swamp of managed corporate stories which you'd be better off ignoring.

Conclusion

In summary, information resources have never been so accessible and up to date. Though there is still a gap in the communication levels between those deemed definitive stakeholders (current and potential investors) and others, the gap is closing and the richness and value of the extra information to which they have access are diminishing and eroding.

Having undertaken your financial analysis based upon the annual report and financial statements of an entity, you will undoubtedly be left with more questions than you have answers. Turning to these additional sources – earnings statements, investor presentations, conference calls, CSR reports, newspapers, corporate websites, social media – will provide you with an almost inexhaustible secondary data set which can be used to support (or contradict) your initial observations.

COMPREHENSION QUESTIONS

1 Discuss what is meant by the term 'stakeholder salience' and why it might be important to incorporate this theory into a business's communication strategy.

2 In terms of the accounting standard-setting process, provide examples of who might be classified into each of the following categories and explain why you believe this to be the case:

a dormant stakeholders;

b demanding stakeholders;

c definitive stakeholders.

3 Can you explain why analysts might view meetings with management as more important than the annual report?

4 Can you explain why analysts might view conference calls/investor presentations as more important than the annual report?

5 Can you explain why the annual report continues to be a useful document?

6 Describe one occasion where you have been influenced to buy a product or engage in an activity as a direct result of an item of corporate communication, eg social media update; and explain what that was, how it happened and outline why you think it happened this way.

Answers to comprehension questions

1 Stakeholder salience: the salience model is a classification model used for stakeholder analysis and stakeholder management purposes. Originally developed as a project management device, it has been adopted by communication theorists to help understand how to respond to certain groups of users and how to prioritize their information needs.

Stakeholder 'salience' is determined by the assessment of power, legitimacy and urgency:

- Power is defined as the LOA (level of authority) of each stakeholder. In a project-oriented organization the highest LOA is having the power to authorize or stop a project.
- Urgency is the need for immediate action.
- Legitimacy is determining whether or not involvement of a stakeholder is appropriate.

The model allows the project team to determine the relative salience of any given stakeholder. The 'level of salience' assists the project team in setting priority and the amount of attention that will be given to each stakeholder.

2 Stakeholders in the standard-setting process:

(a) Dormant stakeholders – these are stakeholders with power but they lack urgency and legitimacy. Ironically, there is strong empirical evidence that shows that analysts (who are frequently used as a proxy for current and potential investors, ie the primary user group) tend to be dormant stakeholders.

(b) Demanding stakeholders – these are stakeholders who have urgency but lack power and legitimacy. It might be an unfortunate truth, but a truth nonetheless, that groups such as environmental campaigners tend to be demanding stakeholders in the standard-setting process. That is not to say their opinions are not heard!

(c) Definitive stakeholders – these stakeholders have power, urgency and legitimacy. The large accounting firms are often characterized as definitive stakeholders.

3 Meetings: there are several reasons why meetings might be thought to be more important than the annual report, for example:

- They provide a chance to meet face-to-face and, to use an old cliché, 'see into the whites of the representative's eyes'. There is a growing body of work which looks at the influence of behaviours, including body language and tone.

- They provide a chance to ask questions rather than simply be the recipient of facts.

- There is a chance you might learn something new (although reporting regulations prevent the release of private information).

- They provide an opportunity to build a relationship with the management of a firm you're following. In the short run this gives you something to impress your clients with; in the longer term it might provide you with other information opportunities, eg being invited to dinners, conferences, events etc, thus bringing the costs of otherwise expensive proprietary information down.

- And so forth...

4 Conference calls/investor presentations: many of the advantages listed above are the same. The additional advantages are:

- You are given an abbreviated and summarized early report on the financial year by the management and don't have to wait for the full annual report to be released.

- You get the chance to hear the strategy outlined and explained first-hand by senior management.

- You get to hear fellow analysts' questions. This might permit you a different interpretation of information.

5 The annual report: if other information sources contribute greater benefits in a more timely manner, why does the annual report continue to be produced given the huge costs of preparation, audit, production and dissemination? Indeed, this is not a straightforward question. Reasons might include:

- The annual report is independently audited and therefore grants the user an additional level of certainty over its veracity and credibility.

- There is information in the annual report which is not (currently) provided elsewhere, eg the directors' remuneration regulation report.

- The annual report has become a useful repository for both financial and non-financial information.

- The exercise of preparing an annual report might be deemed important from an internal perspective.

- The annual report is a permanent record, accessible at any time from anywhere in the world (assuming the organization is a limited liability entity).

- And so forth.

6 The influence of media: answers will be personal. However, with 13,000 new items of corporate communication bombarding us every day, it is highly unlikely that we are not compelled to act on some of it from time to time. Identifying what, when and where is a field of study all of its own!

Business planning

OBJECTIVE

To provide an understanding of how budgeting fits into the business planning process, and the different approaches which may be taken to budgeting.

LEARNING OUTCOMES

After studying this chapter, the reader will be able to:

- Understand the role of budgeting within the business planning process.
- Distinguish and evaluate different approaches to budgeting.

KEY TOPICS COVERED

- Business planning and the role of budgets in that process.
- The function and uses of budgets.
- The budget-setting process – different approaches.
- Practical budget-setting.
- Flexible budgeting.
- Zero-based budgeting.
- Activity-based budgeting.

MANAGEMENT ISSUES

Managers should be aware of how budgeting contributes to the overall business planning process and be familiar with the range of budgeting approaches available to them.

Introduction

In this chapter we will look at how budgeting fits into the overall framework of decision making, planning and control within an organization. We will also look at some of the range of approaches to budgeting and explore how different approaches are more appropriate to different types of organization.

What is a budget? A budget can be defined as the plans of an organization expressed in quantitative terms. It is usually detailed and sets out the planned income and expenditure of a future period of time. Although budgets are primarily seen as being monetary, operational budgets may also set out non-monetary elements such as stock levels and staffing requirements.

Typically a budget will be broken down into several levels, so that there will be a master budget for the organization and then budgets for different divisions, functions or areas of the business, all of which feed into the master budget.

The budget period will depend upon the needs of the organization. Most organizations prepare detailed budgets for a 12-month period which corresponds with their fiscal year. They may also prepare less detailed budgets for longer periods such as five years or ten years. Equally, many organizations break their annual budget down into shorter periods such as quarterly or monthly. In some cases weekly or even daily budgets may be used if that proves to be a useful management tool.

Why budget?

Budgeting is an important part of the management process – the way in which an organization sets goals and plans actions, allocates resources, controls and measures performance and rewards people. Budgeting plays a central role in all of these activities. It therefore needs to be understood and recognized as something broader than simply a set of numbers for income and expenditure over the next 12 months.

However, despite its widespread use, budgeting is far from perfect as a management tool. Indeed, there is debate within some circles as to how beneficial budgeting is. Some commentators argue that in today's uncertain and complex markets meaningful budgeting is not possible. At the end of this chapter we explore some of the arguments against budgeting and some of the alternatives which have been put forward.

Business planning and control: the role of budgets

A budget needs to be understood as a tool to help managers achieve organizational objectives. First and foremost it is an important element of the planning and control functions within an organization. Figure 5.1 illustrates how budgeting fits into this planning and control process.

A major advantage of budgeting is that it forces an organization to be explicit about setting long-term objectives and short-term goals and planning to achieve these.

FIGURE 5.1   The planning and control process

Without budgeting there is a danger that managers concentrate purely on the day-to-day running of the business. A budget helps identify the resources that are needed, and when they will be needed, so that the right resources are in place at the right time.

The budgeting process, if implemented well, can integrate the many areas of an organization, coordinating activities, communicating strategies, motivating staff, providing accountability and transparency.

Budgets form an important mechanism for *coordinating* actions across different parts of an organization. Each department or division within an organization, by working to their part of the budget, will ensure *goal congruence* in terms of achieving overall organizational objectives.

Budgets form an important part of *communication* within organizations. When a budget is set and communicated throughout the organization, this provides 'top-down' communication by sending clear messages to employees within different divisions as to what is expected of them over the next period. In turn, as budgets are monitored and performance is evaluated against budgets, there is 'bottom-up' communication as this monitoring feeds back important information to senior management as to how actual activities are unfolding in relation to the original business plans.

Budgets can be an important *motivational tool*, particularly if incentives such as financial bonuses are derived from performance against budgets. The effectiveness of budgets as a motivational tool is dependent upon the degree to which employees 'buy into' the budget. This is more likely to occur if they have a meaningful participation in the preparation of the budget. These behavioural issues are explored in more detail later in this chapter.

Budgets also provide *accountability* from managers in terms of the objectives they pursue and the results they achieve. Managers will be responsible for achieving budget targets and reporting on their results.

A communicated budget also provides *transparency* about the allocation of resources within the organization.

Although budgets are primarily forward-looking in terms of planning for the future, managers can also use them to *evaluate* past performance. In the next chapter we will look at this evaluation process in more detail.

Extract 5.1: The use of budgets in practice

A survey of 558 medium and large firms in the United States and Canada in 2010 found that 79 per cent used budgets for control purposes (Libby and Lindsay 2010). A similar survey in 1987 found a comparable figure of 83 per cent of firms used budgets for control.

The budget-setting process

The budget-setting process within most organizations follows certain clear steps. There may be some variation between organizations according to their exact budgeting approach, but Figure 5.2 sets out what is a typical budgeting process for most organizations.

Large organizations will have a budget committee which has overall responsibility for the preparation of the budget. The budget committee is usually made up of managers from all levels and divisions of the organization in order to achieve good cooperation and coordination. The budget committee will oversee the following steps during the budget-setting process:

1 *Communicate budget policy*. The first step in budgeting is to communicate the budgeting policy to all those involved in the budget-setting process. This is to ensure that everybody fully understands the policy and to try to ensure that contributions to the budget are in line with that policy. For example, the budgeting policy may be to increase sales by 5 per cent over the next 12 months while at the same time increasing profit margins by 2 per cent. This policy will form the basis of the individual elements of the budget and will inform the process.

2 *Determine restricting factors*. Before the process of establishing the figures for the different areas of the budget can start, the organization must consider what factors will restrict performance over the budgetary period. There will always be some restricting factors. These may, for example, be the production

FIGURE 5.2 The budget-setting process

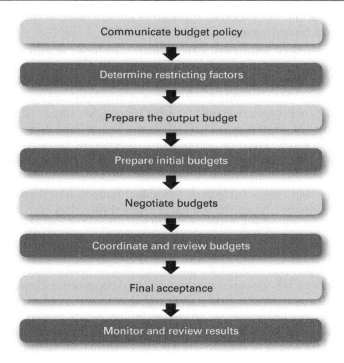

capacity of a factory, the amount of skilled labour available in certain areas of activity, the quantity of raw materials available, or the size and capacity of the market. If these restricting factors are not identified and taken into consideration, there is a serious risk that an unachievable budget will be set.

3 *Prepare the output budget.* For most organizations the logical place to start the budget is with the level of output. This is because it is usually the output which determines the resources required throughout the organization. Output can be determined in terms of sales or level of service provided. For organizations that produce multiple products or services, this budget needs to be broken down into more detail to determine the relative mix of each output element.

Some organizations, such as those in the public sector, may have fixed levels of resources that constrain output according to funding available. However, even in such situations, it is good practice to start with the desired level of output. Even with fixed resources, different levels and mixes of outputs of sales or services can be achieved by allocating resources in different ways.

4 *Prepare initial budgets.* Once the level of output has been determined, initial budgets for the other areas of activity can be established. These budgets will include those for production, purchasing, staffing, advertising and support services. Who is responsible for producing each of these budgets will vary across different organizations and depends upon the budgeting philosophy of the organization. The different approaches are discussed in the section below on practical budget-setting.

5 *Negotiate budgets*. This is not a step which is included within the budgeting process of all organizations. However, when an organization is structured in such a way as to give divisional managers a high degree of autonomy, this is a necessary step. It is particularly important if divisional managers hold budgets for which they become responsible at the monitoring stage and those budgets include costs of services provided by other divisions. The budget-holding manager should be given the opportunity to negotiate the level of service and cost from the service provider. If this step is omitted, budget-holding managers may be disincentivized by budgets they feel unable to work to.

6 *Coordinate and review budgets*. If individual budgets have been produced by the budget-holding manager, and particularly if there has been a negotiation process as set out in step 5 above, it will be essential to coordinate and review individual budgets to ensure that they fit together. One problem with delegation of budget-setting to individual managers is that self-interest may interfere such that individual budgets do not fit together to produce a coordinated overall budget. It is essential that there is goal congruence between individual budgets, that is to say, that they all fit together towards achieving the overall goal of the organization as set out in the budget policy in step 1. One role of the budget committees is to oversee and mediate any negotiation process and to coordinate and review the overall budget before final acceptance.

7 *Final acceptance*. Once individual budgets have been prepared, negotiated and coordinated, there needs to be a final acceptance of the budget as a whole. At this stage the budget can be finalized and will be ready for implementation.

8 *Monitor and review results*. The final stage in the budgeting process takes place once the budget is being implemented. During implementation, actual performance should be measured against budget at regular intervals. Any significant variances from budget should be recorded and investigated, as they represent a deviation from the business plan. If necessary, management action should be taken either to modify activities to bring them back in line with the budget, or to modify the budget to reflect changes which may have occurred since the budget was produced and which were not anticipated during the budgeting process. Different organizations have different approaches towards dealing with budget variances and these are explored in the next chapter which looks in more detail at performance management.

Practical budget-setting

So far in this chapter we have considered the benefits of producing a budget and looked at the overall budget-setting process. In this section we will look at some of the more detailed practical aspects of budgeting.

Levels of budgeting

Large organizations will have several levels of budget which feed into a master budget as illustrated in Figure 5.3.

FIGURE 5.3   Levels of budgeting

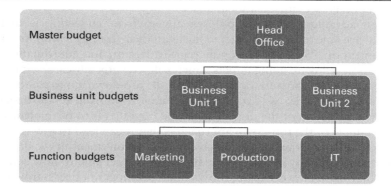

The master budget integrates all the budgets from the different business units of the organization. It will be made up of both the operational budget and the financial budget.

The operational budget comprises those budgets which make up the details of the operations of the business. These will include the sales budget, the production budget, direct labour and purchasing and the overhead budget. These budgets feed into the budgeted income statement.

The financial budget includes the cash budget, the capital budget and the budgeted balance sheet.

Different approaches to budget preparation

Budgeting is sometimes mistakenly seen as a purely accounting function. Although accountants are typically involved in the coordination of the budget-setting process, and in the production of budget-monitoring reports, the budget-setting process should involve employees at all levels within the organization. If line managers as well as senior management are involved in setting budgets, this will ensure greater ownership of the finalized budgets throughout the organization. It will also enable the organization to take advantage of localized and specialist knowledge to ensure a more accurate budget.

The sequence in which budgetary decisions are made is important, as this can have a significant impact on the budget which emerges from the process. The budget-setting process can be classified into two main approaches: a top-down approach or a bottom-up approach.

The top-down approach to budgeting

The top-down approach, as the name implies, involves senior management producing a master budget and then devolving activity targets and expenditure limits down throughout the organization. Once this overarching framework for the budget has been established, the details of the budget, in terms of allocations to individual divisions or activities, can be discussed and negotiated. Under this approach, any budget negotiation becomes one of how best to allocate individual activity budgets in order to best achieve organizational goals.

The main advantage of the top-down approach to budgeting is that senior management are able to set the budget in line with their strategic vision for the future of the organization. This improves policy prioritization and coordination. Senior management can set demanding targets which will strengthen fiscal discipline within the organization. Those organizations which use the top-down approach to budgeting use the budgeting process as part of the communication from senior management as to the strategic vision of the organization and how that is to be implemented.

A disadvantage of the top-down approach is that it can lead to low commitment from employees. If low-tier managers have had no involvement in the design of the budget, they are less likely to take ownership of the budget and to show commitment towards achieving it. However, a top-down approach does not necessarily mean that employees have no input into the budgeting process. The allocation of resources to individual projects and activities can be left open to discussion and line managers can still be given substantial freedom to negotiate detailed spending within their overall budget allocation.

The bottom-up approach to budgeting

When a bottom-up budgeting approach is adopted, budget proposals are produced within each division or section of the organization and then fed upwards. They are then compiled, coordinated and integrated into a master budget.

A characteristic of this approach is that total expenditure tends to be determined through a process of negotiating the details of the budget with each function manager. Because of this, the bottom-up approach often works best in an unconstrained budgeting environment: an environment in which individual line managers are free to put forward expenditure proposals if these can be justified in terms of revenue generation. The approach is less suited to organizations which have fixed expenditure limits; although it can be used in such situations, this will involve substantially more negotiation and adjustment.

The rationale behind the bottom-up approach is greater involvement of divisional managers and employees. If employees are involved in setting the budget they are more likely to be committed to achieving budget targets.

Extract 5.2: Circle bring bottom-up management to the NHS

When Circle became the first private company to take control of a full-service hospital in the UK, it introduced a new management philosophy which moved away from the traditional top-down approach found in the National Health Service. The chief executive of Circle, Ali Parsa, whose background was in the banking industry, believes in incentivizing staff to do things better and more efficiently and delegating power down so that they are able to do so. Staff hold a 49.9 per cent stake in the business, and shares are awarded based on performance. Employees are divided into clinical teams of between 50 and 100, each led by a doctor, a nurse and an administrator. Each team has responsibility for its own budget, financial performance, and how well patients do. Teams meet regularly to monitor performance and have the power to do things differently if they believe they can improve the operation of the hospital. The ideology behind the model is that staff, if given both a financial interest and the power to act, are better at identifying improvements and efficiency changes than managers who are divorced from the day-to-day activities.

This approach also enables senior management to take advantage of the local knowledge and specialist expertise of divisional managers who are 'closer to the ground'. This avoids the situation of senior management setting unrealistic budgets because they don't have a detailed knowledge of the activities and costs involved in achieving objectives within individual functions.

Despite the advantages outlined above, the bottom-up approach does present a number of challenges:

- It can be an extremely time-consuming and costly process to involve a greater number of people throughout the organization.
- It makes it more difficult to ensure congruence towards organizational goals. Individual line managers are likely to put forward budget proposals based upon local needs and wants rather than those which contribute towards those of the organization as a whole.
- It makes it much more difficult for senior management to maintain tight fiscal control. Budget proposals from individual line managers will inevitably argue for increases in expenditure.

There is also a risk that line managers who are allowed to set their own budgets will set themselves undemanding targets, or that they will create 'slack' for themselves to avoid criticism for not achieving targets. Within individual divisions, line managers have little incentive to identify and propose savings that could be used to increase profitability or to finance new initiatives. In a bottom-up budgeting system the budget negotiation process can become an exercise in preserving existing levels of funding and attempting to obtain additional resources.

Another feature of the bottom-up approach is that it is inherently incremental in nature. This makes significant reallocations between sectors or large restructuring of the budget unlikely.

Incremental budgeting

Incremental budgeting involves taking the previous year's figures and adjusting them for any known changes such as inflation, wages increases or changes in level of activity. The major advantage of this approach to budgeting is that the budget-setter has a clear starting point based upon previous actual performance. The disadvantage of incremental budgeting is that any inefficiencies or wastage in budgets may be rolled forward year after year.

Incremental budgeting has had much bad press, particularly from those advocating alternative approaches. Much of this criticism arises out of poor implementation of incremental budgeting rather than the approach itself, and one should not be too hasty in dismissing many of the benefits of this approach. The problem is that many organizations in practice simply take last year's budget and add a percentage to it to allow for inflation. This approach can justifiably be criticized. However, incremental budgeting can still be an extremely good approach if done well. If there are no major changes in the way a business operates, looking at last year's figures as a starting point for the next year makes a great deal of sense. However, these figures must be scrutinized in detail to ensure that any necessary adjustments are made to remove unused budgets and/or inefficiencies and to reflect known changes for the coming year.

Are the top-down and bottom-up approaches mutually exclusive?

In practice, all budget preparation processes will have both a top-down and a bottom-up element. Although there is a clear conceptual difference between the two approaches, all good budget-setting will involve elements of both.

Top-down budgeting should not be seen as a tool for limiting the discretionary powers of line managers. Nor does it eliminate the process of negotiating budgets and choosing between competing programmes and activities. However, some top-down element is essential to provide clarity during the process of prioritization through the focus on organizational-level goals. At the same time, it is not feasible to impose detailed function budgets from above without having some assurance that these will achieve their goals.

The two approaches of top-down and bottom-up do not therefore represent absolutes, but rather differing emphasis of balance during budget-setting. The challenge is to find the right balance which achieves all of the aims of the budget-setting process.

The basic steps of preparing a budget

In the previous section we explained that the overall master budget is made up of an operational budget and a financial budget, each of which is composed of several functional budgets. There may be functional budgets for several business units across the organization. This can mean a lot of individual budgets to coordinate. In order to facilitate this coordination there is a logical sequence to the preparation of a master budget. For commercial organizations the first step will be to forecast sales and to prepare a sales budget. Other operational budgets will then follow from this. Figure 5.4 illustrates a typical budget preparation sequence.

FIGURE 5.4 The budget preparation sequence

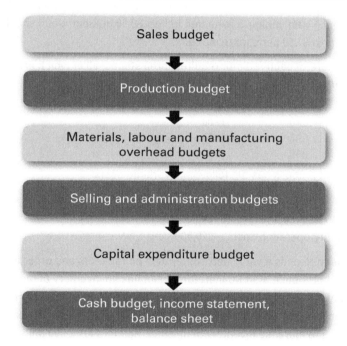

The following example illustrates the budget preparation steps set out in Figure 5.4. The example is kept simple as it is intended to demonstrate clearly the main steps of budget preparation rather than the detailed practical issues which may be involved during each stage.

WORKED EXAMPLE 5.1   Preparing a budget

Rad Co manufactures one model of vehicle radiator which is sold to just one customer, a major car manufacturer. The radiators are incorporated into several different models of vehicle.

The following information has been compiled for the preparation of the budget for the next financial year:

1 Expected sales of radiators for the year are 180,000 units. The expected selling price per unit is $20. All sales are made on credit.

2 The manufacture of each radiator requires 8 metres of tubing and $0.7\,m^2$ of sheet metal. Over the coming year, tubing is expected to cost $0.50 per metre and sheet metal is expected to cost $1.50 per square metre.

3 The manufacture of each radiator requires three stages, all of which are performed by computerized machines:

	Time (hours)	Cost per hour ($)
Cutting	0.10	12.00
Forming	0.13	20.00
Welding	0.15	15.00

4 The production process has the following overhead costs:

	$
Production staff salaries	240,000
Other factory operating costs	320,000

5 The customer demands a very short supply time on radiators and order levels can fluctuate at short notice. Rad Co therefore maintains an inventory of finished units. At the start of the year 8,000 units are expected to be held in inventory. However, in order to ensure a greater buffer against fluctuations in demand, the production director wants to increase inventory of finished radiators to 12,000 units by the end of the year.

6 Inventory of raw materials at the start of the year is expected to be as follows:

Tubing	100,000 m
Sheet metal	$10,000\,m^2$

The production director plans to increase these inventory levels by 5 per cent during the year.

7 Administration and selling overheads are expected to be $500,000.

8 The balance sheet at the start of the year is expected to include the following figures:

	$	$
Share capital		800,000
Retained profits		720,270
Non-current assets: cost	1,400,000	
Less: accumulated depreciation	460,000	940,000
Trade receivables		433,700
Trade payables		69,230
Cash at bank		62,000

9 The customer has been demanding greater credit terms and after some negotiation these will be increased over the coming year such that closing trade receivables are expected to be 20 per cent of the total sales for the year.

10 Closing trade payables are expected to be 8 per cent of the purchases for the year.

11 Planned capital expenditure for the year is $80,000.

12 Non-current assets are depreciated on a straight-line basis at a rate of 15 per cent on cost.

Using this information we will now illustrate how the budget is put together, following the steps set out in Figure 5.4.

The sales budget

The first step will be to produce the sales budget. This will detail both the physical quantity of sales and their financial value. In the example this is a relatively straightforward task as these figures are given:

$$180,000 \text{ units} \times \$20 = \$3,600,000$$

In practice a variety of means will be used in order to establish the physical quantity of sales. These figures may be based upon market research, they may be based upon known contracts or they may be aspirational in terms of increased sales targets. A variety of statistical and mathematical techniques may be used in forecasting sales.

Establishing the sales price is a complex topic in its own right. Chapter 8 of this text examines pricing in detail.

The production budget

The level of production will be derived from the level of sales. Production must be budgeted at a level which meets sales requirements and planned inventory levels. This can be derived as follows:

	Units
Sales	180,000
Less: opening inventory	8,000
	172,000
Add: planned closing inventory	12,000
Production required	184,000

Direct material usage budget

Material usage will be derived from the level of production established above. We have the number of units of production needed and from the information in the example we know how much material is required for each unit. The material usage budget will therefore be as follows:

Tubing	(8 m × 184,000 units)	=	1,472,000 m
Sheet metal	(0.7 m² × 184,000 units)	=	128,800 m²

Direct material purchases budget

Material purchasing must be sufficient to meet production needs and planned levels of inventory. In this example there are only two direct materials to purchase (tubing and sheet metal). Once purchase quantities have been established, these can be costed to establish a purchasing budget:

	Tubing (m)	Sheet metal (m²)
Production usage	1,472,000	128,800
Less: opening inventory	100,000	10,000
	1,372,000	118,800
Add: closing inventory (Opening +5%)	105,000	10,500
Purchase quantity	1,477,000	129,300
Cost per unit	$.50	$1.50
Purchase cost	$738,500	$193,950

Machine usage budget

The machine usage budget will detail the number of hours of running time required for each machine together with the total cost of that operation. In this example (Table 5.1) we can assume that production is within capacity, but in practice it will be necessary to ensure that sufficient machine time is available to meet budgeted production levels.

	Time (hours)	Cost per hour ($)	Total cost ($)
Cutting	0.10 × 184,000 = 18,400	12.00	220,800
Forming	0.13 × 184,000 = 23,920	20.00	478,400
Welding	0.15 × 184,000 = 27,600	15.00	414,000
			1,113,200

Fixed production overhead budget

The figures for production overheads are given in the example:

	$
Production staff salaries	240,000
Other factory operating costs	320,000
Total production overhead	560,000

Administration and selling budget

The figure is provided in the example:

Administration and selling overheads $500,000

Capital expenditure budget

Capital expenditure must be budgeted to meet both the short-term and long-term capital needs of the organization. Chapter 9 of this textbook looks at the capital expenditure decision in detail. In this example the figure is provided:

Planned capital expenditure $80,000

Workings for preparation of financial budgets

Before we can complete the cash budget, the income statement and the balance sheet, we need to calculate values for closing inventory of both finished goods and raw materials and for closing trade receivables and trade payables. From these we can derive a cost of goods sold. We also need to calculate the depreciation charge for the year.

Working 1: Raw materials closing inventory

From the production information we can calculate the value of the closing inventory:

Closing inventory of raw materials:

Tubing	105,000 m × $0.50	=	$52,500
Sheet metal	10,500 m² × $1.50	=	$15,750
			$68,250

Working 2: Finished goods closing inventory

In order to calculate the value of the closing finished goods inventory we need to first calculate the direct cost per unit:

Finished goods cost per unit:	$	$
Direct materials:		
tubing (8 × $0.50)	4.00	
sheet metal (0.7 × $1.50)	1.05	5.05
Machining:		
cutting (0.10 × $12.00)	1.20	
forming (0.13 × $20.00)	2.60	
welding (0.15 × $15.00)	2.25	6.05
Total direct cost per unit		11.10
Units in stock		× 12,000
Closing stock value		$133,200

Working 3: Cost of goods sold

	$
Opening inventory	88,800
Production cost (184,000 × $11.10)	2,042,400
	2,131,200
Less: closing inventory	133,200
Cost of goods sold	1,998,000

Working 4: Depreciation

Depreciation is charged at 15 per cent on cost:

Cost: $1,400,000 (opening balance) + $80,000 (expenditure) = $1,480,000

Depreciation charge for the year: $1,480,000 × 15% = $222,000

Accumulated depreciation: $460,000 (opening balance) + $222,000 = $682,000

Working 5: Closing trade receivables

Closing trade receivables are expected to be 20 per cent of total sales for the year:

$3,600,000 × 20% = $720,000

Working 6: Closing trade payables

Closing trade payables are expected to be 8 per cent of total purchases for the year:

$$\text{Purchases from the direct material purchasing budget}$$
$$= \$738,500 + \$193,950 = \$932,450 \times 8\% = \$74,596$$

Cash budget

The cash budget sets out expected cash receipts and payments throughout the budget period and the impact on the cash balance. This is an outline cash budget and most organizations will prepare a much more detailed forecast of cash flows and cash requirements. This cash-flow planning is looked at in more detail in Chapter 7 of this text.

	$
Receipts	
Cash from trade receivables	3,313,700
(433,700+3,600,000—720,000)	
(opening balance + sales – closing balance)	
Payments	
Payments to trade payables	
(69,230+932,450—74,596)	927,084
(opening balance + sales – closing balance)	
Machine costs (from machine usage budget)	1,113,200
Fixed production overheads	560,000
Administration and selling costs	500,000
Capital expenditure	80,000
	3,180,284
Net receipts (receipts – payments)	133,416
Add: opening cash balance	62,000
Budgeted closing cash balance	195,416

Budgeted income statement

	$
Sales	3,600,000
Less: cost of sales (see working 3)	1,998,000
Gross profit	1,602,000
Fixed production overheads	560,000
Depreciation (see working 4)	222,000
Production profit	820,000
Administration and selling costs	500,000
Budgeted net profit	320,000

Budgeted balance sheets

	$	$
Non-current assets		
Cost (working 4)		1,480,000
Less: accumulated depreciation (working 4)		682,000
		798,000
Current assets		
Raw materials (working 1)	68,250	
Finished inventory (working 2)	133,200	
Trade receivables (working 5)	720,000	
Cash at bank (from cash budget)	195,416	1,116,866
Current liabilities		
Trade payables (working 6)		74,596
Total net assets		1,840,270
Financed by:		
Ordinary share capital		800,000
Retained earnings (720,270+320,000)		1,040,270
		1,840,270

Budgeting in different types of organization

The previous section outlined the basic budget-setting process. This is a generic process which is relevant to most types of organization. However, there will be some variation and significant differences between different types of organization. Some of these special considerations are set out below.

Production businesses

The budget set out in Worked Example 5.1, although simple, is typical of that for a production business. Many production businesses use a standard cost system to establish their production budgets. A standard cost is the business's estimated cost of producing a product based upon previous experience of material usage and time taken together with up-to-date material costs, direct labour costs and factory over-head costs. Standard costing is examined in more detail in Chapter 6.

Service businesses

Organizations that provide services have a number of characteristics which make the budget-setting process different from production businesses. Service-based businesses include professionals and others who primarily sell their time and skills rather than a tangible product. Service providers usually have a higher proportion of fixed costs than manufacturing businesses. A very large part of those fixed costs will be employee costs, as services are provided by people rather than manufacturing plants. Also, services cannot be stored in the same way as physical inventory. This means that if the sale of a service is missed, that opportunity can be gone for ever. Service businesses therefore tend to focus their budget-setting process around employee costs and ensuring high utilization of employees.

Public-sector and not-for-profit organizations

Public-sector organizations include government and local government and public services such as health services, police, fire service and the army. Other not-for-profit organizations will include charities.

The aim of budgeting for a not-for-profit organization is to maximize the benefits from expenditure given the resources available. Budget allocations should reflect current organizational priorities and spending should be contained within sustainable levels.

A comparison of private- and public-sector budgeting is provided in Table 5.2.

TABLE 5.1   A comparison of private- and public-sector budgeting

Private sector	Public sector
Market driven	Resource constrained (ie funded by taxation)
Resources influenced by market demand	Resources controlled by government through grant settlements
Reliance upon external sales	Activity politically determined
Need for flexibility	Fixed budgets
Profit oriented	Service oriented
Single or limited number of objective(s)	Multi (and often conflicting) objectives
Outputs identifiable and measurable	Outputs subjective and qualitative

Not-for-profit organizations sometimes approach budgeting in a different sequence by preparing expenditure budgets first. However, levels of expenditure should be derived from planned levels of activities, which are 'outputs' in the same way as sales are for commercial organizations.

Merchandising businesses

If an organization is a merchandiser it buys in products to sell on, either wholesale or retail, and undertakes no direct production itself. In this case there will be no production budget. Rather, such organizations will have a merchandise purchasing budget.

Limitations and problems with budgeting

At the beginning of this chapter we mentioned that some commentators have criticized budgeting as a management tool. In this final section we will conclude the examination of business planning by discussing some of the perceived limitations and problems of the budgeting techniques we have covered and looking at the alternatives which have emerged in recent years.

Extract 5.3: Frustrations with budgeting

A survey conducted in 2000 which questioned financial executives about their current experience with their organizations' budgeting revealed that 84 per cent of participants were frustrated with their organizations' budgeting processes. (Comshare, 2000)

The dissatisfaction with current budgeting practices has resulted in practice-led developments in two directions: some practitioners are seeking to improve the budgeting process and make it more relevant, whereas others claim that budgeting should be abandoned altogether.

Should organizations budget?

Budgeting has been criticized by both practitioners and academics as being outdated and unsuitable for the uncertainty involved in the rapidly changing post-industrial business environment: budgeting is seen as consuming too much managerial time and the benefits are not worth the cost; budgets inhibit firms from adapting to changes in a timely manner owing to their fixed nature; budgeting is disconnected from strategy, thereby putting it out of kilter with the competitive demands facing firms; and the use of budgets as a performance measure leads to unreliable performance evaluation and promotes dysfunctional behaviour in employees. The Beyond Budgeting Round Table (BBRT) is an international network of organizations that seek to find business planning and control tools that could replace budgeting and help organizations become more adaptive to change. The BBRT website contains a list of 10 specific criticisms of budgeting.

Extract 5.4: The Beyond Budgeting Round Table

The Beyond Budgeting Round Table (**www.bbrt.org**) sets out 10 explicit criticisms of budgeting:

1 Budgeting prevents rapid response.

2 Budgeting is too detailed and expensive.

3 Budgeting is out of date within a few months.

4 Budgeting is out of kilter with the competitive environment.

5 Budgeting is divorced from strategy.

6 Budgeting stifles initiative and innovation.

7 Budgeting protects non-value-adding costs.

8 Budgeting reinforces command and control.

9 Budgeting demotivates people.

10 Budgeting encourages unethical behaviour and increases reputational risk.

We will examine some of these criticisms and other issues with budgeting in more detail below. However, it should be understood that this criticism from the BBRT is not an attack directed at business planning *per se*, but rather the management model which it perceives as lying behind traditional budgeting approaches. It calls this the 'command and control' management model – one which involves senior executives commanding and controlling the organization from a corporate centre. Budgeting is perceived as a symptom of this management model which restricts and constrains organizations that need to be more flexible and able to respond quickly to the business environment.

We would like to examine three particular problems of budgeting in more detail. These are the cost of budgeting, some negative behavioural aspects of budgeting and the problems of budgeting in a volatile business environment.

Cost

Budgeting requires a considerable amount of time and effort which can use up and divert valuable resources. As with any other 'expenditure' within a business, benefits should outweigh the costs. If an organization feels that it is not getting value for money from its budgeting, it needs to look at how it can increase the value of the budgets produced or how it can cut the cost of budgeting.

The value of budgets can be increased by using them more effectively as tools for controlling operational costs and for ensuring that organizational goals are met.

Good budgets can be particularly effective in controlling cash flow and thereby reducing the need for bank borrowing.

There are several ways in which the costs of budgeting can be reduced. One way is to use a rolling budget (see below for details). Another way is through the effective use of computerization which can both increase the efficiency and speed of budget preparation and increase the usefulness of budgets by incorporating strategic tools such as sensitivity analysis and scenario-building.

Defenders of traditional budgeting point out that although budgeting can be time-consuming and costly, it is not as resource hungry as some of the alternatives proposed by its critics.

Behavioural aspects of budgeting

Budgeting is, at its core, a human activity and as such it is subject to all the behavioural problems found in any area of human endeavour. The behavioural side of budgeting is a vast topic which cannot be covered comprehensively within a textbook such as this. However, this section aims to set out some of the key issues and arguments around the human dimension of budgeting that can limit the accuracy and usefulness of budgets.

The first issue is commonly referred to as **bounded rationality**. This can be explained as the fact that, when budgeting, we are looking to the future and cannot possibly know what will happen. The accuracy of budgets will therefore be limited by the boundaries of our abilities to predict the future. This problem is often compounded by the fact that budgets tend to be built on the assumption that the future will resemble the past. A second and related problem is the fact that budgeting often involves dealing with vast amounts of data. Even with the use of computers to help assemble and process these data, there will be a human element in interpreting and analysing them. Often the amount of data available is too much for people to be able to use effectively as part of their decision making.

Another human problem with budgeting is that people often stick with trusted strategies, particularly if the incremental approach to budgeting is used. The usefulness of budgets is therefore limited by users' inability to break out of habitual patterns of behaviour. Related to this problem is a similar issue which is sometimes called **satisficing** behaviour. This refers to the fact that managers will choose workable solutions to problems rather than optimal solutions. Typically, if a solution to a problem is being sought, once a workable solution is found it will be operationalized. It is not human nature to continue to seek alternative solutions once a workable solution has been found.

Budget preparation can often involve dealing with conflicting objectives. The budget negotiation process can be viewed as a **game** played between senior management and line managers. Line managers, if given freedom to set their own budgets, may follow personal objectives which conflict with those of the organization as a whole. In particular, managers will exaggerate their need for resources and will set themselves targets which they know they can meet. At the same time, senior management, aware of these tendencies, will attempt to restrict resource allocation to that which is necessary to maintain anticipated activity levels. Research has shown that where managers are able to put forward their own spending proposals, resource requirements can be over-estimated by up to 30 per cent.

There is another gaming problem which relates to managerial behaviour once budgets have been allocated. **The hockey-stick effect** refers to the tendency for budget holders to make sure that all of their budgeted funds are spent by the end of the budget period, irrespective of whether such spending is necessary. This is often done out of fear that an underspent budget will be cut in the future – managers seek to 'use' their budget before they lose it. Managers may hold back on spending during the year and then suddenly increase spending just before the end of the budget period in order to bring spending up to the budget limit. This behaviour manifests itself in a spending pattern which, if graphed, looks like a hockey stick, hence the name.

Budgeting in a volatile business environment

Opponents of budgeting argue that budgets are only useful tools in a stable business environment in which future events can be predicted with reasonable accuracy. However, the modern post-industrial business environment has proved to be anything but stable, being characterized by constant change, innovation and technological development. This means, it is argued, that budgets are often out of date and irrelevant even before they are implemented.

Defenders of budgeting point out that even in a volatile business environment there is still a need for forecasting and planning. It could be argued that cash-flow planning becomes even more important as business volatility increases. The beyond budgeting approach advocated by the Beyond Budgeting Round Table and its supporters still includes cash-flow forecasts and rolling cost forecasts. Many academics and management consultants therefore argue that the need is not to move beyond budgeting but rather to improve budgeting.

Extract 5.5: Beyond budgeting at Statoil

Statoil, the Norwegian oil company, has eliminated traditional budgeting from the company's management and reporting processes. The company's management saw budgeting as a barrier to what they wanted to achieve as a global oil exploration company in a turbulent, dynamic and demanding business environment. The problem with traditional budgeting, as they saw it, is that it tries to achieve too many things with one set of figures. Traditional budgeting is used to control costs, allocate resources and set targets. By trying to achieve all three of these objectives, traditional budgeting falls prey to manipulation and gaming from employees: managers will set themselves undemanding targets in order to achieve bonuses; a requirement to spend within budget stifles innovation and change in response to the business environment.

Statoil no longer uses budgets for oil exploration. Rather, under the new 'Ambition to Action' regime the business aims to get the optimum cost level to maximize value. There is a differentiation between good and bad costs. Good costs generate more income than you put in. The new approach aims to give more freedom and responsibility to managers. There is still planning, forecasting and monitoring, and the business uses KPIs (key performance indicators). However, the performance regime used attempts to move the management mindset from a mechanical adherence to milestones and triggers to a holistic understanding of business performance.

Improving business planning and budgeting

Not all critics of budgeting suggest that the process should be abandoned. There has been strong interest in recent years, both among academics and practitioners, in improving budgets to make them more useful for the current business environment. Key elements which have been identified for improving the process are better communication and collaboration. In particular, rather than budget negotiation being a process of arguing for and justifying budget allocations, it should be a process of sharing and exploring views of the future operating environment.

Although there is an advocacy for going 'beyond budgeting', the mainstream of current thinking on budgeting focuses on improving the budgeting process. This includes better integration between strategic planning and budgeting, better feeding of business intelligence into the budgeting process, greater inclusion and teamwork and less bureaucracy. These measures will reduce the cost of budgeting and improve its effectiveness.

Three widely used developments of budgeting are rolling budgets, zero-based budgets and activity-based budgets. We will therefore look at these developments in a little more detail.

Rolling budgets

A rolling budget is sometimes also called a continuous budget. This approach involves always having a 12-month ongoing budget. Rather than set a budget for a fixed 12-month period, the organization at the end of every month will add another month to their budget so that there is always a 12-month budget in place. The advantage of this approach is that managers' attention is continuously placed on what will be happening over the next 12 months, rather than the remaining months of a fixed-period budget. The process often also involves revising the 11-month budget that was already set.

The rolling budget is extremely useful for organizations that have uncertain levels of activities and need to respond by adjusting their capacity and operating levels. For example, a building contractor may operate a rolling budget in order to ensure that labour and equipment are in place during busy periods but that they are not idle when work is not available. This approach enables both greater flexibility and tighter control through its frequent revision and updating. However, the process can be resource-intensive and time-consuming as the organization is effectively continuously producing a budget. It also requires a more flexible management approach, as managers may find themselves working to constantly changing budgets. If not implemented and managed well, this can lead to confusion and frustration.

Zero-based budgeting

Zero-based budgeting (ZBB) involves building the budget without reference to what happened in the past. The idea behind ZBB is to avoid some of the pitfalls of incremental budgeting. These include continuing existing inefficiencies and failure to re-evaluate how things are done. The ZBB approach starts each budget afresh, rather than basing the budget on historical data from previous periods. Managers must make a case for resources and their budget will be zero unless they can justify the budget allocation they require. The advantage of this approach is that every activity is questioned and has to be justified in terms of costs involved and benefits accrued. Resources are therefore allocated according to results and needs and wasteful budget 'slack' is eliminated. The approach also encourages managers to question the way resources are being allocated and to look for alternatives.

Many organizations and particularly the health sector have seen substantial benefits from using ZBB. It can result in an organization radically changing its cost structures, cutting substantial amounts from overhead and support costs whilst increasing efficiency and competitiveness. It encourages managers to be forward thinking in terms of identifying what activities and resources will be needed to compete in future market conditions. Because this is done on a ground-up basis rather than an incremental approach of targeting areas where costs can be cut, managers must justify what to keep rather than what to remove. This can produce far more substantial changes in cost and performance.

The ZBB process is therefore particularly useful for organizations which have recently experienced substantial structural change such as an acquisition or a merger which may have left a legacy of unnecessary overhead costs. Also, changes in the competitive environment may create increasing pressures on costs such that an organization needs to re-examine the way it delivers its goods or services.

The ZBB process is both complex and time-consuming. This can also make it costly such that ultimately there has to be a payoff in terms of the costs and benefits. The process can also create internal conflict within organizations as managers are forced to compete annually for budget allocation. ZBB has also been criticized for focusing on short-term benefits to the detriment of longer-term strategic development.

Although ZBB is a good idea in principle, many organizations have found that in practice it is best combined with incremental budgeting. It can be useful to prepare a zero-based budget periodically; to do so continually year after year offers little benefit, particularly if there are no major changes to the way the organization is operating. Some organizations have therefore incorporated ZBB by using it only every few years or when a major change occurs within the organization. Between the ZBB sessions they revert to an incremental approach.

The ZBB approach became very popular in the 1970s, having originally been developed at Texas Instruments in Dallas (Pyhrr, 1973). However, due largely to the practical problems outlined above, many companies implemented the approach in some form and found that it did not work for them. It has fallen out of popularity in recent years. It is, however, still used in many areas of the public sector.

Extract 5.6: ZBB at InBev

InBev, the Belgium-based brewing company, has successfully used zero-based budgeting as a tool for cutting unnecessary costs after acquisitions, enabling it to become the largest brewer in the world. The management team at InBev have a reputation for ruthless efficiency in cost-cutting in new acquisitions to ensure that they create value. They have achieved this by extending their ZBB practices to newly acquired subsidiaries, requiring businesses to justify every expense each year.

Activity-based budgeting

One approach to improving the budgeting process which has gained popularity over the past decade is activity-based budgeting (ABB).

The most comprehensive model of ABB has been developed by the Consortium of Advanced Management, International (CAM-I), published in a book entitled *The Closed Loop* in 2004. This model is illustrated in Figure 5.5.

FIGURE 5.5   Activity-based budgeting

Private sector	Public sector
Market driven	Resource constrained (ie funded by taxation)
Resources influenced by market demand	Resources controlled by government through grant settlements
Reliance upon external sales	Activity politically determined
Need for flexibility	Fixed budgets
Profit oriented	Service oriented
Single or limited number of objective(s)	Multi (and often conflicting) objectives
Outputs identifiable and measurable	Outputs subjective and qualitative

ABB focuses on the activities of an organization rather than its departments or products. The approach is based upon the concept that costs are driven by activities. It focuses on how activities add value within the organization and expresses budgets in terms of activity costs. This is in contrast to the traditional approach to budgeting which involves focusing on the input of resources and identifying those in terms of functional areas.

The advantage of ABB is that the cost of activities within the organization are clearly highlighted in a way that does not happen in the traditional budgeting approach. These activities can then be linked back to the mission and strategic goals of the organization.

ABB has developed many of the ideas of ZBB and can be linked with activity-based costing as part of a more general activity-based management approach.

This approach has been popular with many public-sector organizations such as law enforcement and health care, as it enables such organizations to identify the costs of the individual services they provide.

Conclusion

This chapter has explored how budgeting is an important part of the management process. We have seen how corporate strategies can be deployed across business activities and departments through the use of budgets. We have examined different approaches to the budget-setting process and looked at the details of how a budget is prepared. We have also looked at budgeting within its wider managerial context and examined some of the criticisms of budgeting practices, together with some recent developments. This prepares the ground for the next chapter (Chapter 6) which looks at how budgets, once set, can be integrated into organizational performance management.

COMPREHENSION QUESTIONS

1 What benefits may an organization derive from a formal budgeting process?

2 What are the elements of a master budget?

3 Explain the difference between incremental budgeting and zero-based budgeting.

4 What are the advantages and disadvantages of a 'bottom-up' approach to budgeting?

5 How would the budget-setting philosophy of a service provider differ from that of a manufacturing business?

6 Discuss the potential conflict between using a budget as a motivational device and as a means of control.

7 Identify and comment on three behavioural problems that might be experienced in a system of budgetary control.

Answers on pages 203–205

Exercises

Answers on pages 205–208

Exercise 5.1: Selecting a suitable budget-setting approach

You have been elected onto the budget committee of a hospital and have been tasked with reviewing the approach taken by the hospital towards budget-setting. The hospital has a relatively stable level of income which comes from government allocations. At the same time it has a very high proportion of fixed costs which are largely made up of salary and wage costs. The hospital engages in a wide and diverse range of activities.

Required:
Identify and discuss the factors which should be considered when selecting a suitable budget-setting approach for the hospital.

Exercise 5.2: The objectives of budgeting

Ingram Co is a small engineering company. The company does not have a computerized accounting or budgeting system, but rather the chief accountant manually produces a budget each year in conjunction with the senior management team.

The managing director has expressed concern at the time and cost of producing the budget each year, and has asked whether any short cuts could be taken.

Required:
Write a memo to the managing director which:

(a) explains the objectives of budgetary planning and control systems;

(b) identifies and explains the stages involved in the preparation of budgets;

(c) identifies ways in which the budget-setting process could be improved for Ingram Co.

Exercise 5.3: Budgetary information

Khan Co is a publishing business. The budget committee is scheduled to meet very soon to discuss plans for next year's budget-setting process. One item on the agenda is the sources of information that will be needed in order to set next year's budget.

Required:
Write a short briefing document for the budget committee which sets out the main sources of information that should be used in setting next year's budget.

Exercise 5.4: Budgetary style

Chin Co, an architectural services firm, uses a top-down budgeting approach. The budget is prepared by Michael Chin, the CEO, and once finalized it is distributed to departmental managers for implementation. Michael Chin sees the budget as an important means of improving company performance and he therefore sets extremely demanding sales targets. Employees receive wage bonuses based upon their performance against the budget.

Required:
Discuss the likely impact that Michael Chin's budgeting style will have upon employee and business performance at Chin Co.

Answers to comprehension questions

1. (a) Improved planning: budgeting forces management to plan for the future, not just in broad terms, and also in detail.

   (b) Improved control: budgets set expected levels of activity and the process of comparing actual results against budget and investigating significant differences improves control of organizational activities.

   (c) Better coordination of activities: budgeting is a means of tying together the activities of different departments within an organization to ensure goal congruence.

   (d) Better communication: budgeting provides both a top-down and a bottom-up means of communication within an organization. Senior management communicates its operational expectations to employees through the budget. Actual business activities throughout the organization are communicated back to senior management through the budget-monitoring process.

(e) Motivation: the budget provides a means of assessing employee performance and can be the basis of rewards such as bonuses or promotion within the organization.

(f) Delegation: the budgeting process allows senior management to delegate responsibility and authority to make financial decisions to budget holders.

2 The master budget is the comprehensive summary and compilation of the individual budgets of an organization. The master budget will usually be made up of two parts: the operational budget and the financial budget. The operational budget sets out the details of the income-generating activities of the organization, including revenues and expenses. The financial budget details the inflows and outflows of cash and the assets and liabilities of the organization. For large organizations the master budget will be broken down into different levels so that feeding into the master budget will be budgets for individual business units and feeding into these budgets for different functions and departments within each business unit.

3 An incremental budgeting approach involves using prior-year figures as a starting point for producing the next year's budget. The prior-year figures are adjusted for any known changes such as inflation, wage increases, or changes in levels of activity to arrive at the figures used for the next year's budget.

ZBB ignores prior-year figures and derives the figures for the next year's budget by looking at expected activities and estimates of their costs. Advocates of ZBB claim that this produces more accurate budgets as prior-year inefficiencies are not rolled forward as would be the case with incremental budgeting.

4 The main advantages of a bottom-up approach to budgeting are greater accuracy because of the local knowledge of those involved in setting the budget, together with greater commitment to the budget from managers who have been involved in the budget-setting process.

Disadvantages of the bottom-up approach are that it is more time-consuming and costly, coordinating the budget and maintaining tight fiscal control is more difficult, and this approach leaves more scope for managers to engage in 'gaming' practices.

5 Service providers usually have a higher proportion of fixed costs than manufacturing businesses. A very large part of those fixed costs will be employee costs, as services are provided by people rather than manufacturing plants. Also, services cannot be stored in the same way as physical inventory. This means that if a sale of a service is missed, that opportunity is gone for ever. Service businesses therefore tend to focus their budget-setting process around employee costs and ensuring high utilization of employees.

6   For a budget to be effective as a motivational device, managers must 'buy into' that budget: they must believe that they can reasonably meet budget targets. This may mean setting less demanding targets and this will be done if management wish to use the budget as a means of exerting tight fiscal control.

7   Three behavioural factors that might be experienced in a system of budgetary control might include:

   (i)   Budget holders may build slack into the figures to provide for an easy life, rather than operating in the most efficient way.

   (ii) Lack of ownership of the budget on the part of budget holders due to the imposition of the figures without appropriate consultation and transparency in their calculation may lead to a lack of commitment.

   (iii) Budgets can be a great motivator by setting the agenda for future performance but they can also demotivate if they are seen as unrealistic.

Answers to exercises

Exercise 5.1: Selecting a suitable budget-setting approach

It is important to consider the culture within the hospital when deciding upon the level of participation in the budgeting process. Any significant changes in the level of participation, either an increase or a decrease, may produce resistance from line managers. For example, if senior medical staff are used to participating in the budget-setting process, they may resent any reduction in their input. This may result in a lack of cooperation and a lack of incentive to meet budget targets. On the other hand, an increase in participation for those not used to such involvement may create anxiety and stress. Training will be required for managers who have no prior experience of budgeting.

   A top-down approach to budgeting will ensure that expenditure is maintained within the fixed income levels. As a high proportion of the hospital's costs are fixed and therefore uncontrollable, this also suggests a centrally controlled top-down budget. However, a level of participation will be necessary in order to empower and motivate staff.

   For routine activities which have been conducted over several years, an incremental approach would be most suitable. This will enable the budget committee to establish realistic ongoing operating costs and to identify areas for potential savings.

Any new activities may benefit from a zero-based approach to budgeting. The budget will be built from the ground up, based upon the aspirations and plans for the new activity.

When there is a large proportion of fixed costs, it can be difficult to control and monitor these. An activity-based budgeting approach may be beneficial here. This will enable the allocation of these fixed costs to individual activities which will allow for better benchmarking and monitoring.

Exercise 5.2: The objectives of budgeting

(a) It is important that Ingram Co continues to produce budgets, as budgeting is widely acknowledged as being an important managerial tool for planning and control. Specifically, budgeting aids management in the following activities:

(i)   short-term and long-term planning and forecasting;

(ii)   coordinating activities between different divisions of the business;

(iii) communicating plans to managers and employees;

(iv)   motivating employees;

(v)   controlling activities;

(vi)   evaluating and rewarding performance.

(b) It is true that the budget preparation process can take a lot of time and effort. However, it is important that budgets are prepared properly and that they accurately reflect the long-term objectives of the business in order for them to be a useful management tool.

There are a number of steps which should be followed in order to ensure an accurate budget. These include:

(i)   communicating details of budget policy;

(ii)   determining restricting factors;

(iii) initial preparation of individual operating and financial budgets;

(iv)   negotiation of budgets;

(v)   coordination and review;

(vi)   final acceptance.

(c) An obvious improvement which Ingram Co can make is to computerize the budget-setting process. This will both speed up the process and improve the accuracy and usefulness of budgets.

A computerized budget, produced on a spreadsheet for example, is much easier to adjust and revise than one which has been produced manually. Not only will this help in the negotiation and coordination of budgets, but it will also allow more sophisticated budgetary modelling such as scenario-building and 'what if' analysis. Also, computerization will take the focus away from simply compiling the numbers and allow management to focus more fully on the real planning process.

Once the budget has been computerized, it will be relatively easy to incorporate actual results and perform variance analysis to enable ongoing monitoring of actual performance against the budget. This also means that budgets can easily be adjusted later in the year if this is necessary.

The process of changing from manual to computerized budgets may not save time in the first year, but in future years the process will take much less time as managers can simply take the existing spreadsheet and adjust it for known changes.

Exercise 5.3: Budgetary information

The budget committee will need to gather information from a wide range of sources in order to ensure that the budget for the coming year is accurate and truly reflects the strategic aims of the business. The sources of information can be classified into two main groups: internal sources of information; and external sources of information.

Internal sources of information will include:

1   the organization's short-term and long-term plans;

2   previous year's actual results;

3   operational changes from previous year;

4   staff training requirements;

5   capital expenditure plans and any non-current asset requirements.

External sources of information will include:

1   an analysis of the firm's economic environment, including market trends and the activities of competitors;

2   estimations of inflation;

3   forecasts of exchange-rate movements for overseas sales and purchases;

4   suppliers' price changes.

Exercise 5.4: Budgetary style

Chin Co uses a top-down budgeting approach. As operational managers are not involved in the budget-setting process, they are less likely to take ownership of the budgets and strive to work to achieve them. This may have a negative impact on staff morale as employees feel that their views are not being taken into account. Furthermore, the company misses the opportunity of gaining ideas and incorporating the knowledge and experience of operational managers into the budgets. This means that budgets are less likely to be accurate and workable.

The difficult sales targets set by Michael Chin may be unachievable. This will have a negative impact on staff morale and upon performance. If employees feel that they are not able to achieve their performance-related bonuses, they may not be motivated to try to achieve targets. This can create a corporate culture of getting away with doing the bare minimum.

If sales targets are over-estimated, related operational costs may also be too high. As a consequence, when the projected sales are not achieved, profit margins will be reduced. The business may well be overstaffed for its actual level of sales, which means that employees may be idle some of the time. This is both demotivating for employees and costly to the business.

Budgets and performance management

OBJECTIVE

To provide an understanding of the role of budgets, standards and variance analysis in performance evaluation.

LEARNING OUTCOMES

After studying this chapter, the reader will be able to:

- Interpret a variance report and assess its implications for management intervention.

- Identify behavioural aspects of budget management.

- Recommend strategies to prevent or remedy adverse behavioural aspects of budget management and to harness positive aspects.

- Evaluate alternative views on performance management.

KEY TOPICS COVERED

- Standard costing and variance analysis.

- Profit-related performance measures.

- Performance measurement in not-for-profit organizations.

- Behavioural aspects of performance management: gaming; achievement motive; creative accounting.

- Alternative views on performance management: activity-based costing (ABC); balanced scorecards (BSC); just-in-time (JIT); and total quality management (TQM).

MANAGEMENT ISSUES

The primary concern of managers is not the calculation and production of performance management data, but rather their interpretation and analysis.

Introduction

In this chapter we will build upon your knowledge from Chapter 5 by looking at the way feedback on actual performance is compared against budget to enable appropriate management decisions and action.

In its broadest sense, performance management is about ensuring that the goals of the organization are consistently met in an effective and efficient manner. It is a multidisciplinary activity that includes aspects of human resource management, financial management, operations, marketing and systems management and management accounting as well as strategic planning and analysis. There are therefore many perspectives on performance management.

In order to better understand how this chapter fits into the wide-ranging activity of performance management, it is useful to sub-categorize performance management into two broad areas – strategic and operational – although in practice these often overlap.

Strategic performance management is concerned with implementing the strategy of the organization and, if necessary, challenging the validity of that strategy as a means of achieving organizational goals.

Operational performance management is concerned with managing operations to ensure that they stay in line with the corporate strategy. An operational performance management system can therefore be understood as a set of metrics used to quantify and measure the activities of the organization to give feedback to managers on their actions.

It is this latter area of performance management that is the primary focus of this chapter, although we will touch on some broader strategic issues. We will look at the sources of management information for goal-setting and performance management and the different performance measures which can be used, both financial and non-financial. We will also look at practical aspects of performance management both in the private sector and in the not-for-profit and public sectors.

The calculation of costing information for performance management can be a complex arithmetic exercise. This information is usually produced by accountants and presented to managers in the form of performance management reports. This chapter therefore focuses on the interpretation and analysis of performance data rather than their production.

Attempts to measure organizational performance are only meaningful with reference to some benchmark against which efficiency and effectiveness can be judged. It is therefore essential that the right frame of reference is chosen. Much of the development in academic thinking and business practice over the past few decades has been focused around establishing an appropriate framework of reference against which performance should be measured. In this chapter we will look at some of the arguments behind recent developments and consider multidimensional sets of performance measures which include both internal and external measures of performance together with financial and non-financial measures.

No matter what the approach towards performance management, there are some important principles which must always be followed. These relate to how responsibility for managing the budget is broken down within the organization and how individual managers are held accountable for the way they manage performance.

Responsibility centres

The first general principle of performance management is clear delineation of responsibility. Within large organizations, responsibility for managing the master budget is broken down into different areas and delegated to line managers. The different budget sub-units are usually referred to as **responsibility centres**. A responsibility centre is the organizational unit (division, section, branch or geographic region) that is headed by a manager who is responsible for its activities and results. There are four main types of responsibility centre: a cost centre; a revenue centre; a profit centre; and an investment centre.

Cost centre

In a cost centre the manager is responsible for managing costs only. The budget is allocated to cost centres for those areas of the business which generate costs but not income. For example, a production manager in a factory producing shoes will be responsible for managing the cost of production but not for any revenues earned from selling the shoes.

Revenue centre

In a revenue centre the manager will be accountable for the level of revenue earned. For example, a book retailer with a chain of 20 bookstores will have a manager responsible for the sales revenue generated by each store. The manager may also have responsibility for some selling expenses, but this responsibility will be limited, as the main costs of running the store such as property costs and staffing costs will be managed by the central office.

Profit centre

In a profit centre the manager will be responsible for both costs and revenues and therefore also profit. The manager of a profit centre usually has more autonomy than the manager of a cost or revenue centre, as increased costs can be incurred and justified if they result in higher profits.

Investment centre

In an investment centre the manager will be responsible not just for costs and revenues but also for managing the level of investment required to earn the revenues. Performance will therefore be measured not just in terms of profitability but also in terms of asset turnover or return on capital employed (ROCE). The performance measures for investment centres are examined in more detail later in this chapter.

The controllability principle

The second general principle of performance management is controllability. A manager should only be held responsible for the things over which he or she has control. If line managers are to be given responsibility for budget areas and held accountable for the performance against budget, it is important that delegated budgets are separated into two elements: controllable and non-controllable. Controllable elements are those which are influenced by factors over which the manager has control, whereas non-controllable elements are those which are beyond the manager's control. This level of segregation is not always easy and will depend upon the structure and systems of the organization.

For example, material prices will normally be regarded as non-controllable by a production manager if price increases are due to external market forces. On the other hand, material prices will be regarded as controllable if the manager has control over the timing and source of material purchases. Material costs may exceed budget because the manager failed to purchase sufficient materials on time and had to source extra at short notice from an alternative supplier at a higher cost.

Profit-related performance measurement

In this section we will look at how financial performance can be measured and evaluated for cost centres, revenue centres and profit centres. Worked Example 6.1 provides a simple illustration of a monthly budget for a manufacturing business. We will look at how actual performance is reported against this budget and examine some of the techniques used by managers to better understand why actual performance has differed from budget.

WORKED EXAMPLE 6.1   Woodburn Co – performance against budget

Woodburn Co makes and sells wood-burning stoves. It has only one model – the 'Optiburner'. The budget for November predicts sales of 200 stoves, giving a profit for the month of $9,000. The budget is made up as follows:

TABLE 6.1

		$
Sales revenue	($180 per unit × 200 units)	36,000
Direct materials	($10 per m² × 3.5 m² × 200 units)	7,000
Direct labour	($12 per hour × 1 1/4 hrs per stove × 200 units)	3,000
Variable overheads	($8 per hour × 1 1/4 hrs per stove × 200 units)	2,000
Fixed overheads	($180,000 per year ÷ 12 months)	15,000
Total expenses		27,000
Operating profit	(Sales revenue – Total expenses)	9,000

At the end of November the accountant of Woodburn Co prepares the report set out in Worked Example 6.2. This report shows the actual results against the original budget. The original budget was for sales of 200 units whereas actual sales have been 230 units.

WORKED EXAMPLE 6.2   Fixed budget variance report for Woodburn Co

TABLE 6.2

	Actual results $	Variance $		Original budget $
Sales revenue	40,250	4,250	F	36,000
Direct materials	8,349	1,349	A	7,000
Direct labour	3,105	105	A	3,000
Variable overheads	2,760	760	A	2,000
Fixed overheads	16,000	1,000	A	15,000
Total expenses	30,214	3,214	A	27,000
Operating profit	10,036	1,036	F	9,000

The difference between the budgeted figure and the actual figure is reported in the middle column and is called a **variance**. Where actual results are better than budget the variance is reported as 'favourable' (F), as is the case with sales revenue which exceeds budget by $4,250. Where actual results are worse than budget the variance is reported as 'adverse' (A), as is the case with direct material costs which exceeds budget by $1,349.

The report shows actual results against the original budget. It is therefore not surprising to find that the actual profit differs from the budget, as actual sales were 230 units against a budget of 200 units. A budget that remains unchanged even if the organization deviates significantly from the originally planned level of activities is called a **fixed budget**.

A problem with comparing actual outcomes with the original fixed budget is that this gives limited information. If managers are to be able to identify problems and decide on appropriate action, they must understand *why* actual costs differ from the budget.

In Worked Example 6.2 actual sales have exceeded the budget by 30 units (or 15 per cent). It would therefore be reasonable to expect costs also to be greater than budget. From the variance report we can see that this is indeed the case. However, what we are not able to ascertain is whether these costs are still reasonable for the level of sales actually achieved. In order to obtain this level of detail we need to be able to 'flex' the budget to reflect the actual level of activity.

A **flexed budget** is one which has been adjusted in order to take account of any differences between actual levels of activity and the original budgeted level of activity. For most organizations this approach has many advantages over fixed budgeting. Accurate estimation of actual levels of activity can be difficult and flexing the budget allows for improvement and refinement of original estimations. It can also help reveal problem areas in the original budget and provide management with the opportunity to correct them.

Flexing the budget is particularly important if actual levels of activity become significantly different from the original budget owing to external factors. Monitoring against a budget which is no longer relevant can produce meaningless budget performance reports. It is far more useful to be able to compare wage costs and material costs against what they are expected to be for actual levels of sales rather than original and no longer relevant levels of sales.

In order to flex the budget, the original (fixed) budget figures are adjusted to what they would have been for the actual level of sales. Worked Example 6.3 shows a budget variance report after the budget has been flexed. In this example the original (fixed) budget would have been calculated before the start of the accounting period. The flexed budget, on the other hand, is not produced until after the accounting period, as it is only then that the actual level of activity is known.

WORKED EXAMPLE 6.3 A flexed budget variance report for Woodburn Co

TABLE 6.3

	Actual results $	Flexed budget variance $		Flexed budget $	Fixed budget variance $		Original (fixed) budget $
Sales revenue	40,250	1,150	A	41,400	5,400	F	36,000
Direct materials	8,349	299	A	8,050	1,050	A	7,000
Direct labour	3,105	−345	F	3,450	450	A	3,000
Variable overheads	2,760	460	A	2,300	300	A	2,000
Fixed overheads	16,000	1,000	A	15,000	0		15,000
Total expenses	30,214	1,414	A	28,800	1,800	A	27,000
Operating profit	10,036	2,564	A	12,600	3,600	F	9,000

With the use of a flexed budget it is possible to analyse the total variance into two columns:

The **fixed budget variance** is the difference between the original fixed budget and the flexed budget. This variance reflects the change in costs that would be expected due to the changed level of activity.

The **flexed budget variance** is the difference between the actual results and the flexed budget. This shows the variance between actual costs and the costs that would be expected for the actual level of activity.

The calculation of the variances shown in Worked Example 6.3 enables managers to obtain a more detailed analysis of the difference between actual profit and budgeted profit for a given period of activity. When total variance is divided between a fixed budget variance and a flexed budget variance, it is usually the flexed budget variance which is most useful to managers in assessing organizational performance, as this variance shows the difference between actual costs and what costs should have been for the actual level of activity.

However, even with total variance broken down into fixed budget and flexed budget variance, there is still a limited amount of information available to managers. The usefulness of variance analysis is greatly enhanced if the organization uses standard costing. This enables the analysis of variances in much greater detail.

Extract 6.1: CIMA guidance on performance reporting

CIMA (the Chartered Institute of Management Accountants) produced the following guidance on performance reporting. The ideal monthly management pack for reporting to the board should be between 10 and 20 pages and contain the following elements:

- Executive summary with a synopsis of KPIs and identifying all key issues.

- Action plan specifying corrective actions and contingencies with best/worst-case scenarios.

- P&L account showing period and cumulative positions with highlighted variances against budget – and major variances. Trend analysis shown graphically.

- Projected outturn recalculated on the basis of actual performance and action plans.

- Profiled cash flow summarizing actual and projected receipts, payments and balances on a regular basis to year-end.

- Capital programme – analysis of progress of major capital schemes showing percentage completion, current and projected expenditure, completion cost and timescale.

- Balance sheet showing working capital position in tabular form or using performance indicators, eg debtor and creditor days.

SOURCE: CIMA (2003)

Standard costing

A standard cost is the planned cost of producing one unit of a product, or in some cases the planned cost of a process. This standard is usually based upon a reasonable expectation of the time and materials involved that allows for idle time and material wastage which would be a normal part of the way a business operates.

Budgeting and standard costing are not the same thing and it is possible to budget without the use of standard costs. However, there is an interrelationship between the two activities in that a budget can be seen as being made up of standard costs multiplied by the expected level of activity. For example, if the standard labour cost of producing one unit of a product is $6 and the budgeted level of production is 5,000 units, then the budget for production labour will be $30,000 (5,000 × $6). Standard costs are therefore a useful tool in budget-setting and if the business wishes to undertake a detailed analysis of actual performance against budget, it is helpful to have standard costing information underpinning the budget.

In practice there are a number of different ways of setting standards and different organizations use different types of standard. Standards are usually classified as being either basic, ideal or attainable:

- A **basic standard** is one which represents a constant standard that will not change over time.
  - This type of standard is not widely used. It is found in some manufacturing industries that have products with long life cycles and processes which remain unchanged over many years of production.
  - By keeping the same standard over a long period the company is able to assess the efficiency of performance across several years.
  - This type of standard is not appropriate for businesses that have changing processes and practices or fluctuating prices, as it would not give a meaningful measure of actual performance. Also, it would be an impractical measure for a business producing non-standardized products or services which are made to customer specifications.

- An **ideal standard** represents the cost of producing a product in perfect conditions, with maximum efficiency and no wastage.
  - The rationale for the use of an ideal standard is to set the highest target possible and to strive towards this, rather than being satisfied with less than optimum performance.
  - In practice an ideal standard will never be achieved and therefore actual performance will always be below standard.
  - This may be demotivating for employees and would be an inappropriate standard to use if bonuses were attached to performance evaluation.

- A currently **attainable standard** makes allowances for normal levels of wastage and lost time and represents the cost under normal but efficient levels of activity.
  - Such a standard represents an achievable target and is therefore more appropriate for performance measurement.
  - The concept of being 'attainable' is not fixed and therefore an attainable standard can be set at a relatively easy or difficult level for performance management purposes.
  - In practice such standards need to be demanding enough to provide sufficient incentive for employees to improve beyond current levels of efficiency, but not so demanding as to prove to be a disincentive.

Whichever approach is adopted towards standard-setting, it is important that the standards used are accurate. The method of deriving standards is therefore extremely important and will vary across different types of organization. Some businesses use what is known as the **engineering approach** which involves industry engineers and operation managers defining processes, routines and exact material usages and costing these. This approach is likely to be used if an ideal standard or a highly demanding attainable standard is desired. It will also be used for a new product or process for which the company has no past actual performance data. A second approach involves analysing actual past costs, removing unwanted inefficiencies and setting a standard based upon this. Businesses operating in a competitive industry will often attempt to **benchmark** their costs against those of competitors. They will obtain information on the actual performance of their competitors and set standards to match or undercut these. Many organizations use a combination of the above approaches.

Extract 6.2: Benchmarking and performance at Samsung

Samsung, the South Korean-based multinational conglomerate, arrived at its current world-leading position through a process of benchmarking and refinement. When he succeeded his father as Samsung Group chairman in 1987, Lee Kun-Hee set about transforming the conglomerate from a Korean competitor to a global leader. Mr Lee insisted that the Group's subsidiaries should measure their performance against global leaders in their field, rather than benchmark against other Korean companies. Business units that did not measure up to global performance, such as sugar and paper processing, were divested even though they were profitable, because they were not capable of achieving leadership in global markets. Investment was concentrated on a handful of businesses deemed capable of competing globally. Mr Lee also increased the autonomy of successful businesses by eliminating cross-business subsidies and below-market transfer prices, thereby freeing the businesses to compete more effectively in global markets.

Standard costing and variance analysis

The use of standards enables a more detailed level of variance analysis than that which we saw in Worked Example 6.3. This is illustrated in Figure 6.1. In particular, the use of standards enables flexed budget variances to be analysed into two key elements. These are generally referred to as a volume variance and a rate variance.

A **volume variance** measures the efficiency with which resources are used by showing the difference between actual usage and standard usage. This can refer to the volume of sales (sales volume variance), usage of materials (material usage variance) or the time taken by direct labour to complete a process (labour efficiency variance). This volume difference is multiplied by the standard cost to show the impact upon profit.

A **rate variance** (which may also be called a price variance or a cost variance) measures the difference between the actual price paid for something (eg materials or labour) and the expected (standard) price. This difference in price is multiplied by the actual quantity used to show the total impact upon profit. In some cases it is possible to break this rate variance down into even more detail through the calculation of **mix and yield variances**.

FIGURE 6.1 Analysis of profit variance

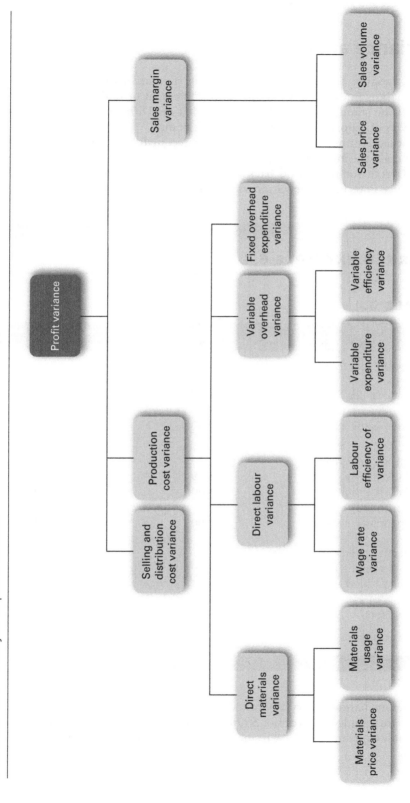

Variance analysis

When variance analysis is performed using standard costing, it is usual to present that analysis in the form of an operating statement or budget reconciliation report. There is no standard format for this information. Different organizations use different styles of report and give them different names.

Worked Example 6.4 presents a budget reconciliation report for Woodburn Co, based upon the information given in Worked example 6.1. This report reconciles the actual profit for the period back to the original budgeted profit and analyses this difference in terms of the variances set out in Figure 6.1.

WORKED EXAMPLE 6.4 Budget reconciliation for Woodburn Co

TABLE 6.4

	$		$		$
Budgeted net profit					9,000
Sales variances:					
Sales margin price	−1,150	A			
Sales margin volume	3,600	F	2,450	F	
Direct cost of variances:					
Material price	−759	A			
Material usage	460	F	−299	A	
Labour rate	1,035	F			
Labour efficiency	−690	A	345	F	
Production overhead variances:					
Fixed overhead expenditure	−1,000	A			
Variable overhead expenditure	0				
Variable overhead efficiency	−460	A	−1,460	A	1,036
Actual profit					10,036

The reconciliation report in Worked Example 6.4 provides a reconciliation between the original budgeted profit of $9,000 and the actual profit of $10,036. The following analysis examines the variances set out in that budget reconciliation in more detail.

Sales variance

The sales variance is expressed not in terms of sales price but rather sales margin, that is to say, the profit margin from sales. The reason for this is that managers will be primarily interested in the impact which changes in sales have upon profitability. The total sales variance is broken down into two elements, the price variance and the volume variance.

From the sales margin price variance, the manager can see the impact upon profitability of any changes from the budgeted price. In the Woodburn Co example the sales margin price variance is adverse ($1,150A), which means that the actual sales price was less than the budgeted sales price. As this is a simple example we can calculate the actual sales price: $40,250 (actual sales revenue) ÷ 230 (actual units sold) = $175. The budgeted sales price was $180, therefore the sales department discounted the stoves sold by $5 each. This reduction in sales price has cost the company $1,150 in lost profit.

However, this is not the full story. If we look at the sales margin volume variance we can see that the reduction in price has generated an increase in volume of sales with a favourable variance of $3,600. The importance of breaking the total sales variance down into a price and volume variance is that it enables the manager to evaluate whether the reduction in sales price was beneficial to the company. In this case we can see that it was. The reduction in sales price adversely affected profit by $1,150 but the resultant increase in volume increased profits by $3,600. Therefore, the net impact was to increase profit for the month by $2,450.

Materials variance

The total materials variance is broken down into a price variance and a usage variance. The price variance measures the cost of materials against budget and the usage variance measures the amount of material used in comparison to what was expected for the actual level of production.

In the Woodburn Co example the material price variance is adverse ($1,150A), which means that materials cost more than was expected, but material usage variance is favourable ($460F), which means that fewer materials were used than would be expected for the volume of production. In practice these two variances are often inter-related and the reason for one may lie with the other. For example, it could be that the material price variance is adverse because better-quality materials which cost more were purchased. In turn, this increase in quality may have resulted in less wastage and therefore a favourable usage variance. If this was a strategy employed by Woodburn Co, management can assess its overall success by looking at the total materials variance. This is adverse ($299A), which would suggest that buying more expensive materials and using less has not been beneficial to the business because this has reduced profit for the period by $299. This is of course an over-simplification and material usage variances can arise for other reasons, such as labour inefficiencies, faulty production or mistakes that require products to be scrapped. Managers always need to investigate variances carefully to understand why they have occurred.

If multiple materials are used in a manufacturing process and it is possible to vary their mix, for example by substituting one material for another, then the material usage variance can be further analysed into mix and yield variances. The material mix variance measures the financial impact of varying the mix of materials. If a more expensive material has been used rather than a cheaper one, or the mix between the two has changed, then the overall cost of materials will be higher. The material yield variance measures the efficiency of turning inputs into outputs. A certain quantity of materials input should produce a certain quantity of outputs. If the mix of materials is changed, the quantity of output may be adversely affected and this will show an adverse material yield variance, even if the change in mix shows a favourable variance.

Labour variance

The total labour variance is divided into a rate variance and an efficiency variance. The rate variance provides information about the hourly cost of the labour (ie the rate at which labour was paid) and the efficiency variance assesses how efficient labour was in comparison to the standard time it should take to build a stove. In this case the labour rate variance is favourable ($1,035F) and the labour efficiency budget is adverse ($690A). This may suggest that lower-paid and perhaps less experienced labour was employed and because of their lack of experience they have been less efficient. The overall labour variance is $345 favourable, which indicates that this change in labour strategy has been financially beneficial to the business.

A phenomenon which should be taken account of when assessing labour variances is the **learning curve**. If employees are involved in a new task, they will become more efficient as they learn how to do this more effectively. The learning curve is also seen with increases in volume of production. As production increases, staff usually become more efficient so that the cost per unit decreases. However, this increase in efficiency comes at a declining rate and will top out at some point.

Two other important factors are **idle time** and **wastage**. Idle time will relate to the labour efficiency variance and wastage will normally relate to the material usage variance but can be connected to labour variances because less experienced employees are more likely to increase wastage of materials. Levels of idle time and wastage can be categorized into 'normal' and 'abnormal' and it is important that a performance management system is able to differentiate between the two.

Normal idle time or wastage will be due to the way a production process operates and so will be expected and should be built into efficiency measures. For example, employees may be idle during the recalibration or refitting of machinery. This does not mean that managers should not be concerned about reducing 'normal' idle time or wastage, but this is a matter of improving or re-engineering systems and procedures, rather than one of employee performance management. Abnormal idle time or wastage, on the other hand, is not expected as part of a normal production process and should be investigated as a matter of employee performance management.

Fixed overhead expenditure variance

Fixed overheads, by definition, are not expected to change with levels of activity. Therefore, any variance in fixed overhead costs will be due entirely to changes in level of expenditure which should not have occurred just because of changes in production volume. In the Woodburn Co example there is an adverse fixed overhead variance of $1,000. This should be investigated as there is no reason for fixed overhead costs to increase just because of the higher level of sales.

Variable overhead expenditure variance

It is normal to allocate variable overhead costs based upon labour hours. As a result, any variances in direct labour efficiency (as seen in the direct labour efficiency variance) will also impact upon variable overhead costs. Because of this, the total variance is broken down into an efficiency variance and an expenditure variance. In the example it can be seen that the variable overhead variance of $460A is entirely due to the adverse labour efficiency already identified and not to any change in actual expenditure.

This analysis illustrates how variances on their own do not provide answers for managers, but rather they direct managers towards asking the right questions. Variance analysis can be seen as an example of **management by exception**. That is to say, by focusing on variances, management's attention is directed to those areas of the business that are not performing according to plan. Many regard this as an efficient management approach.

Extract 6.3: Standard costing in practice

KPMG, the international accountancy firm, in association with CIMA (the Chartered Institute of Management Accountants), carried out a global survey into the use of standard costing in 2010. Their report found widespread use of standard costing but highlighted serious shortcomings in the standard costing information used in many large manufacturing organizations. Some businesses were using outdated standards and standards which contained uncontrollable costs in their performance management.

It was found that the best companies use more than one type of standard to support different areas of decision making. Effective performance management focused on variance analysis and remedial action in controllable areas of performance. In addition, in order to deal with economic volatility these businesses undertook frequent updates of their standards to keep them relevant and useful for performance management.

Exercises: now attempt Exercise 6.1 on page 239

Performance management in investment centres

The manager of an investment centre is not just responsible for the costs, revenues and profits of that centre, but also for the investments made in order to earn those profits. Investment centres therefore need performance measures which address the efficiency of investments, that is to say they address both income and assets. In this section we will look at the most commonly used investment centre performance indicators.

Return on investment (ROI)

The return on investment (ROI), which is synonymous with ROCE, is the most commonly used performance measure for evaluating investment centre financial performance. The ROI measures the level of income earned in relation to the assets employed to earn that income. This is usually expressed in the following formula:

$$ROI = \frac{\text{Operating income}}{\text{Total assets}} \times 100\%$$

Expert view 6.1: ROI

ROI is also used to evaluate potential investments in the form of accounting rate of return (ARR) and so is discussed in more detail in Chapter 9. The difference is that in investment appraisal the technique is applied to estimates of future income, but for performance measurement it is applied to historic income, ie that which has already been earned.

The popularity and widespread usage of ROI can be attributed to the fact that, because it gives a measure as a percentage, it allows for easy comparison of performance between different businesses, business divisions and the same business division over time.

A second and related measure sometimes used in investment centres is the capital turnover. This measures sales revenue in relation to assets and shows how efficiently the centre is using its assets to generate sales:

$$\text{Capital turnover} = \frac{\text{Sales revenue}}{\text{Total assets}} \times 100\%$$

This measure may be more appropriate for a division that is primarily responsible for income generation and has little or no control over costs.

Residual income (RI) and economic value added (EVA)

Residual income presents an alternative means of measuring income against assets of an investment centre. Whereas ROI measures performance in percentage terms, RI measures it in absolute terms. RI is calculated with the following formula:

$$RI = \text{After-tax operating income} - (\text{Cost of capital} \times \text{Invested assets})$$

The cost of capital charge deducted from operating income is the company's weighted average cost of capital (WACC) multiplied by the total assets invested in the division. It represents the cost of financing the assets of the division and hence the minimum acceptable level of income for the division. RI is therefore a measure of the surplus or residual which the division earns over and above the minimum required by the company's investors.

In the early 1990s Stern Steward & Co consultants made some refinements to residual income and termed their new measure **economic value added (EVA)**. This measure has been widely adopted over the past 20 years and research suggests that up to 25 per cent of businesses now use it to evaluate divisional performance.

$$EVA = \text{Adjusted after-tax operating income} - $$
$$(\text{Cost of capital} \times \text{Adjusted average invested capital})$$

For EVA the operating income and capital invested are both adjusted to bring them closer to approximation of equivalent cash figures. This is to remove distortions which occurred owing to the way income and capital have to be reported for financial accounting purposes.

WORKED EXAMPLE 6.5   Investment centre performance

The following information relates to the performance of an investment centre:

Total assets of division	$500,000
Sales revenue of division	$770,000
After-tax operating income	$65,000
Adjusted after-tax operating income	$70,000
Adjusted total capital of division	$560,000
Cost of capital	12%

Using these figures we can calculate the performance of the investment centre:

Return on investment:

$$ROI = \frac{\text{Operating income}}{\text{Total assets}} = \frac{\$65,000}{\$500,000} = 13\%$$

Capital turnover:

$$\text{Capital turnover} = \frac{\text{Sales revenue}}{\text{Total assets}} = \frac{\$770,000}{\$500,000} = 154\%$$

Residual income:

RI = Operating income − Cost of capital charge
= \$65,000 − (\$500,000 × 12%) = \$5,000

Economic value added:

EVA = Adjusted after-tax operating income −
Cost of invested capital × Adjusted average invested capital
= \$70,000 × (\$560,000 × 12%) = \$2,800

Which is the best measure: ROI or EVA?

As ROI and EVA represent two very different measures of divisional performance, the question naturally arises as to which is the better. In practice each of the two measures has both advantages and disadvantages:

- The advantage of ROI is that it enables easy comparison between divisions and different companies, particularly if they are of different sizes. Also, managers are usually more comfortable dealing with percentages.

- The disadvantage of ROI is that it can encourage divisional behaviour which is not in the interest of the business as a whole. For example, if a division has a current ROI of 20 per cent it will be reluctant to invest in a new project which offers a return of only 15 per cent, as this new project would reduce the average ROI for the division. But if the overall ROI of the company is 12 per cent, the new project with a return of 15 per cent represents a good investment because it will increase the company ROI. When using the ROI measure it is possible for the interests of the division and the business as a whole to conflict.

EVA overcomes this problem by moving focus away from percentages, but in doing so it suffers from the disadvantage of being an absolute measure and therefore being less useful for comparison with other divisions or businesses of a different size. A major advantage of EVA is that because it makes a charge for the capital used, it raises managers' awareness that capital has a cost and that the balance sheet needs to be managed just as carefully as the income statement. The EVA enables managers to assess a proper trade-off between the two.

Non-financial performance indicators

The usefulness of financial measures and variance analysis as a management control and performance measurement system has been challenged by some commentators.

One criticism is that currently used financial measures arose in manufacturing businesses operating in a relatively stable business environment and as such they offer insufficient focus on quality for modern service-oriented businesses. They are also focused on the short term, which means that management decisions will be directed towards short-term financial gains at the potential cost to long-term sustainability and development. Another criticism is that the speed of change in the modern business environment is a barrier to effective standard-setting and variance analysis. Some commentators have gone as far as to claim that standard costing is now obsolete. Others have suggested that it can be updated to incorporate qualitative considerations to make it more suitable for modern businesses.

In *Relevance Lost*, an influential book published in 1987, the authors Johnson and Kaplan outlined the limitations of short-term financial measures of performance and argued for the use of more non-financial measures. Johnson and Kaplan claimed that short-term financial measures have become less relevant in a modern business environment characterized by rapid change, innovation and shorter product life cycles. They proposed that a range of non-financial performance measures should be used, covering not just operations, but also marketing and research and development.

Johnson and Kaplan encouraged the use of performance indicators that will better predict an organization's long-term goals rather than just short-term financial performance. This should, for example, include measures of efficient product design, flexible production capability, quality, delivery time and customer feedback. One result of these criticisms has been the development of what has come to be known as the **balanced scorecard**.

The balanced scorecard

The balanced scorecard (BSC) was developed in the early 1990s as a performance management tool which addresses some of the criticisms of traditional finance-focused measures discussed above. It's best-known proponents are Kaplan and Norton who published an article in the *Harvard Business Review* in 1992 followed by a book, *The Balanced Scorecard*, in 1996. Since then it has become the most widely adopted performance management framework.

The principle of the balanced scorecard is that it presents a mix of financial and non-financial performance measures which are derived from corporate strategy and which focus on the main activities required to implement that strategy. Kaplan and Norton proposed three non-financial areas and one financial area to provide four 'perspectives' on performance (see Figure 6.2). A company should choose a small number of performance measures (typically five or six) to reflect performance from each of these perspectives and attach targets to each measure which indicate expected levels of performance.

Financial perspective

The financial perspective considers the organization's performance from the point of view of the shareholders. The primary concern is how well the organization is creating value for its owners. Kaplan and Norton suggested three core areas that

FIGURE 6.2   The balanced scorecard

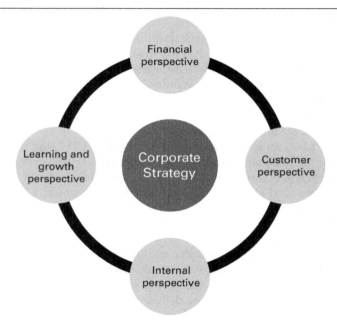

should drive the business strategy: revenue (growth and mix); cost reduction; and asset utilization.

Customer perspective

This perspective considers the organization's performance from the point of view of customers. The organization should understand its customer profile and the market segments in which it competes.

Internal perspective

This perspective is concerned with the internal workings of the organization and what must be done well in order to satisfy customers. It involves identifying critical business processes. Kaplan and Norton identified three key areas of added value: the innovation process; the operations process; and the post-sales process.

Learning and growth perspective

This perspective focuses on continual improvement and innovation within the organization. It involves a recognition that markets, products and processes are continually changing and that in order to continue satisfying customers and making good financial returns the organization must keep learning and developing. An emphasis of this perspective is continued investment in infrastructure – systems, organizational procedures and people, in order to provide the capability to perform and improve in the other three perspectives.

Using a balanced scorecard

The four perspectives detailed above are those initially put forward by Kaplan and Norton. In practice, each organization should choose perspectives which it feels are most appropriate to its corporate mission and strategic vision. It should then select performance measures and set targets in line with these perspectives. Extract 6.4 shows an extract from the balanced scorecard of a major electricity utility supply company.

Extract 6.4: Balanced scorecard for an electricity utility supplier

Objectives	Performance measures	Targets
Financial perspective		
Maximize returns	• ROCE	15%
Profitable growth	• Revenue growth	12%
Leveraged asset base	• Asset utilization rate	90%
Manage operating costs	• Operating costs per customer	$125
Customer perspective		
Industry-leading customer loyalty	• Customer satisfaction rating	90%
Internal perspective		
Business growth	• Percentage of revenue from deregulated products or services	10%
Continued public support	• Customer satisfaction (5-point scale)	4.5
Customer service excellence	• Promised delivery percentage	97%
Optimize core business	• Percentage rated capacity attained	90%
Learning and growth perspective		
Market-driven skill	• Strategic skill coverage ratio	85%
Employee satisfaction	• Employee satisfaction rating (5-point scale)	4.5
World-class leadership	• Leadership effectiveness rating (5-point scale)	4.5

Development of the BSC

Since its introduction in the early 1990s the balanced scorecard has attracted some criticism. One early criticism was that the model developed by Kaplan and Norton focused primarily on the needs of US-based SMEs and as such was not very useful to other types of organization. This has led to a number of variant models (with alternative perspectives or different numbers of perspectives) aimed at being more appropriate to a broader range of organizations. A further criticism has been the focus on shareholders to the detriment of other stakeholders. Current thinking on business strategy emphasizes the importance of well-rounded stakeholder management. There is also little empirical evidence to support the claim that the use of the balanced scorecard produces better financial performance. Despite this, the balanced scorecard and its various derivatives are still extremely popular and widely applied by commercial businesses, non-profit organizations, schools, colleges, government bodies and the military.

Kaplan and Norton have gone on to develop their ideas since the initial introduction of the balanced scorecard. In their latest book *The Execution Premium*, published in 2008, they incorporate the balanced scorecard into a broader **execution premium process (XPP)**, a broader holistic system of implementing and monitoring strategy.

Exercises: now attempt Exercise 6.3 on page 240

Performance measurement in not-for-profit organizations

A not-for-profit organization (NPO) is one which does not aim to earn profits for the owners. Rather, revenues allocated, earned or donated are used in pursuit of the organization's goals. NPOs typically refer to charities and public service organizations such as education, health, police, fire service and social welfare. However, NPOs can also include museums, churches, religious organizations, sports organizations and political organizations. Not-for-profit status is a legal status which will vary from country to country.

NPOs face unique challenges in assessing their performance as the performance measures used by commercial organizations are in many cases not relevant. For example, the variance analysis examined in Worked Example 6.4 above was concerned with the impact upon profitability of actual performance against budget. As generating profits is not a goal for NPOs, this approach to performance measurement is not appropriate. The challenge for NPOs therefore is to find alternative performance measures which better suit their organizational goals and aims.

Not only are NPOs different from commercial organizations in not being unified by a profit motive (Table 6.5), they are also a heterogeneous category, having a wide range of goals which lead to a wide range of activities. These activities and goals are often seen as intangible and difficult to quantify. This increases the challenge of finding appropriate performance measures.

However, there are some points of commonality that allow for a general framework of performance management. The activities of NPOs can in most cases be categorized into three key areas: fundraising, management and programme implementation. Adequate performance management therefore needs to include measurement of performance in each of these areas.

TABLE 6.5 The features which typically make NPOs different from commercial businesses

- There are no shareholders to whom management have a primary responsibility to provide a financial return.
- Generating profits is not a goal of the organization.
- NPOs often provide services or goods free of charge.
- Income is received from individuals or organizations that are different from those receiving the benefits of the organization's work.
- Those providing resources to the NPO often do not expect a financial return in the same way as private-sector investors.

One performance measure which is common to most NPOs is the proportion of resources spent on management and fundraising as opposed to carrying out programme activities. A smaller proportion of resources spent on management and fundraising is seen as a positive performance indicator, and this measure is frequently used by tax authorities and watchdog organizations when rating NPO performance.

Although the proportion of total resources spent on programme activities is important, it is not in itself an adequate performance measure. Good performance is not just about spending money. It is possible for an NPO to spend a high proportion of its total resources on programme activities but for it to be ineffectual in reaching its goals. Performance measurement for NPOs must therefore focus on output and outcomes as well as inputs. It is therefore useful to clarify these three important concepts of inputs, outputs and outcomes:

Inputs can be defined as all the resources used to carry out the organization's mission and implement projects and programmes. This will include financial resources (earned, allocated or donated) and also staff and volunteer time.

Outputs are the level of services provided by the NPO. Outputs will usually be measured in non-financial terms and will depend upon the goals of the organization. For example, an anti-malaria charity may report the number of mosquito nets distributed; a hospital heart surgery department may report the number of operations performed; a college may measure the number of people attending workshops or training classes; a humanitarian charity may report the number of people provided with shelter, food and water following a disaster.

Outcomes are the effects which services provided (outputs) have on the organization's stated mission. Outcome measures should focus on how well outputs are achieving organizational goals. These measures attempt to gauge how effective the organization is being. For example, the anti-malaria charity may report the number of cases of malaria in the area in which it is working; the college may report the number of students entering new jobs.

There are many approaches to performance measurement in NPOs, but all are based around three important factors often referred to as the '3Es': economy, effectiveness and efficiency. This framework provides a focus for NPO performance measures which cover inputs, outputs and outcomes:

Economy is concerned with achieving goals within given levels of resource input. Most NPOs operate with restricted resources and must therefore be able to achieve their goals effectively with a limited budget. For example, a hospital with a fixed level of funding must be able to operate within its fixed budget, without overspending, regardless of how effective or efficient it is.

Effectiveness is concerned with achievement of outcomes and focuses upon the organization's goals. For example, a drug rehabilitation clinic may have a corporate mission of reducing the number of people dependent upon illegal drugs. That clinic may treat a large number of patients at a low cost and thereby be deemed efficient. However, if a high proportion of those patients relapse, the clinic may be deemed to have low effectiveness in achieving its goals.

Efficiency is concerned with the relationship between inputs and outputs. Efficiency measures look at the amount of resources used to achieve outputs. For example, two care homes may both provide similar levels of care for the same number of residents, but if one does so at a considerably lower cost than the other, it can be considered to be more efficient.

NPO efficiency can be measured in each of the three key areas of activity: fundraising, management and programme implementation. There may be external benchmarks for efficiency, or it may be possible for an organization to track its efficiency performance over time with reference to past data. For example, a hospital heart surgery department could calculate the cost per operation performed. This could then be compared to similar data from other hospitals or tracked over several years to measure the efficiency of the department.

Value for money (VFM) as a public-sector objective

In many public sector organizations the principle of the 3Es is implemented under the term **value for money (VFM)**. VFM can be defined as the optimal use of resources to achieve the intended outcomes. An organization is said to be achieving high VFM when there is an optimum balance between the 3Es: relatively low costs (economy), high productivity (efficiency) and successful outcomes (effectiveness).

NPO performance measurement: an example

Extract 6.5 presents a balanced scorecard developed by the Kenya Red Cross Society. The mission of the society is 'to work with vigour and compassion through our networks and with communities to prevent and alleviate human suffering and save lives of the most vulnerable'. The society's strategic vision is 'to be the most effective, trusted and self-sustaining humanitarian organization in Kenya'.

From this mission statement and strategic vision the society has derived the following four perspectives: beneficiary/stakeholder; financial stewardship; business processes; and organization capacity. Each of these perspectives has been given a small number of objectives against which performance measures and targets have been set. These are set out below.

Extract 6.5: NPO Balanced scorecard

Objective	Performance measure	Target
Perspective: beneficiary/stakeholder		
Improve livelihoods	• Households that meet minimum standards	50% 20%
	• Reduction on relief aid in target communities	100%
	• Lives saved during emergencies	
Increase contribution to national policy	• Activities supported by legal framework	100% 75%
	• Appropriate national policies contributed to	100%
	• Projects aligned to appropriate national policy	
Enhance community ownership	• Average age of projects running after completion	10 yrs
	• Contribution to project budget by community	20% TBD
	• Projects replicated by community and partners	
Increase access to services	• Services within the standard distance	95% TBD
	• Beneficiaries reached	75%
	• Information available to stakeholders	
Perspective: financial stewardship		
Optimize resource utilization	• Percentage of core cost to total cost	30% TBD
	• Cost per beneficiary	

Objective	Performance measure	Target
Perspective: business processes		
Improve service delivery	• Increase in integrated programme	80%
	• Programme success	95%
	• Programme standards compliance	100%
Strengthen partnerships	• Active partnerships	95%
	• Formal partnerships	95%
	• Partner confidence score	80%
Strengthen disaster risk management (DRM) processes	• Incidences responded to on time	100%
	• Compliance to DRM process standards	100%
		20%
	• People assisted	
Perspective: organization capacity		
Strengthen branch network and infrastructure	• Branches meeting minimum standards	100%
		60%
	• Participation in membership activities	TBD
	• Income raised locally	
Internalize the economic engine	• Core costs paid from own funds	50%
	• Funding gap	100%
	• Growth in disaster fund	20%
Improve human resource alignment	• Job satisfaction index	95%
	• Staff retention	TBD
	• Appropriate skills and competencies	TBD
		80%
	• Percentage of hours spent on projects	
Improve health and safety	• Emblem awareness index	TBD
	• Reduce incidences to staff	ZERO
	• Safety compliance score	100%
Improve knowledge management	• Evidence-based decision making	100%
	• Documentation and dissemination of lessons	95%
		TBD
	• Employee information awareness	

Behavioural aspects of performance management: gaming and creative accounting

Performance measurement has an impact on the environment in which it operates and will influence the behaviour of those whose performance is being measured. Deciding what to measure, how to measure it and what targets to set will all influence employee behaviour. Sometimes this can have unintended negative consequences.

One important consequence of the increased emphasis on performance measures is the pressure that performance measurement puts on employees. Research shows that the increasing demands of performance measurement systems can increase tension, frustration, resentment, suspicion, fear and mistrust in employees. This in turn reduces employee job satisfaction, increases absenteeism and has been shown to result in a reduction in long-term performance.

Other research has identified how employees respond to performance measures. One consequence is that 'what gets measured gets done'. If employees know that their performance is being measured, they will inevitably focus on achieving those targets against which they know they will be assessed. This may be to the detriment of other areas of performance. A further problem is that multiple and diverse performance measures may generate tension and conflict between performance targets. This can cause confusion and distrust of performance measures and can prove to be demotivating.

Another behavioural risk of setting performance measures is that managers will take actions to improve their measured scores through 'creative accounting' without improving underlying performance. Many examples of such practices can be found across a wide range of industries. For example, hospitals that are assessed on the length of waiting lists have redefined and delayed the point at which a patient enters the waiting list. Repair and maintenance departments that are assessed on how quickly they respond to repair requests similarly redefine and delay the point at which a request is formally recognized and therefore when the 'clock starts ticking'. In many cases these changes, which are effectively a manipulation of the definition of waiting time, mean that there is no actual improvement in performance.

A further problem can arise with benchmarking, which is a process intended to assess and improve performance. Sometimes managers will use benchmarking to defend rather than improve poor performance. The manager will focus on explaining why their department or organization performed poorly against the benchmark, citing factors that make their situation different from those against which it is being assessed. In such cases, the benchmarking exercise leads to little or no improvement in performance.

Exercises: now attempt Exercise 6.4 on page 241

External influences on performance

All organizations, whether they be profit-seeking or not-for-profit, are experiencing increased external scrutiny and pressure to meet the expectations of external stakeholders. Current academic work on external financial reporting is greatly concerned with impression management and measures of corporate social responsibility. As a consequence, performance management is increasingly being used to assess the impact of organizational actions on stakeholders outside the organization.

These developments are reflected in the widespread use of the balanced scorecard and other similar models of performance management which include measures of the impact of the organization's performance on customer satisfaction, employee satisfaction or local community satisfaction. This in turn has shaped the way in

FIGURE 6.3 PEST analysis: a framework of focusing managers' attention on those external factors (political, economic, social and technological) that may impact upon organizational performance

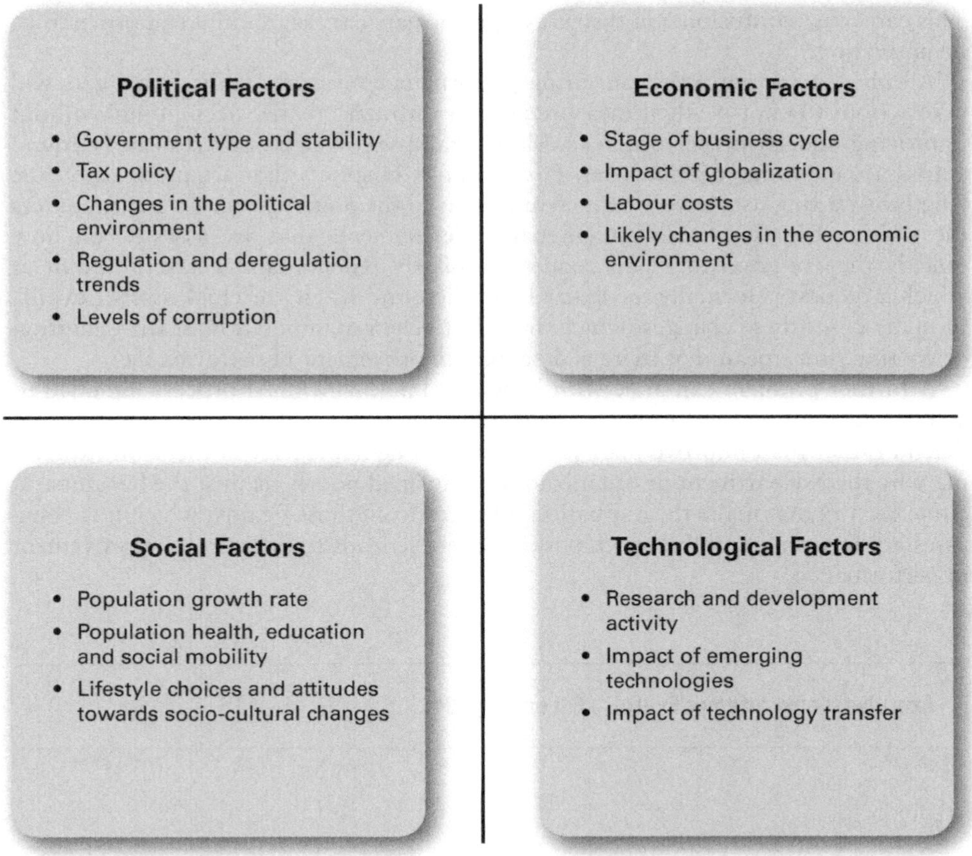

Political Factors

- Government type and stability
- Tax policy
- Changes in the political environment
- Regulation and deregulation trends
- Levels of corruption

Economic Factors

- Stage of business cycle
- Impact of globalization
- Labour costs
- Likely changes in the economic environment

Social Factors

- Population growth rate
- Population health, education and social mobility
- Lifestyle choices and attitudes towards socio-cultural changes

Technological Factors

- Research and development activity
- Impact of emerging technologies
- Impact of technology transfer

which performance management systems are developed and the kind of performance measures that are used. Techniques are now widely used to assist management in identifying and assessing those external factors which can impact on organizational performance and which therefore need to be taken into consideration in performance management. These include tools such as PEST analysis (Figure 6.3) and Porter's five forces model.

There has also been an increased need to interpret performance in the light of external considerations and, in particular, societal ethical issues that may impact on business performance. Performance measurement is now turning to factors such as carbon footprinting, sustainable use of resources, ethical sourcing of materials, employee welfare, pollution and recycling.

Performance management in modern business systems

Recent developments in management accounting such as target costing, life-cycle costing, just-in-time (JIT), throughput accounting and total quality management (TQM) have changed the nature and use of performance measures within many organizations. This raises the question of whether traditional performance measurement accounting techniques such as standard costing still have a place in modern business systems.

One of the common features of the techniques mentioned above is a move towards viewing the organization more holistically as a system or flow of processes rather than a collection of individual activities. Management attention is therefore directed towards improving overall performance rather than optimizing the performance of individual areas in isolation. This can lead to some conclusions about performance that are counter-intuitive to those focused on traditional measures.

For example, throughput accounting is concerned with improving the overall efficiency of total production processes. There is a focus on identifying and removing bottlenecks in production systems. Businesses employing the principles of throughput accounting have often found that overall performance is improved by allowing an increase in idle time in some areas of the system and by substantially reducing production batch sizes. Under traditional variance analysis idle time is seen as an evil which should be eradicated. Equally, it can be hard to grasp how overall financial performance can be improved by cutting batch sizes, as this means a greater number of smaller orders, more set-ups (with a resultant increase in idle time) and more deliveries. These factors all results in higher costs. However, because throughput accounting looks at the holistic picture, such changes can substantially reduce inventory levels which in turn reduces the amount of money the business has tied up in inventory, together with cutting costs of damaged, lost and obsolete inventory. Also, smaller batch sizes can result in a more flexible approach to production which means meeting customer needs more closely and more quickly. This can give the business an important competitive advantage. As a result of these changes, sales volumes and production throughput can be significantly increased. This can create economies of scale which can lower operating costs to offset the higher costs associated with smaller batch sizes.

So these new accounting techniques together with new approaches to manufacturing have brought new challenges for control and performance measurement. There is a change in emphasis towards performance measures that encompass both financial and non-financial aspects, such as measures of on-time deliveries, reduction in inventory, cooperation with suppliers, process cost reduction, quality improvement, reduced cycle time and product complexity.

Furthermore, these new techniques bring with them the aims of continuous innovation, change and development. For example, a JIT approach involves continuous improvement and a commitment to constant change. Performance measurement systems are required that encourage employees to focus on the critical elements of efficient operations and to provide effective links across the value chain. Continuous improvement and innovation are also important aspects of TQM. This approach needs performance measurement systems that incorporate benchmarking against industry competitors and the integration of quality and strategic information. Within this context, traditional management accounting performance measures can be regarded as an impediment. Focus has moved from recording and reporting costs and cost variances against budget, to understanding and controlling the causes of costs. Organizations need organic and flexible performance management systems.

However, these new developments do not totally negate the usefulness of standards and standard costing. In many organizations they have been integrated into these new techniques. For example, target costing, with its emphasis on continuous improvement, requires a review of resources used in the past to identify where fewer resources might be used in the future. This can involve reviewing old standards and setting new standards for improvement.

Extract 6.6: Performance management at Toyota

Toyota, the Japanese manufacturing giant, employs the philosophy of just in time as part of its performance management and production control systems. The company calls its approach the Toyota Production System (TPS). The company's philosophy is to 'make only what is needed, when it is needed, and in the amount needed'. This approach means that the focus of performance management is upon the flow of parts into production and the flow of items through the production process. Parts should be available just when they are needed within the production process and they should be available in the right place at that time. Toyota concentrates its performance management on measuring and fine-tuning work cycle times, workflow, optimum movement of products and reducing waste time, materials and capacity.

Exercises: now attempt Exercise 6.2 on page 240

Conclusion

We started this chapter by describing how performance management is a multidisciplinary activity which extends beyond accounting to virtually every area of organizational management. We have described some of the basic principles of performance management and looked in some detail at traditional techniques. We have also looked at recent developments in performance management and how tools and techniques have responded to changes in modern management practices. In particular, this chapter has emphasized how performance management has moved away from purely financial measures to a broader perspective which encompasses non-financial aspects of performance and the considerations of external stakeholders.

COMPREHENSION QUESTIONS

1 What are the four main ways of delegating responsibility for budget management?

2 What are the advantages and disadvantages of using flexible budgets?

3 What type of standard costing system would be most appropriate for a manufacturing business that uses budget targets as part of its employee motivation and reward package?

4 Compare the relative advantages of ROI and EVA as divisional performance measures.

5 What are the four perspectives of the balanced scorecard as originally recommended by Kaplan and Norton?

6 Explain how the concept of VFM can be used to measure performance in a public-sector organization.

7 Explain how performance measures may have unintended behavioural consequences.

Answers on pages 242–243

Exercises

Answers on pages 244–246

Exercise 6.1: Evaluating cost variances

Walkon Co manufactures wooden flooring. The company buys timber which it cuts to standard-length boards, sands and polishes to sell on to builders. The variance analysis shown in Table 6.6 has been produced for the production department for the last accounting period.

TABLE 6.6

	$
Material price variance	20,000 (F)
Material usage variance	25,000 (A)
Labour rate of variance	14,000 (A)
Labour efficiency variance	18,000 (F)
Variable overhead expenditure variance	13,000 (A)
Variable overhead efficiency variance	8,000 (F)
Fixed overhead expenditure variance	10,000 (F)

F = favourable variance; A = adverse variance

In response to the variance analysis the production manager has made the following comments:

1 We were experiencing poor staff morale and a high staff turnover so I increased wage rates during the period. I believe that this has improved staff morale and produced a positive benefit to the company.

2 I was able to source an alternative supplier of raw materials. I negotiated a very good price which I believe has saved the company a considerable amount of money.

3 We had a large sanding machine which I felt was not being sufficiently used and was therefore costing the business too much money. I sold this machine and hired a sander only when we needed one.

Required:
Comment on the performance of the production department based upon the variance analysis and the comments from the production manager provided above.

Exercise 6.2: Total quality management

Coat Co manufactures men's clothing. The company has for many years operated a traditional standard costing and variance analysis approach to performance management. The marketing director has recently been on a training course about quality improvement and has suggested that the company moves to a TQM approach to performance management. His recommendation will be considered at the next meeting of the board of directors.

Required:
Write a brief report which considers some of the practical issues that Coat Co would face should the company decide to change from a standard costing to a TQM approach to performance management.

Exercise 6.3: Non-financial performance indicators

Jake Designs is a small firm which specializes as a consultant in product packaging and marketing within the cosmetics industry. The company recently appointed a new finance director, Katie Williams. In her first meeting with the CEO of Jake Designs, Jake McLeod, Katie expressed concerns at the limited focus of the current performance management system. Katie explained that, although the current system provided good details of the financial performance of the business, it is also important to include non-financial performance indicators, particularly those which will provide a better indication of the future performance of the business. She has suggested that the following performance measures should be reported to the board of directors:

- number of customers;
- average fees per customer;
- average job completion time;
- employee turnover rate;
- employee job satisfaction;
- level of customer satisfaction;
- percentage of revenue from new customers.

Jake McLeod is sceptical about Katie's suggestion. He is concerned that these additional performance measures will just cause more work for the accounting department and may act as a distraction from more important tasks such as ensuring that invoices go out promptly and customers pay on time.

Required:
Explain why the inclusion within the performance management system of the non-financial information suggested by Katie will provide a better indication of potential future success of the business.

Exercise 6.4: Negative behavioural consequences

Tools4U Co operates a chain of tool hire stores across the country. Tool purchases and store staffing levels are managed centrally, so each store is treated as a revenue centre, with the store manager being responsible for the level of sales revenue earned, but not the costs. Store managers earn a bonus of 10 per cent of their salary if the outlet exceeds sales revenue targets for the year.

Required:
Identify how a store manager may be able to manipulate results in order to gain more frequent bonuses.

Answers to comprehension questions

1   The level of budgetary responsibility delegated to an individual manager will depend upon a number of factors such as organizational structure and management philosophy. Budgetary responsibility is usually categorized into one of the following four types:

   (a)   Cost centre – the manager of a cost centre is responsible for managing costs only.

   (b)   Revenue centre – the manager of a revenue centre is responsible for managing revenues only.

   (c)   Profit centre – the manager of a profit centre is responsible for managing both revenues and costs, and therefore the profit of the centre.

   (d)   Investment centre – the manager of an investment centre will be responsible for costs and revenues and also the level of investment in non-current assets.

2   A flexible budgeting approach enables the business to adjust its original budget to reflect the actual level of activity. This approach is useful for businesses with uncertain or unstable levels of activity as it enables them to fine-tune budgets. This in turn provides more useful levels of information for management.

   However, a flexible budgeting approach is not appropriate for an organization that has a fixed level of funding. Such an organization needs to operate within the confines of the original budget. In such cases, a fixed budgeting approach would be more appropriate.

3   The effectiveness of budgetary targets in improving employee performance will depend on how achievable employees perceive the target to be. If targets are too low this may actually pull performance downwards from where it would have been with no targets at all. If targets are too high then employees may give up and again performance will be reduced from what it could be. It is therefore important that standards which provide demanding but achievable budget targets for employees are used.

   It would be best for this business to use attainable but demanding standards. If ideal standards were used, actual performance would consistently fall below budget targets and this would have a demotivating effect on employees rather than act as an incentive. Basic standards are inappropriate in this situation as they are unlikely to provide suitably demanding targets for employee motivation. Standards which are attainable by employees based on current working practices should be set. However, management can make these demanding in order to maximize employee performance.

4 ROI (return on investment) measures the performance of a division by taking its operating income as a percentage of the assets employed to earn that income. Because the measure is a percentage, this enables easy comparison between different divisions and different companies of different sizes. However, the disadvantage of ROI is that the metric discourages managers from investing in new projects which offer a return less than existing ROI, even if that project represents a good investment for the business as a whole.

   EVA overcomes this disadvantage of ROI by measuring performance in absolute terms. Any investment which offers a return above that required by the company as a whole will appear favourable using the EVA measure. Also, because EVA incorporates a charge for capital, it focuses managers' awareness on the fact that capital has a cost and that both the income statement and the balance sheet are important when considering performance levels.

5 The four perspectives of the balanced scorecard are *financial, customer, internal* and *learning and growth* (sometimes referred to as *innovation*). Kaplan and Norton maintained that the business should measure its performance from all four of these perspectives and not just from a financial perspective.

6 Value for money can be defined as the optimal use of resources to achieve the organization's intended outcomes. This is usually measured using the '3E's' of economy, effectiveness and efficiency. Economy refers to the organization successfully operating within given resources. Effectiveness refers to how well the organization achieves its intended outcomes. Efficiency refers to the relationship between inputs and outputs.

7 When employees know that their performance is being measured in certain areas, they will concentrate their efforts on ensuring that they meet these performances and will be less inclined to perform well in other areas that are not being measured. For example, if the customer services department of a business is being measured on how quickly it answers telephone calls, it may concentrate on answering and dealing with calls quickly rather than on the quality of the service provided to customers. Such problems mean that any performance indicators and targets must be chosen very carefully to avoid negative behavioural consequences.

Exercise 6.1: Evaluating cost variances

The variances reported for the last accounting period appear to reflect some of the decisions made by the production manager. When assessing these variances it is important to consider the whole picture and the interrelationships between the different variances.

Material variances

It is clear that the production manager has negotiated a better price on purchases. This has saved the company $20,000 in material purchase costs. However, the adverse material usage variance suggests that this cheaper supply of wood may have been of an inferior quality. There will inevitably be wastage in converting timber into floorboards. In this case the usage variance is $25,000 adverse. This represents a considerable increase in the amount of wastage. Furthermore, the cost of this additional wastage outweighs the saving in purchase price of the material. In retrospect, the change to a cheaper supplier may not have been a wise move.

Labour variances

The production manager gave staff a wage increase during the period and the effectiveness can be seen in the adverse labour rate variance of $14,000. The production manager claims that this increase has improved staff morale and performance. The labour efficiency variance appears to bear out this claim as this shows an $18,000 favourable variance. This labour efficiency variance must also be evaluated in conjunction with the material usage variance. An adverse material usage variance is often associated with an adverse labour efficiency variance. In this case the labour efficiency variance is favourable despite the adverse material usage variance. It would therefore appear that the production manager is correct and the wage increase awarded to the production staff has had a beneficial impact on the company. The adverse labour rate variance is more than offset by the favourable labour efficiency variance, with a net benefit of $4,000 for the company.

Overhead variances

The production manager sold the sanding machine which he believed was being under-utilized and therefore costing the company too much money. The impact of this sale can be seen in the favourable fixed overhead expenditure variance. No longer owning this machine is saving the company $10,000 per accounting period.

However, in place of this machine the manager is now hiring in sanding equipment when needed. These higher costs will be reflected in the variable overhead expenditure. As the variable overhead expenditure variance is $13,000 adverse, this would suggest that the decision was not a good one. Even though the sanding machine may have been idle much of the time, it was still costing the company less than hiring in the machine when needed.

Exercise 6.2: Total quality management

Standard costing and TQM involve different cultures and therefore a change from one to the other would require a change in the mindset of all employees. The most significant cultural change would be a move in emphasis from one of quantity to one of quality. The focus of standard costing is reducing costs. This can be totally at odds with a TQM culture in which favourable changes may involve increasing costs.

There will also be a change in allocation of responsibilities within the company. A standard costing system allocates responsibility for variances to individual departments. If a TQM system were adopted, every employee would be seen as equally responsible in the quality assurance process.

There would also be changes in attitudes towards waste and idle time. A standard costing system makes allowances for waste and idle time. This is contrary to the TQM philosophy which aims to eliminate both of these issues.

The TQM approach is based upon a philosophy of continuous improvement which would involve moving away from the idea of working to fixed standards. Employees would need to adjust to working in an environment where regular small changes to processes and procedures were the norm.

Exercise 6.3: Non-financial performance indicators

Katie Williams is effectively suggesting a balanced scorecard approach towards performance management. This approach involves producing a range of performance measures which cover four important perspectives on business performance:

- the financial perspective;
- the customer perspective;
- the internal perspective;
- the learning and growth perspective.

The reason for including performance measures in relation to these additional perspectives (customer, internal, and learning and growth) is that these are the factors which will lead to good financial performance in the future. The problem with financial performance indicators is that they generally only give a measure of past performance. Good financial performance in the past is no guarantee of good financial performance in the future.

The business needs to ensure that it is continuing to meet the needs of clients so that they do not go elsewhere. Likewise, the business needs to look at how it is operating in order to ensure that costs remain low and operational performance is effective. Non-financial measures are often regarded as indicators of future financial performance because good performance in these measures will lead to good financial results. For example, good levels of customer satisfaction will lead to customer retention and the attraction of new customers. Similarly, high staff morale and low staff turnover result in skill retention and reduced recruitment and training costs.

Exercise 6.4: Negative behavioural consequences

A store manager may attempt to improve his bonuses by manipulating profit. If the manager anticipated that sales were going to fall below targets, he might take action in order to boost the level of sales in the year.

As the manager is responsible for sales revenue and not costs, he may be tempted to undertake activities which boost sales but not necessarily profit. This might include offering discounts to customers in order to attract more sales, or offering 'free' extras such as extended hire or the hire of additional equipment at no further cost.

If the manager suspected that he was not going to meet his targets as he got close to the year-end, he might raise some invoices early for orders he knew were going to come in immediately after the year-end. The manager could raise these invoices before the year-end (and not actually send them out to the customer) so that the sales will be recorded before the year-end and overall sales for the year increased. This, of course, represents fraudulent activity and Tools4U Co should implement suitable internal controls to prevent such practices.

Cash flow

OBJECTIVE

To provide an understanding of the importance of cash management to a business and the impact of management strategies on cash flow and liquidity.

LEARNING OUTCOMES

After studying this chapter, the reader will be able to:

- Discuss the importance of cash management to a business.
- Interpret a cash budget and identify potential problems.
- Formulate strategies for improving cash flow and liquidity.

KEY TOPICS COVERED

- The cash-flow cycle.
- Information which a cash budget provides, and why this is important.
- The format and construction of a cash-flow forecast.
- The evaluation of different decisions which impact on cash requirements (financing of asset purchases, credit terms to customers).
- Strategies for improving cash flow.

MANAGEMENT ISSUES

Managers need the ability to evaluate the impact of managerial decisions and strategies on cash requirements. They also need to be able to analyse cash budgets and use them to make appropriate managerial decisions.

Introduction

Planning and managing cash flows lies at the centre of business success. We hear many aphorisms which confirm how important this is: 'cash is king' and 'cash is the lifeblood of the business' are two commonly used expressions. Why is this the case? Quite simply, a business cannot survive without cash. It is possible for a business to function for several years without making a profit provided that it still has cash. But once the cash runs out the business will very quickly fail. This was the fate of many so-called 'dot-com' businesses in the 1990s.

> **Extract 7.1: Cash flow and small business failure**
>
> Dun and Bradstreet, one of the world's leading credit rating agencies, report that 90 per cent of small business failures are caused by poor cash flow.

Why does a business need cash?

Cash is needed in a business for a number of reasons: to purchase inventory and to pay wages, rent, utility bills etc. A business also needs cash to purchase assets such as machinery, equipment, vehicles and premises. In addition, cash is needed to pay dividends to investors, pay interest on loans and pay any taxes due. On top of this, at any one time a business may have cash tied up in current assets such as inventory and accounts receivable. This will be a normal part of operating the business, but the more money that is tied up in assets the greater the cash requirement for the business. For example, if a business offers credit to its customers, this will delay the receipt of cash from sales and will in turn increase the amount of cash the business needs because it still needs to pay wages and other bills. In a similar fashion, if a business increases its levels of inventory it will also increase its need for cash.

What is cash flow?

Cash flow refers to the ways in which cash moves in and out of a business through receipts and payments and also how it circulates within the business to be tied up in various assets such as inventory of accounts receivable. This flow of cash is represented in Figure 7.1. How quickly that cash flows and how much cash is tied up in assets will dictate the cash requirements of the business.

Cash flow within a business is usually categorized into three different aspects:

- **Operating cash flow**: cash flowing in and out of the business from normal day-to-day operations such as receipts from sales and payments for wages, purchases of inventory, utility bills and rent.

- **Investment cash flow**: the flow of cash in and out of the business relating to the purchase and sale of non-current assets.
- **Financing cash flow**: cash inflows from new financing such as new equity or loans and cash outflows from repayment of financing and payment of interest and dividends.

These three aspects of cash flow are all included within Figure 7.1.

FIGURE 7.1   Cash flows in a typical business

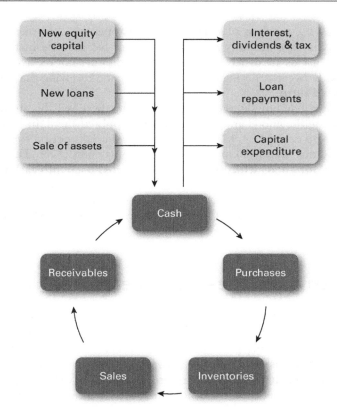

The **cash-flow cycle** (sometimes known as the **cash conversion cycle**) refers to the circular flow of cash shown at the bottom of Figure 7.1. During the normal operations of a business, cash gets tied up in working capital: cash is used to pay for purchases and becomes tied up in inventory. This inventory must be sold and the sales revenue collected from customers before it is converted back into cash. The cash-flow cycle measures the length of time in days that it takes for a business to convert purchases into cash. This is an important metric as it can provide the foundation for establishing how much cash the business needs. The faster cash flows around this cycle, the less is tied up in working capital and therefore the less cash the business needs. Figure 7.2 shows this cycle for a typical business.

FIGURE 7.2 The cash conversion cycle

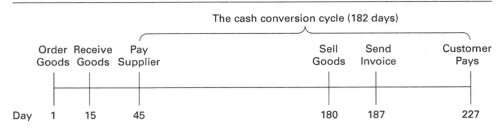

Figure 7.2 shows a timeline of what typically happens within the business from ordering goods in to eventually receiving payment for the sale of those goods to a customer. The goods are ordered in on day 1 but they are not received until day 15. This time lapse between ordering the goods (day 1) and receiving the goods (day 15) is known as **lead time**.

If the business has bought the goods on credit, there will be another time lag between receiving the goods and paying for the supply of them. In Figure 7.2 there is a time lag of 30 days (45 – 15) which is a typical credit period for a supplier. At this point the clock starts ticking on the cash conversion cycle. The business has paid out money for goods which will not be converted back into cash until they are sold and the customer has paid. The cash conversion cycle is therefore the time lapse between paying a supplier and receiving payment from the customer. In Figure 7.2 the supplier is paid on day 45 and the customer pays on day 227. The cash conversion cycle is therefore 182 days (227 – 45).

How much cash does a business need?

The amount of cash which a business chooses to hold will always be a trade-off between costs and benefits. Both holding too much cash and holding too little cash can have a cost to the business. On the one hand, there is a cost to holding cash and so the more cash the business holds the greater the cost. This is usually measured as an **opportunity cost**, that is to say, the return that could have been earned by invest-ing the cash in other assets. On the other hand, there is also a cost to raising cash if it is not available when needed. So if a business holds too little cash, this will also create costs. This will be either the cost of converting assets into cash (by selling them) or the cost of arranging loans.

Cash, unless it is held in a high-interest investment account, represents shareholders' capital that is not being put to work earning a return for the investors. There will therefore be a pressure to reduce the amount of cash the business holds. The lower the cash balances, the lower the amount of capital the business uses to operate. Reducing cash will improve the return on capital employed (ROCE), as demonstrated in Worked Example 7.1.

WORKED EXAMPLE 7.1   Cash balance and ROCE

Quint Co earns a profit before interest and tax of $280,000. The company has total capital of $1,850,000. The current ROCE is therefore:

$$\text{ROCE} = \frac{\$280,000}{\$1,850,000} = 15.14\%$$

Included within the capital of $1,850,000 is a cash balance of $300,000. The finance director decides that the company does not need to hold this cash and therefore uses it to repay a loan.

This action will reduce the capital of the business to $1,550,000. This in turn increases the ROCE:

$$\text{ROCE} = \frac{\$280,000}{\$1,550,000} = 18.06\%$$

The company is therefore able to increase its financial performance (as indicated by ROCE) without any change in the level of profit simply by reducing its cash balance.

Extract 7.2: Cash mountain at Microsoft

Microsoft, the US software giant, generates over US$20bn in excess cash every year and consequently is sitting on a mountain of cash. You might think that this is an enviable position to be in, but in fact it is a major headache for the company. This is an unutilized asset that is substantially lowering the ROCE. How does Microsoft deal with this? Large cash balances require large investments to use them up and the most expensive investments are usually acquisitions – buying up other companies. This is why we see Microsoft making a series of high-cost takeovers – Hotmail, Skype, Firefly, CompareNet, Yammer... the list is long. Microsoft has recorded over 150 corporate acquisitions since 1987. They need to in order to use up all that cash.

Although Worked Example 7.1 demonstrates that holding too much cash can have a negative impact on the business's financial performance, if the business does not hold sufficient cash it can experience trading problems (such as **overtrading**) which will also have a negative impact on profitability and shareholder returns. This means that a business is constantly seeking to hold just enough cash to meet its needs, but no more than is necessary. Managing cash is a constant balancing act between having too much cash and not enough.

Expert view 7.1: Cash flow and overtrading

Overtrading is a problem which hits many businesses. It occurs when the business tries to grow too quickly and has insufficient funds to pay the increasing costs which accompany an increase in sales. A growing order book may seem like good news, but it also creates a demand for more cash within the business. Meeting growing levels of sales also requires increases in working capital: more inventory and more money tied up in trade receivables. Extra orders may also mean overtime payments to employees and the purchase of more equipment. A business therefore needs to manage its growth carefully to ensure that it can be funded.

The amount of cash which an individual business needs to hold will depend upon the nature of its operations and the attitudes of its managers. Financial theory categorizes the reasons for holding cash into four 'motives':

- the transaction motive;
- the precautionary motive;
- the speculative motive; and
- the compensating balances motive.

The transaction motive

Any business will need to hold a certain amount of cash in order to pay the day-to-day bills. For most businesses, there will be a gap between receiving cash from sales and needing cash to make payments to employees and for purchases, utilities and equipment. The greater this gap, the more cash the business will need to hold. This cash may be held directly by the business (in cash registers and secure safes) or may be held in non-interest-bearing bank accounts. Some businesses hold a balance of cash in deposit accounts which earns some interest. Because such accounts provide easy access to cash, interest rates are usually low; better returns will be available elsewhere.

The precautionary motive

Most businesses will wish to hold a certain reserve of cash in case of emergencies. This will include unforeseen and unexpected expenses and may be referred to as 'financial slack'. If a business does not have a certain amount of slack in its cash balances, it may have to raise money quickly and in the short term if an unexpected need arises. This could prove to be very costly. Research has shown that although holding precautionary cash balances has a cost, this is less than the cost of having to raise cash at short notice when an emergency arises.

Extract 7.3: Cash holdings and the rise of the precautionary motive

You might expect that the improvements in information and financial systems over recent years have enabled businesses to reduce their cash holdings. In fact, the opposite is true. The average cash to assets ratio of industrial companies in the United States has more than doubled since 1980. Research has identified that this trend correlates with industry risk – ie businesses are holding more cash to protect themselves against riskier cash flows: the precautionary motive. The situation is amplified by the fact that new manufacturing technologies have reduced inventories and receivables, thus tying up less cash in other assets.

The speculative motive

Businesses will also hold cash in order to be able to take advantage of unexpected opportunities such as new investments, changes in interest rates and favourable fluctuations in exchange rates. Good investments may be missed if the business does not have funding readily available. If interest rates are low, businesses will typically maintain higher speculative balances of cash; if interest rates are high, businesses will commit these balances to high-yield investments.

Extract 7.4: ING Direct and Emirates – speculative gains

Businesses that have sufficient cash funds available at the right time are able to benefit from unexpected opportunities. The benefit is often greater if competitors are not in a similar position to take up the opportunity:

At the time of the Icelandic banking crisis, ING Direct snapped up the deposits being offloaded by failing Icelandic banks.

Emirates bought up the new Airbus A380 at a time when other airlines had insufficient funds due to the industry downturn after 11 September 2001. This gave Emirates a competitive advantage as the A380 had greater range, passenger capacity and fuel economy than the planes being used by competitors.

The compensating balances motive

Most businesses that maintain current accounts with commercial banks are required to maintain a minimum balance in their account. This minimum balance, referred to as the compensating balance, is to compensate the bank for the services they provide and essentially provides the bank with free use of the business's money. If such a balance is not maintained, higher fees are normally imposed by the bank.

Methods of establishing cash balances

A number of models have been developed to assist managers in establishing appropriate cash levels. In this chapter we will look at the two most popular and widely used models: the Baumol–Tobin model and the Miller–Orr model. Each model takes a very different approach to establishing the cash balance that a business should hold.

The Baumol–Tobin model of cash management

The Baumol–Tobin model is a transaction-based model which assumes that a business's demand for cash is consistent over time and can be predicted with certainty. As a business uses its available cash it will need to convert investments into cash by selling them. This will incur transaction costs and therefore there is an incentive to minimize the number of such sales. However, if large quantities of cash are converted each time, there will be a high opportunity cost of lost interest because of holding cash balances rather than investments. The model therefore attempts to establish optimum cash balances by determining the amount of cash that should be converted from investments each time cash is required.

The Baumol–Tobin model therefore attempts to establish optimum cash balances by quantifying the trade-off between the opportunity costs of holding too much cash and the transaction costs involved in holding too little cash. This trade-off can be represented diagrammatically as shown in Figure 7.3.

The opportunity costs represent the interest forgone by holding funds as cash rather than placing them in an investment. These costs rise with the size of the cash balance.

The trading costs represent the costs of having to raise cash in the short term either by liquidating assets or by taking out a loan. The lower the size of the cash balance, the higher these trading costs will be.

If frequent small conversions to cash are made, average cash balances will be low and opportunity costs minimized, but trading costs will be high owing to the high frequency of transactions. See Figure 7.4.

On the other hand, if large quantities of investments are converted to cash, trading costs will be minimized but average cash balances and therefore opportunity costs will be high. See Figure 7.5.

Using the Baumol–Tobin model, the business attempts to minimize the total costs of holding cash, which will be made up of both trading costs and opportunity costs. Thus, the optimal cash balance (ie that which has the lowest total cost to the business) is found where the opportunity cost equals the trading cost (see Figure 7.3).

FIGURE 7.3   The cost of holding cash

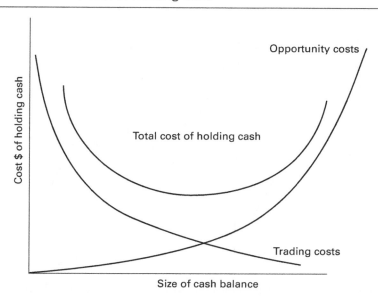

FIGURE 7.4   Frequent cash conversions

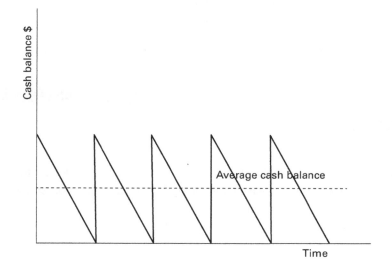

FIGURE 7.5   Infrequent cash conversions

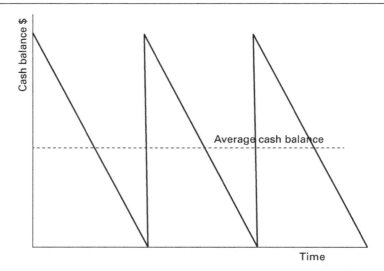

The Baumol–Tobin model determines the optimum quantity of cash to convert each time cash is required. This quantity is represented mathematically by the expression:

$$C = \sqrt{\frac{2TF}{K}}$$

Where: C = the optimal cash order quantity
             T = the total amount of cash needed in a period
             F = the cost of selling assets to raise cash
             K = the opportunity cost of holding cash (the interest rate)

WORKED EXAMPLE 7.2   The Baumol–Tobin model

The following information relates to Ergin Co: the fixed cost of selling assets to raise cash is $500; cash outflows exceed cash inflows by $9,000 per week; the interest rate earned on marketable securities is 5 per cent.

   What is the optimum cash balance for Ergin Co?

Answer
Using the Baumol–Tobin model:

$$C = \sqrt{\frac{2TF}{K}} = \sqrt{\frac{2 \times \$9,000 \times \$500}{5\%}} = \$13,416$$

So when the Ergin Co requires cash, it should convert $13,416. This means that the average cash balance carried by the business will be approximately $6,708 (13,416 ÷ 2).

The Baumol–Tobin model suggests that when interest rates are high, cash balances should be kept to a minimum. However, the model is based upon a number of assumptions, which reduces its usefulness in complex real-world situations. The model assumes that:

- Cash outflows are predictable and even over time.
- Cash inflows are predictable and regular.
- Day-to-day cash needs are funded from a bank current account.
- A 'buffer' of short-term investments is held which can be liquidated to provide cash when needed.

In practice these assumptions do not hold true for most businesses. In particular, cash inflows and outflows are not even and regular and can be difficult to predict. Therefore a more useful model for cash management is one which allows for irregularity and fluctuations in cash flows. One such model is the Miller–Orr model.

The Miller–Orr model of cash management

The Miller–Orr model provides a method of cash management for businesses that do not have uniform cash flow and therefore find it difficult to predict levels and timing of cash inflows and outflows. The model allows for daily variations in the cash balance within prescribed control limits known as the **upper limit** and the **lower limit**.

The model is applied by firstly deciding upon a minimum acceptable cash balance (the lower limit). This is set by management and will be used to establish a buffer of cash for emergencies. The lower limit will depend upon how much risk of a cash shortfall management are willing to accept. This in turn will depend upon the consequences (and costs) of experiencing a cash shortfall together with how quickly and easily the business can access additional funds.

Having established this minimum cash balance, the Miller–Orr model can be used to establish a maximum cash balance (the upper limit) and a **return point**. The return point represents the optimum cash balance. Cash is then managed as follows:

If cash levels reach the upper limit, an amount is transferred into investments in order to bring the cash balance back down to the return point.

If cash levels drop to the minimum level, an amount is converted from investments into cash to bring the cash balance back up to the return point.

This principle is demonstrated in the diagram in Figure 7.6.

The difference between the upper limit and the lower limit is known as the **spread**. This is calculated using the formula shown in Figure 7.7.

FIGURE 7.6 Cash limits

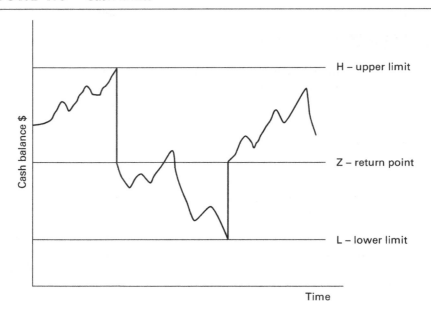

FIGURE 7.7 The spread formula

$$\text{Spread} = 3\left[\frac{\tfrac{3}{4} \times \begin{array}{c}\text{transaction} \\ \text{costs}\end{array} \times \begin{array}{c}\text{variance of} \\ \text{cash flows}\end{array}}{\text{Interest rate}}\right]^{1/3}$$

In the figure:

- The transaction costs represent the cost of converting short-term investments into cash or vice versa.
- The variance of cash flows is a measure of the fluctuation in the cash flows and therefore cash balances. The assumption underlying the Miller–Orr model is that although cash balances can fluctuate randomly, these fluctuations are normally distributed. It is therefore possible to calculate a mean balance and standard deviation of cash balances based upon past data (Variance = Standard deviation^2).
- The interest rate represents the return that can be earned by converting cash into marketable securities or other similar investments.

Both the variance and interest rates should be expressed in daily terms.

Once the spread is calculated, the return point can be found using the following formula:

$$\text{Return point} = \text{Lower limit} + (1/3 \times \text{spread})$$

We will now see how this model is applied using a simple illustration in Worked Example 7.3.

WORKED EXAMPLE 7.3　The Miller–Orr model

Zetoc Co sets its minimum cash balance at $5,000 and estimates the following:

- Transaction costs = $500 per sale or purchase of short-term investment.
- Standard deviation of cash flows = $1,200 per day (therefore variance = $1.44m per day).
- Interest rate = 7.3 per cent per year (= 0.02 per cent per day).

Given the lower limit of $5,000, what upper limit and return point should Zetoc Co set for its cash management?

Answer

Using the formulae above:

$$\text{Spread} = 3[(3/4 \times \$500 \times \$1.44m) \div 0.02\%]^{1/3} = \$41,774$$
$$\text{Therefore the upper limit} = \$5,000 + \$41,774 = \$46,774$$
$$\text{And the return point} = \$5,000 + (1/3 \times \$41,774) = \$18,925$$

This means that Zetoc Co should try to maintain its cash balance at around $18,925 (in practice this will probably be rounded to $19,000 or even $20,000 for convenience).

If the cash balance rises as high as $46,774, the company should transfer $27,849 ($46,774 − $18,925) from the bank account into short-term investments in order to bring the balance back down to $18,925. On the other hand, if the cash balance falls as low as $5,000, the company should convert $13,925 ($18,925 − $5,000) of short-term investments back into cash to bring the balance up to $18,925.

Exercises: now attempt Exercise 7.1 on page 285

Cash forecasting: the cash budget

A business needs to produce a cash budget alongside the budgeted income statement and balance sheet in order to ensure that the business holds sufficient cash to achieve the targets set within the operational budget. A cash budget (sometimes referred to as a **cash-flow forecast**) shows the amount and timing of cash receipts and cash payments. In doing so, it also predicts the amount of cash the business will need.

A cash budget may be produced on a daily, weekly or monthly basis dependent upon the volatility of cash flows of the business and the need for level of detail. In this section we will show you how the cash budget is a useful tool for planning the business's future cash needs and how it can be used to inform management strategies.

The format and construction of a cash budget

Cash-flow planning is central to good cash management. It is therefore important that managers are able to produce and understand cash budgets. The following example demonstrates how to produce a simple cash budget for a business.

WORKED EXAMPLE 7.4   A simple cash budget

Pascal starts a furniture-making business. Budgeted sales and purchases for the first six months of his business are:

	Jan $	Feb $	Mar $	Apr $	May $	Jun $
Sales	5,000	6,000	6,500	7,000	6,000	7,000
Purchases	4,000	6,000	4,000	4,000	3,500	4,000

1 Pascal anticipates that 50 per cent of his sales will be for cash and 50 per cent on credit terms of one month.

2 Inventory will be kept very low and bought in the month it is sold. Inventory is paid for with cash as it is bought.

3 Workshop rent is $1,200 per month, paid on the first day of each month.

4 Pascal has a van. This costs $400 per month. Pascal pays all van costs in cash.

5 Pascal starts the business with an opening bank balance of $5,000.

Required:
Prepare a cash budget for the first six months of Pascal's business.

Answer:
There are a number of logical steps in producing a cash budget:

• Forecast sales.

• Forecast cash receipts from sales.

• Forecast cash payments.

• Estimate end-of-period cash balances.

In this simple example we will show you how to carry out each of the steps and to compile the information into a cash budget.

Forecast sales

When preparing a cash budget it is necessary to determine cash receipts in two steps. Firstly, a budget must be established for sales. In the second step this sales forecast is translated into a cash receipts forecast. The reason for these two steps is that the cash budget is concerned with the timing of cash receipts and sales do not necessarily translate directly into cash, particularly if sales are made on credit.

Worked Example 7.4 is relatively straightforward and we are given predicted sales figures. In practice, these would have to be established based upon market research, known contracts or past trends. A variety of statistical and mathematical techniques may be used in forecasting sales.

	Jan	Feb	Mar	Apr	May	Jun
	$	$	$	$	$	$
Sales	5,000	6,000	6,500	7,000	6,000	7,000

For many businesses the pattern of sales is not even throughout the year, but rather is seasonal. For example, 40 per cent of toy sales occur in the six weeks before Christmas. Accurately establishing this pattern can be extremely important for cash-flow planning.

Forecast cash receipts from sales

Once a sales forecast has been prepared, it is necessary to determine when those sales will be collected as cash receipts. If sales are made on credit, there will be a delay between the point of sale and the point of cash receipt.

In Worked Example 7.4 Pascal predicts that 50 per cent of his sales will be for cash and 50 per cent on one month's credit. Based upon this prediction we can establish when cash from sales will be received. For the purposes of this exercise we will assume that cash from cash sales is received immediately and that cash from credit sales is received in the following month. In practice, all customers may not pay on time and some cash receipts may be even later. However, we will keep it simple for this example.

In the table below, the forecast sales for each month are split so that 50 per cent of the money is received in that month (the cash sales) and 50 per cent is received in the following month (the credit sales). For example, January's forecast sales of $5,000 will be received in cash as $2,500 in January and $2,500 in February.

	Jan	Feb	Mar	Apr	May	Jun
	$	$	$	$	$	$
Sales	5,000	6,000	6,500	7,000	6,000	7,000
Cash sales	2,500	3,000	3,250	3,500	3,000	3,500
Credit sales	0	2,500	3,000	3,250	3,500	3,000
Total receipts	2,500	5,500	6,250	6,750	6,500	6,500

Of course, 50 per cent of the cash from June's sales will be received in July, but as this lies outside our six-month budget period we can ignore this.

Forecast cash payments

Cash payments should be recorded when they are expected to be made. You should start with those payments that are fixed amounts due on known dates, such as loan repayments, interest charges, rent or any other standing payments. Payments to creditors should be scheduled based upon predicted purchase patterns and known credit periods.

In Worked Example 7.4 we are given a schedule of purchases and told that these purchases are made in cash. We are also given information about workshop rent and van running costs. This information can be used to produce a schedule of cash payments as set out below:

Payments:	Jan	Feb	Mar	Apr	May	Jun
	$	$	$	$	$	$
Inventory	4,000	6,000	4,000	4,000	3,500	4,000
Rent	1,200	1,200	1,200	1,200	1,200	1,200
Van	400	400	400	400	400	400
Total	5,600	7,600	5,600	5,600	5,100	5,600

Estimate end-of-period cash balances

Finally, we can combine our cash receipts and cash payments forecasts to establish the net increase or decrease in cash balance each month. This allows us to estimate end-of-period cash balances. In Worked Example 7.4 we are told that the opening cash balance will be $5,000. Using this information we can now create a full cash budget. This is set out in Table 7.1.

Table 7.1 shows the total expected cash receipts and cash payments in each month and the resultant increase or decrease in the cash balance. For example, in January total receipts are $2,500 whereas total payments are $5,600. This will result in a decrease in cash balance of $3,100. As the opening cash balance is $5,000, this means that the closing cash balance will be only $1,900. As $1,900 is the closing cash balance in January, it will also be the opening cash balance for February.

It can be seen from this cash budget that if the projected pattern of cash receipts and payments occurs, Pascal will run out of money by the end of February when the closing cash balance is predicted to be negative $200. This means that either he will have to put in place arrangements to borrow money in February or he will have to change his plans somehow to avoid this negative cash situation. However, we can see from the forecast that this situation is only temporary and by the end of March cash balances should be positive again until the end of the six-month period of the forecast.

It is the fact that the cash budget allows us to identify potential problems such as this in advance that makes them so useful. In the next section we will look in more detail at how cash management can be improved by concentrating on the key areas that cause cash problems for businesses.

TABLE 7.1   Cash budget for Pascal

	Jan $	Feb $	Mar $	Apr $	May $	Jun $
Cash receipts						
Cash sales	2,500	3,000	3,250	3,500	3,000	3,500
Credit sales	0	2,500	3,000	3,250	3,500	3,000
Total receipts	2,500	5,500	6,250	6,750	6,500	6,500
Cash payments						
Inventory	4,000	6,000	4,000	4,000	3,500	4,000
Rent	1,200	1,200	1,200	1,200	1,200	1,200
Van	400	400	400	400	400	400
Total payments	5,600	7,600	5,600	5,600	5,100	5,600
Increase/(Decrease)	(3,100)	(2,100)	650	1,150	1,400	900
Opening balance	5,000	1,900	(200)	450	1,600	3,000
Closing balance	1,900	(200)	450	1,600	3,000	3,900

Exercises: now attempt Exercise 7.2 on page 285

Cash management: strategies for improving cash flow

There are certain key areas that always have the potential to cause cash problems for any organization. Good cash management therefore needs to focus on these four key areas:

- managing accounts receivable;
- managing accounts payable;
- managing inventory;
- strategic financing of assets.

The first three areas in this list are concerned with the amount of money tied up in working capital. Managing these three areas is therefore known as **working capital management**. Good working capital management can substantially reduce the amount of cash a business needs.

The fourth area of asset financing is equally important. Research has shown that one of the greatest growth barriers to businesses is an inability to finance new assets for growth. We will therefore examine different methods of financing assets and how these impact upon cash flows.

Managing accounts receivable

Extract 7.5: The reality of offering credit

Around 90 per cent of businesses that operate in industry or wholesale offer credit to their customers. In addition, around 40 per cent of retail sales are made on credit. This means that accounts receivable are a cash management issue for the vast majority of businesses.

Good management of accounts receivable can substantially reduce the cash needs of a business. On the other hand, poor management of accounts receivable is often a source of cash-flow problems, particularly in small businesses. Effective management of accounts receivable involves four key steps:

- formulating an appropriate credit policy;
- setting credit levels;
- credit control; and
- debt collection.

Credit policy

Cash flow can be improved by offering shorter credit periods to customers and thereby reducing the amount of cash tied up in accounts receivable. The best credit policy from a cash-flow point of view is to offer no credit and trade in cash sales only. That would mean that cash is received as soon as a sale is made. However, in many industries it is common practice to offer credit to customers and a business would not be able to trade if it did not offer credit terms similar to those of competitors.

Many businesses offer early settlement discounts on their invoices to encourage customers to pay earlier. Although this technique can be successful, it is not necessarily financially beneficial to the business. The discount offered must be weighed up against the cost of the outstanding debt, as illustrated in Worked Example 7.5.

WORKED EXAMPLE 7.5   Credit policy and early settlement discounts

Mahmoud Co trades in an industry in which it is usual practice to offer 30 days' credit on all sales. Analysis of Mahmoud Co's sales ledger reveals that customers on average actually take 38 days to pay.

The sales director has suggested that the company increase its credit period to 60 days, which he says will make Mahmoud Co more attractive to customers and will increase sales by 5 per cent. The finance director has suggested that if the credit period is extended, the company should also offer an early settlement discount of 2 per cent for payments made within 14 days. He believes that 25 per cent of customers will take advantage of the early settlement discounts and that this will counterbalance the extended credit taken by other customers.

The company has annual sales revenue of $5 million and earns a contribution of 40 per cent on sales. Accounts receivable are financed by an overdraft which has an annual interest rate of 6 per cent.

Should the company change its credit policy in the way suggested by the sales director and the finance director?

Answer

The current collection period on accounts receivable is 38 days. This means that the average balance on accounts receivable is $520,548 ($5m sales × 38/365).

If the new credit policy is implemented, the average collection period will increase to (25% × 14 days) + (75% × 60 days) = 49 days. Sales will also increase by 5 cent to $5.25 million per year. The level of accounts receivable will therefore increase to: $5.25m × 49/365 = $704,795.

With this increase in outstanding accounts receivable, financing costs will increase by ($704,795 – $520,548) × 6% = $11,055 per annum. The discount offered to early settlers will cost $5.25m × 25% × 2% = $26,250. However, from the 5 per cent increase in sales the company will earn additional contribution of $250,000 × 40% = $100,000.

Therefore, there will be a net financial benefit to the company of $62,695 ($100,000 – $26,250 – $11,055) by changing the credit policy and offering early settlement discount. Mahmoud Co should implement the policy change.

Credit analysis

The second step in good credit management is to set appropriate credit levels for customers. This involves assessing the creditworthiness of customers and deciding how much credit you are going to extend to them.

Businesses should make use of credit references and other sources of information. They should analyse the accounts of potential new customers for signs of liquidity problems and potential bankruptcy problems.

Assessing creditworthiness is not just a one-off task for new customers. Credit level should be constantly reviewed and checks frequently made on customers. Sales staff can be very helpful in obtaining information about customers, such as rumours and reputation within the industry. They are also in regular contact with customers and therefore are able to feed back their impressions from dealings with the customers and visits to their premises.

It is frequent practice to extend little or no credit to new customers and to gradually extend credit limits as customers prove their creditworthiness by prompt payment of invoices.

Credit control

Once credit limits have been set, they need to be constantly monitored and controlled. There are two aspects to this task. Firstly, the company must ensure that no customer exceeds their credit limit. Before any new order is accepted the current outstanding balance from the customer should be checked to make sure that the new order does not take the customer over their credit limit. For example, if a customer had a credit limit of $15,000 and currently had outstanding invoices of $12,000, an order worth $4,000 would not be processed until the customer had paid off at least $1,000 of the outstanding balance.

The second aspect of good credit control is ensuring that customers pay on time. One of the most frequently used tools for this task is the **aged debtors report**. This is a report generated from the sales ledger which shows the outstanding balance from each customer broken down by age of the debt. An extract from an aged debtors report is shown in Table 7.2.

Table 7.2 shows an extract from an aged debtors report for a company which offers 30 days' credit to customers. This report enables managers to identify if there are problems with any customers and to initiate action to chase outstanding debts. In the report it can be seen that the first account, Adam Co, has no amounts outstanding outside of the 30-day credit period. However, Benson Co and Cantor Co both have outstanding invoices which have not been paid within the credit period.

Benson Co has an outstanding balance of $27,613.59, all of which is more than 60 days old. This would suggest that there is a problem with this customer. No further credit sales should be made to the customer and action should be taken to recover the outstanding balance.

TABLE 7.2 Aged debtors report

Customer	Total $	<30 days $	30–60 days $	60–90 days $	>90 days $
Adam Co	15,981.81	15,981.81	–	–	–
Benson Co	27,613.59	–	–	18,279.03	9,334.56
Cantor Co	18,516.37	17,935.70		580.67	–

Cantor Co appears to be paying invoices within the credit period, with the exception of one small invoice for $580.67. This might suggest that there is a dispute on the invoice. This needs to be investigated and resolved.

Debt collection

Even with a good credit policy in place and frequent credit checks on customers, it is necessary to ensure that debts are collected promptly. The longer a debt is outstanding, the greater the likelihood that the customer will never pay and the business will incur a **bad debt**.

To ensure prompt payment, invoices should be sent promptly. Ideally, invoices should be sent as soon as goods are shipped. If an account becomes overdue an action should be taken immediately. There is a series of escalating follow-up actions which can be taken if an invoice is not paid on time:

- Send the customer a statement of their account which highlights overdue balances and late payment penalties.
- Telephone the customer to ask for payment.
- Send a formal letter to the customer reminding them that payment is overdue and late payment penalties will be incurred.
- Visit the customer in person (this will usually be done by a member of the sales department) to discuss the outstanding balance and secure payment.
- Send a solicitor's letter threatening legal action if the balance is not paid.
- Hand the debt over to a debt collection agency that will enforce payment on behalf of the company.

If the customer is consistently failing to pay invoices on time, the business should restrict credit to that customer until all outstanding bills are cleared.

Invoice discounting and debt factoring

Even if a business follows all of the steps above for good credit management it may still find itself having a large amount of money tied up in accounts receivable. For example, if the business operates in an industry in which it is necessary to offer credit to customers, it may not be able to avoid having large balances of accounts receivable. If this is the case, there are some ways in which the business can free up this cash.

One such method is **invoice discounting**. This involves using accounts receivable as collateral against borrowing from a finance company. The finance company will typically lend up to 80 per cent of the value of outstanding sales invoices. As invoices are paid and new ones are issued, the amount of borrowing available will be adjusted to maintain that fixed percentage. Interest will be charged on the amount borrowed and usually the finance company also charges a monthly service fee.

In order for invoice discounting to work, the finance company must be confident of the creditworthiness of customers. Borrowing available is rarely greater than 80 per cent of total outstanding invoices as this provides the finance company with a margin for bad debts. Also, a finance company may refuse to lend against certain invoices if it feels that they represent a high risk. As security, the finance company providing the loan will take a **floating charge** over the accounts receivable of the business.

Expert view 7.2: Fixed and floating charges

Anyone lending money to a company will want some security against that loan. It is therefore usual to take a charge against an asset of the company. For example, a lender may take a charge against one of the business's buildings. In the event of default on the loan the lender has the legal right to seize the asset, sell it and recoup the amount they are owed. If this charge is against a clearly identified asset, it is known as a fixed charge. However, in the case of some assets such as accounts receivable it will be difficult to fix the charge against any one asset as individual invoices are constantly being raised and paid off. In this case the lender will raise a floating charge over the class of assets in general.

Invoice discounting can prove to be a very effective and flexible means of raising extra cash for a business that has no other options. The business will only pay interest on the amount it borrows, which will not necessarily be the full amount available. The system essentially works rather like an overdraft but it is usually more expensive than a bank loan or overdraft and therefore would only be used if these were not available.

Another method of releasing cash from the sales ledger is **debt factoring**. Unlike invoice discounting, which is borrowing against the value of accounts receivable, debt factoring involves actually selling sales invoices on to a third party called a factor. Some banks offer factoring services or the factor may be a specialist financial company. If an invoice is sold to a factor a cash advance (typically around 80 per cent of the invoice value) is made immediately. The balance of the invoice value less the factor's fee is then paid upon settlement of the invoice by the business's customer. The factor may or may not take on the risk of bad debts. Usually this is an optional extra which carries an increased fee.

The debt-factoring company may also take on responsibility for managing the sales ledger and chasing and collecting unpaid sales invoices. Although there is obviously an additional cost of this service, it can be beneficial as a form of outsourcing; as the factor has expertise in this task it can reduce bad debts, speed up debt collection and free management time to concentrate on core activities.

A related but less frequent method of raising cash against accounts receivable is **forfaiting**. This is sometimes used by exporting businesses and involves selling individual export sales invoices using a method similar to debt factoring.

Exercises: now attempt Exercise 7.3 on page 286

Managing accounts payable

Just as a business needs to collect its accounts receivable as soon as possible in order to improve its cash flow, it can also improve cash flow by paying creditors as late as possible. The ultimate cash-flow position for a business is to buy on credit and sell for cash, such that cash is received from customers before payments must be made to suppliers. In this way, sales finance purchases. Unfortunately, for most businesses this is not the case and so extra cash is needed to 'buffer' the timing difference between converting accounts receivable to cash and having to pay creditors.

The longer the cash conversion cycle (the time gap between collecting accounts receivable and paying creditors), the more cash the business will need. Therefore, good management of accounts payable can involve extending credit periods as far as possible. In the first instance, the business should seek to get favourable credit terms from its suppliers. It should then carefully manage its payments to stretch these credit terms as far as practicable. However, the business should always take care against stretching it too far as it could result in the supplier suspending the account. This could disrupt trading and also result in poor credit ratings which cause the business difficulty in setting up accounts with new suppliers.

If suppliers offer discounts for early payment, the business needs to balance the advantage of reduced purchase costs against the cost of having to make the payment earlier.

Good management of accounts payable also involves ensuring that only valid invoices are paid. It is therefore important that the business has in place a good system of **internal controls** to check physical receipts of inventory against invoices and to note any omissions or damage.

WORKED EXAMPLE 7.6   Should you take a cash discount?

Red Co purchases supplies at a cost of $5,000. The supplier's standard credit terms are 30 days, but the supplier offers a 2 per cent discount if the invoice is paid within 10 days. Red Co has an overdraft which incurs an interest charge of 0.05 per cent per day.
    Should Red Co take the early payment discount?

Answer

If Red Co takes the early payment discount it will save $100 on its purchases. However, it will also incur higher interest charges on the overdraft as follows:

$$\$4,900 \times 20 \text{ days} \times 0.05\% = \$49$$

As the early payment discount outweighs the additional overdraft interest charges, Red Co should make the early payment. It will be $51 ($100 − $49) better off by doing so.

Managing inventory

Holding inventory can be very expensive, particularly if the goods held are of high value or large quantities are involved. This can mean a substantial amount of cash tied up in inventory. So why do businesses carry inventory? In practice, there are a number of reasons:

- Stocks of finished goods may be held as a buffer where there is fluctuation and uncertainty in patterns of demand. If it is difficult to predict patterns of demand, a high level of inventory will be necessary to ensure that inventory does not run out at those times when demand is high. Some businesses with seasonal sales (such as firework manufacturers) will carry high levels of inventory throughout much of the year because they will be producing throughout the year for sales over a very short period.

- Running out of inventory may carry a cost to the business. If no stock is available customers will buy from a competitor. This could mean not only a lost sale but also a lost customer.

- Some businesses manufacture in batches, such that they will produce a large quantity of one item and then retool the production system to run a batch of another inventory item. This method of operating may be necessary to achieve economies of scale through large runs of production or it may be a requirement of the manufacturing process. In either case, it will result in the business carrying inventory to ensure that all items are available even when they are not being produced.

- A business may purchase large quantities of raw materials at a time in order to take advantage of bulk discounts. This will result in the business carrying inventory.

- Most retailing businesses need to carry sufficient inventory for the shop to look full in order to be attractive to customers.

The amount of inventory carried needs to be just right – not too much and not too little, as each carries a cost to the business.

The costs of carrying too much inventory include:

- the opportunity cost of having money tied up in inventory;
- higher storage costs;
- increased handling and insurance costs;
- increased costs of inventory deterioration, obsolescence and theft.

On the other hand, the costs of carrying too little inventory include:

- the cost of unfulfilled orders;
- the cost of lost customers;
- idle machines and employees if raw material inventory runs out.

Inventory management

Good inventory management is a matter of minimizing the costs associated with holding inventory, whether they be the costs of holding too much or the costs of holding too little inventory. There are many inventory control models which tell a business how much inventory to order and when to order it in order to minimize costs. In this chapter we will look at four approaches to inventory management:

- the inventory turnover ratio;
- inventory reorder levels;
- ABC inventory management;
- the economic order quantity model;
- just-in-time inventory management.

The inventory turnover ratio

The most common method of analysing and assessing inventory levels is to use the inventory turnover ratio. This ratio shows a business how many days' worth of inventory it is holding on average throughout the year. It is expressed by the following formula:

$$\text{Inventory holding (in days)} = \frac{\text{Average inventory}}{\text{Cost of sales}} \times 365$$

Inventory can be measured against sales turnover, but it is better to use cost of sales because inventory is recorded at cost and therefore you are comparing like with like. Also, it is possible to use the end-of-year inventory balance but if inventory levels change seasonally, using an average balance is a more accurate measure.

The inventory turnover ratio can be useful for benchmarking the level of inventory the business holds in two ways:

Firstly, inventory holdings can be analysed over time to see if the inventory levels are changing in relation to the level of sales (as reflected in cost of sales). If inventory days are increasing, this may suggest unnecessary stockpiling or it may reveal that the business is holding obsolete and unsaleable inventory. If inventory levels are falling over time, this may reflect more efficient inventory management or it could be a result of inefficient management which may result in stockouts and lost sales.

Secondly, the ratio enables comparison with industry rivals. If the business finds that it is holding inventory for longer than its competitors, it should be concerned that it is not operating as efficiently as it could in its inventory management. Too much cash is being tied up in inventory and this has a cost for the business.

WORKED EXAMPLE 7.7   Comparing inventory turnover

The following data are being extracted from the most recent financial statements of Ant Co and its two main competitors, Ben Co and Crab Co:

	Ant Co	Ben Co	Crab Co
	$m	$m	$m
Cost of sales	140.0	50.2	300.8
Opening inventory	17.5	4.2	21.8
Closing inventory	19.1	4.6	23.2

Using these data, the respective inventory turnover ratios can be calculated:

Ant Co:

Average inventory = (17.5 + 19.1)/2 = 18.3
Inventory turnover = (18.3 ÷ 140.0) × 365 = 48 days

Ben Co:

Average inventory = (4.2 + 4.6)/2 = 4.4
Inventory turnover = (4.4 ÷ 50.2) × 365 = 32 days

Crab Co:

Average inventory = (21.8 + 23.2)/2 = 22.5
Inventory turnover = (22.5 ÷ 300.8) × 365 = 27 days

This analysis shows that Ant Co is holding its inventory for considerably longer than its competitors. This would suggest that it is carrying too much inventory and needs to adjust its inventory management policy.

Lead time and buffer stock

If a business uses inventory in a fairly regular and consistent manner, its inventory levels will look like the graph in Figure 7.8.

The business will manage its inventory level in the following manner:

- Firstly, it will establish a **buffer stock** which represents the minimum inventory it wishes to carry. This is an insurance against stockouts and the disruption which they would cause.

- Secondly, the business needs to calculate the **lead time** on receiving new inventory. This is the time delay between placing an order and actually receiving delivery of the inventory.

FIGURE 7.8   Inventory reorder level

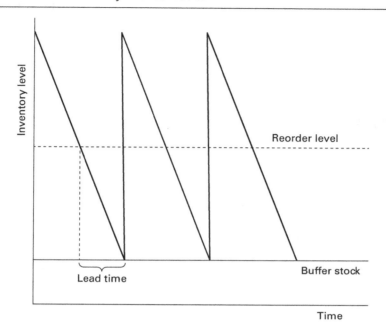

- Using this information, the business can work backwards from the buffer stock level, using the lead time, to establish the level of inventory at which a new order should be placed – the **reorder level**. As inventory falls to this level the inventory management system should trigger an order to the supplier.

Many businesses use a computerized inventory control system which is linked to the ordering system and in some cases also linked to the supplier's sales and stock dispatch systems so that the whole process is automated. This automation can substantially reduce the lead time on inventory delivery and consequentially reduce the quantity of inventory that the business needs to carry. When taken to the extreme, this results in just-in-time inventory management (see below).

Economic order quantity (EOQ) model

The EOQ model is an approach to inventory management which attempts to minimize the costs of holding inventory. The model recognizes that there are two opposing sets of costs which need to be balanced and attempts to do so by calculating the optimum quantity of inventory to order at any one time:

- If large quantities of inventory are ordered at a time, the business will incur higher costs in storage and handling; there will be a higher cost of inventory obsolescence, damage or loss; and the opportunity cost of having cash tied up in inventory will be greater.

● If small quantities of inventory are ordered each time, orders will need to be placed more frequently and levels monitored more closely. This will increase order costs.

Figure 7.9 illustrates how these opposing sets of costs lead to a total cost of stock-holding which has an optimum (ie minimum) cost when storage costs = order costs.

FIGURE 7.9   The economic order quantity

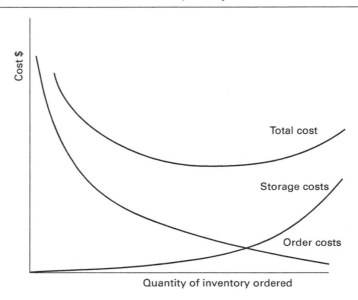

This relationship can be expressed with the following formula:

$$EOQ = \sqrt{\frac{2C_OD}{C_H}}$$

Where: C_H is the cost of holding one unit of stock for one year
C_O is the cost of ordering a consignment of stock
D   is the annual demand

Therefore, when using the EOQ model, the amount of inventory held by the business will be dictated by the most economic quantity to order. This will be the quantity which minimizes the total cost of holding inventory. The method is illustrated in Worked Example 7.8.

WORKED EXAMPLE 7.8   Optimizing inventory order levels

The management of Pantar Co wishes to minimize the business's inventory costs. The company accountant has identified the following costs and figures in relation to inventory item P31:

- Annual demand for P31 is 80,000 units.
- P31 costs $3.00 per unit.
- Inventory management costs for P31 are:
  - Ordering cost: $15.00 per order
  - Holding cost: $2 per unit per year.

Required:
Calculate the total cost of inventory for P31 if Pantar Co applies the EOQ.

Answer
The EOQ for P31 will be:

$$= \sqrt{(2 \times 15 \times 80{,}000/0.5)/2} = 1{,}095 \text{ units}$$

Therefore, the number of orders placed in a year will be:

$$= 80{,}000/1{,}095 = 73 \text{ orders per year}$$

The annual ordering cost:

$$= 73 \times \$15 = \$1{,}095 \text{ per year}$$

The average inventory of P31 held by Pantar Co will be:

$$= 1{,}095/2 = 547.5 \text{ units}$$

The annual holding cost:

$$= 547.5 \times \$2 = \$1{,}095 \text{ per year}$$

(Note that the annual ordering cost = annual holding cost at the optimum level as illustrated in Figure 7.9.)

Inventory purchase cost:

$$= 80{,}000 \times \$3 = \$240{,}000$$

Total cost of inventory with EOQ policy:

$$= \$240{,}000 + \$1{,}095 + \$1{,}095 = \$242{,}190 \text{ per year}$$

ABC inventory management

ABC inventory analysis is a method of prioritizing different inventory lines in order to focus management attention on the most critical areas of inventory. It employs the **Pareto Principle** – the principle that 80 per cent of overall revenue is based upon only 20 per cent of inventory items. This means that not all inventory lines are equally important. Efficient management means focusing on the most important lines and less on other areas of inventory. For this reason the technique is also sometimes known as **selective inventory control**.

When applying the ABC approach all inventory is evaluated and divided into three categories – A, B or C – as illustrated in Table 7.3.

TABLE 7.3   ABC Inventory analysis

Category	Inventory quantity (%)	Inventory value (%)
A	12	72
B	28	18
C	60	10
Total	**100**	**100**

- Category A contains inventory that is most important to the business. The category usually contains items that are carried in relatively low quantities but have a high individual value. This inventory needs a high degree of attention. The business has a lot of money tied up in the inventory but it carries low quantities and so could easily run out. The usage of this category of inventory needs careful forecasting and the level should be closely monitored.

- Category B inventory needs less sophisticated management than category A. This is an intermediate category between A and C.

- Category C contains inventory that has low value but is carried in high volumes. This requires much less close management than category A. The business can apply the simplest control possible to this area of inventory.

Expert view 7.3: ERP and ABC analysis

Many businesses operate enterprise resource planning (ERP) systems. These are integrated computer software modules which support the different process areas of the business. This can include financial accounting, management accounting, customer relationship management, project management, supply chain management, manufacturing processes and human resource management. **ABC inventory analysis** is usually built into these systems.

Just-in-time (JIT) inventory management

JIT is an approach to inventory management that has gained popularity in recent years as part of a broader **lean manufacturing** approach. It is usually integrated into a materials requirement planning (MRP) system.

Expert view 7.4: Lean manufacturing

Lean manufacturing is a management philosophy which was developed within the Japanese manufacturing company Toyota. The focus of lean manufacturing is to ensure that any expenditure results in the creation of value for the end customer. Any activity or expenditure which does not add value is seen as wasteful and therefore a target for elimination. The approach involves removing unnecessary processes and material movements, streamlining systems to remove idle time or unnecessary delays, and reducing inventory levels.

As with the other inventory management techniques we have already examined, the aim of JIT is to minimize inventory costs. However, the JIT approach focuses primarily on minimizing inventory holding costs through efficient monitoring of inventory usage and placing orders so that they arrive only when needed. The goal is to minimize the amount of cash tied up in inventory, thereby improving ROCE.

Successful operation of a JIT inventory system requires good forecasting of production requirements, short and predictable lead times, and good coordination with suppliers. Good communication both up and down the supply chain is critical. Implementing JIT inventory management often involves integrating information systems with suppliers, and good communication is critical. Although many businesses have successfully implemented JIT and have increased efficiency and cost savings as a result, it is important to recognize that the system also has drawbacks. By removing buffer stock the business has no emergency fallback in case of disruption in the supply chain.

Advantages of JIT:

- A JIT system eliminates the cost of holding inventory.
- Inventory obsolescence is avoided.
- Cash is freed up for investment in other activities.
- Warehouse space can be freed up for other value-adding activities.
- Production can be more flexible and responsive to customer requirements.

Disadvantages of JIT:

- There is no 'buffer stock' so late delivery of inventory will cause disruption in production.

- The business becomes vulnerable to disruptions in the supply chain caused by labour strikes, transportation problems or information system problems.
- It is more difficult to respond to unexpected fluctuations in demand.

Extract 7.6: JIT at Dell Computers

Dell, a leading supplier of personal computers, revolutionized the industry by using JIT systems. Dell takes orders directly from a customer and builds computers to that customer's order, an approach to production which is known as a **pull system**. The company keeps only five days of inventory on hand, which compares with competitors who have up to 90 days of inventory.

This approach has given Dell a competitive advantage over its rivals which enabled it to become the market leader in personal computers. The reduced time to market enables Dell to keep up to date with technological advancements so that customers are always offered the latest-specification computers. Dell has achieved this by integrating the entire value chain from delivery and sales back to design and development.

Exercises: now attempt Exercise 7.4 on page 286

The financing of asset purchases

One of the greatest cash demands for businesses is the purchase of new assets such as machinery, equipment or vehicles. Research has shown that the inability to finance the purchase of new assets is one of the greatest barriers to growth for businesses.

If a business does not have the cash available to purchase new assets, it will need to raise more cash by issuing new shares or by taking on a new loan. However, if the business is not able to raise cash by these means, there are alternative methods of financing the purchase of new assets which reduce the demands on cash flow.

One alternative method of financing assets is to use a **hire purchase (HP)** agreement. This is a legal contract through which the purchases are made through a series of payments over time. In reality the purchaser is hiring the asset and making a series of (typically monthly) rental payments. Once these rental payments equal the cash purchase price plus an agreed interest charge, ownership of the asset passes to the purchaser. If the purchaser defaults on the rental instalments, the owner may repossess the asset. The main advantage of an HP agreement is that it removes the need to have the purchase price in cash up front. The purchaser is able to spread the cost of the asset over time through a series of payments.

Another method of financing the purchase of new assets is to lease those assets rather than purchase them. There are two types of lease which a business could enter into: a finance lease or an operating lease.

A lease is a contractual arrangement through which a party owning an asset (the lessor) gives use of that asset to a second party (the lessee) in return for a series of rental payments. Ownership of the asset remains with the lessor.

A **finance lease** is usually defined as one in which the risks and rewards of ownership of the leased asset are transferred to the lessee but not the actual ownership. The lease term is all or most of the life of the asset. The total rental payments throughout the lease period add up to the cash price of the asset plus a finance charge. Responsibility for repair and maintenance of the asset may remain with the lessor, but often this becomes the responsibility of the lessee. In many cases, ownership of the asset is transferred to the lessee at the end of the lease term.

An **operating lease** is one in which the lease term is short in comparison to the life of the asset. Operating leases are commonly used to acquire equipment or vehicles for short-term use. For example, if you went on holiday and leased a car for a week, that would be an operating lease. Under an operating lease the lessor remains responsible for maintenance and repair of the asset, which can be an advantage for the lessee. However, this will be reflected in the lease cost. If an asset is required infrequently for short periods, using an operating lease can be a smart way of easing cash flows, as it removes the need to tie up valuable cash in an infrequently used asset. On the other hand, it can be an expensive option if the asset is leased too frequently.

The decision of whether to enter into a finance lease or an operating lease will obviously depend upon an assessment of how long an asset is required and how frequently it will be used. A finance lease is essentially an alternative means of financing the acquisition of an asset. On the other hand, an operating lease is a means of acquiring the use of an asset for short periods of time without having to tie up cash in the purchase of that asset.

There are also tax and accounting disclosure implications for businesses deciding between hire purchase, finance leasing and operating leasing. These may have an impact on the finance method chosen.

Interpreting and analysing a cash-flow forecast

Now that you have learnt how to produce a simple cash-flow forecast, we will look at a more complex example and learn how to analyse and interpret it. Within larger organizations it will usually be the case that cash-flow forecasts are produced by the accounting department. As a manager you will be using that forecast to make both operational and strategic decisions.

Expert view 7.5: Cash-flow forecasting

Large organizations usually have a specialist division within the accounting department that is dedicated to cash planning and cash-flow forecasting. This is usually known as the **treasury department**.

Worked Example 7.9 sets out a cash-flow forecast for the start-up of a new business. We will take a detailed look at this forecast and identify any potential problems which may be looming for the business. We will also identify any changes to business plans that could be recommended in order to improve the business's cash flow and cash position.

WORKED EXAMPLE 7.9   Cash-flow analysis

Jill has recently been made redundant from her job as a designer. She has decided to use her redundancy money to realize her dream of starting a business which manufactures and sells high-quality greenhouses. In order to start the business Jill has applied for a business start-up loan from the bank. The bank requires a business plan, which includes a cash-flow forecast. Jill has prepared the cash budget for the first six months of the business (Table 7.4).

In relation to the cash budget, Jill has provided you with the following information:

1 The business will commence on 1 June with $55,000 in the bank. $30,000 of this will come from Jill's redundancy money. The remaining $25,000 will come from a business start-up loan.

2 Jill will rent a workshop unit on an industrial estate. This will cost $900 per month, payable at the start of each month.

3 A van will be bought in June at a cost of $12,000.

4 General workshop costs (light, heat, power etc) and the van's running costs are expected to be $400 per month.

5 Jill will also lease a Land Rover Discovery car starting in June. The monthly lease payments will be $450, payable on the 10th of each month.

6 The greenhouses will be sold to local garden centres. Sales are expected to be as follows:

	June	July	Aug	Sept	Oct	Nov
Number of greenhouses	10	15	15	20	25	30

The sales price of each greenhouse will be $4,000. In order to stimulate interest from customers, Jill has offered two months' credit.

7 Purchases of materials, which will be on one month's credit, are expected to be as follows:

June	July	Aug	Sept	Oct	Nov
$30,000	$20,000	$20,000	$35,000	$50,000	$60,000

8 Jill will initially employ a workshop manager at a cost of $1,500 per month and two further staff at a cost of $1,000 per month each, payable on the last day of the month. When sales reach 20 greenhouses per month, she will employ an additional person at a cost of $700 per month. Jill will herself draw $1,750 cash each month from the business.

9 Jill wishes to undertake a substantial advertising campaign to launch the business. This will cost $8,000 in the first month and $1,000 per month for a further two months, payable in the month incurred.

10 The machinery and equipment needed will be bought immediately at the start of June. Most can be bought second-hand for $12,000 cash. Other machinery, costing $25,000, will be bought new on two months' interest-free credit.

11 Repayments on the business loan, including the interest element, will be $1,200 per month. These will be payable on the 15th of the month, commencing in July.

TABLE 7.4

Receipts	June $	July $	Aug $	Sept $	Oct $	Nov $
Sales	0	0	40,000	60,000	60,000	80,000
Payments						
Materials	0	30,000	20,000	20,000	35,000	50,000
Wages	3,500	3,500	3,500	4,200	4,200	4,200
Drawings	1,750	1,750	1,750	1,750	1,750	1,750
Workshop	900	900	900	900	900	900
Advertising	8,000	1,000	1,000			
General	400	400	400	400	400	400
Van	12,000					
Land Rover	450	450	450	450	450	450
Equipment	12,000		25,000			
Loan		1,200	1,200	1,200	1,200	1,200
	39,000	39,200	54,200	28,900	43,900	58,900
Increase/(Decrease)	(39,000)	(39,200)	(14,200)	31,100	16,100	21,100
Opening Balance	55,000	16,000	(23,200)	(37,400)	(6,300)	9,800
Closing Balance	16,000	(23,200)	(37,400)	(6,300)	9,800	30,900

Required:

Analyse Jill's cash budget and make any recommendations which you feel would improve her cash management.

Answer

The cash budget reveals that despite starting the business with an investment of $55,000, Jill will very quickly run out of cash. In both of the first two months of business there is a predicted fall in cash of nearly $40,000. This means that by the end of the second month of trading Jill will have to find another $23,200. By the end of the third month this amount will have increased to $37,400. These forecast figures would suggest that unless Jill secures a substantial additional source of finance (nearly $40,000), her business will fail within two months.

Alternatively, Jill can make changes to her business plans to reduce the cash requirements of the business. In this way Jill may be able to launch her business successfully without the need for an extra $40,000.

We would suggest that Jill makes the following changes to her business plans:

Inventory management

The forecast shows that Jill intends to buy a substantial amount of raw material inventory in the first month. This means that cash will be tied up in inventory that may not be realized as cash for several months. We recommend that Jill buys materials as they are needed and not create a large inventory. She should seek out suppliers who are able to supply quickly so that she can manage the business successfully with relatively low levels of inventory.

Management of accounts receivable

Jill is proposing to offer an extremely generous credit period to new customers. The impact of this is that there will be no cash receipts for the business for the first two months. The business cannot afford such a generous credit policy. Jill should therefore aim to gain orders from customers without the need for such a long credit period. If she can gain sufficient customers in the first few months offering only a one-month credit period, this will increase the cash inflow into the business by $40,000, substantially easing the cash-flow problem.

Jill should also consider using either invoice discounting or debt factoring to release some of the cash that will be tied up in debtors.

Expenditure plans

Excessive expenditure can be a drain upon the cash flow of a business. Jill therefore needs to look at areas of her business plan where she can cut expenditure to keep cash within the business.

One potential area is Jill's own planned drawings from the business. Jill plans to draw $1,750 from the business each month, right from the very start of the business. Jill should look at her own personal spending and reduce this amount to the absolute minimum that she can manage to live on for the first few months of the business. Then, once the business is well established and cash flows are eased, she will be able to draw more money in the future.

Another potential area for savings is the advertising plans. Jill plans to undertake a substantial advertising campaign to launch the business. This will cost $8,000 in the first month and $1,000 per month for a further two months. As Jill intends to deal with local garden centres she may be able to secure sufficient sales through personal contact and negotiation. This will reduce or totally remove the need for the advertising campaign. Alternatively, Jill can still advertise using cheaper methods.

Purchase and financing of assets

Substantial cash expenditure on new vehicles (the van and the Land Rover) and new equipment is planned. Jill should look both at her needs and at the planned method of financing the purchases.

Jill plans to buy a van in the first month of the business at a cost of $12,000. This cost could be spread if Jill purchased the van on a finance deal or lease. This would substantially ease the cash flow in the first few months of the business.

Jill should also consider whether the Land Rover is necessary and if so, whether she needs to buy it so soon after the launch of the business. Jill may aspire to driving a Land Rover but a cheaper vehicle may be sufficient for her needs until the business is established and has more cash available.

Jill plans to buy a substantial amount of equipment ($37,000) within the first few months of the business. The cost of this would be spread if the equipment could be bought on a finance deal. This may prove more expensive if the equipment cannot be bought second-hand using a finance deal, but Jill needs to balance out the cash-flow benefits of a finance deal with the reduced cost of second-hand equipment.

Repayments on the business loan are $1,200 per month. Jill could try to negotiate a longer period for the loan so that the repayments could be spread over more months and thereby reduced in the critical first months. Alternatively, she could ask for a deferment in the repayments so that she does not need to make any payments in the first two or three months.

Management of accounts payable

Purchases will be made on one month's credit. Jill should try to negotiate a longer credit period with her suppliers or seek out alternative suppliers who are willing to offer more credit. In addition, she could seek early payment discounts with suppliers.

Conclusion

In this chapter we have looked at the importance of cash management. We have explored the reasons for holding cash and the different motives which determine the level of cash a business will hold. We have examined models which aim to assist managers in optimizing cash levels within the business. We have also explored how good management of different assets within the business, such as inventory, accounts receivable, accounts payable and non-current assets, can greatly improve the cash-flow requirements of the business. Lastly, we have explored the importance of cash-flow planning and how managers can use cash-flow budgets to inform planning decisions.

COMPREHENSION QUESTIONS

1 Explain the business problems that may be associated with holding insufficient cash balances. What are the problems of holding too much cash?

2 Distinguish between the transaction motive and the speculative motive for holding cash. How do these two motives differ in terms of their impact upon the level of cash held?

3 Explain how a business can benefit from a cash forecast, even if it already has an income and expenditure forecast and a balance sheet forecast.

4 Discuss the assumptions which underpin the Baumol–Tobin model of cash management and explain how they may limit the usefulness of the model for some businesses.

5 Explain the difference between a finance lease and an operating lease as a means of financing the purchase of an asset.

6 Discuss the ways in which factoring and invoice discounting can assist in the management of accounts receivable.

7 Explain what you understand by the terms 'buffer stock' and 'lead time' and briefly consider any stock policy that would minimize or eliminate such costs.

Answers on pages 286–288

Exercises

Answers on pages 288–291

Exercise 7.1: Managing the cash account

The management of Darum Co have set a minimum cash balance of $7,500. The average cost to the company of making deposits or selling investments is $24 per transaction. An analysis of cash flows over the last 12 months reveals a standard deviation of $2,000 per day. The average interest rate on investments is 4.6 per cent.

Calculate the spread, the upper limit and the return point for the cash account of Darum Co using the Miller–Orr model. Explain the relevance of these values for the cash management of the company.

Exercise 7.2: Cash-flow forecasting

Jade opens a sandwich shop. She sells sandwiches directly over the counter for cash, but also provides buffet lunches for local businesses. These customers are allowed one month's credit.

Budgeted sales for the first six months of the business are as follows:

	Jan	Feb	Mar	Apr	May	Jun
	$	$	$	$	$	$
Counter sales	4,000	3,500	3,500	4,000	4,000	5,000
Buffet sales	4,000	5,000	3,000	4,000	3,500	4,000

Purchases of bread and fillings are all made locally for cash. Expected purchases are:

	Jan	Feb	Mar	Apr	May	Jun
	$	$	$	$	$	$
Purchases	3,000	3,000	3,000	4,000	3,500	4,000

1 Jade employs two assistants in the shop. Each is paid a monthly salary of $1,000. This is payable on the 25th of the month.

2 Shop rent is $700 per month. This is paid on the first day of the month.

3 Shop heat and light costs are $300 per quarter, payable in arrears in March and June.

4 The bank balance on 1 January is $1,000.

Required:

(a) Prepare a cash-flow forecast for the first six months of Jade's business.

(b) Comment on changes which Jade might make in order to improve her cash flow.

Exercise 7.3: Managing accounts receivable

Andro Co makes all its sales on credit and allows its customers 30 days' credit. However, analysis of the financial statements shows that the average accounts receivable period in the last financial year was 70 days. This has increased from 50 days in the previous financial year. In addition, bad debts as a percentage of sales increased from 3 to 6 per cent. The CEO has expressed great concern at these figures and has asked for your assistance in improving the management of accounts receivable.

Required:
Write a report to the CEO of Andro Co which details ways in which the company could improve the management of its accounts receivable.

Exercise 7.4: Inventory management

Rio Co currently employs an inventory management policy of reordering inventory when levels fall to 3,500 units. This reorder level allows for the lead time of two weeks and maintains a buffer stock.

The company orders 10,000 units at a time. Forecast production demand during the next year is 70,000 units. The cost of placing and processing an order is $300, while the annual cost of holding a unit in the warehouse is $1.50. These costs are expected to be constant during the next year.

Required:

(a) Calculate the cost of the current ordering policy.

(b) Determine whether a saving could be made by using the EOQ model.

Answers to comprehension questions

1   If a business holds insufficient cash:

- Payments to suppliers may be delayed, causing credit problems and disruption in supply.

- Emergency loans or overdrafts, which cost the business more than is necessary, may be required.

- Opportunities for good investment may be missed.

- The business may ultimately become insolvent

If a business holds too much cash:

- ROCE will be reduced.
- The cost of capital may increase.
- The business may become a target for acquisition.

2 The transaction motive refers to holding cash in order to be able to pay day-to-day bills. The speculative motive refers to holding cash in order to be able to take advantage of unexpected investment opportunities. The amount of cash held due to the transaction motive will depend upon the cash conversion cycle of the business. The longer this cycle (for example, due to offering extended credit to customers), the more cash the business will need in order to continue with day-to-day transactions. The amount of cash held due to the speculative motive will depend upon the attitude of management and the investment opportunities available to the business. If interest rates are low, businesses will typically maintain higher speculative balances of cash. On the other hand, if interest rates are high, the opportunity cost of holding cash balances may outweigh the speculative benefits.

3 An income and expenditure forecast will enable a business to forecast its future levels of income and profitability. A balance sheet forecast enables a business to forecast levels of assets and liabilities. Although both of these forecasts are important to the business, neither provides a prediction of the cash requirements of the business. A business needs to produce a cash budget in order to ensure that the business holds sufficient to cash to meet the targets set within the income and expenditure budget. A cash budget shows the amount and timing of cash receipts and cash payments. It helps a business predict future cash needs and plan to meet any potential shortfalls.

4 The Baumol–Tobin model of cash management makes the following assumptions:

- Cash outflows are predictable and even over time.
- Cash inflows are predictable and regular.
- Day-to-day cash needs are funded from a bank current account.
- A 'buffer' of short-term investments is held which can be liquidated to provide cash when needed.

Although many businesses do have consistent cash flows, many have cash flows that are irregular or unpredictable. If this is the case, a more useful model for cash management is one which allows for the regularity and fluctuations in cash flows. One such model is the Miller–Orr model.

5   In a finance lease the risks and rewards of ownership of an asset is transferred to the lessee but not the actual ownership. The lease term is all or most of the life of the asset. The total rental payments throughout the lease period add up to the cash price of the asset plus a finance charge. Responsibility for repair and maintenance of the asset may remain with the lessor, but often this becomes the responsibility of the lessee. In many cases ownership of the asset is transferred to the lessee at the end of the lease term.

In an operating lease the lease term is short in comparison to the life of the asset. The lessor remains responsible for maintenance and repair of the asset.

6   Factoring and invoice discounting are two ways in which a business can release the cash tied up in accounts receivable. Debt factoring involves a company handing over administration of its sales ledger to a financial institution with expertise in this area. This may be a bank or a specialist factor company. The factor will offer finance to the company, usually based on up to 80 per cent of the face value of invoices raised. The loan is repaid as customers settle invoices, with the balance being passed to the company after deduction of a fee equivalent to an interest charge on the cash advanced. Invoice discounting is an alternative way of raising finance against accounts receivable. Rather than employing the credit management and administration services of a factor, a number of invoices are offered as collateral against borrowing. This approach can be considerably cheaper than factoring.

7   Buffer stock is a minimum level of inventory that a business holds in order to protect itself against stockouts. Lead time refers to the time lag between placing an order for new inventory and actually receiving it. A stock policy which seeks to minimize or eliminate the costs of buffer stock and lead time is the JIT approach. This approach involves careful coordination with suppliers to ensure that new inventory arrives just as it is needed.

Answers to exercises

Exercise 7.1: Managing the cash account

Spread: using the Miller–Orr model the spread can be calculated as follows:

Daily interest rate = 4.6% / 365 = 0.014% per day (0.00014)
Variance of cash flows = $2,000^2 = $4,000,000 per day
Transaction cost = $24 per transaction
Spread = $3 \times ((0.75 \times \text{transaction cost} \times \text{variance})/\text{interest rate})^{1/3}$
= $3 \times ((0.75 \times 24 \times 4,000,000)/0.00014)^{1/3}$ = $24,036

Upper limit:
   Lower limit (set by management) = $7,500
   Upper limit = 7,500 + 24,036 =$31,536
Return point:
   Return point = 7,500 + (24,036/ 3) = $15,512

Relevance for cash management

The Miller–Orr model takes account of uncertainty in relation to receipts and payment by setting limits within which cash balances can be allowed to fluctuate. If cash balances fall to the lower limit, an amount of cash equal to the difference between the return point and the lower limit is raised by selling short-term investments. If cash balances rise to the upper limit, an amount of cash equal to the difference between the upper limit and the return point is transferred into short-term investments. The model therefore helps Darum Co to decrease the risk of running out of cash, while avoiding the opportunity cost of having unnecessarily high cash balances.

Exercise 7.2: Cash-flow forecasting

(a) Jade's sandwich shop – cash flow forecast. See Table 7.5.

TABLE 7.5

	Jan	Feb	Mar	Apr	May	Jun
Cash sales	4,000	3,500	3,500	4,000	4,000	5,000
Credit sales		4,000	5,000	3,000	4,000	3,500
Total	4,000	7,500	8,500	7,000	8,000	8,500
Expenses						
Purchases	3,000	3,000	3,000	4,000	3,500	4,000
Salaries	2,000	2,000	2,000	2,000	2,000	2,000
Shop rent	700	700	700	700	700	700
Heat & light			300			300
	5,700	5,700	6,000	6,700	6,200	7,000
Net movement	(1,700)	1,800	2,500	300	1,800	1,500
Opening balance	1,000	(700)	1,100	3,600	3,900	5,700
Closing balance	(700)	1,100	3,600	3,900	5,700	7,200

(b) Improvements to cash flow: The current cash-flow forecast suggests that Jade will require additional funding of $700 by the end of the first month of trading. She may be able to avoid this by taking one or more of the following actions:

- require a deposit or partial payment in advance from the buffet customers;
- seek credit for purchases from some of her suppliers;
- delay employment of a second assistant until February or March when she has more funds available.

Exercise 7.3: Managing accounts receivable

Report to CEO of Andro Co

Management of accounts receivable

The information made available to me concerning accounts receivable indicates that there are two areas of concern:

- the increasing level of bad debts as a percentage of credit sales; and
- the excessive credit period being taken by credit customers.

Reducing bad debts

Bad debts have increased from 3 to 6 per cent of credit sales in the last year. This figure could be reduced by introducing a credit policy which ensures that the creditworthiness of new customers is assessed before they are extended credit. Andro Co needs to introduce a formal policy which sets out how this should be done. For each new customer, information should be gathered from a variety of sources such as trade references, bank references and credit reference agencies. The solvency and credit history of all new customers should be evaluated. The terms of the credit offered will be based upon this assessment of default risk.

Reduction of average accounts receivable period

Customers have taken an average of 70 days' credit over the last year rather than the 30 days offered by Andro Co. As this is more than twice the formal credit period offered, there is clearly a problem in collecting outstanding accounts receivable.

Andro Co should check the credit offered by its competitors. It may well be the case that competitors are offering a longer credit period (for example, 60 days) and that Andro's credit policy is therefore out of line with the industry.

Andro Co should have a clear policy for managing outstanding accounts receivable balances. This should include the following actions:

- Statements should be regularly sent to customers detailing any amounts outstanding.

- An aged accounts receivable analysis should be produced at the end of each month to identify customers with overdue balances.

- Any customers with outstanding accounts should be contacted to encourage payment.

- Customers with overdue accounts should be denied further credit until those accounts are settled.

- Customers with overdue accounts should be charged interest on those balances.

Andro Co could also consider introducing an early settlement discount as a positive means of encouraging customers to settle their accounts sooner.

Exercise 7.4: Inventory management

Cost of current ordering policy:

Ordering cost = $300 × (70,000/10,000) = $2,100 per year

Weekly demand = 70,000/52 = 1,346 units per week

Consumption during 2 weeks' lead time = 1,346 × 2 = 2,692 units

Buffer stock = reorder level less usage during lead time = 3,500 − 2,692 = 808 units

Average stock held during the year = 808 + (10,000/2) = 5,808 units

Holding cost = 5,808 × $1·50 = $8,712 per year

Total cost = ordering cost plus holding cost = $2,100 + $8,712 = $10,812 per year

Cost using the EOQ:

EOQ = $((2 \times 300 \times 70,000)/1·5)^{1/2}$ = 6,481 units

Number of orders per year = 70,000/6,481 = 11 per year

Ordering cost = $300 × 11 = $3,300 per year

Holding cost (including buffer stock) = $1·50 × (808 + (6,481/2)) = $6,073 per year

Total cost of EOQ-based ordering policy = $3,300 + $6,073 = $9,373 per year

Saving for Rio Co by using EOQ-based ordering policy = $10,812 − $9,373
= $1,439 per year

Pricing decisions

OBJECTIVE

To provide an understanding of the factors, both internal and external to the business, that should guide the pricing decision.

LEARNING OUTCOMES

After studying this chapter, the reader will be able to:

- Recommend appropriate costing methods for pricing.
- Assess the potential impact of different competitive environments on pricing.
- Identify appropriate pricing strategies to fit different markets and products/services.

KEY TOPICS COVERED

- Costing and pricing – different approaches to costing.
- Consumer behaviour and pricing.
- Competitor behaviour and pricing.
- Pricing new products or services.
- Product life cycle and pricing.
- Special pricing strategies.

MANAGEMENT ISSUES

Pricing is not an exact science. Much of the detailed mathematics of the economics of pricing is impossible to apply in practice. Managers need an understanding of the broad principles which should guide them in the pricing decision.

Introduction

In this chapter we will examine the factors which a business needs to take into consideration when establishing the most appropriate price for its products or services. In practice, pricing strategies can be both short term and long term and businesses will employ a combination of pricing strategies to achieve their corporate goals. For example, a business may have a long-term goal of being a high-quality provider and will have a long-term strategy of setting prices high to reflect this. However, the business may reduce prices in the short term in order to improve cash flows, increase market share or deter competitors.

Some of the factors involved in pricing may appear obvious. For example, it is important to take into consideration the costs of delivering a product or service in order to ensure that profit is made or at least costs are covered. However, how those costs are established is not necessarily always obvious or simple. Also, a business needs to be mindful of its customers and competitors when establishing pricing strategy. How will customers and competitors react to your prices? In some circumstances this may be an extremely important question, because if you get it wrong you will lose all your customers to your competitors. The pricing decision can therefore be said to be made up of 3 C's: costs, customers and competitors (Figure 8.1).

FIGURE 8.1 The pricing decision

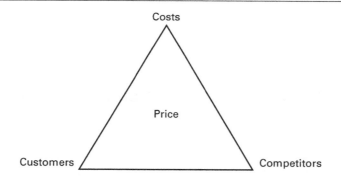

Another way of looking at this is to say that there are three different perspectives which need to be considered when making a pricing decision:

The accountant's perspective: this perspective is concerned with the relationship between revenues and costs. The sales price must be set at such a level as to ensure that revenues exceed costs in order to generate a profit.

The economist's perspective: this perspective is concerned with the competitive environment in which the business operates. Different market types have an impact on the ability of a business to control its own pricing.

The marketer's perspective: this perspective is concerned with the way in which customers react to prices and how pricing should be integrated into the overall marketing mix.

The accountant's perspective can be said to be inward-looking in that it is concerned with the internal workings of the business and how these generate costs. The economist's perspective and the marketer's perspective are both outward-looking in that they are concerned with the business's external environment and how that impacts upon price.

In this chapter we will look at each of these perspectives in turn to establish a good understanding of the factors involved, and then we will see how all three perspectives can be combined into coherent pricing strategies.

The accountant's perspective – costing and pricing

Understanding the cost of delivering a product or service is important to all organizations. Profit-seeking organizations have at least to break even and not-for-profit organizations need to cover their costs.

The way in which a business will establish the cost of delivering its goods or services will depend upon the way that the business operates and the information that is available. In this section we will look at several well-established costing methods and the circumstances to which they are most suited:

- absorption costing and full-cost-plus pricing;
- marginal-cost-plus pricing;
- activity-based costing and pricing;
- life-cycle costing and pricing.

Absorption costing and full-cost-plus pricing

Absorption costing, which is aimed at establishing the full cost of production, originally arose in manufacturing businesses operating in a relatively stable environment. When using the absorption costing approach, sales price is determined by calculating the full cost of a product or service, including relevant overhead costs, and then adding a percentage mark-up to achieve the desired level of profit.

WORKED EXAMPLE 8.1   Pricing using absorption costing

Grogstore Co manufactures stainless-steel beer barrels. The manufacturing depot has two production departments: cutting and welding. The direct costs of producing each barrel are as follows:

Materials:	$2\,m^2$ of stainless steel @ $3 per m^2
Labour – cutting:	15 minutes per barrel @ $14 per hour
Labour – welding:	20 minutes per barrel @ $18 per hour

Budgeted overhead costs for next year are:

	$
Property costs	92,000
Managers' salaries:	
Cutting department	25,000
Welding department	28,000
General administration costs	143,000
Machine power	28,000

The following information relates to each of the production departments:

	Cutting	Welding	Total
Floor space (sq. m)	35	25	60
Number of employees	6	10	16
Labour hours	9,000	17,000	26,000

What price should Grogstore charge for the barrels if it wishes to earn a profit mark-up on total costs of 30 per cent?

Solution

The first step in establishing a full-cost price is to identify all the direct costs of manufacturing a barrel. These will include the costs of materials and labour which go directly into the barrel:

	$
Materials: (2 m² @ $3 per m²)	6.00
Labour: cutting (15 minutes @ $14 per hour)	3.50
Labour: welding (20 minutes @ $18 per hour)	6.00

Once total direct costs have been established, the relevant parts of overhead costs are incorporated into the product cost. This is done through a method known as the '3 A's' of absorption costing: **allocate**, **apportion** and **absorb**.

This method involves attributing overhead costs firstly to relevant production cost centres, and then from the cost centre to the individual product.

Expert view 8.1: Cost centre

A cost centre is a department or segment of the business to which costs are allocated or apportioned.

In the case of Grogstore Co we can identify two production cost centres: the cutting department and the welding department. This is, of course, a very simple example and in reality most organizations will have many cost centres.

All overhead costs which can be directly attributed to a given cost centre should be **allocated** to it. For example, as there is a manager responsible for the running of each department, his or her salary can be allocated to that department.

	Cutting	Welding
	$	$
Allocated costs:		
Managers' salaries	25,000	28,000

Overhead costs which do not relate directly to one cost centre but rather relate to the running of the business as a whole are then apportioned to each cost centre in the most appropriate and fair way. For example, the property costs can be **apportioned** based upon space occupied by each cost centre:

Cutting department share of property costs: 35/60 m^2 × $92,000 = $53,667
Welding department share of property costs: 25/60 m^2 × $92,000 = $38,333

In a similar manner, administration costs can be apportioned between the two production cost centres based upon the number of employees in each department, and the machine power cost can be apportioned based upon the number of hours worked in each department (labour hours). This will result in the total cost allocation and apportionment between the two production cost centres shown in Table 8.1.

TABLE 8.1

	Cutting $	Welding $	Total $
Allocated costs:			
Managers' salaries	25,000	28,000	53,000
Apportioned costs:			
Property costs (floor space)	53,667	38,333	92,000
Admin costs (no. of employees)	53,625	89,375	143,000
Machine power (hours worked)	9,692	18,308	28,000
Total	141,984	174,016	316,000

There is no fixed basis for apportionment of costs. The method used will depend upon perceptions of what is most appropriate and what information is available. The most important factor is fairness – the allocation and apportionment of costs must fairly reflect the extent to which the cost centre contributes to the generation of those costs.

Once all overhead costs have been allocated or apportioned to production departments and a total cost calculated for each department, that cost is 'absorbed' into individual products by calculating an **overhead absorption rate (OAR)**. This OAR is usually based upon the level of activity (or amount of time) contributed from each department in the making of a single product.

Therefore, for the cutting department of Grogstore Co the OAR can be calculated based upon labour hours as follows:

$$OAR = \frac{\text{Total overhead costs}}{\text{Labour hours worked}} = \frac{\$141{,}984}{9{,}000 \text{ hrs}} = \$15.78 \text{ per hour}$$

This means that for every hour of work done in the cutting department, $15.78 will be charged to the product. As each barrel requires 15 minutes of cutting department time, it will be charged $3.95 ($15.78 × 15/60 minutes) of cutting department costs.

The OAR for the welding department will be:

$$OAR = \frac{\text{Total overhead costs}}{\text{Labour hours worked}} = \frac{\$174{,}016}{17{,}000 \text{ hrs}} = \$10.24 \text{ per hour}$$

As each barrel requires 20 minutes of welding department time, it will be charged $3.41 ($10.24 × 20/60 minutes) of welding department costs.

We can now establish the total cost of producing each barrel, including the relevant overhead costs (Table 8.2).

TABLE 8.2

	$
Direct costs:	
Materials: (2m² @ $3 per m²)	6.00
Labour – cutting: (15 minutes @ $14 per hour)	3.50
Labour – welding: (20 minutes @ $18 per hour)	6.00
Overhead costs:	
Cutting department (15 minutes @ $15.78 per hour)	3.95
Welding department (20 minutes @ $10.24 per hour)	3.41
Total cost:	$22.86

An appropriate sales price can now be calculated by adding the required profit mark-up of 30 per cent:

$$\text{Sales price per barrel} = \$22.86 \times 130\% = \$29.72$$

Expert view 8.2: Mark-up and margin

Once a full cost has been established for a product, the price is calculated by adding mark-up to that full cost. This mark-up is usually a standard percentage which is established by management. For example, a company may decide to add a mark-up of 25 per cent to all its products. If product A has a full cost of production of £80, the sales price will be calculated as:

Sales price of Product A = £80 × 1.25 = £100

At this point it is worth discussing the difference between mark-up and margin, as these are two terms which are frequently confused: mark-up is profit expressed as a percentage of costs; whereas margin is profit expressed as a percentage of sales price.

A simple illustration will show the significance of understanding the difference. Imagine a product that has a cost of £60 and a sales price of £80. This means that the profit will be £20.

$$\text{Mark-up} = \frac{\text{Profit}}{\text{Cost}} = \frac{£20}{£60} = 33\%$$

$$\text{Margin} = \frac{\text{Profit}}{\text{Price}} = \frac{£20}{£80} = 25\%$$

Problems with full-cost-plus pricing

Although full-cost pricing is in theory a method of always ensuring that all costs are covered and a known profit is earned, there are a number of problems with implementing this method in practice.

Firstly, the technique requires the estimation of some important figures, such as annual overhead costs and the volume of output. These figures will not be known for certain until an accounting period is complete, yet they are needed at the start of an accounting period if a price is to be established. Although the technique theoretically establishes the total cost of a product, in practice this is just an estimation and not the actual cost. There is therefore always a risk that estimates are inaccurate and the method does not establish an accurate cost for pricing.

Another problem is that the basis of apportioning and absorbing overheads may well be arbitrary and may result in an unfair or appropriate apportionment of overhead costs between different products and services. This may result in some products or services being overpriced, which could make them uncompetitive. For example, one of the authors once worked in a business division which operated from the old premises of the business after the other divisions had moved into new premises. This building was far too big for the needs of the division and was half empty. Despite this, the division was charged for the full running cost of the premises.

A further disadvantage is that by simply calculating the full cost as it currently stands and adding a mark-up to this, there is no incentive within the system to reduce costs. When we look at pricing within the competitive environment later in this chapter, it will be seen that this can be a significant issue.

Marginal-cost-plus pricing

One way of overcoming some of the problems of full absorption cost pricing is to avoid the process of estimating and apportioning overhead costs. Also, for some businesses, the basic variable costs of production are easy to identify, but overheads are less easy to apportion and allocate. In this case, sales price is determined by adding a profit mark-up to the marginal (variable) cost. This method of costing is widely used in retailing and in professional services.

A retailer can easily identify the cost of products bought in for resale and can establish a consistent gross profit margin by applying a mark-up to this cost. Different retailing businesses have different levels of mark-up. In clothing retailing it is usual to have mark-up on purchase cost of 400–500 per cent. However, in food retailing where volumes of sales are higher, profit margins are much lower and mark-up on direct costs may be as little as 25 per cent.

The marginal-cost-plus pricing method is also frequently used by professional service firms such as solicitors and accountants. For such businesses the direct cost of delivering a service will be the salary of the solicitor or accountant working for the client. The price charged to the client will be based upon a multiple of that salary. This is illustrated in Worked Example 8.2.

WORKED EXAMPLE 8.2   Marginal-cost-plus pricing

A solicitor is paid a salary of £30 per hour. For every hour which she spends working for a given client, that client will be charged £30 × 300% = £90. This price will cover the direct cost of the solicitor's salary and any office overhead costs, and will leave a profit for the firm.

Exercises: now attempt Exercise 8.3 on page 323

Activity-based costing (ABC) pricing

Activity-based costing is a method of costing which was developed to address some of the criticisms of absorption costing discussed above. In a bid to identify and apportion costs more accurately, this approach attributes costs to different organizational activities, rather than departments. The method therefore uses the concept of **cost pools** – the collection of costs which relate to a given activity.

Under absorption costing, different overhead costs will be apportioned to a department which may undertake a range of activities. For example, the production department may accumulate costs for ordering, receiving and holding inventory, machining, assembly, packaging and dispatching. Under ABC these would be identified as separate activities with separate cost pools. The difference between the two approaches to costing is illustrated in Figure 8.2.

Once costs have been apportioned to activities, the **cost driver** for each activity is determined. The cost driver is the metric which best explains why resources are consumed by a particular activity and therefore why the activity incurs costs. The cost driver provides an explanation of the size of the cost pool. This system of activity-based costing is best illustrated with an example which compares the approach with that of traditional absorption costing.

FIGURE 8.2   Traditional absorption costing vs ABC. (a) Traditional absorption costing system; (b) activity-based costing system

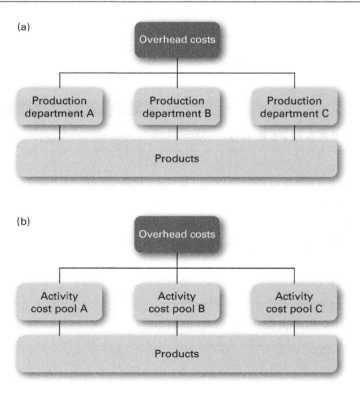

WORKED EXAMPLE 8.3   Activity-based costing and pricing

Pedal Co manufactures a range of different bicycles, including the A-series and the B-series. The A-series is a bicycle aimed at serious sports riders. The company makes and sells 200 of these each year. The B-series is a leisure bicycle. The company makes and sells 5,000 of these each year.

The bicycle frames are made in the company's factory, but all other components, including wheels, are bought in from other suppliers. The factory has a normal production capacity of 10,000 direct labour hours each year.

Production overhead costs relating to receiving raw materials and bought-in components are $240,000 per year. These costs have been identified as relating to the following activities:

Receiving 225 consignments of frame tubing	$90,000
Receiving 250 consignments of components	$150,000

The A-series requires 60 frame-tubing consignments and 50 component assignments. The B-series requires 50 frame-tubing consignments and 75 component assignments.

The direct costs of producing each model of bicycle are as follows:

	A-series	B-series
Direct materials:	450	90
Direct labour:	(2.5 hours@ $16 p.h.) 40	(1.5 hours@ $16 p.h.) 24
	$490	$114

The company applies a standard mark-up on its products of 40 per cent.

Required:
Compare the total cost and therefore the price of the two models of bicycle using traditional absorption costing and activity-based costing.

Answer: Traditional absorption costing

If Pedal Co uses traditional absorption costing, the $240,000 production overhead costs would be absorbed into each model of bicycle using an OAR based upon production time:

$$OAR = \frac{\text{Total overhead costs}}{\text{Labour costs worked}} = \frac{\$240,000}{10,000} = \$24 \text{ per hour}$$

Therefore the total cost and price of each model would be:

	A-series	B-series
Direct costs	$490	$114
Overhead costs	(2.5 hours@ $24 p.h.) 60	(1.5 hours@ $24 p.h.) 36
Total cost	550	150
Price (40% mark-up)	$825	$210

Answer: Activity-based costing

If activity-based costing is used, the overhead costs will be apportioned based upon cost drivers. In this case the cost drivers are receiving the frame tubing and receiving the components. The absorption rate based upon these cost drivers will be:

Receiving frame tubing = $90,000 ÷ 225 = $400 per consignment
Receiving components = $150,000 ÷ 250 = $600 per consignment

These costs will be apportioned to the two models of bicycle based upon the level of activity which each model generates:

	A-series	B-series
Direct costs	$490	$114
Receiving frame tubing	($400 × 60/200) 120	($400 × 50/5,000) 4
Receiving components	($600 × 50/200) 150	($600 × 75/5,000) 9
Total cost	760	127
Price (40% mark-up)	$1,064	$178

This ABC analysis suggests that more overhead costs should be apportioned to the A-series and less to the B-series. This in turn has a knock-on effect on the prices which the company should be charging for each model of bicycle.

Advocates of ABC argue that this calculation provides a much more accurate analysis of the true cost of producing each model of bicycle because the technique is more sensitive to how activities give rise to the overhead costs.

Life-cycle costing and pricing

With many modern high-technology products, life cycles have become much shorter and more costs are incurred at a pre-production stage in research, development and design. This means that direct production costs can be a relatively small part of the overall cost of the product. In such cases it is more useful to identify the costs across the whole life cycle of the product and use these as the basis of establishing a suitable price.

FIGURE 8.3 Life-cycle pricing

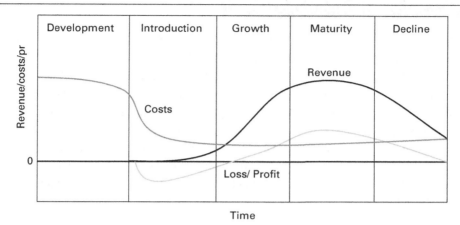

All products can be seen as having a life cycle, from development through to withdrawal from the market. This life cycle, as illustrated in Figure 8.3, has different stages during which costs and revenues will have differing patterns. During development, costs will be incurred but no revenues are earned yet. At the introduction stage, sales may be slow to pick up, meaning that initial sales revenue will be low. At the same time, costs may be relatively high because there is insufficient sales volume to generate economies of scale. In the growth stage, sales begin to pick up and grow rapidly and the product becomes more profitable. During the maturity stage, sales will stabilize at a maximum level. This is usually the most profitable period for a product. As the product enters its final stage of decline, sales and profitability will fall off until the point where management are forced to withdraw the product from the market.

Life-cycle costing recognizes the fact that in order to make a profit, revenues must cover all costs whether they are incurred pre-production, during production or post-production. This focus on costs across the whole life cycle has many advantages. Firstly, focusing on all costs will help management see opportunities for cost reductions. Secondly, many costs will be linked across the life cycle and therefore opportunities for reducing costs later can be identified at an earlier stage. For example, better design may reduce production costs and changes in manufacturing processes may reduce end-of-life decommissioning costs.

A further dimension of life-cycle pricing is the recognition that different pricing strategies may be adopted at different stages in the product's life cycle. The best choice of pricing strategy at any given stage will depend upon customers' perceptions, competition and the nature of the product being sold. All of these factors, together with the appropriate strategies, will be discussed as we progress through this chapter.

Conclusions: costing for pricing

A major disadvantage of all the costing methods examined above is that they are entirely inward looking. That is to say, they ignore the impact which price has on demand. By simply calculating the costs of production and adding a mark-up for profit, one is assuming that the customer will be willing to pay the price that is arrived at through these calculations. In reality, customers are not concerned with how much it cost to make a product. Rather, they are interested in the value the product provides them and they will be reluctant to pay a price which does not offer good value. Furthermore, the internal focus ignores the activities of competitors. If competitors are producing similar products at lower costs, they will be able to undercut the business's price. It is therefore important to consider these external factors and these are the subject of the following sections.

The economist's perspective

From the economist's perspective we look at the competitive environment of the business and how this will impact on pricing strategy. There are two aspects of economic theory which we want to consider in relation to pricing. The first is the concept of the price elasticity of demand. The second concept is that of market type or market context: the competitive conditions in which the business operates.

Price elasticity of demand

Generally speaking, as the price of a product or service increases, the demand for it will decrease. However, the amount by which that demand decreases will vary across different products or services, for a number of reasons (which will be explored later in the chapter). The relationship of this change in demand to a change in price is known as the **price elasticity of demand (PED)**. Economists measure this with the following formula:

$$PED = \frac{\text{Percentage change in demand}}{\text{Percentage change in price}}$$

The greater the percentage change in demand in relation to a given price change, the more '**elastic**' that demand is said to be. If a 10 per cent increase in price creates a 30 per cent fall in demand, demand is said to be relatively *elastic*. On the other hand, if a 10 per cent increase in price creates only a 5 per cent fall in demand, demand is said to be relatively *inelastic*.

It is important for a business to understand how elastic the demand is for its products or services, as this price elasticity of demand will have an impact on the success of different price strategies. For example, if a business knows that the demand for its products is relatively inelastic, it would not pursue a strategy of cutting prices in order to try to stimulate demand. The importance of this relationship is explained in the following section.

Price elasticity of demand and total revenue

In order to appreciate the importance of price elasticity of demand upon pricing strategies, it is necessary to understand the relationship between demand, price and total revenue. In Figure 8.4 total revenue is represented by the area enclosed by the lines P_1, A, D_1. This area is a graphical representation of the fact that *price × demand = revenue*:

FIGURE 8.4 Total revenue

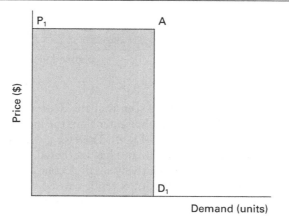

Now look at Figure 8.5 where the price is reduced from P_1 to P_2. That reduction in price stimulates an increase in demand from D_1 to D_2. In this example, demand is relatively **inelastic** in relation to price so that the decrease in price creates a relatively small increase in demand. Now look at the relative change in total revenue as

FIGURE 8.5 Price inelasticity

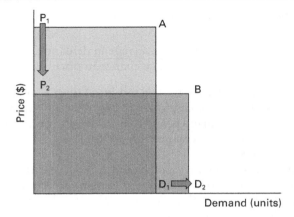

FIGURE 8.6 Price elasticity

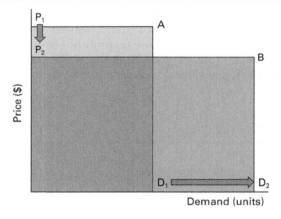

indicated by the shaded boxes. It can be seen that the decrease in revenue resulting from the price cuts (box P_1–P_2–A) is much greater than the increase in revenue resulting from the increase in demand (box D_1–D_2–B). Therefore, overall revenue falls as a result of the cut in price, even though demand has increased.

On the other hand, in Figure 8.6 a relatively small decrease in price creates a large increase in demand. In this case the loss of revenue caused by the fall in price (box P_1–P_2–A) is more than offset by the increase in revenue from the greater demand (box D_1–D_2–B). As a result, overall revenue will increase due to the price cut.

What determines elasticity?

The graphs above serve to illustrate the way in which the price elasticity of demand can be a hugely important factor when it comes to pricing. Therefore, it is important for a business to understand what determines the elasticity of demand for its products or services. Managers also need to understand how they can take measures to change the price elasticity of demand. Generally speaking, it is more beneficial for a business to have low price elasticity of demand. This means that managers will seek methods for reducing elasticity. In this section we will look at the factors which determine the price elasticity of demand and look at how it may be possible to manipulate those.

The relative price of the goods

The more expensive that something is, relatively speaking, the more elastic demand will be. For example, if a bar of chocolate costs $0.50 and the price increases by 20 per cent to $0.60, this increase is unlikely to have a major impact upon demand. On the other hand, if a car costing $25,000 increases in price by 20 per cent to $30,000, this increase will decrease demand as it will put the car out of the affordable price range of some existing customers.

The price of other goods

Economists identify two different categories of related goods or services, the price of which can have an impact upon the price of other goods or services.

The first category is *complementary* goods. These are products which go together, such as video games and gaming consoles. If the price of a complementary good increases, this may have a negative impact upon the demand of your product. For example, if the price of gaming consoles increases so that fewer people can afford them, then fewer people will be buying games (see Extract 8.1).

The second category is *substitute* goods. These are goods which a customer could buy instead of the item we are trying to price because they can be substituted in its place. An example is two mobile phones from different manufacturers with similar specifications. If the price of a competitor's phone is less than the price of your similar model, a customer will buy the competitor's phone as it represents better value.

Consumer income

Products or services can be categorized in terms of how their price elasticity of demand changes with levels of consumer income. Some items, known as *staple goods*, will have a relatively stable level of demand, regardless of consumer income. A simple example might be a basic foodstuff such as potatoes or rice. Generally speaking, people tend to eat the same amount of potatoes or rice, regardless of their level of income. An increase in income will not increase demand for this type of goods.

A second category of goods, known as *luxury goods*, will be subject to an increase in demand as consumers' income increases. This will include items such as expensive holidays, luxury cars and jewellery.

A third category of goods, known as *inferior goods*, will be subject to a fall in demand as consumers' income increases. These goods may not actually be inferior in terms of quality, but they are in terms of consumers' perception. Therefore, for example, a consumer on a low income may buy a pair of cheap unbranded denim jeans. If that consumer has an increase in income, he or she may stop buying the cheap jeans in favour of more expensive brand-name clothing.

Tastes and fashions

Tastes and fashions can have a significant impact on the elasticity of demand for products and services. It is not unusual to see the latest 'must have' children's toy, usually linked to a recently released film, selling at a very high price and yet parents are falling over each other to buy it. On the other hand, last season's clothes can usually be found in the bargain bin when nobody wants to buy them, even at a fraction of their original price.

Expectations

If customers expect the price of a product to increase in the near future, this can increase demand in the short term. An example of this is seen in the UK each year before the Chancellor's budget. The usual expectation is that the Chancellor will increase taxation on vehicle fuel. This leads to large queues at filling stations the evening before the budget, as drivers rush to fill their vehicles in expectation of an increase in fuel prices.

Obsolescence

Aside from changes in taste and fashions, goods can also become obsolete. This is particularly the case with high-technology products. Once a new version with a higher specification has been released, demand for the older version usually falls off very quickly and customers are not willing to buy that product even at a substantially reduced price. Another issue, related to obsolescence, is how long a product lasts. If a product has a relatively short life before it wears out or breaks, then over a long period customers will buy more of that item. However, this must always be balanced with customer expectations of value. If a product wears out or breaks sooner than the customer thinks it ought to, the customer may boycott that item in the future.

Pricing within market context

The second aspect of economic theory that is important to pricing is market type, or market context. This refers to the competitive conditions in which the business operates. This can refer to the number and type of competitors and the ability of a business to differentiate itself from competitors.

Economists identity four types of market:

- perfect competition;
- monopoly;
- monopolistic competition;
- oligopoly.

Each of these different types of market has an implication for the business's ability to determine its own pricing strategy, and therefore whether it is a *price setter* or a *price taker*. It is therefore extremely important for a business to understand what type of market it operates in and how this will impact on it.

Perfect competition

Perfect competition describes the situation in which there are many buyers and sellers in a market, none of whom is big or powerful enough to influence the market. New sellers can freely enter the market at any time and all firms operating within the market are selling products or services which are difficult to differentiate, so that they are essentially identical. This means that customers are likely to choose between the products or services of different businesses purely upon the basis of price. The consequence is that an individual business will find it very difficult to set a price which differs from that of every other seller in the market. This situation is illustrated in Worked Example 8.4.

WORKED EXAMPLE 8.4 Perfect competition and pricing

Imagine a large fruit and vegetable market in which there are 30 stalls all selling oranges which were purchased from the same wholesaler and are therefore indistinguishable in quality. If 29 of the stalls sell the oranges at $0.50 each, what will happen if one stall attempts to sell the oranges at $0.60 each? The likely outcome is that the more expensive stall will be unable to sell any oranges, as customers, freely able to see the price and quality of the oranges at all the other stalls, will buy oranges elsewhere. On the other hand, what would happen if one stall dropped its price to $0.40 per orange? Again, because customers are able to compare prices and quality freely, they will all rush to the one stall to buy the cheaper oranges. This will force all of the other stallholders to reduce their price to $0.40. The ultimate outcome is that the original price-cutting stall will have no price advantage and all stallholders will have lost profit by selling their oranges at a lower price.

The implication is therefore that the closer to perfect competition the market conditions are, the more difficult it will be for an individual firm to set its own prices. Each firm selling within that market will be forced to go along with the prevailing market price.

It is interesting that the internet and, in particular, price comparison sites have made information much more freely available to customers and have created a situation very close to perfect competition for many retailers.

Monopoly

A monopoly describes a situation where a market is dominated by one major seller. In this situation customers will have little or no option to buy from an alternative supplier. This gives the monopoly business far more control over pricing. A business can have a monopoly through ownership of patents or copyrights or through access to limited resources. Any aspect of the market which creates a barrier to entry for other firms can result in a monopoly.

Provided that there is not a very high level of elasticity of demand, a monopoly will be able to charge higher prices and customers will continue to buy from them, simply because they have no other option. Because this creates a situation in which the supplier can potentially abuse customers, many jurisdictions have created competition laws to prevent or restrict monopolies. In the UK many industries have been broken up to remove monopolies in an attempt to create more price competition among suppliers. Examples include electricity and gas suppliers, telecommunications and rail transport.

Monopolistic competition

Monopolistic competition describes a market in which there are multiple buyers and sellers, but sellers are able to differentiate their products or services from those of their competitors. This means that if you are able to persuade customers that your product is somehow better than that of your competitors, for example by having better features or being of a better quality, you will be able to charge a higher price.

The market for many common products and services can be seen as falling into this category. Businesses operating in such a market tend to spend a lot of money on marketing to establish brand loyalty and to convince customers that their products should be purchased in preference to those of competitors.

Oligopoly

Oligopoly describes the situation where a market is dominated by a small number of suppliers selling similar products or services. A surprisingly large number of markets are oligopolies: car manufacturers, computer manufacturers, petrol and oil suppliers, gas and electricity suppliers and mobile telephone providers are all oligopolies. When there is an oligopoly, even though there are multiple suppliers in competition, the suppliers are few enough in number to be able to cooperate and work together to control prices. An example of this is OPEC, the group of oil producing nations that work together to control oil prices.

Extract 8.2: The perils of trading with an oligopoly

The supermarket industry in the UK is a well-known oligopoly, being dominated by four major businesses: Tesco, Sainsbury, Asda and Morrisons. This means that leading food producers must trade with the supermarkets, which consequently dominate their order book and squeeze their profit margins. However, smaller food producers are often unable to deal with the major supermarkets and therefore sell to independent retailers. As this is a more open market, it enables them to charge more reasonable prices and earn higher profit margins.

The marketer's perspective

The marketer's perspective on price is concerned with the impact that price will have upon consumers' perception and purchasing behaviour. Price is therefore one of the 4 P's of the marketing mix, the others being product, promotion and place.

Expert view 8.3: the marketing mix

The marketing mix is that set of factors which are regarded as being crucial in marketing a product or service. Since the 1960s this has been commonly referred to as the **4P's**: *price, product, promotion* and *place* (McCarthy, 1960). However, this model has been refined and developed over time so that there is now a **7P's** model of the marketing mix (*price, product, promotion, place, people, process* and *physical evidence*) which is considered to be more appropriate for marketing services rather than products. Also, more recently a **4C's** model has been proposed as being a more consumer-focused view of the marketing mix. This has two alternative versions, the first being *consumer, cost, communication, convenience* (Schulz *et al*, 1993) and the second being *commodity, cost, communication, channel* (Shimizu 1973). Regardless of the variation in detail and emphasis, in all these models of the marketing mix the *price* or *cost* to the consumer is highlighted as being a key factor.

The impact of price on consumer behaviour

From a marketing perspective, price is important because it has an impact on the customer's perceived value of the product. It is therefore not so much the price itself but the customer's perception of that price which is important. If customers can be convinced that a higher price represents good value for a product or service, they will be willing to pay a higher price.

In the section on the economist's perspective we looked at a number of factors which can affect the price elasticity of demand. The marketer is equally concerned with these factors, as good marketing may be able to reduce the price elasticity of demand. That will enable the business either to charge higher prices or to gain more customers at existing prices.

Expert view 8.4: Product positioning

In a competitive market it is important to make your products or services stand out from those of your competitors, an activity which is known as *product positioning*. There are several academic models of product positioning which look at different aspects of what is important to customers, but pricing is widely recognized as being key. Generally speaking, businesses will want to charge the highest price they can, but their ability to persuade customers to pay a higher price will depend upon customers' perception of the quality of what they receive for their money. The model in Figure 8.7 illustrates how price maps against quality in product positioning.

The product positioning price/quality model shows four general strategies which a business might follow (A, B, C or D). Of the four quadrants available, only quadrants C and B offer sensible strategies. Strategy A is to charge a lower price for a high-quality product. This strategy will certainly attract customers but it will not be one which maximizes profit for the firm. Strategy B is to charge a high price for a high-quality product. This is a strategy followed by many businesses that sell luxury products. Customers are willing to pay a higher price because they believe that what they are getting is a better product. Strategy C is to sell a lower-quality product at a low price. This is another common strategy. The business will charge a low price and thereby gain a high volume of sales, so that even if the profit per item is low the overall profitability will be high. Strategy D is to sell a low-quality product at a high price. This strategy is unlikely to succeed in the long term as customers will realize that they can get better-quality products at the same price elsewhere.

Many businesses combine strategies B and C by offering a range of products at different qualities and different prices. For example, most major supermarkets have a budget low-cost range, a normal range and a luxury high-cost range of foods.

FIGURE 8.7   Product positioning

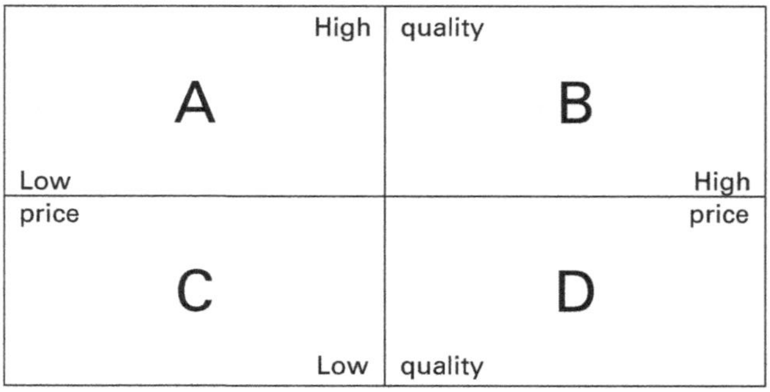

Price perception

Customers are looking for good value from any product or service they buy and will therefore be unwilling to pay a price which they believe does not offer value. The level of sensitivity to price will generally vary with the absolute price being charged. That is to say, most customers will unhesitatingly buy something which is relatively cheap, say $0.50, but will stop and think before buying something which is more expensive, such as $1,000. (As explained in the economist's perspective above, this will also vary according to the level of the consumer's disposable income.)

If customers are looking for value from a product, it can be useful to make customers believe that a product is cheaper than it actually is. It is therefore not unusual to see products priced at $9.99 rather than $10, or $79.99 rather than $80. The objective of this pricing, which is sometimes known as *psychological pricing*, is to overcome any perceived price barriers that customers may have. A customer may consider $10 to be too expensive, so pricing the product at $9.99 makes an important psychological difference.

Perception of quality

If customers perceive a product or service to be of a higher quality, they will be willing to pay a higher price. It is the customer's perception of quality rather than the actual quality itself which is important. This is why many businesses invest in heavy advertising which emphasizes the quality of their products.

Perception of difference from other products

Differentiating your products from those of competitors is another way of persuading customers to pay a higher price. This involves persuading customers to buy based upon other elements of the marketing mix, such as special or unique features of the goods, special promotion activities, brand loyalty, and place (where the goods or services can be obtained).

Consumer ethics

Goods or services which satisfy customers' ethical concerns can command higher prices. For example, customers will be willing to pay higher prices for free-range eggs, fair-trade products, carbon-neutral products, sustainable products or foodstuffs which have been farmed organically in order to reduce damage to the environment.

Differentiating customers

Another important aspect of marketing is the recognition that not all customers will behave in the same way. For a given product within a given market, some customers will have relatively high price elasticity of demand whereas other customers will have relatively low price elasticity of demand. An important skill in marketing is identifying and targeting different groups of customers according to their willingness to pay. An example of this is supermarkets which have a 'value' range of products for thrifty customers, a normal range of products for the majority of customers, and a premium or luxury range of products for better-off customers.

Combining the three perspectives: establishing an appropriate pricing strategy

Now that we have looked at the different issues which go into the pricing decision and the factors which influence prices, we can look at how organizations should consider these when establishing pricing strategies. Figure 8.8 sets out a range of different pricing strategies. Before we look at these in detail, we need to consider some general principles. Firstly, the long-term pricing strategy of an organization should be in line with the organization's mission and broader strategic objectives. Secondly, any pricing strategy adopted should always be informed by all three C's of pricing discussed above: costs, competitors and customers.

Broadly speaking, there are three considerations that will help the business frame an appropriate pricing strategy. These relate to the following questions:

1 Are we pricing a new or existing product or service?
2 Are we going to a new or existing market?
3 Are we a volume-driven or a price-driven business?

New product or existing product?

If a business is launching a new product or a product with substantial new features (ie one that is not currently offered by any competitor), there will be no competition for that product. This may mean a relatively inelastic demand and a high level of interest in the product. On the other hand, if the business is launching a product which is similar to those already available from competitors, it needs to compare that new product with those already available. Are the features comparable? Are there new or unique features? These factors will impact upon the business's ability to charge higher prices. For example, when Apple launched the iPad there were no comparable products available. This, together with the relative price inelasticity of the market, enabled Apple to charge high prices for their new product. However, as other competing manufacturers launched similar products they had to price more competitively in recognition of the fact that there were several substitute products available.

New market or existing market?

If a business is entering an existing market where other similar products are already on sale, they will need to analyse what competitors are charging and set their prices accordingly. On the other hand, if a business is entering a new market where there is no existing competition, pricing will be based upon expectations of what customers are willing to pay.

Volume driven or price driven?

Businesses that have large fixed overhead costs tend to be volume driven in their pricing strategy. For example, an airline will have a largely fixed cost of operating a flight. It will therefore manipulate its prices in order to fill all the seats on an aeroplane whilst covering those fixed costs. In a similar manner, supermarkets have high fixed costs. They price to sell a high volume of products at a low margin. On the other hand, businesses that are price driven tend to have low fixed overheads. Such businesses do not need high volumes of sales.

Pricing strategies

Having considered these overriding issues, let us look at the range of pricing strategies available. These can be seen as a range of pricing positions in relation to the prices of competitors, as illustrated in Figure 8.8.

FIGURE 8.8 Price-positioning strategies

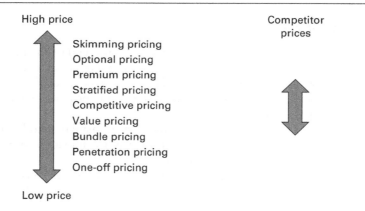

High price

Competitor prices

Skimming pricing
Optional pricing
Premium pricing
Stratified pricing
Competitive pricing
Value pricing
Bundle pricing
Penetration pricing
One-off pricing

Low price

1) Market skimming pricing

A market skimming pricing strategy involves launching a new product at a very high price and then gradually reducing the price over time. This strategy is often used to launch a new technology product which has little or no competition. It takes advantage of the fact that demand for the new product will be relatively inelastic for some customers. This strategy is effectively a type of price discrimination which segments the market in terms of how long customers are willing to wait before obtaining the new product. For example, if a new specification of smart phone is launched, some customers, referred to as *early adopters*, will want to buy that new phone immediately, with little regard to the cost. The seller is therefore able to charge a very high price at launch. On the other hand, some consumers will only buy that new phone once the price is substantially lower, and they are willing to wait several months after launch before buying it.

Price skimming is by necessity a short-term strategy applicable only to the launch stage of a new product, as it relies on the uniqueness and novelty of the new product. As competitors launch comparative products this will put downward pressure on prices. A business also has to be careful in the timing of reducing the price. If prices are kept high for too long, a relatively small volume of sales will be achieved and there is a risk that a competitor may develop an alternative product which goes on to take a higher volume of the market.

2) Optional pricing

Optional pricing is another method of segmenting the market in order to maximize profit. This strategy is used by many car manufacturers. Rather than just offering one version of a particular model of car, the manufacturer will offer a basic model with a range of enhancement options at additional cost. These options will include larger and more powerful engines, alloy wheels, leather interiors, more electric and electronic gadgetry and so on. By offering a range of different versions of the car at different prices the business is able to capture a wider range of customers and to make more profit from those customers willing to pay for the higher specifications.

3) Premium pricing

Premium pricing is a strategy of setting prices at the top end of the range offered by competitors. A business using this strategy is not trying to compete on price. Rather, it will concentrate on competing through the other elements of the marketing mix, such as product quality or features, ease of access to the product or service (ie availability) or the way the product is promoted.

Establishing a strong brand name to reduce price elasticity enables a business to charge premium prices. Strong branding also reduces the impact of substitute goods. Coca-Cola is an example of strong product branding.

Ethical products also tend to be premium priced as they are meeting non-price-based consumer needs.

Extract 8.3: Premium pricing at MV Agusta

The iconic Italian motorcycle brand MV Agusta has a reputation built upon a racing heritage, stylish Italian design and high performance. The company opts for a niche marketing strategy that emphasizes this reputation and is enhanced by celebrity customers such as actors Brad Pitt, Tom Cruise and Angelina Jolie, and former Formula One world champion Michael Schumacher.

The company has a strategy of maintaining the essence of this brand and focusing on high-quality product development. Part of this strategy is charging premium prices for its products.

4) Stratified pricing: Price discrimination and market segmentation

Price discrimination is the practice of charging different prices to different customers for the same product or service. This practice is common in a number of industries. For it to be successful it is important that the market for the product and service can be successfully segmented such that customers are not able to move between the different price brackets. One example of market segmentation is peak and off-peak travel. Customers are charged different prices for the same service depending on when they use that service. A business using this strategy is taking advantage of the fact that those customers who will need to travel during peak commuting times have little flexibility about when they travel. There is therefore relatively little elasticity of demand, so prices can be increased. On the other hand, customers travelling for leisure generally have more flexibility about when they travel. They can be attracted to use buses or trains during off-peak times by making this cheaper.

A second form of *stratified pricing* involves producing a range of similar products but with different features to meet the needs of different customers. An example of this is the different classes of air travel available. Three passengers may all fly from Paris to New York at the same time on the same aeroplane. However, each will pay a different price (and receive a different level of service) by flying economy class, business class or first class. The airline divides the market for air travel into three different market segments.

Extract 8.4: Stratified pricing wins Apple the US market

The world of mobile phones is dominated by two major players: Apple and Samsung. Apple is known for its premium pricing strategy and perhaps because of this Samsung has achieved a higher volume of smartphone sales across the world. However, towards the end of 2012 Apple ended Samsung's four-year lead in the US mobile phone market. With the launch of the iPhone 5, Apple also offered lower-priced, old versions of the iPhone, shipping an estimated 17.7 million phones to the United States in the last three months of 2012. This **stratified pricing strategy** provided a range of phones to satisfy the needs of more budget-conscious consumers. Apple's share of the market increased from 25 to 34 per cent in one year.

5) Competitive pricing

A competitive pricing strategy will be adopted by a business operating in a market that is close to perfect competition. These market conditions make it difficult for the firm to charge prices that are significantly higher or lower than those of competitors. The business will therefore price its products very close to the price of competitors.

6) Value pricing

Value pricing involves selling a product which is of similar quality to that of competitors at a lower price. The aim of this strategy is to attract customers by offering better value than competitors. Although this strategy can mean that the business is potentially not maximizing its profit from each sale, the aim is to increase sales volume so that overall profitability is increased. This strategy uses the consumer psychology in the product positioning model discussed earlier in this chapter.

Extract 8.5: Value pricing at Amazon – a strategy for market monopoly

Amazon, the online retailer, has established a business model that enables it to operate at very low profit margins – often 2 per cent or less – whilst delivering a high-quality service and cheaper products than the competition. It is estimated that Amazon now has over one-third of the entire e-commerce market in the United States. This strong position has enabled Amazon to undercut new market entrants and increase its dominance of the e-commerce world. In addition, the online retailer has steadily squeezed out high-street bookshops and DVD retailers.

---

7) Bundle pricing

Bundle pricing is often used by retailers to entice customers to spend more. Typical bundle pricing strategies include 'buy one get one free' (BOGOF) or 'three for the price of two'. Such a strategy decreases the profit margin on each product sold, but increases the volume of sales such that the retailer can achieve an overall higher level of profit. Usually this is a short-term pricing strategy.

Another strategy commonly used by retailers, particularly supermarkets, is that of the *loss leader*. A loss leader is a product which is priced below cost in order to attract customers into the store. The rationale behind the loss leader is that it will attract customers who will then buy other products whilst in the store. This must be a short-term pricing strategy for any one product.

In some cases, prices may be deliberately set very low, even giving away products for free, by a dominant business in the market in order to cut out competitors. This is known as *predatory pricing*, a practice which is illegal under competition law in most legislations.

8) Penetration pricing

Market penetration pricing is the strategy of introducing a new product at a very low price in order to entice consumers to buy that product. In some cases, this may involve selling at a price which is lower than the cost of production. (As mentioned above, this is known as a *loss leader*.) Once the product is established in the market, the price can be brought back up in line with competitors' prices. This is therefore a strategy for increasing market share through sales volume and will only succeed if there is a relatively high level of price elasticity.

This is a good strategy to adopt when launching a new product into an existing market which already contains several similar products. The goal of the business launching the new product is to encourage customers to switch to their product because of its lower price. An example is the launch of a new washing powder. There are already several different brands of washing powder on the market. By launching the new washing powder at a low price the business should achieve two important objectives. Firstly, they will make their product more attractive than that of their competitors. Secondly, by gaining relatively high levels of sales very quickly they will be able to establish economies of scale, thus reducing the cost per unit. Once customer habits have been established in buying the new product, the business can increase the price so that it is in line with those of competitors.

9) One-off pricing

One-off pricing has been kept as a separate category here because it relates to certain unusual pricing situations. It is at the bottom end of the pricing scale in Figure 8.8 because the strategy usually (but not necessarily) involves selling at a very low price. This pricing strategy will be used by a business that has surplus inventory that could not otherwise be sold. Rather than setting a price to recover the full cost of the product, the business recognizes that any price which covers selling costs will put the business in a better financial position than if it kept the otherwise unusable inventory. This principle is illustrated in Worked Example 8.5.

WORKED EXAMPLE 8.5   One-off pricing

Glaze Co manufactures window units. The company took an order for 50 windows from a customer that subsequently went bankrupt and never paid for or collected the windows. The windows cost $20,000 to manufacture. Another customer has placed an order for similar windows. Glaze Co could change the specification of the 50 windows it already has in stock to meet the needs of a new customer at a further cost of $5,000. It has no other use for the windows which otherwise would be scrapped. Glaze Co usually adds a mark-up of 30 per cent to the cost of windows in arriving at a sales price.

What is the minimum price that Glaze Co should accept from the new customer for the 50 windows?

Answer
In this case Glaze Co should ignore the $20,000 it has already spent on manufacturing the windows. If it costs only $5,000 to adapt the windows to the needs of the new customer, any price above $5,000 will put Glaze Co in a better financial position than not selling the windows and having to scrap them. The company should therefore be happy to negotiate any price above $5,000.

Exercises: now attempt Exercise 8.1 on page 322

Target pricing and target costing

Target pricing is an approach to pricing which combines the three elements discussed in this chapter (cost, competitors and customers). It does so in a manner which recognizes the importance of cost on profitability, whilst ensuring that the competitive focus on customers and competitors leads cost considerations rather than being subsumed by them. The technique originated in Japan in the 1960s, but by the 1980s it was being widely used by a range of businesses across the world.

Target pricing involves examining the market and customer preferences in order to determine in advance what the optimum price would be. The business then sets itself the target of producing the goods or services at a cost which will enable a profit at the target price. This process typically involves the following five steps:

1 Develop a new product based upon analysis of customer needs and demands.

2 Set a target price that is based upon customers' perceived value of the product.

3 Set a target profit margin. This will be based upon the required return on investment. (See Chapter 6 for more details of return on investment.)

4 Derive the target cost of production by subtracting the target profit from the target price.

5 In many cases there will be a cost gap between actual cost per unit and the target cost per unit. Techniques such as **value engineering** and **kaizen** (see below) can then be used to bring actual costs as close as possible to target costs.

This process is illustrated in Figure 8.9.

FIGURE 8.9   The target costing process

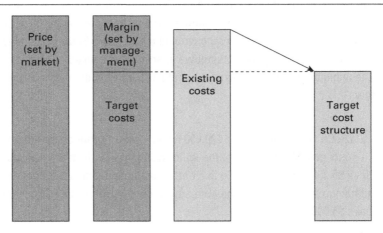

Value engineering

Value engineering is a customer-focused approach to product design. It involves identifying those parts of a product or service that add value and equally importantly eliminating those features which do not add value. The aim of value engineering is to maximize value to the consumer whilst minimizing costs.

Value engineering focuses on the planning and design stage of a product's life cycle and strives to ensure that products are designed in such a way that it is possible to produce them to target costs. Some features, although desirable, may be much too expensive to manufacture. Sometimes minor changes at the design stage can create huge efficiency savings once manufacturing commences. If such matters are not dealt with at the planning stage, it may be impossible to meet target costs no matter how efficient the production process is.

In practice, activity-based costing will be an important tool at the product design stage, as it will help in decision making about how product features will translate to manufacturing costs. By understanding the cost drivers a business will be better able to control its costs.

Kaizen

Kaizen is a Japanese term which refers to a philosophy of continuous improvement in operations. In practice, it means continually examining the manufacturing processes and business systems of the organization in order to identify and implement efficiency changes which will reduce costs. The focus of kaizen is typically on small improvements, rather than large and drastic changes to production processes. An example of a kaizen improvement can be as simple as moving the location of a parts trolley by one metre in order to improve the efficiency and speed at which an operative works.

Exercises: now attempt Exercise 8.2 on page 323

Conclusion

This chapter has examined the factors that go into the pricing decision and has set out a range of pricing strategies used across different industries. In practice, the pricing decision can be very difficult. It may not be possible to obtain the information needed to make some of the evaluations set out in this chapter. Furthermore, many markets are volatile and the factors underpinning pricing are constantly changing. The pace of change of technology and new innovation in many products and services makes the life cycle of a product and the competitive environment extremely uncertain. This means that managers must continually review their pricing strategies and the costing, competitor and consumer factors which underpin them.

COMPREHENSION QUESTIONS

1 Distinguish between the three main perspectives on pricing and identify the main concerns of each perspective.

2 What are the 3C's of pricing and how does each impact upon price?

3 Distinguish between full-cost and marginal-cost pricing.

4 Explain the concept of life-cycle costing and how this relates to pricing.

5 If a product is known to have a low price elasticity of demand and a company reduces its price in order to stimulate demand, would you expect this to lead to increased or decreased overall sales revenues?

6 Publisher Co sells both paper books and e-books. If the company reduces the price of its e-books, should it expect demand for paper books to increase or decrease?

7 Explain how customers' expectations can impact upon the price they are willing to pay for a product.

8 What is price skimming and under what circumstances is it an appropriate pricing strategy?

Answers on pages 323–324

Exercises

Answers on pages 325 – 326

Exercise 8.1: Pricing strategy

XTA Co is about to launch a new personal computer called the *Eye* which the user wears like a pair of glasses. Interaction with the computer is through eye movement and voice. No competitors are offering such an advanced product, but two competitors are expected to launch a similar device within the next six months. Market research has indicated that there is a great deal of customer excitement about this new computer and there have been several favourable articles in leading computer magazines.

Required:
Set out a pricing strategy for the new product, explaining why you consider it to be the most appropriate.

Exercise 8.2: Target pricing

ACT Motors, a large vehicle manufacturer, is seeking to launch a new family saloon car. The market for such cars is already well established and highly competitive.

Required:
Explain the main steps ACT Motors should take in developing a target price for the new family saloon car.

Exercise 8.3: Marginal-cost-plus pricing

Printit Co provides rapid printing and design services to the public and small businesses. The business, which has 12 employees, operates out of a high-street shop which includes office space. The company undertakes 400 to 500 jobs each month. It currently operates a full-cost-plus pricing system, and as each job is unique it must be priced individually. The accountant, who works part-time, is struggling to keep on top of the task of pricing each job. She has suggested that the company should move to a marginal-cost-plus pricing system as this would make pricing much easier.

Required:
Discuss the advantages and disadvantages for Printit Co of changing to a marginal-cost-plus pricing system from its existing full-cost-plus pricing system.

Answers to comprehension questions

1 The three main perspectives on pricing are the accountant's perspective, the economist's perspective and the marketer's perspective. The accountant is primarily concerned with the relationship between revenues and costs and seeks to set a price which will generate the desired level of profit. The economist is primarily concerned with the competitive environment and the impact which price will have upon the behaviour of competitors and customers. The marketer is primarily concerned with the way in which a customer perceives the goods or services provided and sees price as one element that contributes to that perception.

2 The 3C's of pricing are: costs, customers and competitors. A business must set the price which covers its costs, is attractive to customers and enables it to compete with competitors.

3 Full-cost pricing involves calculating the full cost of producing an item for sale. This will include an apportionment of indirect and overhead costs. Marginal-cost pricing involves calculating only the direct costs of an item and adding sufficient mark-up to cover indirect and overhead costs. Each method has advantages and disadvantages and which is the most appropriate will depend upon the circumstances of the business.

4 Life-cycle costing involves costing a product over its entire life cycle rather than calculating the immediate cost of producing a unit now. The aim of using life-cycle costing for pricing is to ensure that a product makes a profit overall. It is more appropriate than traditional techniques for pricing those products which have a short life cycle and involve high pre-production costs. For such items the pre-production costs may be far more significant than ongoing production costs and it is important to ensure that these are incorporated into the price to ensure overall profitability.

5 If the product has a low price elasticity of demand, a change in price will result in a relatively small change in demand. Therefore, if the price is reduced, demand is unlikely to increase by very much. As a result, overall revenue will be reduced.

6 Paper books and e-books can be seen as substitute goods. Therefore, if the price of e-books is reduced, we can expect the demand for paper books to decrease.

7 There are a number of aspects of customer expectations which will impact upon price. For example, if customers expect supply to decrease or stop in the future, they may be willing to pay higher prices to obtain a product now. Equally, if customers expect prices to increase in the future, they will be willing to pay more now.

8 Price skimming is usually used at the launch of a new product. The strategy works best for products which have previously been unavailable or have new features. The strategy involves launching with a very high price and then gradually bringing the price down over time. This strategy takes advantage of the fact that the price elasticity of demand is not the same for all customers: some customers will be willing to pay a high price to have the product immediately, whereas other customers will not buy the product until the price falls. By starting with a high price and bringing the price down over time, the company is able to maximize the profit it earns from the product.

Answers to exercises

Exercise 8.1: Pricing strategy

The most appropriate pricing strategy for the *Eye* would be price skimming. This would involve launching the product at a relatively high cost. As there is already a lot of marketing excitement about the product, there is likely to be a substantial number of customers who will be willing to pay a premium price in order to be among the first users of this new personal computer.

Once competitors bring similar products onto the market, XTA Co can reduce the price of the *Eye* to make it more competitive. This strategy will enable XTA Co to maximize profits whilst there is no competition for the *Eye*, but then compete or even undercut competitors once they enter the market.

XTA Co will have first-mover advantage in the market. By the time competitors place their products, XTA Co will already be established with customers. Furthermore, the company will hopefully have achieved sufficient volume of sales to bring unit production costs down through economies of scale. This will enable the company to match competitors' prices or undercut them while still earning higher levels of profit.

Exercise 8.2: Target pricing

ACT Motors should take the following steps in developing a target price for the new family saloon car:

Step one: the company must develop a new car which meets customer needs in order to attract adequate sales. Market research should be undertaken in order to establish the features which customers most desire and preferably identify features not provided by competitors.

Step two: a target price should be set based upon an analysis of customers' perceived value of the new car. Market research should be undertaken in order to establish an appropriate price. If the new car has significant new features not available from competitors, a premium pricing strategy may be chosen by setting the price higher than that of competitors. Alternatively, a value pricing strategy could be adopted by offering a product which is comparable with those of competitors at a slightly lower price.

Step three: senior management should set the desired profit margin for the new car. This will be based upon company policy and will be in line with strategic targets for return on investment or return on sales.

Step four: the target cost of the new car will be derived by subtracting the target profit margin from the target price.

Step five: projected actual costs should be analysed against target cost and steps taken to reduce actual costs should they be in excess of the target costs. This will involve techniques such as value engineering and kaizen.

Exercise 8.3: Marginal-cost-plus pricing

The current pricing system used by Printit Co involves identifying all of the costs involved in each job, including the relevant proportion of overhead costs, and adding the desired profit margin. A marginal-cost-plus system would need to identify only those costs incurred as a consequence of the job being undertaken. In this case, that would involve the costs of staff time and any materials consumed.

For a business like Printit Co, overhead costs will include the property, computer and printing equipment. These costs are unlikely to vary with the number of jobs undertaken.

Investment decisions

OBJECTIVE

All organizations have to make investment decisions through the process of acquiring, replacing or upgrading premises, equipment or vehicles, hiring new staff, investing in training, or changing systems and procedures. Such decisions must make strategic sense for the organization, but they must also make good financial sense. It is because of this that managers at all levels find themselves involved in the financial evaluation of investments, whether it be in preparing proposals or evaluating options. This chapter therefore aims to provide the understanding necessary for managers to participate in the financial evaluation of investment opportunities.

LEARNING OUTCOMES

After studying this chapter, the reader will be able to:

- Assess the financial impact of an investment using traditional techniques.

- Evaluate the strengths and weaknesses of the above techniques.

- Demonstrate an awareness of alternative techniques.

- Explain the role of financial assessment within the wider strategic assessment of investment decisions.

KEY TOPICS COVERED

- Traditional investment appraisal techniques.

- The strengths and weaknesses of individual appraisal techniques.

- The use and abuse of investment appraisal techniques.

- Financial analysis within the overall context of investment planning.

- Non-financial factors in investment appraisal.

- Alternative strategic approaches to investment appraisal.

MANAGEMENT ISSUES

- Managers need to be able to interpret and evaluate the results of financial investment appraisal calculations, rather than perform the calculations. This chapter therefore focuses on those skills.

- The apparent sophistication and precision of financial investment appraisal techniques can mask shortcomings and behavioural aspects of their application. This chapter therefore includes evaluation of frequently used techniques within a wider behavioural context.

Introduction

Investment appraisal is the process of deciding which projects or assets to invest in. In this chapter we will look at how to evaluate investments from a financial point of view and how such financial analysis fits into the overall investment decision process. Investment appraisal should always be understood within the wider context of strategic formulation and implementation. Although such matters are beyond the scope of this textbook, this chapter will look at how non-financial factors, risk levels and wider strategic concerns can impinge upon the more traditional concerns of the immediate economic return from an investment.

Investment appraisal, sometimes referred to as capital investment appraisal, is concerned with organizational decisions about investment in equipment, machinery, buildings or other long-term assets. This can include a range of types of decision such as replacement of existing assets, investing in new IT or equipment to reduce operating costs, expansion through purchasing new buildings or equipment, improving delivery service or staff training. However, the principles apply equally to investments in shares in companies, whether made by businesses or individuals. Therefore the techniques looked at in this chapter are equally relevant to both businesses and individuals who are involved in making investments.

The importance of good investment appraisal lies with the strategic and financial importance of the investments made. Investments will shape the future of the organization. Such investments often involve large resources. Wrong decisions can be costly and difficult to reverse and will have a direct impact on the organization's ability to meet its strategic objectives.

From a financial point of view, an investment involves making a cash outlay with the aim of receiving future cash flows in return. At a basic level, assessing the financial viability of an investment involves simply comparing costs with benefits, and ensuring that the benefits outweigh the costs. However, in practice this can prove difficult, as identifying and measuring the costs and benefits from an investment can be a complex task. This chapter will address some of the problems of investment cost–benefit analysis and look at how techniques have developed in order to meet these problems.

In order to help make investment decisions, a common method of appraisal is required; one which can be applied equally to a whole spectrum of investment situations and which will enable the decision-maker to assess individual investments and compare alternative investment opportunities.

Investment appraisal – the basics

In this section we will consider the important questions which should be asked when an investment is being evaluated. Imagine that you are offered an investment opportunity as follows: 'Invest $1,000 with me now and I promise that I will make you rich.' Before you hand over your money, what is the information that you need in order to evaluate this investment opportunity effectively?

Firstly, you would want some clarification on how 'rich' the investment would make you. In other words, you want some information on the *return* that the investment offers.

Secondly, you would also want to know *when* you will become rich. You therefore need more information on the *timing* of returns from the investment. There would be a significant difference between receiving a return immediately and receiving the same return in 10 years' time. This is referred to as the **'time value of money'**. This principle recognizes that the sooner you receive a return, the more valuable that return is to you.

Thirdly, you would also want some more information on the *risks* involved in your investment. If you are going to invest $1,000, what is the risk that the promised return never materializes (or that you lose the whole $1,000)?

Therefore, we can say that in evaluating a potential investment we need information about three key issues: *risk*, *return*, and *timing*.

Having established these basic principles we can now look at the techniques most frequently used in practice by businesses for investment appraisal, and examine how these techniques address the questions raised above.

Traditional evaluation techniques

There are three techniques which are in common usage in evaluating capital investment decisions:

- payback period (PP);
- accounting rate of return (ARR);
- discounted cash flow (DCF).

The last of these techniques, discounted cash flow, can be divided into two different methods of application: net present value (NPV) and internal rate of return (IRR).

In order to examine each of these techniques we will look at how they are applied to a simple investment opportunity, as set out in Worked Example 9.1.

WORKED EXAMPLE 9.1

Soundzgud Co is a manufacturer of hifi equipment. The company is currently considering the launch of a new amplifier called the 'Window Rattler'. Research indicates that the company can expect sales of its new amplifier as shown in Table 9.1.

TABLE 9.1

Year	1 $'000	2 $'000	3 $'000	4 $'000	5 $'000	6 $'000
Revenue	600	800	800	700	500	400

The machinery needed to produce the 'Window Rattler' will cost $1,200,000. However, at the end of six years this machinery can still be used for other products and is expected to then have a value of $150,000. The machinery will be purchased as soon as the decision to manufacture has been approved by the board of directors.

The company accountant has forecast the production costs for the 'Window Rattler' (Table 9.2).

TABLE 9.2

Year	1 $'000	2 $'000	3 $'000	4 $'000	5 $'000	6 $'000
Production costs	320	410	410	350	250	200

The production costs exclude depreciation, which the company normally charges on a straight-line basis. The company uses a discount rate of 15 per cent to evaluate new investments.

Expert view 9.1: Common notation conventions

Because of the importance of timing, any cash flows or profits in relation to an investment must be allocated to a particular accounting period. With the use of computer spreadsheets, an accurate analysis of timing can be made to the nearest month or even week or day. However, as all cash flows used in investment appraisal are forecasts, and therefore by their very nature estimated, it is often not possible to identify when they will occur to such a high level of accuracy. Therefore, the most common convention for investments which will run over several years is to identify cash flows by year and to assume that they will arise at the end of the year. Obviously, this may not be the actual pattern of cash flows.

A significant difference between profit and cash flow is that profit is recorded using the accruals principle. That is to say, sales and purchases are recorded when the transaction takes place rather than when any underlying payment is made. This means that, in practice, profit may be allocated to a different period from the underlying cash flow. However, for simplicity, in this example it will be assumed that cash flows occur in the same period in which accounting costs or revenues arise.

Another significant difference between profit and cash flow is depreciation. This is an accounting adjustment rather than a cash payment.

A common convention in recording the timing of cash flows or profits is to use the term t_0 to denote an item which occurs immediately, t_1 to denote an item which occurs in one year's time, t_2 for two years' time and so on. Hence, the cash flows forecast for the 'Window Rattler' can be recorded as shown in Table 9.3.

TABLE 9.3

Timing	Cash flow	$'000
t_0 (Immediately)	Cost of machine	(1,200)
t_1 (1 year's time)	Net cash inflow (600–320)	280
t_2 (2 years' time)	Net cash inflow (800–410)	390
t_3 (3 years' time)	Net cash inflow (800–410)	390
t_4 (4 years' time)	Net cash inflow (700–350)	350
t_5 (5 years' time)	Net cash inflow (500–250)	250
t_6 (6 years' time)	Net cash inflow (400–200)	200
t_6 (6 years' time)	Residual value of machine	150

We can now go on to examine how each of the investment appraisal techniques deals with this information.

Payback period (PP)

The payback period is the length of time it takes for an initial investment to be re-paid out of the net cash inflow from a project. The easiest way to calculate this is to establish the cumulative net cash-flow position at the end of each year of the invest-ment. Applied to the example of the 'Window Rattler' the payback period can be calculated as shown in Table 9.4.

TABLE 9.4

Timing	Cash flow	$'000	Cumulative $'000
Immediately (t_0)	Cost of investment	(1,200)	(1,200)
1 year's time (t_1)	Net cash inflow	280	(920)
2 years' time (t_2)	Net cash inflow	390	(530)
3 years' time (t_3)	Net cash inflow	390	(140)
4 years' time (t_4)	Net cash inflow	350	210

There is no need to take this calculation further than four years as we can see that the initial cost of the investment is paid back sometime between three and four years. At the end of three years there is still another $140,000 to pay back, but after four years the initial cost plus a further $210,000 has been paid back. If we stick with the assumption that all cash flows arise at the end of the year, we would say that this investment has a payback period of four years. However, if we assume that the cash inflows arise evenly throughout the year, we could calculate the payback period to a fraction of year as follows:

Initial cost still not paid back after three years = $140,000
Net cash inflow in year four = $350,000

Therefore the remaining balance of $140,000 would be paid back in $140,000/$350,000 = 0.4 of a year.

The payback period is therefore 3.4 years.

Simply knowing that this investment would take 3.4 years to pay back does not in itself tell us whether this is a good investment. An evaluation has to be made as to whether this is an acceptable payback period. However, if two or more alternative investments are being compared, they can be ranked in terms of their payback period, with the shortest being the most attractive.

In practice, businesses which use this technique have predetermined payback periods. These tend to differ according to type of investment. For example, an investment in IT equipment may be required to pay back within two years. On the other hand, investment in a new building may be required pay back within 20 years:

- Standard Life, a pensions and life assurance company, set itself a payback period of five years for any new products launched.

- Next, a UK-based retailer, uses a payback period of 18 months when investing in a new clothing store. However, when the business opened its first Home and Garden store in 2011, it set a payback period of 25 months.

Evaluation of PP

Having examined how the payback period works as an investment technique, we can evaluate how well it addresses the three questions we set at the beginning of this chapter. The payback period, by its very nature, tells us something directly about *timing*. In doing so, it also tells us indirectly about an important aspect of *risk*, because a shorter payback period can be equated with a lower level of risk. However, the technique tells us very little about *return* other than the fact that the initial outlay is recovered. Payback period can therefore be seen as more of a *risk* appraisal tool than a measure of *return*.

In fact, in terms of addressing return, the technique has some major shortcomings. Firstly, it ignores cash flows outside of the payback period and in doing so ignores total return. Consider Worked Example 9.2 which compares two potential investments.

WORKED EXAMPLE 9.2

TABLE 9.5

Timing	Cash flow	Investment A: $'000	Investment B: $'000
Immediately (t_0)	Cost of investment	(600)	(600)
1 year's time (t_1)	Net cash inflow	200	200
2 years' time (t_2)	Net cash inflow	200	200
3 years' time (t_3)	Net cash inflow	200	200
4 years' time (t_4)	Net cash inflow	10	400
5 years' time (t_5)	Net cash inflow	5	600
6 years' time (t_6)	Net cash inflow	5	800

Both Investment A and Investment B have identical payback periods of three years and are therefore equally attractive according to the payback period technique. However, in years 4 to 6 the cash returns of Investment A fall substantially. In comparison, the cash returns of Investment B continue to rise. Looking at this full picture, Investment B is clearly a better alternative, as the same initial investment offers a much greater overall return. But this fact is not revealed by the payback period method of analysis. To take this example a step further, consider the implication of Investment A offering a $400,000 return in year 1. This would make the payback period two years. Investment A would therefore be favoured using the payback period method of evaluation, even though Investment B offers a much higher overall return. An issue to be aware of when using this technique, therefore, is that it favours short-term returns rather than highest overall returns.

A second shortcoming is that the technique ignores the timing of cash flows within a payback period. Consider Worked Example 9.3, again of two investments with identical payback periods.

WORKED EXAMPLE 9.3

TABLE 9.6

Timing	Cash flow	Investment A: $'000	Investment B: $'000
Immediately (t$_0$)	Cost of investment	(600)	(600)
1 year's time (t$_1$)	Net cash inflow	500	50
2 years' time (t$_2$)	Net cash inflow	50	50
3 years' time (t$_3$)	Net cash inflow	50	500

Both investments take exactly three years to pay back the initial cost. However, Investment A has repaid the bulk of this initial cost by the end of the first year. There is therefore a significant difference between the two investments in that we can say Investment A is less risky. Were the investment to stop suddenly for some reason at the end of year 2, the business making Investment A would have already recovered a substantial part of the initial cost, whereas the business making Investment B would have lost most of this money.

Despite the shortcomings, payback period is an extremely popular investment appraisal technique in practice. Several surveys of businesses conducted over the past 40 years have all shown that, despite the rise in popularity of more sophisticated techniques, payback period remains the most widely used means of investment appraisal, being used by around 80 per cent of businesses. Its strength lies in its simplicity – it is not difficult to calculate or to understand. Most importantly, it appeals to a basic human level of psychology. Anyone having made a substantial investment understands that there is an initial period of anxiety concerning the risk of that investment. The point at which the investment has repaid its initial outlay is an important psychological landmark as it means that the initial capital investment has not been lost. It is because of this that payback period becomes an extremely important technique when a company has liquidity constraints or severe limitations on the availability of financing. The technique is also most useful for projects which are known to have a short life and require a quick repayment of investment.

Extract 9.2: Disney buys Star Wars

In 2012 Disney bought Lucasfilm, the company behind the Star Wars films, for US$4bn. How does this purchase price stack up in terms of return on that investment? The main value comes from the potential earning of future films. Disney has announced that it plans to release three new Star Wars films, one every three years, starting in 2015. The last three Star Wars films generated around US$1.5bn each at the box office. Such films usually cost around US$0.5bn to make and market, so that would generate Disney net cash flows of US$3bn. In addition, Lucasfilm has ongoing revenue of around US$0.9 billion per year from existing films, video games and related consumer products. There is an obvious risk in terms of the success of future films, but the last three Star Wars films were a box office success despite not being well received by many fans. These cash-flow forecasts would suggest a payback period as short as five years. Not bad for a brand that has been financially successful for the past 35 years and looks set to continue long into the future.

Accounting rate of return (ARR)

The term 'accounting' in accounting rate of return refers to the basis of calculation of this technique, which is accounting profits. Unlike the other techniques examined in this chapter which all use cash flow, ARR is calculated on the accruals basis, ie using profit.

The ARR is sometimes referred to by other names. In the United States it is more widely called return on investment (ROI). Other names include average rate of return, book rate of return or unadjusted rate of return. It is also sometimes called return on capital employed (ROCE). However, as will be seen below, this name is more appropriately applied to divisional or overall company performance, rather than the tool for investment appraisal. This multitude of names reflects both the wide usage of the technique and the fact that there is a range of definitions as to its calculation.

Although there are different ways of calculating ARR, which will be discussed below, we will concentrate on the most commonly applied calculation. This takes the 'return' on an investment as being the average accounting profit after depreciation and expressing this as a percentage of the average investment over the life of the project:

$$\text{ARR} = \frac{\text{Average annual profit}}{\text{Average investment}} \times 100\%$$

Applying this formula to our investment scenario in Worked Example 9.1, the average annual profit can be calculated by dividing the total profit for the investment by the number of years over which this profit is earned.

The total profit before deducting depreciation is $1,860,000 ($280,000 + $390,000 + $390,000 + $350,000 + $250,000 + $200,000).

The total depreciation can be calculated as the initial cost less the residual value of the investment = $1,200,000 − $150,000 = $1,050,000.

$$\text{The average annual profit} = \frac{(\$1,860,000 - \$1,050,000)}{6 \text{ years}} = \$135,000$$

Because the company charges depreciation on a straight-line basis, the average investment will be the value halfway between the initial cost and the residual value:

$$\text{Average investment} = \frac{\text{Initial cost} + \text{Residual value}}{2}$$

$$\text{Average investment} = \frac{\$1,200,000 + \$150,000}{2} = \$675,000$$

$$\text{Therefore the ARR} = \frac{\$135,000}{\$675,000} \times 100\% = 20.0\%$$

Once calculated, this ARR of 20 per cent can be compared with a predetermined minimum acceptable return for the company. For example, if Soundzgud has a predetermined requirement of a return on investments of 15 per cent, the above return of 20 per cent would be acceptable.

Evaluation of ARR

Unlike payback period (and the discounted cash-flow techniques we will look at later in the chapter), the ARR evaluates investments based upon profits. The other techniques use cash flows. There are both advantages and disadvantages to this use of profit.

The main advantage of ARR is that it calculates the performance of an investment in terms of profit returns, which is in line with the most often reported figure for overall company performance. ARR provides a measure which is directly comparable with ROCE, which is the most common measurement of the financial performance of a business as a whole.

ROCE is measured as:

$$\text{ROCE} = \frac{\text{Profit}}{\text{Capital employed}}$$

It can therefore be seen that there is direct comparison between the formula for ARR and that for ROCE. They are both measuring the same thing – the level of profit in relation to the capital invested in order to earn that profit: ARR measures this at the level of the individual investment; ROCE measures it at the divisional or company level.

It makes sense to use a measure for evaluating new investments which reflects the way the performance of the whole business will be evaluated. By comparing the ARR of a new investment with the existing ROCE of the whole business, managers are able to assess the potential impact of that new investment on the financial performance of the business as a whole. If a new investment has an ARR which is lower than the existing ROCE, that investment will reduce the future ROCE of the business. On the other hand, a new investment with an ARR greater than the existing ROCE will increase that ROCE in the future.

Despite the advantages outlined above, ARR suffers from some major deficiencies which have caused the technique to be criticized by many academic commentators. However, it is still widely used in practice, so you need to be aware of these deficiencies and their implications:

- ARR uses the accruals concept, that is to say, it is calculated from profit rather than the cash flow. Profit is far more judgemental and therefore easily manipulated than cash flow. For example, profits from an investment will vary with different methods of stock valuation and depreciation calculation. This means that it is more difficult to obtain an objective measure of performance. If ARR is being used to make comparisons between different organizations, problems will arise in comparing the figures.

- ARR is a relative measure: it measures profit returns in relation to the amount invested. This makes it possible to compare the profitability of investments of different sizes, but it means that if ARR is used to choose between two or more projects, a small project may have a higher ARR than a larger project whilst giving a much smaller absolute profit.

- There is no universally accepted basis of calculating the figures used for either the profit from an investment or the capital invested to earn that profit. This means that, in practice, erroneous comparisons may be made between investments because one is not comparing like with like. One major problem is that there is disagreement over whether the ARR calculation should use average capital invested (as shown in the example above) or initial investment. The argument for using the initial investment is that this is the cost of the investment and therefore reflects the return required to recover that cost. The more widely accepted average capital invested method argues that the ARR calculation should take into account the fact that the initial cost is written off over the life of the investment, and that an average return therefore needs to reflect the average value of the capital investment. Neither method is wrong; they simply reflect different principles.

- The technique ignores the timing of profits, as the averaging used in the calculation of ARR removes all information about timing of receipts and payments. Consider Worked Example 9.4 in which three different investments each lasts four years:

WORKED EXAMPLE 9.4

TABLE 9.7

Profits ($'000)	Investment A	Investment B	Investment C
Year 1	850	50	250
Year 2	50	50	250
Year 3	50	50	250
Year 4	50	850	250

All three investments offer an average annual profit of $250,000. However, there are significant differences in both the evenness and the timing of this profit. This information, which may be important in an investment decision, is lost in the ARR calculation through the process of averaging. ARR is therefore blind to the **time value of money**.

- Another problem arises because of this averaging process. It renders the technique unsuitable for comparing investments of different lengths. If an investment offers long-term but diminishing profits, then as each year of a lower profit is added to the calculation the average profit will be pulled downwards. Consider Worked Example 9.5 in which two investments have the same initial cost of $1 million with no residual value. However, Investment A has a life of only three years whereas Investment B has a life of six years:

WORKED EXAMPLE 9.5

TABLE 9.8

Profits ($'000)	Investment A	Investment B
Year 1	300	300
Year 2	300	300
Year 3	300	300
Year 4	–	200
Year 5	–	150
Year 6	–	100

For the first three years both investments offer the same level of profits. However, Investment B continues to deliver profit for a further three years, albeit at a lower level. Investment B offers a total profit return of $1,350,000 from an initial investment of $1 million, whereas investment A offers a total profit return of only $900,000 from the same initial investment.

However, when we calculate the ARR of each investment, Investment A appears to be the more attractive simply because the average annual profit is higher:

$$\text{ARR (investment A)} = \frac{\$300}{\$500} \times 100\% = 60\%$$

$$\text{ARR (investment B)} = \frac{\$225}{\$500} \times 100\% = 45\%$$

Discounted cash flows and the time value of money

The final two investment appraisal techniques we will examine in this section both involve the use of **discounted cash flows**. Discounting a cash flow involves making adjustments for the time value of money, that is to say, to reflect the fact that *when* you receive money has an impact upon its **value** to you.

Here is a simple example to illustrate this principle: Would you prefer to receive $100 now or $100 in two years' time? I would imagine that you would answer that you would prefer to receive the $100 now, for a number of reasons:

- There is always the risk that you will not actually receive the $100 in two years' time.
- The effect of inflation means that you can buy more with your $100 now than you will be able to in two years' time. Hence it is more valuable to you now.

- You could take the $100 now and invest it for two years, after which you would have more than $100.

We will look at risk and inflation later in this chapter, but at this point we can examine the issue of earning interest in more detail. In the example above, deciding between $100 now or $100 in two years' time was relatively easy. However, what if I offered you a choice of $100 now or $108 in two years' time? You need some means of comparing the two amounts to decide which is the more attractive. One way in which you could do this is to ask: 'What would $100 received now be worth if I invested it for two years?'

Compounding and discounting

Let us assume that you can invest your $100 received now at an interest rate of 5 per cent. At the end of one year you will have $105 ($100 × 1.05). At this point, the principle of **compound interest** starts to apply, because in the second year you will earn interest not only upon your original $100 but also upon the $5 interest you earned in the first year. Hence, at the end of two years you will have $110.25 (($100 × 1.05) × 1.05).

Because the formula calculating this is $100 × 1.05 × 1.05 = $100 × 1.05², we can generalize this as:

$$A = P \times (1 + r)^n$$

Where: A = the amount received in the future
         P = the original amount invested
         r = the interest rate earned
         n = the number of years the investment runs

This technique gives you a way of comparing the $100 offered now with the $108 offered in two years' time. You can calculate that if you take the $100 now and invest it for two years at 5 per cent, you will end up with $110.25. You would therefore be better off taking the $100 now rather than the $108 in two years' time.

This technique works well for a simple investment scenario such as that given above. However, it is not so useful if the investment is a little more complex.

What if you were offered the alternative of $100 now or $55 in one year's time and a further $55 in two years' time? In this case you cannot use the compounding technique shown above, because there is no single time in the future to which you can compound the $100 received now. We therefore need to modify the technique.

The one point in time which we can always use consistently is now (the present moment). So rather than asking the question 'what will $100 received now be worth at some point in the future?', we ask 'what would the money received in the future be worth if received now?' By asking the question this way we can compare monies received at several different points of time in the future.

Let us go back to the choice between $100 received now and $108 received in two years' time. Rather than **compounding** the $100 forward, we **discount** the $108 back to today's date by asking the question: 'What would I need to receive now to have the equivalent of $108 in two years' time?' Another way of looking at this is to ask: 'If I can earn interest at 5 per cent per year, how much do I need to invest now in order to end up with $108 after two years?' We can calculate this by using the formula which we established above:

$$A = P \times (1 + r)^n$$

We used this formula before to calculate the value of A (the amount received in the future) when we already have the value of P (the amount invested now). We simply need to rearrange the formula to start with A, the amount receivable in the future ($108), and calculate the value of P:

$$P = \frac{A}{(1 + r)^n}$$

An alternative way of stating this formula is:

$$P = A \times \frac{1}{(1 + r)^n}$$

If we apply this formula to our example:

$$P = \$108 \times \frac{1}{1.05^2} = \$97.96$$

This means that if we wanted to receive $108 in two years' time we would have to invest $97.96 now. In terms of the time value of money, receiving $108 in two years' time is the equivalent of receiving $97.96 now. We can compare the two alternatives: receive $100 now or receive an amount in two years' time which is the equivalent of receiving $97.96 now. We end up with the same decision as we did before – it is better to take the $100 now.

What of the second scenario in which you were offered the alternative of $100 now or $55 received at the end of one year and a further $55 received at the end of two years? The calculation is a little more complex, but we can evaluate these alternatives using this new discounting technique. We do this by taking each of the future amounts and discounting them back to their present value and then adding them together as follows:

Present value of $55 received in one year's time:

$$= \$55 \times \frac{1}{1.05} = \$52.38$$

Present value of $55 received in two years' time:

$$= \$55 \times \frac{1}{1.05^2} = \$49.89$$

Therefore, receiving $55 in one year's time plus $55 in two years' time is the equivalent of receiving $52.38 + $49.89 = $102.27 now. We are now able to evaluate this choice. In this case we would be better off taking the two future amounts as their present value is more than the $100 offered now. (In fact, we can measure precisely that we would be $2.27 better off in today's terms by taking the future amounts: $102.27 – $100 = $2.27).

Discount tables

The fraction by which we multiply the future cash flow A in order to calculate its present value P is known as the *discount factor*. This, as was shown above, is calculated using the following formula:

$$\frac{1}{(1 + r)^n}$$ where: r = the discount rate applied

n = the number of years

Because we use the same formula every time to calculate a discount factor, a standard set of values can be set out in a table which provides the discount factor for common discount rates and time periods. A discount factor table is available in Appendix D.

Net present value (NPV)

The NPV technique uses the principle of discounting cash flows explained above. The NPV of an investment is the sum of the present values of all cash flows which arise as a result of undertaking that investment.

The present value (P) of a single sum, A, receivable in n years' time, given an interest rate (discount rate) of r, is given by:

$$P = A \times \frac{1}{(1 + r)^n}$$

Let us now see how this technique works when applied to the Soundzgud Co investment in Worked Example 9.1. The discount rate we need to apply to the cash flow from the project is 15 per cent. The relevant discount factors have been extracted from Appendix D. We can present the NPV calculation as shown in Table 9.9.

TABLE 9.9

	Cash flow $	Discount factor (15%)	Present value $
t_0 (Immediately)	(1,200,000)	1.000	(1,200,000)
t_1 (1 year's time)	280,000	0.870	243,600
t_2 (2 years' time)	390,000	0.756	294,840
t_3 (3 years' time)	390,000	0.658	256,620
t_4 (4 years' time)	350,000	0.572	200,200
t_5 (5 years' time)	250,000	0.497	124,250
t_6 (6 years' time)	200,000	0.432	86,400
t_6 (6 years' time)	150,000	0.432	64,800
Net present value			**$70,710**

From this calculation it can be seen that the NPV of this investment is $70,710. This can be interpreted as meaning that the company will be $70,710 better off, in today's terms, by undertaking this investment.

There is therefore a simple rule for interpreting NPV calculations: If the NPV is positive, the company will increase its wealth by undertaking the investment, which is therefore financially viable; if the NPV is negative, the company would decrease its wealth by undertaking investment and the investment should therefore be rejected.

The NPV technique can be seen as a more sophisticated means of investment appraisal than the payback period and the ARR. Unlike the payback period, NPV takes account of the entire cash flow of the project; unlike ARR, NPV takes account of the timing of earnings from an investment. The further into the future a cash flow arises, the more it is discounted. This reflects the increased risk and uncertainty of cash flows as they lie further into the future.

Not only is NPV more sophisticated in the way that it takes account of *timing*, *risk*, and *return*, but it is also a technique which is capable of incorporating more sophisticated and subtle analysis of investments. We will see this as we look at more complex investment scenarios later in the chapter.

Internal rate of return (IRR)

Internal rate of return is a second discounted cash-flow technique which works on the same mathematical principles as NPV, but uses discounting to give an answer in a slightly different format.

In the NPV calculation above, we discounted the cash flow from the Soundzgud investment at 15 per cent to produce a positive NPV of $70,710. The implication of this positive NPV is that the actual return of the investment is greater than 15 per cent. The discount rate which we apply in calculating the NPV represents the minimum acceptable return. A positive NPV means that this minimum return has been exceeded and this is why investments with a positive NPV should be accepted.

Another way of using the DCF technique would be to calculate the actual discounted cash-flow return of the investment and compare that to our minimum acceptable return of 15 per cent. This is known as the internal rate of return, as it is the rate of return 'internal' to, ie within, the project.

In practice, the IRR will be the discount rate which gives an NPV of zero. With a computerized spreadsheet, calculating this discount rate is relatively straightforward. However, if a computer is not available, the IRR can be estimated as demonstrated below.

Returning to the Soundzgud investment in Worked Example 9.1, the NPV at 15 per cent was a positive value of $70,710. This means that the IRR of the investment must be greater than 15 per cent. We can therefore choose a discount rate greater than 15 per cent and recalculate the NPV to see if we are closer to the IRR. (Remember, the exact IRR would give an NPV of zero.) Let us discount the project again using a discount rate of 20 per cent (Table 9.10).

TABLE 9.10

Timing	Cash flow $	Discount factor (20%)	Present value $
t_0 (Immediately)	(1,200,000)	1.000	(1,200,000)
t_1 (1 year's time)	280,000	0.833	233,240
t_2 (2 years' time)	390,000	0.694	270,660
t_3 (3 years' time)	390,000	0.579	225,810
t_4 (4 years' time)	350,000	0.482	168,700
t_5 (5 years' time)	250,000	0.402	100,500
t_6 (6 years' time)	200,000	0.335	67,000
t_6 (6 years' time)	150,000	0.335	50,250
Net present value			$(83,840)

This time we get a negative NPV of −$83,840. This means that the IRR must lie somewhere between 15 and 20 per cent. We can establish the IRR more accurately using a mathematical technique called *linear interpolation*. This is done by applying the formula:

$$IRR = A\% + \frac{NPV\ at\ A\%}{(NPV\ at\ A\% - NPV\ at\ B\%)} \times (B\% - A\%)$$

Where: A% = the lower discount rate
B% = the higher discount rate

Applied to our calculations for the Soundzgud investment we get:

$$IRR = 15\% + \frac{\$70,710}{(\$70,710 + \$83,840)} \times (20\% - 15\%) = 17.3\%$$

So in this case we can say that the investment offers an internal rate of return of 17.3 per cent. We can then compare this to an acceptable minimum level of return in the same way as we did with the ARR technique.

Extract 9.3: EDF – IRR in the energy industry

Investment in energy infrastructure in the UK involves a delicate partnership between the government and the private sector. Adequate returns are critical to attracting suitable private-sector investment. The government is seeking to increase investment in low-carbon energy infrastructure, but this can represent a high risk to investors who consequently require high returns. Investors in gas-fired power plants typically expect an IRR of around 10 per cent, whereas investors in wind generation expect an IRR of 10 to 13 per cent.

The government can reduce the returns demanded by reducing the risk. In 2013 the UK government struck a deal with EDF Energy, the French energy company, to subsidize the building of a new nuclear power plant at Hinkley Point in Somerset. The plant has an estimated build cost of £16bn, which is too high to represent a viable investment. The government is therefore offering various incentives, including guaranteeing EDF's income in order to create an IRR of 10 per cent from the plant. Industry experts estimate that this will add up to a subsidy of £7 per household per year. The complexity of this deal underscores the importance of IRR for investors. Without an adequate return on the investment, no new power plants would be built and the UK would risk facing power shortages.

Evaluation of IRR

The IRR is used in the same way as ARR, by comparing with a predetermined acceptable value. However, the IRR uses discounted cash flows rather than average profits, and therefore has all the advantages we identified when looking at the NPV technique: it takes account of risk, timing and returns.

However, one major drawback of the IRR technique is that it will not work with investments which have what are known as 'non-conventional' cash flows. A conventional investment cash flow is one which involves an initial cash outflow followed by a series of cash inflows. With some investments, net cash flows can flow both inward and outward throughout the life of the project. For example, investment in a nuclear power plant may involve initial cash outflows followed by many years of cash inflows and then substantial cash outflows as the power plant is decommissioned at the end of its life. The IRR technique cannot cope with cash flows such as this, as mathematically it will produce more than one value. It is possible to modify the IRR technique to work around this problem, but such calculations are beyond the scope of an introductory text such as this.

Although DCF techniques are more sophisticated in integrating the factors of risk, timing and returns, they do have some drawbacks which have led to criticism. The process of discounting cash flows inevitably leads to a favouring of investments which offer returns in the shorter term. It has been suggested that this leads to short-termism and a reluctance to make investments which offer strategic benefits which may be more long-term and more difficult to quantify. Also, the techniques have been criticized as being inadequate for evaluating new technology investments as they are unable to evaluate non-quantifiable issues. We will look at some methods for addressing these problems later in the chapter.

Exercises: now attempt Exercise 9.1 on page 363

Incorporating real-world complexities into investment appraisal

So far we have examined the main investment appraisal techniques using a relatively straightforward example. However, in the real world, investment appraisal decisions will be more complex and need to take into account issues such as inflation and the impact of taxation. In this section we will examine some of these real-world complexities and look at how they can be incorporated into our calculations.

Establishing an appropriate discount rate

The discount rate used in an NPV calculation represents the minimum acceptable rate of return for the investor. In practice, a wide variety of methods can be used to determine appropriate discount rates. Most organizations establish a discount rate based upon either the weighted average cost of capital (WACC) or the capital asset pricing model (CAPM). Explanation of these techniques is beyond the scope of this textbook. However, whatever method is used in practice, it is based upon certain principles. The rate of return from an investment should be sufficient to cover the cost of financing that investment and should incorporate an assessment of the risk. In simple terms, the more risky an investment is perceived to be, the higher the discount rate used to evaluate it. Hence one important way in which risk assessment is incorporated into investment appraisal is through adjustment of the discount rate used in NPV calculations.

Deciding what to count: relevant cash flows

One of the most common mistakes in investment appraisal in practice involves using the wrong figures. This can mean including costs which should not be counted, or omitting costs or revenues which should be included. These mistakes can lead to inappropriate investment decisions, with disastrous consequences for future business operations.

An important principle in decision making, therefore, is that only those costs or revenues which are affected by the decision should be considered. A frequent error is to include costs which will be incurred anyway, even if the investment were not made. These may include, for example, the costs of employees working on a project, but who would be paid anyway, regardless of whether or not the project goes ahead. In a similar way, factory costs, administration and head office costs which will not change as a result of the project should not be included.

Likewise, costs already incurred, even if they relate to the investment, such as market research or product development already completed, should not be included in an investment appraisal calculation. This is because these costs, having already been incurred, cannot change as a result of making the investment.

Therefore, as a simple rule of thumb, you should include in investment appraisal calculations only those costs or revenues which will change as a result of undertaking the investment (see Worked Example 9.6 below).

Opportunity costs

Opportunity costs are a category of costs used only in decision making. They can be extremely important in assessing the true financial impact of an investment. An opportunity cost can be defined as the cost of an alternative that must be forgone in order to pursue a certain action. Opportunity costs arise from the recognition that committing resources to one project means that they cannot be used on other projects. This may mean that there is a cost to the business in terms of the lost 'opportunity' of using that resource elsewhere. For example, using a production facility to make one product means that that facility cannot be used to make a different product, even though the alternative may be extremely profitable. This example may be obvious, but some opportunity costs are less obvious. For example, opening a new store may draw business away from existing stores in the same area, reducing their profits.

By incorporating opportunity costs into investment appraisal calculations, a business is able to quantify the loss of other potentially profitable opportunities and thereby ensure that the most profitable course of action is taken. To ensure that this is the case, opportunity cost is always measured in terms of lost **contribution** from the use of a particular resource.

Expert view 9.2: Contribution

Contribution = Revenue – Variable (direct) costs

WORKED EXAMPLE 9.6   Relevant costs and opportunity costs

Zebra Co is a paint manufacturer that is planning to launch a new range of fast-drying paints. The directors of Zebra Co have asked you to help evaluate the financial viability of the new paint range. Which of the following amounts would you include in an NPV calculation?

A   A proportion of head office administrative costs calculated at $18,000 per year.

B   Depreciation on the new paint manufacturing plant purchased for the project.

C   Salaries of 10 new workers hired to operate the new plant.

D   Financing costs of $25,000 per year on the loan to purchase the new plant in (B) above.

E   The salary of $35,000 per year of the manager running the new plant. This manager ran one of the other manufacturing plants and has been transferred to this job because of his experience. In his absence, the other plant is being run by a new manager hired as a replacement for the duration of this project. The new manager has a salary of $28,000 per year.

Answers

A   Head office costs will be incurred regardless of whether or not the new range of paints is launched. These costs should therefore not be included in an NPV calculation as they are not relevant.

B   Depreciation is not a cash flow. This cost should therefore not be included.

C   The salaries of new workers are a relevant cost and should therefore be included in the NPV calculation.

D   Financing costs should not be included in the cash flows to be discounted. The cost of financing the investment will be incorporated into the discount rate used to evaluate the investment.

E   This is an example of an opportunity cost. The additional cost to the business of using the experienced manager on this project is the $28,000 it costs to replace him in his old job. The amount which should be included in the NPV calculation is therefore $28,000 per year, rather than $35,000 per year.

Taxation

Tax payments can have a significant impact on investment cash flows and should therefore be taken into account. There are four aspects of taxation which are relevant to investment appraisal:

1 Income tax paid on profits from an investment will represent a cash outflow for a business and therefore needs to be incorporated into the NPV calculation. Because of the importance of timing, when tax is paid can make a difference.

2 Interest on any debt financing is an allowable expense against income tax. The method of financing an investment will therefore impact upon tax cash flows.

3 Any tax losses may give rise to tax relief on other profits which can reduce the amount of taxation payable.

4 Capital allowances are the income tax equivalent of depreciation. They provide tax relief on the investment in assets which will reduce the cash outflows for income tax. For projects involving large investments in buildings, plant or equipment, capital allowances can be significant and can have a major impact upon the cash flows of the investment.

Because these aspects of taxation can have a significant impact upon the cash flows from an investment, it is important to ensure that taxation is always considered and incorporated into investment appraisal calculations.

Inflation

Inflation decreases the purchasing power of future cash inflows, making them worth less. Therefore inflation can create distortions when attempting to assess the time value of money and in calculating returns from investments. For example, a rate of return of 12 per cent could be reduced to 8 per cent in real terms after taking inflation into account. It is therefore important to incorporate the impact of inflation into the return on investments and to be clear whether a quoted rate of return includes or excludes inflation.

To avoid this confusion, different terms are used. If an interest rate includes the effect of inflation, it is referred to as the 'money rate'. Just to add the potential for confusion, this is sometimes also known as the 'nominal' or 'market' rate. On the other hand, 'real' interest rates are stated after adjusting to remove inflation. The adjustment is done as follows:

$$(1 + \text{real rate of interest}) \times (1 + \text{rate of inflation}) = (1 + \text{money rate of interest})$$

Note that the real rate is multiplied by inflation, not added, to give the money rate.

WORKED EXAMPLE 9.7 Adjusting for inflation

a The real rate of return which a business requires from its investments is 12 per cent and inflation is currently 4 per cent. What is the money rate of return which the business needs to apply for investment appraisal?

> *Answer*: The money rate of return = 16.5 per cent (1.12 × 1.04 = 1.165).

b A business experiences a money rate of return of 18 per cent on an investment. Over that same period inflation was 5 per cent. What is the real rate of return on the investment?

> *Answer*: The real rate of return = 12.4 per cent (1.18 ÷ 1.05 = 1.124).

Dealing with inflation in investment appraisal calculations

There are two ways in which the impact of inflation can be incorporated into investment appraisal calculations:

Money method: the first method is to use 'money' cash flows (ie those cash flows which include inflation) and to discount these using the 'money' discount rate (ie the discount rate which incorporates the effect of inflation).

Real method: the second method is to use cash flows which exclude the impact of inflation and to apply the 'real' discount rate.

Which of these techniques is used in practice will depend upon how the cash-flow forecast for an investment has been compiled. If the cash-flow forecast is in 'today's terms', without consideration of the impact of inflation, it is easier to use the real method. On the other hand, if cash-flow forecasts have been compiled looking at actual amounts payable or receivable in the future (and therefore incorporating inflation), the money method should be used.

WORKED EXAMPLE 9.8 Dealing with inflation

A company is considering investing $100,000 in a project which will give returns of $50,000 in current terms for three years. The money rate of return required by the company is 14 per cent and inflation is currently 4.6 per cent. What is the NPV?

Money method

TABLE 9.11

Year	Real cash flow $	Money cash flow (inflated by 4.6%)	Money discount factor @14%	Present value $
0	(100,000)	(100,000)	1.000	(100,000)
1	50,000	52,300	0.877	45,867
2	50,000	54,706	0.769	42,069
3	50,000	57,222	0.675	38,625
Net present value				26,561*

Real method

TABLE 9.12

Year	Real cash flow $	Real discount factor @9%	Present value $
0	(100,000)	1.000	(100,000)
1	50,000	0.917	45,850
2	50,000	0.842	42,100
3	50,000	0.772	38,600
Net present value			26,550*

Real discount rate = 9 per cent (1.14 ÷ 1.046 = 1.09)

The small difference of $11 between these two calculations (Tables 9.11 and 9.12) is due simply to rounding.

Exercises: now attempt Exercise 9.2 on page 364

Annuities

If the level of cash flow from an investment is the same from year to year, it is referred to as an annuity. If this is the case, there is an easier way of calculating the NPV by using annuity tables. Annuity tables show the present value of $1 received every year, starting one year from now and going on for n years. A set of annuity tables is available in Appendix E.

WORKED EXAMPLE 9.9   Annuity

A company is considering investing in a project which will cost $10,000 and will yield cash inflows of $3,000 per year for five years. No scrap value is expected at the end of the project and the company uses a discount rate of 12 per cent to evaluate investments. Should the investment be accepted?

Answer:

TABLE 9.13

Year	Cash flow $	Discount factor	Present value $
t_0	(10,000)	1.000	(10,000)
t_1–t_5	3000	3.605	10,815
NPV			815

As the investment gives a positive NPV of $815, it should be accepted.

Capital rationing: the profitability index

Capital rationing refers to a situation in which there is a limited supply of capital to finance investment projects. In this situation, a company cannot accept all projects with positive NPVs if the costs of implementation will exceed the supply of capital. The company will therefore need to choose between alternative investments.

In practice, capital rationing arises for one of two reasons:

Hard rationing: capital markets will always supply a limited amount of capital. A company therefore may not be able to raise sufficient capital to finance all available projects.

Soft rationing: the company may have sufficient funds available but has chosen to restrict its capital investment for strategic reasons.

When faced with a situation of capital rationing a company should allocate available capital so as to maximize returns on the capital invested. Individual investment proposals should therefore be considered in terms of their rate of return (ie NPV divided by capital required). This ratio is sometimes known as the profitability index:

$$\text{Profitability index} = \frac{\text{Net present value}}{\text{Initial capital cost}}$$

WORKED EXAMPLE 9.10 Capital rationing

A company has $10 million available to fund new projects in the current year. It has identified five potential investments and calculated the NPV on each investment as shown in Table 9.14.

TABLE 9.14

Investment	NPV	Capital required
A	$2m	$4m
B	$1m	$3m
C	$0.4m	$0.5m
D	$0.5m	$0.75m
E	$1.6m	$4m
Total		$12.25m

The company cannot undertake all five projects because this would require a total capital commitment of $12.25 million. In order to choose where to invest the $10 million available, the company will rank the proposals according to their rate of return, ie the ratio of NPV/Capital required (Table 9.15).

TABLE 9.15

Investment	NPV/Capital required	Ranking
A	$2m/$4m = 50%	3rd
B	$1m/$3m = 33%	5th
C	$0.4m/$0.5m = 80%	1st
D	$0.5m/$0.75m = 67%	2nd
E	$1.6m/$4m = 40%	4th

Based upon this ranking the company would invest in projects C, D, A and E in that order of preference. This would use a total capital of $9.25 million. Although this leaves $0.75 million unused, it is unlikely that project B could be subdivided such that 0.75/3.0 or 25 per cent of the project could be undertaken.

Replacement decisions

All of the investment scenarios we have looked at so far have involved investing in new assets. However, in reality, many investment decisions involve replacing existing assets. An important decision for a company is how long to retain an asset such as machinery or a company vehicle before replacing it. It is possible to use NPV calculations to determine the optimum time at which to replace an asset.

When using NPV for replacement decisions the technique is modified slightly. Firstly, the NPV is calculated in the normal way, and then the figure is adjusted to determine the 'annualized NPV'. The company should then replace an asset at the point when the annualized NPV is maximized.

WORKED EXAMPLE 9.11   Replacement decisions

A company purchases a machine for $15,000. The machine can be used for up to three years before it will be replaced by an identical machine which will be used in the same production process. The following figures have been estimated (Table 9.16).

TABLE 9.16

Year	1	2	3
Net revenue $	9,000	7,500	4,500
Scrap value $	6,000	4,500	1,500

The company uses a discount rate of 10 per cent for project appraisal. Should the machine be replaced after one, two or three years?

Answer

If the machine is replaced at the end of year 1, the NPV will be as shown in Table 9.17.

TABLE 9.17

Year	t_0	t_1	NPV
Cost of machine	(15,000)		
Net revenues		9,000	
Scrap value		6,000	
Total	(15,000)	15,000	
Discount factor	1	0.909	
Present value	(15,000)	13,635	(1,365)

If the machine is replaced at the end of year 2, the NPV will be as shown in Table 9.18.

TABLE 9.18

Year	t_0	t_1	t_2	NPV
Cost of machine	(15,000)			
Net revenues		9,000	7,500	
Scrap value			4,500	
Total	(15,000)	9,000	12,000	
Discount factor	1	0.909	0.826	
Present value	(15,000)	8,181	9,912	3,093

If the machine is replaced at the end of year 3, the NPV will be as shown in Table 9.19.

TABLE 9.19

Year	t_0	t_1	t_2	t_3	NPV
Cost of machine	(15,000)				
Net revenues		9,000	7,500	4,500	
Scrap value				1,500	
Total	(15,000)	9,000	7,500	6,000	
Discount factor	1	0.909	0.826	0.751	
Present value	(15,000)	8,181	6,195	4,506	3,882

Each of the NPVs is then 'annualized' by dividing it by the annuity factor for the number of years the investment runs:

Replaced after one year: ($1,365) ÷ 0.909   = ($1502)

Replaced after two years: $3,093 ÷ 1.735   = $1783

Replaced after three years: $3,882 ÷ 2.486   = $1562

Replacement after two years gives the highest annualized NPV. This is therefore the replacement strategy which the company should follow.

Investment appraisal within context

So far in this chapter we have looked at the main techniques of investment appraisal and how they can be applied to different investment decisions. We will now look at some of the practical considerations of investment appraisal and some of the problems involved in applying these techniques in practice.

There are a number of problems to be found in the way these investment appraisal techniques are actually used in practice. We will focus on three main aspects of practice:

Firstly, the techniques we have examined have a very narrow focus on tangible factors which can be quantified financially. In practice, many investment decisions can involve factors which are difficult to quantify or which are intangible, for example investing in a new computer system in order to improve customer service, or investment in research and development for new product features.

Secondly, the highly computational nature of the techniques, particularly NPV, means that, in practice, managers can get lost in the details of the calculations and lose sight of the fact that they are based upon forecasts which may not be accurate and which in all likelihood will not actually work out.

Finally, the narrow focus of traditional investment appraisal techniques (typified by the concept of relevant cash flows) means that they can fail to capture the richness of investment decisions within the context of a wider organizational strategy. In reality, managers will not just invest for immediate financial return, but also for wider strategic reasons such as increasing operational flexibility, gaining competitive advantage or providing more strategic options in the future. Furthermore, within today's business context, managers must consider more than just immediate financial returns to the business's owners; the interests and requirements of other stakeholders such as employees, customers, suppliers, wider society and the environment can be equally important in investment decisions.

Integrating qualitative factors

One of the problems with traditional investment appraisal is that it tends to lead to an analysis of tangible financial issues in isolation from other important elements of the investment decision. When qualitative considerations are brought into an appraisal, the exercise becomes more complex, even if all the elements being considered are still tangible.

Let us take the example of a company that is investing in a new computerized customer management system (CMS). This new CMS will be integrated into the existing IT-based financial system and will be available in all offices through a new computer network. When doing a financial investment appraisal, there are a number of questions which may be difficult to answer:

- *What tangible costs should be included?* The tangible costs of new networks and other computer hardware can easily be identified. However, what is not so easy to establish is the proportion of these costs which should be allocated to the CMS investment. The network will be of benefit to all departments and all systems, and any new computers or workstations will be used for a number of other functions.

- *How should intangible costs be measured?* Some of the costs of implementing the new CMS system will be intangible and difficult to measure. For example, management time spent on developing and reviewing the new system will be a distraction from other activities; there may be disruption to existing work as a new system is implemented; staff learning to use a new system will be slower and less productive. In such cases it may be possible to record and measure the amount of time spent on the project, but it is not so easy to record and measure the impact which this has on other activities and productivity levels.

- *Diminishing returns from benefits.* If the rationale for implementing the new CMS is to improve customer services, then how far should this go? More and more features could be added to the CMS at an ever-increasing cost. How many of these features should be adapted? In a similar manner, increased processing power will provide information faster. It may be possible to identify that there is a clear advantage in obtaining information in two hours rather than two days. But would it be better to obtain that information in two minutes, or even in two seconds?

- *How should intangible benefits be measured?* The problem with implementing any new investment (particularly an IT investment) aimed at improving the availability of information or quality of service is that the costs are usually tangible and easily identified, whereas the benefits are intangible. Traditional NPV calculations are not able to capture such intangibles, which means that any investment appraisal will inevitably result in a negative NPV. In many cases, the identification of costs is much easier than the identification of benefits. This is particularly the case where the benefits sought from an investment are intangible. There are therefore three options available in this case:

1 *Ignore the benefits*: the traditional approach is to ignore intangibles and focus only on that which can be measured in financial terms. Unfortunately, this could result in negative NPVs and the rejection of investments, simply because the benefits are not immediately financially quantifiable.

2 *Quantify the benefits*: a common approach is to attempt to quantify the benefits so that they can be incorporated into a traditional investment appraisal calculation. Although this may work in some cases, it may be extremely difficult to quantify some benefits or it may result in a loss of richness of information about the benefits of investment.

3 *Change the approach*: the balanced scorecard. A third alternative is to move away from a purely financial analysis to one which incorporates non-financial benefits. This approach tries to integrate qualitative and quantitative dimensions of evaluation within one exercise and can be termed a balanced scorecard approach. To use such a balanced scorecard approach in investment appraisal requires the decision-maker to weigh up the various quantitative and qualitative aspects of the investment and to give a 'score' to each aspect so that each investment can be given an overall score, which allows comparison between alternatives.

WORKED EXAMPLE 9.12   Balanced scorecard approach

Investment appraisal of new customer management system:

Financial benefits:

- NPV $x.

Non-financial benefits:

- x per cent of users happy with quality;

- x per cent of users happy with scope;

- x hours saved per month.

Exercises: now attempt Exercise 9.3 on page 365

Addressing risk: the variability in outcomes

In investment appraisal, risk is about the variability of outcomes. When we talk about investment risk we mean that the actual outcome may not be as we expect. In all the examples that we have looked at so far, calculations have been based upon one 'best guess' set of outcomes. Unfortunately, in reality, 'best guess' will hardly ever be the actual outcome. Therefore, one way of further incorporating risk assessment into investment appraisal is to analyse the range of possible outcomes. There are three main ways of doing this: sensitivity analysis; scenario analysis; and probability analysis.

Sensitivity analysis

Sensitivity analysis is a simple but powerful technique which is used extensively in practice. It examines the impact on the project return of changes in individual variables such as the investment cost, the level of cash flows and the life of the investment. The technique is applied by adjusting each major variable in an NPV calculation until the NPV equals zero (ie the point at which the investment is no longer financially viable). This gives the decision-maker an indication of how much of a change can be tolerated in each variable. If an NPV of zero is arrived at with a relatively small change in a variable, the investment is very sensitive to the value of that variable. Sensitivity analysis makes it easier to identify weaknesses in forecasts. It is an extremely good way of identifying key factors that will need careful monitoring once the project has commenced. It could also be used to evaluate whether further action should be taken to minimize risk, for example interest-rate hedging or the use of currency derivatives to manage exchange-rate risks.

Scenario analysis

Whereas sensitivity analysis is useful in isolating and identifying changes in individual variables, it is not realistic in its presumptions. In reality, it is more likely that several or all variables will change at the same time, depending upon the circumstances. Scenario analysis addresses this by predicting how multiple variables will change under different conditions, for example under improved economic conditions, or if an economic downturn occurs. It is normal for this type of financial modelling to be done using computer spreadsheets.

Probabilities and expected values

Sensitivity analysis and scenario analysis introduce the idea of using a range of different forecasts rather than a single calculation. However, they can make decision making more difficult because they give no indication of the likelihood that each of a range of different outcomes may occur. A second problem is that a range of different scenarios will give a range of different NPV values, some of which may be negative. Does that mean the investment should not be made? It is no longer possible to use the simple rule that a positive NPV means a financially viable investment.

WORKED EXAMPLE 9.13   Probability analysis

A method to overcome these problems is used by some investment analysts. This involves identifying a range of different outcomes and attaching a probability to each outcome. These probabilities can be used to calculate a weighted average of the NPVs of each different scenario as shown in Table 9.20.

TABLE 9.20

Scenario	NPV $	Probability	NPV × Prob
A	(100,000)	0.2	(20,000)
B	200,000	0.3	60,000
C	300,000	0.4	120,000
D	500,000	0.1	50,000
ENPV = (NPV × Prob) =			210,000

This weighted average of $210,000 is known as the expected net present value (ENPV). It offers the advantage of once more providing a single figure which can be used to evaluate the investment. If the ENPV is positive, the investment is financially viable. However, care should be taken in using this technique as the ENPV does not reflect the outcome which will actually occur. For example, the decision-maker in Worked Example 9.13 should always remember that there is still a 20 per cent chance that the investment will have a negative NPV of –$100,000.

Other methods of assessing risk

There are a number of other methods which are becoming increasingly popular as means of modelling the uncertainty around investment cash flows as the availability of sophisticated computerized spreadsheets and increased processing power has made possible the use of more complex mathematical techniques.

The Monte Carlo simulation method involves the use of a probability distribution and random numbers to estimate net cash-flow figures. If this is repeated many times, a distribution of possible NPVs is derived from which it is possible to ascertain the uncertainty surrounding the project. Similar methods for modelling uncertainty include the use of Markov chain theory and fuzzy set theory. These methods allow unknown cash flows to be represented by a range of inexact ('fuzzy') numbers for the purposes of modelling NPV outcomes.

Taking a broader strategic view

So far we have looked at investment appraisal as an isolated financial exercise. The techniques we have examined, although widely used, have been criticized for not taking into account wider strategic considerations. In this last section we will therefore look at some recent developments in investment appraisal which have been aimed at integrating a broader strategic focus into the financial evaluation of individual investment decisions.

Real options

The traditional investment appraisal techniques we have examined in this chapter take a very narrow financial focus. This is exemplified by the concept of relevant cash flows, whereby any cost or revenue deemed not to be relevant to an investment is excluded from the calculation. However, when looking at an investment from a wider strategic perspective, a business may wish to build in flexibility which will give it options in the future. For example, if investing in a new production facility, a company may build a new factory which is twice the size of that needed for current production capacity. It will do this in anticipation of future growth. The problem with applying traditional approaches to investment appraisal in this case is that the extra cost of the large factory in relation to the revenues based upon current capacity may result in a negative NPV.

The concept of real options borrows from financial options, which are options to exchange a financial asset such as a share for cash. A real option is the option to exchange a real asset for some other asset. For example, buying a prime plot of land can give a food retailer a real expansion option to acquire the revenues from a new outlet by paying the cost of building a new store on that land. The further option to sell the land in the future, should the new store prove to be less profitable than anticipated, is a real abandonment option.

Value chain analysis

One way of evaluating a project's strategic issues as well as its cash flows is to undertake value chain analysis. This involves identifying strategically important value-creating activities. The 'value chain' is that set of activities which link from basic raw materials through to the ultimate end product. Focusing on these activities involves finding opportunities to enhance customer value or lower production costs. It has been found in practice that value chain analysis can produce very different investment decisions from those using traditional techniques, as the linkages between different activities within the value chain become an important aspect of the decision process.

Cost-driver analysis

Cost-driver analysis borrows from the concepts of activity-based costing which were examined in Chapter 8. It involves identifying those cost drivers which flow from the organization's investment decisions. By making these connections more explicit, the organization is able to identify the impact on future cash flows which an investment will make.

Competitive advantage analysis

Competitive advantage analysis involves evaluating whether an investment's benefits are consistent with the organization's competitive positioning strategy, such as cost minimization or differentiation. Projects can be ranked according to their ability to contribute towards the organization's chosen strategy.

Extract 9.4: Cisco – integrating the wider strategic picture

Cisco Systems is a US multinational corporation based in San Jose, California, that designs, manufactures, and sells networking equipment. During the economic boom of the late 1990s and early 2000s, middle managers were given great freedom to acquire business start-ups for the technology and ideas. However, during the economic downturn that followed, Cisco tightened up their investment procedures by creating an investment review board that met monthly to vet potential acquisitions. Managers proposing acquisitions were required not only to demonstrate the potential financial benefits but also to draw up detailed integration plans.

Conclusion

This chapter has examined a multitude of investment appraisal techniques. It has presented those techniques traditionally used for investment appraisal together with some more recent innovations. In particular, we have evaluated each technique, pointing out its strengths and weaknesses. The reader will have noted that all the techniques presented in this chapter have both strengths and drawbacks. It might therefore be concluded that reliance upon one technique alone may lead to sub-optimal decision making or even to failure. On a practical level, therefore, it makes sense for an organization to use a mixture of techniques in order to eliminate or minimize the drawbacks of each individual technique used.

We hope that as a result of studying this chapter the reader will have a better understanding of how different investment appraisal techniques should be applied, will be able to use them more effectively to evaluate investments and will be able to identify and avoid common mistakes in the application of the techniques.

COMPREHENSION QUESTIONS

1 Why is good investment appraisal important to organizations?

2 What are the three main factors that should be considered when appraising a potential investment?

3 What are the main drawbacks of the payback method of investment appraisal?

4 Explain the concept of the time value of money.

5 What is the 'discount rate' used in NPV calculations and how is it arrived at?

6 What is an opportunity cost and why should it be included in an investment appraisal calculation?

7 In what ways can taxation impact upon cash flows from an investment?

8 Explain two ways in which risk assessment can be incorporated into investment appraisal.

Answers on pages 366–367

Exercises

Answers on pages 368–372

Exercise 9.1: Basic computations

A company is considering investing in a new production facility at a cost of $120 million. The new facility is expected to produce annual cost savings as set out in Table 9.21. The facility is expected to have a useful life of eight years, before becoming obsolete and requiring replacement. The company has a policy of depreciating all assets on a straight-line basis.

TABLE 9.21

Year	Annual cost savings
1	$30m
2	$35m
3	$40m
4	$45m
5	$30m
6	$26m
7	$15m
8	$15m

Required:

Evaluate the investment using the following techniques:

(a) Payback period – the company considers a capital investment to be acceptable if it pays back within four years. Should the company make the investment?

(b) ARR – what is the accounting rate of return on the average capital employed?

(c) NPV – if the capital investment has a required rate of return of 12 per cent, what is its net present value? Should the company make the investment?

Exercise 9.2: Understanding principles

Freshfare Co is a food retailer with 25 stores in the south of the country in which it operates. The board of directors are currently considering expansion into the north of the country by opening a large new store in a major northern city.

The investment in the new store is estimated to cost $40m. This will be financed mainly through a new bank loan of $35m at a cost of 8 per cent a year. The investment is expected to pay back within three years with an IRR of 22 per cent.

You have been asked to make a presentation on the proposed investment at the next meeting of the board of directors. The directors have raised some queries regarding the calculations in the investment appraisal and would like you to address the following points in your presentation:

1 A feasibility study for the new store has already been completed at a cost of $28,000. This cost has not been included in the investment appraisal calculations.

2 The interest payments on the bank loan of $35m will be payable quarterly. These payments have not been included in the investment appraisal calculations.

3 The chief accountant proposes to charge 5 per cent of central office administration costs to the new store. This charge has not been included in the investment appraisal calculations.

4 The company has a policy of depreciating all new investments on a straight-line basis over four years. No depreciation charge has been included in the investment appraisal calculations.

5 When the new store opens, it will be managed by one of the company's most experienced store managers. This manager earns $40,000 per year and this cost has been included in the investment appraisal calculations. When the manager moves to the new store, her assistant manager will be promoted to take over her current job. The assistant manager currently earns $25,000 per year but will receive a salary increase to $30,000 per year when he is promoted.

Required:

Make notes for your presentation to the board of directors which explain the treatment of each of the five issues above. You should state whether you agree with the accounting treatment in each case. If you disagree with the accounting treatment, you should explain why and propose an alternative.

Exercise 9.3: Financial appraisal within context

ANG Co is a manufacturer of high-performance processor chips for smart phones and other mobile devices. The company, based in Europe, has grown rapidly over the last five years. It has been able to compete with global competitors through developing a highly skilled and loyal workforce.

The company forecasts continued growth in existing markets and intends to break into the new markets of China and South East Asia. With this in mind, the directors have been examining options for opening a new factory within the next 18 months.

The directors have identified three possible new sites for the factory. You have been appointed as a business consultant to help the business choose which site to develop.

The financial information for each factory is set out in Table 9.22.

TABLE 9.22

	Factory A	Factory B	Factory C
Initial cost	$150m	$150m	$140m
Expected production life	5 years	5 years	4 years

The company accountant has calculated the information shown in Table 9.23.

TABLE 9.23

	Factory A	Factory B	Factory C
Payback period	3 years	2 years	2 years
Accounting rate of return	29%	29%	32%
Net present value	$25.6m	$39.4m	$28.7m

The NPV is calculated using the company's standard discount rate of 13 per cent. The following further details are provided:

Factory A: This factory will be opened next to the existing factory. This will provide more jobs for people in the area and possible promotion opportunities for existing employees.

Factory B: Factory B will be located in a new enterprise development zone which is situated approximately 150 kilometres from the existing factory. By opening the factory here, the company can take advantage of some generous tax breaks and other incentives offered by the government. Opening this factory will involve moving some of the existing production into the new factory. This will mean making 20 per cent of the existing workforce redundant. (The cost of redundancies is built into the figures above.)

Factory C: This factory will be opened in China. The company will benefit from cheaper labour costs (this is built into the figures above). The company will also be in a strong geographic position to grow sales in the newly opened market in China and South East Asia.

Required:
Write a report to the directors of ANG Co which evaluates each of the three potential investments using the financial and non-financial information provided above. State what further information the directors might need to consider before making a final decision.

Answers to comprehension questions

1   Good investment appraisal is important in ensuring that new investments offer acceptable financial returns and that they contribute towards achieving organizational strategic objectives.

2   The three main factors that should be considered when appraising a potential investment are risk, return and timing.

3   The main drawbacks of the payback method are that:
    -   it ignores cash flows outside of the payback period;
    -   it provides no information about total return;
    -   it does not differentiate between different timing of cash flows within the payback period.

4 The time value of money refers to the fact that when payments are made or received has an impact upon their value to the investor.

5 The discount rate used in NPV calculations is the percentage rate at which the estimated cash flows from the investment are discounted. The discount rate will be arrived at by incorporating the rate of return from the investment required by investors (this must exceed financing costs) adjusted for inflation and the risk of the investment. Investment perceived as being more risky will be evaluated using higher discount rates.

6 An opportunity cost is the cost of an alternative course of action which must be forgone in order to undertake the investment in question. Opportunity cost is measured in terms of financial contribution. It should always be included in investment appraisal calculations to reflect the fact that when resources are limited there is always a cost of diverting them from elsewhere.

7 Taxation impacts upon cash flows from an investment in two main ways: taxation paid on earnings from an investment is a cash outflow; and capital allowances on assets purchased for an investment will reduce the amount of taxation paid by the business.

8 Risk assessment can be incorporated into investment appraisal in a number of ways. These include:

- adjusting the discount rate used in NPV calculations;
- performing sensitivity analysis on investment appraisal calculations;
- undertaking scenario analysis to evaluate a range of different possible outcomes;
- assigning probabilities to different possible outcomes and calculating expected values;
- using mathematical models such as the Monte Carlo simulation method or fuzzy sets.

Exercise 9.1: Basic computations

Payback period

The payback period can be seen by calculating the cumulative cash flow from the investment (Table 9.24).

TABLE 9.24

Year	Cash flow $	Cumulative cash flow $
0	(120)	(120)
1	30	(90)
2	35	(55)
3	40	(15)
4	45	30
5	30	60
6	26	86
7	15	101
8	15	116

The cumulative cash flow shows that the investment pays back within the fourth year. If it is assumed that the cash flow arises evenly throughout the year, the payback period will be:

3 years + (15/45 × 12 months) = 3 years and 4 months

This payback period is within the company's requirement of four years. The investment should therefore be accepted.

Accounting rate of return

Total cash inflow over the eight years of the project = $236m
Total depreciation = $120m (the investment will be fully written off by the end of year 8)

Therefore average profit = ($236m − $120m)/8 years = $14.5m

As the investment will be fully written off by the end of year 8, average investment = ($120m + $0)/2 = $60m.

Therefore, ARR = $14.5m/$60m = 24.2 per cent

Net present value

TABLE 9.25

Year	Cash flow $m	Discount factor (12%)	Present value $m
0	(120)	1.000	(120.00)
1	30	0.893	26.79
2	35	0.797	27.90
3	40	0.712	28.48
4	45	0.636	28.62
5	30	0.567	17.01
6	26	0.507	13.18
7	15	0.452	6.78
8	15	0.404	6.06
Net present value			34.82

The NPV is $34.82m. As this is a positive figure, the investment should be accepted.

Exercise 9.2: Understanding principles

1 Because the feasibility study has already been completed it is a **sunk cost**. Only future costs which will change as a result of the decision to invest should be included in the investment appraisal calculation. It is therefore correct to exclude this cost from the calculations.

2 The cost of financing an investment should not be included within the cash-flow forecasts. It is therefore correct to exclude this cost. When using the IRR technique, financing costs are considered by evaluating whether the predicted IRR is sufficient to meet those costs. In this case the predicted IRR is 22 per cent, which is substantially in excess of the 8 per cent cost of the loan. In any case, it is incorrect to evaluate an investment purely against the source of financing. The investment must meet the overall return requirements of the business and not just the cost of the loan to finance the store.

3 Unless it is expected that central office administration costs will increase as a result of opening a new store, these costs should not be included, as they will be incurred anyway, even if the investment does not go ahead. However, any additional central office costs which are incurred as a result of opening the new store should be included within the investment appraisal calculations.

4   Although it is important to charge depreciation for financial accounting purposes, this charge is not relevant to the investment appraisal. The two methods used to evaluate the proposed investment are payback period and IRR. Both of these techniques use cash flows and depreciation is an accounting adjustment, not a cash flow.

5   This is an example of an **opportunity cost**. It is incorrect to include the salary of $40,000 of the manager in the investment appraisal calculations, because this salary will be paid regardless of whether or not the new store is opened. The only additional cost which the company will incur as a result of opening the new store is the increase in the salary of the assistant manager. The annual cost included in the investment appraisal should therefore be $5,000, the value of the assistant manager's salary increase.

Exercise 9.3: Financial appraisal within context

Consultant's report to the directors of ANG Co

Investment appraisal for the opening of a new factory

Terms of reference

I have been asked to advise the board of directors in relation to its decision to open a new factory in order to extend its production facility. This report sets out my evaluation of the options currently being considered by the board.

Introduction

ANG Co has grown rapidly over the last five years. The company is now seeking to extend its production facility through opening a new factory. In particular, the company intends to break into new markets in China and South East Asia. Any new factory must therefore meet the needs of the company in developing this new market.

Three alternatives have been proposed for the siting of the new factory. The first alternative (Factory A) is to site the factory alongside the existing production facility. The second alternative (Factory B) is to move to a new enterprise development zone approximately 150 km from the existing factory. The third alternative (Factory C) is to open a new factory in China.

Financial evaluation

The cost of each of the investments is very similar. Both of the factories in the existing country will cost $150 million. The proposed factory in China is slightly cheaper at $140 million. All production facilities are expected to have similar lives: the two factories in the existing country will have a production life of five years, whereas the factory sited in China would have a production life of four years.

A financial evaluation of the three options has already been conducted. The potential investments have been evaluated using three commonly used and reliable techniques: payback period; accounting rate of return; and net present value. However, the NPV calculations have all been performed using the company's standard discount rate of 13 per cent. This has therefore not been adjusted to take account of the differing levels of risk involved with each of the three investments. It is therefore important to consider risk and other non-financial factors alongside the financial evaluations which have already been conducted.

Factory A

This option appears the least attractive in terms of the financial evaluations. It has the longest payback period of three years. The ARR is 29 per cent, which matches that of Factory B but is less than the 32 per cent return offered by Factory C. This investment has the lowest NPV of $25.6 million.

However, there are a number of non-financial factors which, when considered, may make this option more attractive. The current success of the business has been built upon a highly skilled and loyal workforce. By building the new factory alongside the existing production facility, the company will be able to take advantage of the skills of the existing workforce. It would also provide an opportunity for promotion and development of existing staff. This is likely to maintain or increase staff morale and enable ANG Co to retain skilled and experienced staff. These factors make Factory A a lower risk option than the other alternatives, and if the discount rate were adjusted to reflect this then the NPV would appear more attractive in comparison with Factory B and Factory C.

Factory B

This is currently the most financially attractive option as it offers the highest NPV of $39.4 million. Although the ARR of 29 per cent is lower than that offered by Factory C at 32 per cent, the NPV is a more reliable measure of the financial viability of the investment.

However, these financial figures should be tempered with consideration of other factors. This option would involve moving a substantial part of production from the existing facility and making 20 per cent of the existing workforce redundant. This is likely to have a significant negative impact on the morale of remaining employees. This may have an impact upon employee motivation and efficiency and may increase staff turnover. The company would also be losing potentially valuable skilled employees. As the new factory would be opened a substantial distance from the existing factory, new employees would have to be recruited. It will be more difficult to supervise and train these new employees alongside existing staff. This will increase the difficulty and timescale of establishing a skilled workforce of the calibre of the existing factory. The company also needs to consider the risks of relying upon tax breaks in a new enterprise development zone. There is a risk that the government may reduce or withdraw these breaks after a short period and this would have a negative impact upon the projected financial figures.

Factory C

This option is financially attractive. It offers the highest ARR, a two-year payback period and a reasonable NPV of $28.7 million. It also requires a slightly lower investment than the other two alternatives, which would save the company $10 million in setup costs. However, the expected production life of this factory is only four years, against a five-year life from the first two options.

The major advantage of this option is that it would put production on the doorstep of the new market which ANG Co is seeking to develop. This may offer several advantages in terms of supply time and reaction to changes in market demands. However, in terms of management control, this option carries the highest risk. The company currently has no experience of operating a production facility in China. The new factory would be at a greater geographic distance from the existing business, which will increase problems of control and communication. The company would also need to recruit a new workforce in an unknown market. This means that the quality and reliability of employees in the new factory will be unknown.

As this option carries the highest risk, the discount rate used in the NPV calculation should have been increased. If the NPV were to be recalculated using a higher discount rate, this option might appear substantially less financially attractive.

Recommendations

Each of the three options offers different strategic advantages to ANG Co. However, they all carry very different risks. Before a final decision is made, it is recommended that the NPV calculations are adjusted to take account of these different risks.

Operational decisions

OBJECTIVE

To enable the manager to incorporate financial evaluation into their operational decision making and problem solving.

LEARNING OUTCOMES

After studying this chapter, the reader will be able to:

- Assess the financial consequences of a range of decision-making situations.
- Define the scope and limitations of the financial techniques applied.

KEY TOPICS COVERED

The chapter will examine a range of operational decisions and the financial techniques which can be used to support them:

- setting sales targets;
- predicting the impact of price changes;
- outsourcing vs in-house operation/production;
- operational restructuring/automation of business processes;
- closing a business segment;
- dropping a product/service line.

MANAGEMENT ISSUES

Managers need to be able to assess the financial impact of operational and tactical decisions.

Introduction

In this chapter we will look at some financial aspects of operational decision making. We introduce some fundamental principles of financial decision making and some core decision-making techniques. Once these techniques are understood, we examine their wider applications and demonstrate their use in a range of typical business decision-making situations. A key skill for managers is understanding which is the most appropriate technique for a given decision.

Operational decision making

All managers are faced with operational decisions. These are decisions concerning the best means of implementing strategies and overcoming problems that are encountered. There is a saying that 'analysis is at the heart of business intelligence': in order to be successful in dealing with the issues they face, managers need a systematic approach towards decision making together with appropriate tools for evaluating the financial impact of different options.

A typical operational decision making process will involve a number of key steps as illustrated in Figure 10.1.

FIGURE 10.1   Decision-making steps

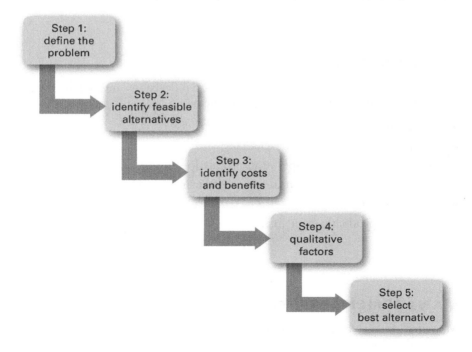

These steps involve:

- Step 1: recognizing and defining the problem or issue which needs to be addressed.
- Step 2: identifying alternative solutions to the problem and eliminating alternatives that are not practically feasible.
- Step 3: identifying the costs and benefits of alternatives in order to establish their financial feasibility.
- Step 4: assessing qualitative factors in the decision that go beyond the immediate financial benefits.
- Step 5: selecting the alternative which offers the greatest overall benefit when considering both financial and qualitative factors.

In this chapter we are primarily concerned with step 3: identifying the costs and benefits of alternatives. However, we will also visit some of the qualitative factors in step 4 that will impinge upon decisions.

We will look at a number of typical operational decisions. In order to examine these different business situations we will explore two key areas of financial decision-making theory in this chapter: cost–volume–profit analysis (CVP) and relevant costing. We will introduce each theory in turn and then demonstrate its application through a number of examples which relate to real-world business decisions.

Cost–volume–profit analysis (CVP)

CVP analysis is the study of the interrelationship between costs and revenues (and therefore profit) at various levels of activity.

Economic models which measure changes in costs and revenues as the volume of activity increases can be complex. However, for the purpose of managerial decision making it is possible to simplify these models in a way that makes them easy to use and therefore more readily useful to the average manager. CVP analysis therefore makes a number of assumptions about how revenues and costs behave as the volume of activity within a business increases. We will look at each of these assumptions in turn.

Revenues

Economic models tell us that as the volume of sales increases, the unit sales price will decrease. Although this may be true when looking at the full spectrum of possible levels of sales, when using CVP analysis for decision making we are usually looking at a relatively narrow range of sales volumes. It is therefore possible to make the assumption that unit sales price will remain constant across all levels of activity.

In this case we can say that total sales revenue will be the volume of sales (in units) multiplied by the unit sales price:

$$\text{Sales revenue} = \text{Units sold} \times \text{Sales price}$$

This relationship between sales revenue and the volume of activity (units sold) is represented graphically in Figure 10.2.

FIGURE 10.2   Revenue

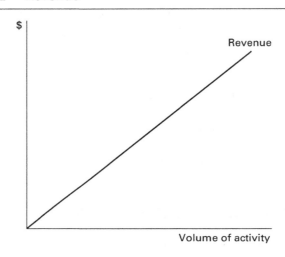

Costs

In financial decision making we usually divide costs into two broad categories: fixed costs and variable costs. This categorization refers to how costs behave in relation to changes in volume of production and sales.

Fixed costs

Fixed costs are unaffected by changes in the level of activity and therefore remain constant or 'fixed' as the volume of activity increases or decreases. An example of a fixed cost is the rent paid on a shop. The rent must be paid even if the shop sells nothing. If the shop does well and sales reach a very high level, the same amount of rent will be paid.

This relationship between fixed costs and the volume of activity is represented in Figure 10.3.

FIGURE 10.3 Fixed costs

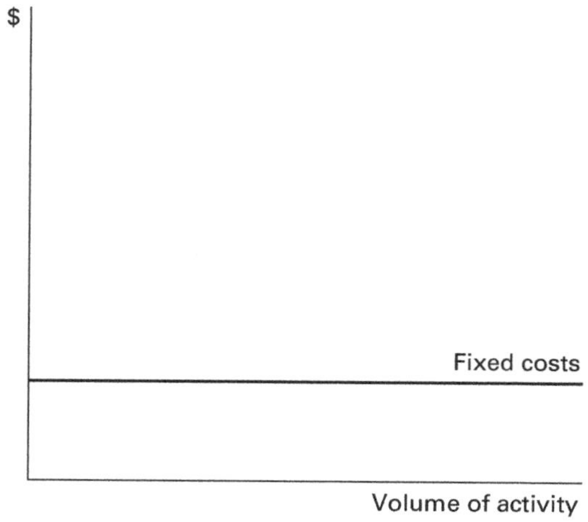

Expert view 10.1: Fixed costs

Some 'fixed' costs may increase if there is a substantial change in the level of activity. For example, a business may employ a manager in its production department. The manager will be paid a fixed salary and this will not change with the level of production. However, if production is increased substantially, for example by moving to 24-hour operations and running two shifts of workers, the business may employ a second manager so that there is one manager for each shift. In this case the cost is said to be a **stepped cost**, because it remains constant over a range of activity (the cost of one manager for one shift), but then increases by a 'step' once the activity goes beyond a certain level (the cost of two managers for two shifts).

A second point to note about fixed costs is that they are deemed to be fixed in relation to the level of activity, but not necessarily over time. Fixed costs may change over time. For example, the rent paid on a shop may be subject to an annual review, with an increase each year. Similarly, a manager paid a fixed salary may have an annual pay rise.

Variable costs

Variable costs are those costs that are directly related to the level of activity and will therefore change as the level of activity changes. For example, the cost of direct materials will increase with the number of units produced.

FIGURE 10.4 Variable costs

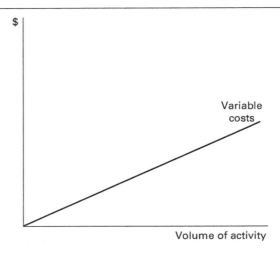

The relationship between variable cost per unit and the volume of activity will vary in different circumstances. For example, in many cases the variable cost per unit will decrease as volume increases, owing to economies of scale. This will be the case when direct labour becomes more efficient as volume increases. It will also be the case if bulk-purchasing discounts are available when buying large quantities of materials. However, in some cases the variable costs per unit may increase as volume increases. For example, higher levels of activity may involve paying employees an overtime premium.

Despite these complicating factors, for financial decision-making purposes we can usually assume that this relationship is linear, as we did with revenues. That is to say, the variable cost per unit will remain the same across all levels of activity. This means that variable costs can be represented graphically, as shown in Figure 10.4.

Total cost

The total cost of an activity will be made up of variable costs plus fixed costs. Therefore we can create a graph to plot total costs by adding these two individual cost elements together. This will give us a graph, as illustrated in Figure 10.5.

Now that we have plotted both revenues and costs on graphs in Figures 10.1 to 10.5, we can incorporate them into one graph as illustrated in Figure 10.6.

The graph in Figure 10.6 shows that up to a certain volume of activity, costs exceed revenue. However, there comes a volume of activity, known as the **break-even point (BEP)**, at which total cost equals total revenue. This is the point at which the business makes neither a loss nor a profit. If the business operates at a volume of activity greater than the break-even point, it will make a profit. On the other hand, if the business operates at a volume of activity less than the break-even point, it will make a loss.

FIGURE 10.5   Total costs

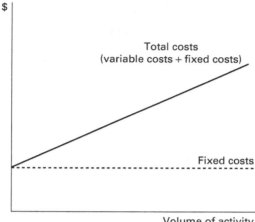

Total costs
(variable costs + fixed costs)

Fixed costs

Volume of activity

FIGURE 10.6   Total revenue and total costs

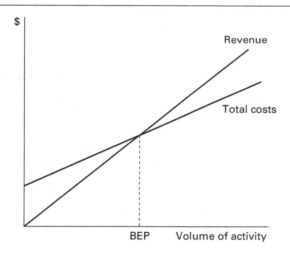

Revenue

Total costs

BEP   Volume of activity

Mathematical approach to CVP analysis

Although the relationship between costs and revenues is easy to see and understand using graphs, it is actually easier to apply to managerial decision making using the following profit equation:

$$\text{Profit} = PQ - (F + VQ)$$

Where: Q = units sold
         P = selling price
         V = unit variable cost
         F = total fixed costs

We can rearrange this formula to express profit in a way which is more useful for decision making:

$$\text{Profit} = Q(P - V) - F$$

Where: $P - V$ =   Contribution per unit

We can use this formula to calculate the break-even point. The break-even point will occur at the volume of sales (ie the value of Q) at which profit is nil.

The graph in Figure 10.6 illustrates that this lies at the value of Q where total revenue = total costs. That is to say, where:

$$PQ = F + VQ$$

If we rearrange this formula in order to find the value of Q, we get:

$$Q = \frac{F}{P - V}$$

Put in plainer English, this formula is:

$$\text{Break-even point (in units)} = \frac{\text{Fixed costs}}{\text{Contribution per unit}}$$

(Remember: contribution per unit = sales price – variable cost per unit)

WORKED EXAMPLE 10.1   Computing the break-even point for sales

Isabel wishes to start a business selling ice cream from a mobile van. She can lease a van at a cost of $206 per week. Isabel has estimated that the van will cost around $70 per week to run. She has also obtained the following prices from an ice cream wholesaler:

Tub of ice cream – 100 portions	$20.00
Box of 100 cones	$10.00

If Isabel sells ice creams at $1.50 each, how many ice creams will she need to sell each week in order to break even?

Answer
We can calculate the number of ice creams that Isabel needs to sell by using the break-even formula. First we need to calculate contribution per unit:

$$\text{Contribution per unit} = \text{Sales price} - \text{Variable cost per unit}$$
$$= \$1.50 - (\$20 + \$10)/100 = \$1.20$$

$$\text{Break-even point (in units)} = \frac{\text{Fixed costs}}{\text{Contribution per unit}} = \frac{\$206 + \$70}{\$1.20} = 230 \text{ units}$$

Therefore Isabel will need to sell 230 ice creams per week in order to cover fixed costs and break even.

Target profit

Obviously Isabel will wish to achieve more than simply break-even with her ice cream business. She will also need to make a profit.

Another application of the CVP technique is to calculate how many units must be sold in order to achieve a target profit. Let's do this for Isabel's business.

WORKED EXAMPLE 10.2   Target profit

Isabel has decided that she needs to earn a minimum profit of $350 per week from her business. How many ice creams will she need to sell each week in order to earn this profit?

Answer

The break-even formula we used in Worked Example 10.1 told us how many ice creams Isabel needs to sell in order to cover her fixed costs. If she wishes to earn a profit of $350, Isabel needs to sell sufficient ice creams to cover fixed costs plus the profit. Hence we can modify the formula we used in Worked Example 10.1 as follows:

$$\text{Target sales (in units)} = \frac{\text{Fixed costs + target profit}}{\text{Contribution per unit}}$$

$$= \frac{\$276 + \$350}{\$1.20} = 522 \text{ units}$$

Therefore Isabel will need to sell 522 ice creams in a week in order to earn a profit of $350.

Margin of safety

In Chapter 9 we introduced the concept of **sensitivity analysis**. Sensitivity analysis involves exploring how susceptible predicted profit levels are to changes in levels of activity. CVP analysis can be a very useful tool for performing such analysis, and one of the most basic methods of doing this is to calculate the margin of safety.

FIGURE 10.7   Margin of safety

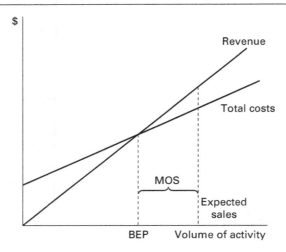

The margin of safety is the gap in units of sales between the expected or target sales and the break-even point. It is a useful measure in that it tells the business how far sales can fall from their expected level before the business starts to make a loss. This is illustrated in Figure 10.7.

We can apply this analysis of margin of safety to Isabel's ice cream business.

WORKED EXAMPLE 10.3   Margin of safety

Isabel expects to sell 550 ice creams each week. The break-even level of sales is 230 ice creams per week. What is Isabel's margin of safety on her expected sales?

Answer

The margin of safety is 320 ice creams (550 – 230). It is more useful to express this as a percentage of the expected sales:

MOS = 320/550 = 58 per cent

This means that sales must fall by more than 320 units or 58 per cent from the expected level of 550 units per week before Isabel will start to make a loss.

The margin of safety is a useful measure of risk. The smaller the margin of safety, the higher the risk that the business will make a loss if it has a poor week of sales.

> **Expert view 10.2: Margin of safety and sensitivity analysis**
>
> In practice, businesses will usually perform CVP analysis using a computer spreadsheet. The use of a computer allows for easy manipulation of the figures so that managers can quickly identify how sensitive predicted profit levels are to changes in different variables.

Change in selling price

Another application of the CVP technique is calculating the impact on profit from changes in price. In Chapter 8 we looked at the relationship between price and demand. Generally speaking, if a business reduces its prices then this will increase demand. However, increased demand at a lower price will not necessarily increase profits. Therefore, before changing prices it is useful to calculate the predicted impact this will have upon overall profit. We can apply this analysis to Isabel's ice cream business.

WORKED EXAMPLE 10.4   Change in selling price

After selling ice creams for several weeks, Isabel has found that she sells 520 ice creams per week on average at a price of $1.50. Isabel's fixed costs are $276 per week and her variable costs are $0.30 per ice cream sold.

Isabel is considering reducing the price to $1 per ice cream in order to increase sales.

(a) What is the minimum number of ice creams that Isabel must sell each week in order to justify the reduction in sales price?

(b) What will be the impact on Isabel's profit if sales increase to 750 units per week at the new price of $1?

Answer

Isabel currently sells 520 ice creams per week at a price of $1.50. Her weekly profit is therefore:

$$\text{Profit} = Q(P - V) - F$$
$$= (520 \times [\$1.50 - \$0.30]) - \$276 = \$348$$

In order to justify a reduction in the sales price Isabel must make at least the same level of profit at the new price of $1.

At the new price the new contribution per unit will be: $1.00 − $0.30 = $0.70. Therefore the minimum level of sales (in units) will be:

$$\text{Target sales (in units)} = \frac{\text{Fixed costs} + \text{Target profit}}{\text{Contribution per unit}} = \frac{\$276 + \$348}{\$0.70} = 892 \text{ units}$$

Isabel must sell at least 892 ice creams each week at the price of $1 in order to make the same level of profit that she currently makes selling the ice creams at $1.50. This represents increasing sales of 372 units (892 – 520) or 71.5 per cent. This analysis shows us that Isabel would need a substantial increase in sales at the lower price in order simply to make the same level of profit. Unless she can be confident of achieving such a large increase in sales, Isabel should not reduce the price to $1. Otherwise she runs the risk of reducing her profits:

> If Isabel's sales increase to 750 ice creams per week at the new price of $1, her profit will fall to $249 per week:

$$\text{Profit} = Q(P - V) - F$$
$$= (750 \times [\$1.00 - \$0.30]) - \$276 = \$249$$

Change in production systems

As well as analysing the impact of price changes on profitability, the CVP technique can be used to analyse the impact of changes in production costs. This is particularly useful for businesses that are making operational changes. For example, the automation of activities is likely to increase fixed costs and reduce variable costs. Because this changes the **operating gearing** (the mix of variable and fixed costs), it will have an impact upon the break-even point, the margin of safety, and profitability at different levels of activity.

Expert view 10.3: Operating gearing

Operating gearing (sometimes called 'operating leverage') describes the relationship between an organization's fixed costs and variable costs:

$$\text{Operating gearing} = \frac{F}{F + V}$$

A greater proportion of fixed costs means a higher operating gearing. Increasing operating gearing makes a business's profits more sensitive to a change in volume of activity. If volume increases, profitability can be greater if operating gearing is higher. However, the effect reverses when volumes fall (see Worked Example 10.5). It is for this reason that businesses with high operating gearing often have to take drastic cost-cutting measures when sales start falling. Managers must be aware of the impact of operating gearing on profits and risk to make good business decisions.

WORKED EXAMPLE 10.5   Change in production systems

Angus Co makes beds. Current production information is:

Materials costs	$80 per unit
Labour costs	$160 per unit
Variable sales costs	$40 per unit
Sales price	$380 per unit
Fixed costs	$1,100,000 per year
Current volume of output	14,000 units per year

The company is considering automating the metal-cutting process, which is the most labour-intensive part of production. This will involve installing a new computerized cutting machine that will have an annual fixed cost of $500,000. However, it is expected that with the new automated cutting, labour costs will fall to $120 per unit.

(a)   Compare the annual profit using the current production method and using the new automated production, if annual sales remain at 14,000 units.

(b)   Compare the annual profit using the current production method and using the new automated production, if annual sales were to fall to 12,000 units.

Answer

If sales remain at 14,000 units per year:

The current contribution per unit = $380 – ($80 + $160 + $40) = $100
Therefore profit = ($100 × 14,000) – $1,100,000 = $300,000

With the new automated cutting process:

Contribution per unit = $380 – ($80 + $120 + $40) = $140
Therefore profit = ($140 × 14,000) – $1,600,000 = $360,000

At current production and sales levels, the proposed automation of the cutting process will increase profits by $60,000.

If sales fall to 12,000 units per year:

Profit using the current production method:

= ($100 × 12,000) – $1,100,000 = $100,000

Profit using the proposed new production method:

= ($140 × 12,000) – $1,600,000 = $80,000

At the reduced level of sales (which represents a fall of less than 15 per cent in sales), the proposed new production method would result in the company earning $20,000 less profit. Therefore, before it goes ahead with the automation, the company should examine its sales forecasts in detail in order to be confident that future sales will not fall. If it cannot be confident of this, it should not change its current production methods.

Advertising campaign

CVP analysis can be used to help managers make decisions regarding discretionary expenditure such as advertising. For example, a company may plan an advertising campaign in order to increase its volume of sales. CVP analysis will help managers assess the potential impact on overall profitability.

WORKED EXAMPLE 10.6   Advertising campaign

Digi Co manufactures laptop computers. The computers sell at $500 and the variable costs of production, sales and distribution are $350 per computer. The company has fixed costs of $9,200,000 per year. Forecast sales for the coming year are 70,000 units.

At a recent board meeting the marketing director argued that Digi Co computers offer good value in comparison to those of competitors. She has therefore proposed an advertising campaign to increase customer awareness of this.

The advertising campaign would cost $350,000 and the marketing director is confident that it would increase sales volume by 4 per cent.

Should Digi Co undertake the advertising campaign?

Answer

If the company undertakes the advertising campaign, fixed costs will increase by $350,000. Total contribution will also increase because of the increase in sales volume:

$$\text{Increase in contribution} = (70,000 \times 4\%) \times (\$500 - \$350) = \$420,000$$

Therefore Digi Co should go ahead with the advertising campaign because the net impact will be an increase in profit of $70,000 ($420,000 − $350,000).

Evaluation of the CVP technique

As can be seen from the worked examples above, CVP is an extremely straight-forward analytical tool. This simplicity is both its strength and its weakness. The strength of the technique lies in the way that it removes many of the complications of the real world in order to provide a sharp focus on the financial impact of decisions. This makes the technique both simple to apply and easy to understand. However, the simplicity of CVP analysis has led to criticism. This criticism focuses mainly on the underlying assumptions. This can be summarized as follows:

- CVP analysis departs from accepted curvilinear models of supply and demand used in economic pricing theory because it uses simple linear formulae for revenues and costs. In other words, CVP analysis ignores price elasticity of demand and economies of scale. Supporters of CVP have responded to this criticism by suggesting that although this is true, the focus of analysis on limited range of activity volumes means that a linear function is a reasonably accurate proxy of the true economic model.

- CVP analysis focuses too much on the short term. It is typically restricted to one accounting period. It therefore ignores longer-term strategic issues.

- CVP analysis usually assumes a single product. The analysis can be used for multiple products but it is necessary to assume a constant sales mix, ie the proportion of different products sold remains the same as the overall volume changes. In practice this rarely occurs. In the real world, changes in volume of sales can result from market conditions that will affect different products or services to differing degrees. This limits the usefulness of CVP analysis for businesses offering a range of products or services.

- CVP analysis assumes a simple, single-stage manufacturing process in which fixed and variable costs can be clearly identified. In the real world, manufacturing processes can be complex, with the interplay of costs being equally so.

- CVP analysis assumes that costs can be categorized into either variable or fixed. It does not allow for costs with more complex behaviour. In the real world, organizations and their activities are complex. It is often difficult to separate costs into clear classifications of fixed and variable.

- CVP analysis assumes that the forces influencing a business are static rather than dynamic. In the real world, changes in volume of sales affect pricing, which in turn can change price elasticity of demand. Changes in volume also affect the cost of materials used in production and the cost of direct labour. CVP analysis ignores these changes and therefore does not reflect the reality that makes up a dynamic complicated market.

All of these criticisms are directed at the simplicity of CVP analysis when used in complex organizations and dynamic business environments. The static nature of CVP analysis means that it must be used with care within a dynamic and complex market. However, this does not mean that the technique is totally without validity. CVP analysis takes a snapshot. This is a useful snapshot provided managers do not think purely in terms of single points in time with nothing changing. There is often great merit in a tool that cuts through the complexities of the real world in order to give simple and straightforward measures for decision-makers.

Cost–volume–profit analysis: summary

This section has demonstrated how CVP analysis can be a useful analytical tool for managers. However, managers must be aware of the limitations of the technique and therefore decide when it is an appropriate tool.

Relevant costing

The concept of relevant costs and opportunity costs were introduced in Chapter 9 in the context of investment decision making. In this chapter we will examine these concepts in more detail and demonstrate how they can be applied to other financial decisions such as: the decision to buy in a product or service or make it in-house, or the decision to drop a product or close a division or segment of the business.

As was the case when we looked at investment appraisal in Chapter 9, it is always assumed when evaluating alternative courses of action that the objective is to maximize the present value of future net cash inflows.

Measuring relevant costs

The relevant costs for decision making are those future costs that will be affected by the decision. Costs that are independent of the decision are not relevant and should not be considered when making that decision.

As a general rule, a cost that is avoidable by choosing one alternative over another is a relevant cost. A cost that is unavoidable, no matter which alternative is chosen, is irrelevant and should not be included in the evaluation of the decision.

FIGURE 10.8   The relevant cost decision

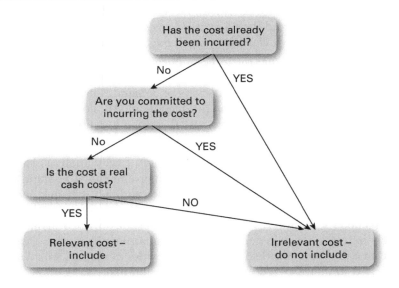

Figure 10.8 sets out a decision tree for deciding whether a cost is relevant to a particular decision.

- The first question to ask is: 'Has the cost already been incurred?' If a cost has already been incurred, it cannot be avoided no matter what decision is made. Such a cost is known as a **sunk cost**; it is irrelevant to any decision and should be ignored. This sounds simple in principle, but often people are confused about the relevance of sunk costs and include them in their considerations.

    For example, a manager may argue that because his organization has invested $500,000 in a new computer system, this expenditure would be wasted if the computer system were abandoned because of problems. Such a manager would argue that the $500,000 is a relevant cost of abandoning the system. However, the reality is that the $500,000 has already been spent, and this cannot change no matter what decision is made now about the future use of the computer system. The only relevant costs in this case would be those future costs incurred to rectify the problems with the system.

- Secondly, you should ask: 'Are you committed to incurring the cost?' In some cases, costs may not yet have been incurred, but the business is committed to those costs no matter what decision is made. If this is the case, the cost is irrelevant and should not be included in the decision-making process.

    For example, a business may enter into a five-year lease of a building. After one year the business thinks that it no longer needs that building and faces the decision of whether or not to move out. If the business is contractually obliged to continue paying the rent for the remainder of the five-year lease term, any future rent will have to be paid no matter what decision is made about the use of the building. The rent cost therefore becomes irrelevant to the decision, even though it has not yet actually been incurred.

- Finally you should ask: 'Is the cost a real cash cost?' Some costs are valid accounting costs that should be included on the profitability analysis, but they are not relevant for decision making. This is the category of costs which relate to accounting adjustments rather than direct cash payments. The main example is depreciation. Each accounting period, a cost will be recorded for the depreciation of non-current assets. However, there is no underlying cash payment relating to this depreciation cost. It is therefore not a relevant cost.

    For example, a business owns a machine which is depreciated on a straight-line basis at $5,000 per year. If the business decides to sell the machine, it will no longer incur the depreciation cost of $5,000. However, this is not a relevant cost and should not be included in the decision regarding selling the machine. The reality is that the underlying cash flow represented in the depreciation charge was the initial purchase of the machine. As this occurred in the past, it is a sunk cost and is irrelevant to the decision. The only costs relevant to the decision to sell the machine would be any extra costs incurred in selling it (such as advertising) together with the revenue received from the sale.

Using relevant costing for decision making

There are two basic steps in using the relevant costing approach to evaluate an operational decision: firstly, disregard costs and revenues that are not relevant to the decision; secondly, use the costs and revenues that remain (ie the relevant costs) to evaluate alternatives, choosing that alternative which offers the greatest net benefit.

Costs do not rigidly fit into the category of 'relevant' or 'irrelevant'. What is a relevant cost will depend upon the circumstances of the decision: costs may be relevant in the context of one decision but not in a different situation. For example, the timescale of the decision often impacts on which costs are relevant. We will look at this issue in more detail below when we compare short-term and long-term decisions for outsourcing.

Let us look at how this principle is applied within the context of common operational decisions.

The make or buy decision

Organizations are regularly faced with what is commonly known as the 'make or buy' decision. This is the decision of whether to make a product (or provide a service) in-house, or to buy that product in from some external supplier. There can be many advantages of buying in from an external supplier:

- Management is freed up to concentrate on activities which may be more important to the profitability of the organization.
- Risks are transferred outside of the organization (to the supplier).
- External suppliers can specialize and create economies of scale which enables them to supply at a much lower cost than the organization is able to achieve.
- Buying in from multiple suppliers creates greater security of supply.
- Buying in services when needed may give an organization greater flexibility and save costs during times when those services are not needed.

During the 1980s the concept of **outsourcing** became extremely popular. As a result, many businesses started to buy in from external suppliers those facilities which had previously always been provided internally.

Extract 10.1: Tom Peters – 'stick to the knitting'

One of the best-known proponents of outsourcing is the management guru Tom Peters, who coined the phrase 'stick to the knitting'. Peters' 1982 book *In Search of Excellence* (written with Robert Waterman) is one of the biggest-selling business books ever. Based upon a study of 43 of the world's most successful (at the time) businesses, the book identifies eight common themes to that success. One of those themes was 'stick to the knitting – stay with the business you know'. One interpretation of this principle, which Peters developed in his later work, was the idea that management should concentrate on their core activities and let others take care of the non-core activities by outsourcing them.

Outsourcing became popular and was widespread practice throughout the late 1980s and into the 1990s. It was seen as a way of keeping businesses lean and flexible – non-core activities could be bought in as needed and at a lower cost than doing the work in-house. Many businesses outsourced payroll services, legal services, recruitment and advertising. Businesses also outsourced areas of manufacturing to overseas suppliers, finding that they could take advantage of cheaper (and un-unionized) labour and avoid regulations, high taxes and other operating costs. Outsourcing also became popular in the public sector, with many areas of public service such as public transport, health care and local services being bought in from private-sector suppliers.

This is a trend which continues in the 21st century in both the public and private sectors.

Short-term vs long-term situations

When faced with a decision which covers only the short term, it is often the case that many costs are unavoidable (and therefore relevant to the decision) because reducing or removing those costs requires measures which take a longer timescale to implement. In the long term, more costs become avoidable. This means that the outcome of a 'make or buy' decision will differ according to whether a short-term or long-term position is considered. This principle is illustrated in Worked Examples 10.7a and 10.7b.

WORKED EXAMPLE 10.7A   Make or buy decision – short term

Scott Co operates a distillery producing Scotch whisky. The main ingredient of whisky is malted barley, which is produced by processing raw barley in order to convert the starch content into sugars.

Scott Co currently produces its own malted barley. However, the directors are considering the option of buying the malted barley in from an external supplier that specializes in malting.

The estimated cost per tonne to Scott Co of producing malted barley in-house is as follows:

	$
Direct labour	80
Direct materials (raw barley)	260
Direct (variable) overheads	180
Fixed overheads (apportioned)	120
	640

The outside supplier has quoted a figure of $580 per tonne for an order of 500 tonnes of malted barley. This is equal to three months' supply.

The share of fixed overheads apportioned to malted barley production will still be incurred whether or not the company purchases the malted barley from an external supplier. Any redundancies of production staff will be subject to three months' notice.

Should Scott Co continue to produce malted barley in-house or should it buy the malted barley from the external supplier?

Answer

On face value, the buy-in option appears more financially attractive: it currently costs Scott Co $640 per tonne to produce in-house, and the external supplier is offering malted barley at $580 per tonne.

However, in evaluating this decision, the directors need to compare the quoted external price of $580 with the *relevant cost* of producing the malted barley in-house. The relevant cost will be those costs which can be reduced or removed if the malted barley is bought in. The fact that this is a short-term contract has an impact on which costs become relevant.

Because the contract is for three months' supply and direct labour is subject to three months' notice on redundancy, direct labour costs cannot be reduced if the malted barley is bought in. This is therefore not a relevant cost. Likewise, the fixed overhead costs will still be incurred if the malted barley is bought in and so this is not a relevant cost. This means that the relevant costs, ie the costs that will be eliminated if the malted barley is bought in, are:

	$
Direct materials (raw barley)	260
Direct (variable) overheads	180
	440

These figures reveal that the short-term contract is not financially viable for Scott Co. The company would be incurring purchasing costs of $580 per tonne, but only reducing its in-house costs by $440 per tonne. This means that the buy-in option would cost the company $140 per tonne more than manufacturing themselves.

However, the situation may change if the company is able to negotiate a long-term contract for supply of malted barley.

WORKED EXAMPLE 10.7B   Make or buy decision – long term

Scott Co is able to negotiate a long-term contract with the outside supplier to deliver 2,000 tonnes of malted barley per year for five years at a cost of $580 per tonne. In the long term the fixed overheads and labour costs can be reduced (with no redundancy costs).

Should Scott Co enter into the longer-term contract for external supply of malted barley, or should it continue to make the malted barley in-house?

Answer

Because Scott Co is able to eliminate both the fixed overhead costs and the labour costs with a long-term contract, all the costs of production become relevant. This means that Scott Co would be saving $640 per tonne by not manufacturing against the cost of buying in of $580 per tonne. This is a net saving to the company of $60 per tonne. In this case, the option of buying in rather than making in-house appears more financially attractive. The final decision should, of course, be made after evaluating wider strategic and qualitative factors. (These are discussed below.)

Extract 10.2: Outsourcing at TagHeuer

TagHeuer, the Swiss watch manufacturer, has a clear 'make or buy' strategy. The company is the world's fourth-biggest producer of luxury watches, after Rolex, Cartier and Omega. Despite this, the company manufactures very little. Watch movements and other components are bought in from external suppliers. Some watch cases are made by a subsidiary, but about half are bought in. Even the final assembly of watches is subcontracted. Only the top-end watches are manufactured internally and that is by a subsidiary.

The company advocates many advantages in this strategy: contracting out manufacturing transfers risk to suppliers; sourcing from multiple suppliers creates security of supply and competitive pricing; management can concentrate on product development and marketing.

Opportunity costs

The concept of an opportunity cost was introduced in Chapter 9. This is a category of cost that will not be found in an income statement. It is used only in decision making. However, opportunity costs can be extremely important in assessing the true financial impact of a decision. This is because, if an organization is operating at full capacity, the decision to engage in one particular activity (for example, to produce a particular good or service) has a cost in terms of not being able to use that capacity for some other activity.

Expert view 10.4: Opportunity cost

An **opportunity cost** is a measure of the opportunity that is lost or sacrificed when the choice of one course of action requires that an alternative course of action be given up. An opportunity cost is always measured financially in terms of lost contribution (Contribution = Sales revenue − Variable costs).

WORKED EXAMPLE 10.7C   Opportunity costs

Let us return to the example of Scott Co considering a short-term three-month contract for buying in malted barley (see Worked Example 10.7a).

Scott Co is currently running at full capacity. The production of malted barley internally required 20 hours of production time that could otherwise be used for chill filtering (another part of the whisky production process). Chill filtering yields a contribution of $8 per hour.

Should Scott Co continue to produce malted barley in-house or should it buy the malted barley from the external supplier?

Answer

Returning to the analysis that we did in Worked Example 10.7a, we established that the relevant cost of producing the malted barley in-house was:

	$
Direct materials (raw barley)	260
Direct (variable) overheads	180
	440

However, because Scott Co is now operating at full capacity, there is also the opportunity cost of using production time for malting barley rather than chill filtering. This opportunity cost is measured in lost contribution:

$$20 \text{ hours} \times \$8 \text{ per hour} = \$160$$

When we include this opportunity cost, the total relevant cost of producing malted barley in-house is:

	$
Direct materials (raw barley)	260
Direct (variable) overheads	180
Opportunity cost	160
	600

This means that the cost of buying in malted barley from the external supplier at $580 per tonne is now more financially attractive than manufacturing in-house. Scott Co should therefore buy in the malted barley over the three-month period and use the internal production facility for chill filtering.

The consideration of qualitative factors in outsourcing

The quantitative factors which we have considered above, ie the relevant costs and the opportunity costs of manufacturing in-house as opposed to buying in, do not give the full picture in decision-making situations. Other, non-financial factors should always be considered, both because they are important in their own right, and also because they might have financial effects which are not immediately quantifiable. Examples of factors which can be difficult to quantify financially are:

- *Redundancies*. Outsourcing an activity invariably results in redundancies. These can have an obvious immediate cost. However, there are other costs which can be more difficult to quantify in terms of lost expertise and knowledge. It is relatively easy to outsource an activity, but far more difficult to reverse that decision once the internal expertise has been lost.

- *Employee morale*. Outsourcing which reduces staffing and results in redundancies can have a negative impact on the morale of remaining employees. This can have a knock-on effect on productivity levels and on employee retention. High staff turnover carries additional costs in terms of recruitment and training of new staff and the loss of experience, knowledge and skills of the employees who leave.

- *Reliance on suppliers*. If goods or services are bought in from an external supplier rather than produced in-house, the organization becomes reliant upon that external supplier. Dealing with a third party is always more complex than dealing with issues in-house as it can involve slower communication, formal contracts and far more bureaucracy.

- *Production flexibility.* External supply usually involves formal contracts which stipulate quantities of goods or services supplied. Although this can provide the security in times of stable trading, it can reduce flexibility if the business's situation changes. For example, if production and requirements reduce substantially, a business may find itself contractually bound to purchase large quantities of supplies it no longer needs.

- *Ability to meet customer requirements.* Many industries experience rapid technological development and change. It is therefore important for businesses to be able to modify and develop their products to meet the changing demands of customers. If items are produced in-house, it is more likely that the business will also have in-house research and development facilities. Therefore, outsourcing, although it may reduce short-term costs, may also reduce longer-term product development and innovation.

- *Control over quality.* Any organization needs to ensure that it has control over the quality of what it produces. Often such control is easier if all operations and therefore communications are in-house. Quality problems can be more difficult to resolve when dealing with external suppliers because of communication, cultural and contractual issues between the two separate organizations.

Extract 10.3: Make or buy – did IBM get it wrong?

When IBM launched the PC in 1981 the business was primarily focused on manufacturing computer hardware. Management were faced with the decision of developing an operating system for the new PC in-house, or outsourcing. They decided to outsource to Microsoft, a relatively new and small software development company. If IBM had been able to anticipate the outcome of this decision, they might well have chosen to develop the software in-house.

The shutdown decision: deleting a business segment

In a changing and developing business environment, organizations are often faced with the decision of whether or not to delete a segment of the business. This can cover a wide range of decision-making situations, because a business 'segment' could be a:

- product;
- type of customer;
- geographic region;
- distribution channel;
- or any other identifiable part of a business.

The Finnish company Nokia is known today as one of the world's leading mobile phone manufacturers. However, the business started as a paper manufacturer and developed over a 100-year period into an industrial conglomerate involved in manufacturing paper, tyres, footwear, electrical cables, televisions, personal computers, consumer electronics, military communication equipment, electronic components, plastics, aluminium and chemicals.

When the Soviet Union collapsed in the early 1990s, Finland suffered a huge recession and Nokia faced financial disaster. Management were presented with some challenging decisions and chose to focus on the rising telecommunications business. All non-telecommunication businesses, which represented nearly 90 per cent of revenues, were sold off.

In 1991, more than a quarter of Nokia's revenue came from Finnish domestic sales. However, with the strategic change and refocusing on mobile phones, Nokia expanded into Europe, North and South America and Asia. By 1998 Nokia had grown to become the world's largest mobile phone manufacturer and continued to hold this position until 2012.

Using relevant costing to evaluate the shutdown decision

The decision to drop a business segment will depend upon the impact the decision has on the overall profitability of the organization. The business segment should be closed only if this results in an increase in overall profit. Therefore, in order to assess its impact, it is necessary to analyse the costs carefully and ensure that only relevant costs are included in the evaluation. This should be done as follows:

- Overall corporate profitability should be analysed by business segment.
- In assessing the profitability of individual segments, only those costs that are relevant to the decision should be included.
- The contribution margin that will be lost by closing the segment should be established by comparing the revenue that will be lost with the costs that will be avoided.

This approach is best seen through the use of an example:

WORKED EXAMPLE 10.8   The shutdown decision

Book Co is a book retailer that has three large stores in three different cities. The budgeted income statement for the company for the next accounting period is as shown in Table 10.1.

TABLE 10.1

	Store A $000	Store B $000	Store C $000	Total $000
Sales	1,000	1,800	1,200	4000
Cost of sales	480	720	510	1710
Gross profit	520	1,080	690	2290
Selling costs:				0
Store staff salaries	140	180	150	470
Store running costs	65	95	70	230
Store expenses	25	40	22	87
Advertising	60	60	60	180
Head office expenses	135	243	162	540
Central warehouse costs	120	200	140	460
Total costs	545	818	604	1967
Net profit/(loss)	(25)	262	86	323

Books are ordered, stored, and dispatched to individual stores from a central warehouse. It is estimated that 60 per cent of the costs of the central warehouse are fixed and 40 per cent are variable.

Store expenses are variable, but store staff salaries and store running costs are fixed. However, all store costs are avoidable if the store is closed. Each store has an advertising budget of $60,000 that is also avoidable if the store is closed.

The directors of Book Co are concerned that Store A is predicted to make a loss. They are therefore considering closing this store. However, before doing so, they have sought your advice as an external business consultant.

Required:
Advise the directors of Book Co on whether they should close Store A, based upon the predicted loss.

Answer

Before a decision is made on closing Store A, the budgeted income statement should be reformatted to clearly identify the relevant costs, ie the costs that would be avoided if the store were closed. This has been done in Table 10.2.

TABLE 10.2

	Store A $000	Store B $000	Store C $000	Total $000
Sales	1,000	1,800	1,200	4,000
Less variable costs:				
Cost of sales	480	720	510	1,710
Store expenses	25	40	22	87
Warehouse costs (40%)	48	80	56	184
Contribution to all fixed costs	447	960	612	2,019
Store specific fixed costs:				
Store staff salaries	140	180	150	470
Store running costs	65	95	70	230
Advertising	60	60	60	180
Contribution to central fixed costs	182	625	332	1,139
Central fixed costs:				
Head office expenses				540
Warehouse costs (60%)				276
Net profit/(loss)				323

The original budgeted income statement suggests that Store A will make a loss of $25,000. Therefore, if the store were closed, the company would expect overall profit to increase by $25,000 to $348,000.

However, the reformatted budget demonstrates that Store A is making a positive contribution of $182,000 towards the common fixed costs. This means that if Store A were closed, overall company profit would fall by $182,000 to only $141,000.

The conclusion should be, therefore, that because Store A is making a positive contribution to common fixed costs, it should remain open. If Store A is closed, this will have a significant negative impact on overall company profit.

> ### Expert view 10.5: Allocated and apportioned fixed costs
>
> In Chapter 8 we looked at the concept of allocating and apportioning fixed costs when establishing the total cost of a department or product. When decision making, it is important to be aware of the distinction between allocated and apportioned fixed costs, because this distinction usually has an impact upon whether the costs are relevant. In Worked Example 10.8 the allocated fixed costs of running Store A were relevant to the decision because they would be avoidable if the store were closed. On the other hand, the apportioned head office fixed costs were not relevant as these costs would still be incurred even if Store A were closed.

Relevant costing: summary

In this section covering relevant costs in different decision-making situations, we have covered the following important points:

- When decision making, only relevant costs should be considered. Any costs deemed not to be relevant should be ignored.
- Relevant costs are those future costs that will be changed by a particular decision. This may include opportunity costs.
- Whether any given cost is relevant will depend upon the situation.
- The time horizon chosen will impact upon what costs become relevant for a given situation.

Conclusion

In this chapter we have covered two important financial decision-making techniques: CVP analysis and relevant costing. CVP analysis enables managers to identify the levels of operating activity that are necessary to avoid losses and achieve targeted levels of profits. It also enables managers to analyse the impact of organizational changes and the related risks. Relevant costing is a useful technique of focusing management attention on those costs that will be affected by decisions.

COMPREHENSION QUESTIONS

1 Explain the concept of 'margin of safety' in CVP analysis.

2 If a business reduces its fixed costs whilst maintaining the same contribution margin, will this increase or decrease its break-even point?

3 Explain what is meant by 'operating gearing'.

4 If a company increases its operating gearing, will this make its profit more or less sensitive to changes in sales volume?

5 Explain three potential weaknesses of CVP analysis as a decision tool.

6 Alpha Co has 200 units of material x in inventory. This originally cost $40 per unit. Alpha Co no longer needs the material x for its original use. It could sell the inventory for $10 per unit. However, the production manager wishes to use the material x in a new project. What is the relevant cost of using the 200 units of material x in the new project?

7 Give an example of a cost which may not be relevant in the short term, but could become relevant in a long-term decision.

Answers on pages 403–405.

Exercises

Answers on pages 405–408.

Exercise 10.1: Target profit

Huath Co has identified that it can optimize its production costs if it sells 200,000 units of its product. The directors wish to make a profit of $300,000. The following costs have been predicted:

Direct material cost	$15 per unit
Direct labour cost	$10 per unit
Variable production overhead cost	$20 per unit
Fixed costs	$400,000 per annum

Calculate the sales price per unit which the company needs to apply.

Exercise 10.2: CVP analysis and price change

Beath Co makes and sells mobile phone batteries. The variable costs of production are $4 and the current sales price is $7. Fixed costs are $35,000 per month and the annual profit of the company is currently $270,000. The volume of sales demand is constant throughout the year.

The company is considering lowering the sales price to $6 to stimulate sales, but is uncertain of the effect on sales volume.

(a) Calculate the minimum volume of sales required to justify the reduction in price.

(b) What would the percentage change in profit be if sales increased to 300,000 units?

Exercise 10.3: CVP analysis and selling price

Luis Co is a manufacturer of precision parts for electric motors. The company has developed a new brush assembly for large industrial electric motors. The company expects to sell 20,000 units of this new product in the following year, and wishes to make a profit of $90,000. Costs are as follows:

Direct material cost	$25 per unit
Direct labour cost	$10 per unit
Variable production overhead cost	$25 per unit
Fixed costs	$70,000 per annum

Required:

(a) Calculate the required sales price per unit.

(b) Calculate the break-even sales price.

Exercise 10.4: Make or buy?

Nuin Co manufactures a number of different components for the oil industry. The management is considering whether to buy in or continue making one of the components (component A). This component currently has a manufacturing cost as follows:

	$
Direct labour (4hr @ $12ph)	48
Direct materials	24
Variable overheads (4hr @ $2ph)	8
Fixed overheads (4hr @ $5ph)	20
	100 per unit

The direct labour, direct materials and variable overhead costs all relate directly to the production of component A and would not be incurred if production of the component stopped. However, the fixed overheads charge is an apportionment of costs which would still be incurred even if component A were not produced.

Required:

Under each of the three (separate) situations below, advise the management of Nuin Co whether component A should be bought in or made in-house:

(a) The purchasing manager has found an external manufacturer that can supply the component A at a guaranteed price of $90 per unit.

(b) The external supplier can offer component A at $90 per unit. If Nuin Co continues to manufacture component A in-house, it will need to install new computer-controlled manufacturing systems which will have a fixed cost of $50,000 per year.

(c) The external supplier can offer component A at $90 per unit. The manufacture of component A in-house requires the use of specialist skilled direct labour. If component A were bought in, that direct labour could be used in the production of component B which is sold for $180 and has a manufacturing cost as follows:

	$
Direct labour (8hr @ $12ph)	96
Direct materials	18
Variable overheads (8hr @ $2ph)	16
Fixed overheads (8hr @ $5ph)	40
	170 per unit

Answers to comprehension questions

1 The margin of safety is the gap, measured in units of sales, between the expected level of sales and the break-even point, ie it is the volume of sales above the break-even point. It is therefore a useful measure of how far sales can fall before the business starts to make a loss.

2 The break-even point in the units is measured as:

$$\text{Break-even point (in units)} = \frac{\text{Fixed costs}}{\text{Contribution per unit}}$$

Therefore, if fixed costs are reduced but the contribution margin remains the same, the break-even point will decrease.

3 Operating gearing describes the relationship between an organization's fixed costs and variable costs:

$$\text{Operating gearing} = \frac{\text{Fixed costs}}{\text{Fixed costs} + \text{Variable costs}}$$

4 If a company increases its operating gearing, it increases fixed costs as a proportion of total costs. This means that total costs will change less with changes in volume of sales. If the volume of sales increases, profitability will increase faster. However, if the volume of sales decreases, profitability will decrease faster.

5 CVP analysis has a number of weaknesses because of the way it simplifies the complexities of the real world:

(a) CVP analysis assumes that unit price remains the same as the volume of sales changes.

(b) CVP analysis assumes that fixed costs remain constant across all volumes of activity.

(c) CVP analysis assumes that variable costs per unit remain constant across all volumes of activity.

(d) CVP analysis assumes that costs can be clearly categorized into either variable or fixed.

(e) CVP analysis typically focuses on one accounting period. It therefore ignores longer-term strategic issues.

(f) CVP analysis usually assumes either a single product or a constant mix of products.

(g) CVP analysis assumes a simple, single-stage manufacturing process.

(h) CVP analysis assumes that the forces influencing a business are static rather than dynamic.

6 The original cost of $40 per unit is a sunk cost and is therefore not relevant. If Alpha Co uses material x in the new project, there will be an opportunity cost of $10 per unit, which is the lost opportunity of earning that revenue from selling the inventory. The relevant cost is therefore $2,000.

7 The only costs that are relevant to a decision are those that will change as a result of the decision. Therefore, any cost that will not change is not a relevant cost. There are many costs which any organization may be unable to avoid in the short term and which would therefore be incurred no matter what decision is

made, but which could be reduced or avoided in the long term. One example is the rental on a building. If there is a contractual agreement to pay the rent, this will continue to be a cost even if the business decides that it will no longer use the building. However, in the longer term the business could sell the lease of the building or let it lapse, thereby removing the cost.

Answers to exercises

Exercise 10.1: Target profit

Using the formula:

$$\text{Target sales (in units)} = \frac{\text{Fixed costs} + \text{target profit}}{\text{Contribution per unit}}$$

$$200,000 = \frac{\$300,000 + \$400,000}{P - [\$15 + \$10 + \$20]}$$

Rearrange:

$$P - \$45 = \frac{\$300,000 + \$400,000}{200,000} = \$10 \qquad \text{Therefore: } P = \$55$$

Huath Co should charge a price of $55 per unit.

Exercise 10.2: CVP analysis and price change

(a) *The minimum volume of sales required to justify the reduction in price:*
Beath Co currently earns an annual profit of $270,000 by selling batteries at $7 each. In order to justify a reduction in the sales price the company must make at least the same level of profit at the new price of $6.
   At the new price the new contribution per unit will be: $6 – $4 = $2. Therefore the minimum level of sales (in units) will be:

$$\text{Target sales (in units)} = \frac{\text{Fixed costs} + \text{target profit}}{\text{Contribution per unit}}$$

$$= \frac{(\$35,000 \times 12) + \$270,000}{\$2} = 345,000 \text{ units}$$

Beath Co must sell at least 345,000 batteries per year at a price of $6 in order to make the same level of profit as it currently does selling the batteries at $7.

We can calculate the current sales volume as:

$$\text{Current sales (in units)} = \frac{\text{Fixed costs} + \text{current profit}}{\text{Current contribution per unit}}$$

$$= \frac{(\$35,000 \times 12) + \$270,000}{\$7 - \$4} = 230,000 \text{ units}$$

Therefore, to earn the same level of profit at a sales price of $6, sales would need to increase by 115,000 units (345,000 – 230,000) or 50 per cent.

(b) *The percentage change in profit if sales increased to 300,000 units:* New profit at sales of 300,000 units:

$$\text{Profit} = Q(P - V) - F$$
$$= (300,000 \times [\$6.00 - \$4]) - (\$35,000 \times 12) = \$180,000$$

If sales increase to only 300,000 units at the new price of $6, profit would fall to $180,000 per year. This is a fall in profit of 33 per cent.

Exercise 10.3: CVP analysis and selling price

(a) *The required sales price per unit*: The sales price must earn sufficient contribution to cover fixed costs and earn the target profit of $95,000. We should therefore use the formula:

$$\text{Target sales (in units)} = \frac{\text{Fixed costs} + \text{target profit}}{\text{Contribution per unit}}$$

$$20,000 = \frac{\$70,000 + \$90,000}{P - [\$25 + \$10 + \$25]}$$

Rearrange:

$$P - \$60 = \frac{\$160,000}{20,000} = \$8 \qquad \text{Therefore: } P = \$68$$

Luis Co should charge a price of $68 per unit.

(b) *The break-even sales price*:

$$\text{BEP (in units)} = \frac{\text{Fixed costs}}{\text{Contribution per unit}}$$

$$20,000 = \frac{\$70,000}{P - \$60}$$

Rearrange:

$$P - \$60 = \frac{\$70,000}{20,000} = \$3.50 \qquad \text{Therefore: } P = \$63.50$$

The break-even sales price is $63.50.

Exercise 10.4: Make or buy?

(a) The relevant production costs for this decision are those costs which would be avoided if in-house production of component A were to stop. These are:

	$
Direct labour (4hr @ $12ph)	48
Direct materials	24
Variable overheads (4hr @ $2ph)	8
	80 per unit

Therefore the relevant cost of producing component A is $80 per unit, compared to the relevant cost of buying in which is $90 per unit. The company should therefore continue to make component A in-house.

(b) If Nuin Co continues to manufacture component A in-house, it will incur an additional fixed cost of $50,000 per year. It will still be worth manufacturing in-house if the volume of production is sufficient to cover the extra cost. (This therefore becomes an exercise in CVP analysis.)

As per the calculations in part (a) above, there is a marginal benefit of $10 per unit in manufacturing component A in-house ($90 – $80). The break-even point for this benefit will be:

$$\text{BEP (in units)} = \frac{\$50,000}{\$10} = 5,000 \text{ units per year}$$

Therefore, if Nuin Co expects to sell more than 5,000 units per year of component A, it will be financially better to continue producing in-house. However, if the company expects to sell fewer than 5,000 units per year, it would be better off by buying in component A.

(c) If the skilled direct labour could be used elsewhere within the business, there is an opportunity cost in using it to produce component A. This opportunity cost will be measured in terms of the lost contribution from component B resulting from using the direct labour to produce component A.

The contribution per unit from component B is:

Sales price – Variable production costs = $180 – ($96 + $18 + $16) = $50

However, each unit of component B requires eight hours of direct labour, whereas each unit of component A requires only four hours of direct labour. Therefore, each unit of component A produced will take away 50 per cent of the contribution from component B, ie $25.

The relevant cost of producing component A is therefore:

	$
Direct labour (4hr @ $12 p.h.)	48
Direct materials	24
Variable overheads (4hr @ $2 p.h.)	8
Opportunity cost	25
	105 per unit

It would therefore be financially better for Nuin Co to buy in component A at $90 and to use the direct labour to produce component B.

APPENDIX A
An introduction to double-entry bookkeeping

Double-entry bookkeeping (bookkeeping, for short) is best taught through t-accounts; named thus because of their shape. T-accounts have a left side and a right side. Hereafter these will be referred to as the DEBIT side and the CREDIT side. This links back to the golden rule of accounting: that every debit must have an equal and opposite credit otherwise your ledgers would not balance.

Over the next few pages we will walk you through each of the Mobius Inc examples, completing the t-accounts as we go.

Bookkeeping comes naturally to a small number of people, but to the majority, however, this is something which needs to be practised and given careful consideration. Regardless of whether you 'get it' within five minutes or five years, for almost everyone there is a 'light-bulb moment' where everything clicks into place and you reflect uncomprehendingly on the times you couldn't see how it worked.

Approaching double-entry bookkeeping

Step 1: Set up your t-accounts

A t-account captures the key information about a transaction:

- the date;
- an outline description of the transaction;
  - note that this is normally the name of the account the other side of the journal entry is going to;
- the value.

For example, our first transaction involves two t-accounts: cash at bank and in hand; and share capital. The cash at bank and in hand t-account would appear as shown in Table A.1.

TABLE A.1 Cash at bank and in hand

Date	Description	$	$	Description	Date

Note that there the '$' or 'value' columns need to be totalled. That is because each t-account needs to 'balance out' at the end of the period of account:

- On the one hand, statement of financial position balances, for example cash at bank and in hand don't stop existing at the end of a period and therefore the amounts left over can be carried forward to the next period.
- On the other hand, income statement accounts, for example rental costs, relate to a period of account and once they have been incurred and paid, they should be closed out.
  - More on this later...

Step 2: Write out your journal entry

Certainly, while you're in the initial learning stages of bookkeeping it is good practice to write out every journal entry. As you progress, you might stop doing this. Note, however, that if you don't write out the entry in full and you make an error (eg a transposition error, post two debits instead of a debit and credit, miss one side of the transaction), tracing the error back is more difficult.

The question states:

Mobius Inc (1)
On day 1, you opt to put financial distance between you and the trading entity and transfer $1,000 from your personal bank account to a bank account you hold in the name of the new enterprise – Mobius Inc.

The journal entry is as follows:

		$	$
Debit	Cash at bank and in hand	1,000	
Credit	Share capital: equity and reserves		1,000

Useful tip

People who struggle with double-entry bookkeeping often don't understand the relevance of posting an entry as either a debit or a credit. The interconnectedness of position and performance provides the clue that we need. The grid below might help you to understand.

First, however, remember the accounting equation:

$$\text{Assets } MINUS \text{ Liabilities } EQUALS \text{ Equity + Reserves}$$
$$(\text{Assets} - \text{Liabilities} = \text{Equity and Reserves})$$

For this equation to work, an increase in assets would necessarily lead to either:

- a decrease in another asset;
- an increase in liabilities; or
- an increase in equity and reserves.

Examples might be:

- a decrease in another asset, eg swapping cash for inventory;
- an increase in liabilities, eg buying inventory on credit from a supplier;
- an increase in equity and reserves, eg selling share capital for cash.

To continue...

We know that the profit is taken to equity and reserves to close it out at the end of a period. A simple double entry effecting both the statement of financial position and income statement (ie performance and position) might be:

- An operating expense being paid, eg rent.
- Cash would reduce (decrease in assets) and the rental cost in the income statement would increase.
  - Assuming this was the only transaction a business undertook during the period of account, at the end of the year this rental expense would be the loss for the period. This balance would be taken to retained earnings (a sub-heading under reserves).
  - Therefore, our accounting equation holds: a decrease in assets is offset by a decrease in equity and reserves.

The accounting equation tells us that there are two equal and opposite sides to every transaction. This can be summarized as shown in Table A.2.

TABLE A.2

	Debit	Credit
Assets and liabilities (excluding equity and reserves)	Assets increase Liabilities decrease (ie positive effect on financial position)	Assets decrease Liabilities increase (ie negative effect on financial position)
Income statement and Equity and reserves	Expenses increase (Revenue decreases) (ie negative impact on performance; reduce profit) Equity and reserves decrease	Expenses decrease (Revenue increases) (ie positive impact on performance; increase profit) Equity and reserves increase

Or, in shorthand (Table A.3).

TABLE A.3

	Debit	Credit
Assets and liabilities (excluding equity and reserves)	+	–
Income statement and Equity and reserves	–	+

Step 3: Post this journal entry to the relevant t-accounts (Table A.4)

TABLE A.4

Cash at bank and in hand					
Date	Description	$	$	Description	Date
Day 1	Initial investment capital	1,000			

Share capital					
Date	Description	$	$	Description	Date
			1,000	Bank	Day 1

Step 4: Close out the t-accounts

Assuming that this is the only transaction, you now need to move your closing balances to a trial balance and then into the financial statements (Table A.5).

TABLE A.5

Cash at bank and in hand					
Date	Description	$	$	Description	Date
Beginning of day 1	Balance brought forward	–			
Day 1	Initial investment capital	1,000			
			1,000	Balance carried forward	End of day 1
		1,000	1,000		
Beginning of day 2	Balance brought forward	1,000			

Share capital					
Date	Description	$	$	Description	Date
			–	Balance brought forward	Beginning of day 1
			1,000	Bank	Day 1
End of day 1	Balance carried forward	1,000			
		1,000	1,000		
			1,000	Balance brought forward	Beginning of day 2

Let's walk through what has happened here.

The original double entry was posted. Both sides were posted correctly and to the appropriate t-accounts.

If this were the only transaction of the day, we need to ask ourselves whether these two balances are position or performance related, ie were they assets or liabilities, or were they revenue or expenses. It is obvious that both cash and share capital are position-related balances. They will continue to be controlled (obligated to settle) by the entity on day 2 given that nothing happened to cancel them out on day 1.

Therefore, these balances have been carried forward (c/fwd) from day 1 to day 2.

You will notice that when the account is closed out, the closing balance which we carry forward is the balancing entry to make the account sum:

- Mobius Inc has $1,000 in the bank at the end of day 1 and none was spent and none generated during that 24-hour period. Therefore, the company has $1,000 at the beginning of day 2.

- Mobius Inc has $1,000 of share capital. No more was sold and none was repurchased during day 1, therefore they close with $1,000 and open the following day with $1,000.

When you open up the account, be careful to bring the brought forward amount down on the correct side, ie the same as it was accumulated; or the opposite of the balancing entry that closed it out. In this case, the cash is c/fwd as a credit to balance the account out, but b/fwd as a debit. Reflecting on the grid above, you'll see that a debit signifies a positive balance and, indeed, we hold $1,000 in the bank. If you had brought this balance forward as a credit, this would mean that you opened with a negative amount of cash (bank overdraft).

Tutor's note: The joy of learning accounting is that it is happening all the time, both to you, with you and all around you. Next time you go into a shop, think about the transaction as a bookkeeping exercise.

- Do you have cash and you want to exchange it for a new pen? If so, you exchange one asset for another (credit cash [reduce asset]; credit equipment [increase asset]).
- Do you pay for your electricity by direct debit? If so, you exchange an asset (credit bank [reduce asset]; debit expenses [reduce profits]).

Step 5: Summarize into a 'trial balance'

A trial balance (TB) is a summary of your t-accounts' closing balances, ie a list of closing balances. Our TB is simple in this instance as we have only two accounts/balances.

Your TB needs to have three columns:

1 account name, eg cash at bank and in hand;
2 debit;
3 credit.

Both debit and credit columns are then summed. If they are not the same value, you have a TB that does not balance and you can therefore conclude that you've made a mistake in your bookkeeping somewhere.

Our TB at the end of day 1 should appear as shown in Table A.6.

TABLE A.6

	Debit (Dr) $	Credit (Cr) $
Cash at bank and in hand	1,000	
Share capital		1,000
	1,000	1,000

NOTE: You will often see debit and credit shortened to 'dr' (DR, Dr) and 'cr' (CR, Cr).

Step 6: Extract the information from the TB and draw up your financial statements

Again in this case, the exercise is straightforward. We only have the statement of financial position entries. We have an asset and the equity (share capital). The statement would appear as follows:

Statement of financial position For Mobius Inc As at the end of Day 1	
Assets	
Current Assets	
Cash at bank and in hand	1,000
Total Assets	1,000
Equity and reserves	
Share capital	1,000
Total	1,000

Tutor's Note: These are the basics of double-entry bookkeeping. We have walked through this example slowly and carefully, explaining points of common error as we go. We will now move up a gear and proceed through the rest of the examples at a slightly speedier pace. If you struggle, however, then come back to these basic points.

Mobius Inc

Day 2

The text states:

On day 2, you borrow $500 from a friend to provide further financial help to your business.

The journal entry would be as follows:

		$	$
Debit	Cash at bank and in hand	500	
Credit	Loan (liabilities)		500

The t-accounts would read as shown in Table A.7.

TABLE A.7

Cash at bank and in hand

Date	Description	$	$	Description	Date
Beginning of day 1	Balance brought forward	–			
Day 1	Initial investment capital	1,000			
			1,000	Balance carried forward	End of day 1
		1,000	1,000		
Beginning of day 2	Balance brought forward	1,000			
Day 2	Loan	500			
			1,500	Balance carried forward	End of day 2
		1,500	1,500		
Beginning of day 3	Balance brought forward	1,500			

Loan account (liabilities)

Date	Description	$	$	Description	Date
			–	Balance brought forward	Beginning of day 2
			500	Bank	Day 2
End of day 2	Balance carried forward	500			
		500	500		
			500	Balance brought forward	Beginning of day 3

Share capital

Date	Description	$	$	Description	Date
			–	Balance brought forward	Beginning of day 1
			1,000	Bank	Day 1
End of day 1	Balance carried forward	1,000			
		1,000	1,000		
			1,000	Balance brought forward	Beginning of day 2
End of day 2	Balance carried forward	1,000			
		1,000	1,000		
			1,000	Balance brought forward	Beginning of day 3

In other words, no change on the share capital account from day 1.

The revised TB at the end of day 2 should read as shown in Table A.8.

TABLE A.8

Day 2	Debit (Dr) $	Credit (Cr) $
Cash at bank and in hand	1,500	
Loan		500
Share capital		1,000
	1,500	1,500

Thus, the statement of financial position as at the end of day 2 should read as follows:

Statement of financial position For Mobius Inc As at the end of Day 2	
Assets Current assets	
Cash at bank and in hand	1,500
Liabilities Non-current liabilities	
Loan	(500)
Net assets	1,000
Equity and reserves Share capital	1,000
Total	1,000

Days 3 & 4

On day 3, Mobius Inc invests $500 of cash by acquiring a new computer.

		$	$
Debit	Non-current assets (computer)	500	
Credit	Cash		500

On day 4, Mobius Inc buys some raw materials worth $400 and holds them as inventories. The cash required to settle the invoices related to these purchases does not need to be found for 10 days as these are the credit terms offered.

		$	$
Debit	Inventories	400	
Credit	Trade payables		400

We now have six t-accounts open:

1 cash at bank and in hand;
2 non-current assets;
3 inventories;
4 trade payables;
5 share capital (remain unchanged during days 3 & 4);
6 loan account (remain unchanged during days 3 & 4).

And they should appear as shown in Table A.9.

TABLE A.9

Cash at bank and in hand					
Date	Description	$	$	Description	Date
Beg of day 3	Bal. b/fwd	1,500			
			500	Inventories	Day 3
			1,000	Bal. c/fwd	End of day 4
		1,500	1,500		

TABLE A.9 *continued*

Non-current assets (computer)

Date	Description	$	$	Description	Date
Beg of day 3	Bal. b/fwd	–			
Day 3	Bank	500			
			500	Bal. c/fwd	End of day 4
		500	500		

Inventories (raw materials)

Date	Description	$	$	Description	Date
Beg of day 3	Bal. b/fwd	–			
Day 4	Trade payables	400			
			400	Bal. c/fwd	End of day 4
		400	400		

Trade payables

Date	Description	$	$	Description	Date
			–	Bal. b/fwd	Beg of day 3
			400	Inventories	Day 4
End of day 4	Bal. c/fwd	400			
		400	400		

Share capital

Date	Description	$	$	Description	Date
			1,000	Bal. b/fwd	Beg of day 3
End of day 4	Bal. c/fwd	1,000			
		1,000	1,000		

Loan

Date	Description	$	$	Description	Date
			500	Bal. b/fwd	Beg of day 3
End of day 4	Bal. c/fwd	500			
		500	500		

The statement of financial position as at the end of day 4 should appear as follows:

Statement of financial position For Mobius Inc As at the end of Day 4	
Assets	
Non-current assets	
Computer	500
Current assets	
Inventories (raw materials)	400
Cash at bank and in hand	1,000
Liabilities	
Non-current liabilities	
Loan	(500)
Current liabilities	
Trade payables	(400)
Net assets	1,000
Equity and reserves	
Share capital	1,000
Total	1,000

Days 5 & 6

Days 5 & 6 introduce performance-related transactions into our accounting. This means that we will need to produce a statement of financial position and an income statement. The bookkeeping remains exactly the same as before.

NOTE: In the interests of economy and ease of reading, we will no longer produce the t-accounts where there have been no changes during the period (in this case, days 5 & 6 eg share capital). We strongly advise that whilst you are in the learning phase, however, you continue to produce all the accounts and get into the habit of opening them up and closing them down.

On day 5, Mobius Inc uses the raw materials to produce 30 units of finished goods stock.

On day 6, half of these are sold for $50 per unit. Cash is received immediately for five of those sold. The remainder were sold to customers on 10-day credit terms.

The first part of this transaction (day 5) is straightforward. We are simply moving an asset from one pot to another. In this case, raw materials are converted into finished goods.

		$	$
Debit	Inventories: finished goods	400	
Credit	Inventories: raw materials		400

The second part, however, is a little more tricky as explained in the main text. We advise you do this in two steps: firstly, the revenue side of the transaction; and secondly, the cost of the transaction (cost of sales), as follows:

		$	$
Debit	Cash	250	
Debit	Trade receivables	500	
Credit	Revenue		750

And then:

		$	$
Debit	Cost of sales	200	
Credit	Inventories: finished goods		200

See Table A.10.

TABLE A.10

Inventories (raw materials)

Date	Description	$	$	Description	Date
Beg of day 4	Bal. b/fwd	400			
			400	Transfer to finished goods	Day 5
			–	Bal. c/fwd	End of day 6
		400	400		

Inventories (finished goods)

Date	Description	$	$	Description	Date
Beg of day 4	Bal. b/fwd	–			
Day 5	Transferred from raw materials	400		Transfer to finished goods	Day 5
			200	Cost of sales	Day 6
			200	Bal. c/fwd	End of day 6
		400	400		

TABLE A.10   *continued*

Cash at bank and in hand					
Date	Description	$	$	Description	Date
Beg of day 5	Bal. b/fwd	1,000			
Day 6	Revenue	250			
			1,250	Bal. c/fwd	End of day 4
		1,250	1,250		

Trade receivables					
Date	Description	$	$	Description	Date
Beg of day 5	Bal. b/fwd	–			
Day 6	Revenue	500			
			500	Bal. c/fwd	End of day 4
		500	500		

Note that these are all statement of financial position accounts and all hold either assets or liabilities which will be carried forward to the next period of account. This is not true of income statement accounts, however. These will be closed out in the period and any balance taken to the income statement (and then through to reserves to be carried forward as a net balance at the end of the period).

The income statement accounts are as shown in Table A.11.

TABLE A.11

Revenue					
Date	Description	$	$	Description	Date
			250	Cash	Day 6
			500	Trade receivables	Day 6
Take to income statement		750			
		750	750		

Cost of sales					
Date	Description	$	$	Description	Date
Day 6	Inventories	200			
			200	Take to income statement	
		200	200		

The financial statements would appear as follows:

Statement of financial position
For Mobius Inc
As at the end of Day 6

Assets	
Non-current assets	
Computer	500
Current assets	
Inventories	200
Trade receivables	500
Cash at bank and in hand	1,250
Liabilities	
Non-current liabilities	
Loan	(500)
Current liabilities	
Trade payables	(400)
Net assets	1,550
Equity and reserves	
Share capital	1,000
Retained earnings	550
Total	1,550

Income Statement
For Mobius Inc
For days 1 to 6

Revenue	750
Cost of sales	(200)
	550

Days 8 to 14

Note: The financial statements are produced in the body of the text and therefore shall not be duplicated here. See Table A.12.

TABLE A.12

Inventories (raw materials)					
Date	Description	$	$	Description	Date
Beg of day 8	Bal. b/fwd	–			
Day 8	Trade payables	800			
			800	Transfer to finished goods	Day 9
			–	**Bal. c/fwd**	**End of day 14**
		800	800		

Trade payables					
Date	Description	$	$	Description	Date
			400	Bal. b/fwd	Beg of day 8
			800	Inventories (raw materials)	Day 8
Day 14	Bank	400			
End of day 14	**Bal. c/fwd**	**800**			
		1,200	1,200		

Inventories (finished goods)					
Date	Description	$	$	Description	Date
Beg of day 8	Bal. b/fwd	200			
Day 9	Transferred from raw materials	800			
			467	Cost of sales	
			533	**Bal. c/fwd**	**End of day 14**
		1,000	1,000		

Operating expenses					
Date	Description	$	$	Description	Date
Day 10	Bank (utilities)	200			
Day 12	Bank (stationery)	50			
Day 14	Bank (web development costs)	750			
			1,000	**Take to income statement**	
		1,000	1,000		

TABLE A.12 *continued*

Cash at bank and in hand

Date	Description	$	$	Description	Date
Beg of day 8	Bal. b/fwd	1,250			
			200	Utilities	Day 10
Day 11	Revenue	1,200			
			100	Scanner	Day 12
			50	Stationery	Day 12
Day 13	Trade receivables	500			
			400	Trade payables	Day 14
			750	Web development costs	Day 14
			1,450	**Bal. c/fwd**	**End of day 14**
		2,950	2,950		

Trade receivables

Date	Description	$	$	Description	Date
Beg of day 8	Bal. b/fwd	500			
Day 11	Revenue	900			
			500	Bank	Day 13
			900	**Bal. c/fwd**	**End of day 14**
		1,400	1,400		

Revenue

Date	Description	$	$	Description	Date
			1,200	Cash	Day 11
			900	Trade receivables	Day 11
Take to income statement		1,800			
		1,800	2,100		

Cost of sales

Date	Description	$	$	Description	Date
Day 11	Inventories	467			
			467	**Take to income statement**	
		467	467		

TABLE A.12   *continued*

Non-current assets (scanner)						
Date	Description	$	$	Description	Date	
Beg of day 8	Bal. b/fwd	–				
Day 12	Bank	600				
			600	Bal. c/fwd	End of day 14	
		600	600			

The trial balance as at the end of day 14 should now read as shown in Table A.13.

TABLE A.13

Day 14	Debit (Dr) $	Credit (Cr) $
Non-current assets (computer)	500	
Non-current assets (scanner)	100	
Inventories (raw materials)	–	
Inventories (finished goods)	533	
Trade receivables	900	
Cash at bank and in hand	1,450	
Trade payables		800
Loan		500
Share capital		1,000
Retained earnings (b/fwd from week 1)		550
Revenue		2,100
Cost of sales	467	
Operating expenses	1,000	
	4,950	4,950

Through to the end of month 1

Mobius (5): Adjustments for non-current assets

The following journal entries relate to the depreciation of the non-current assets which the company acquired during the first two weeks, ie the scanner and the computer:

Depreciation charge against the scanner		
Debit	Depreciation (income statement)	5
Credit	Computer: Accumulated depreciation (statement of financial position)		5

Depreciation charge against the computer		
Debit	Depreciation (income statement)	10
Credit	Scanner: Accumulated depreciation (statement of financial position)		10

Note that the t-accounts for the accumulated depreciation are kept separately to the t-accounts for the original cost of the asset. This is so that later adjustments required – for example, disposal or re-measurement – are simpler.

The entries related to the acquisition of the motor vehicle, the associated loan required to buy the asset and the unpaid interest on that loan would be as follows:

Acquisition of motor vehicle		
Debit	Motor vehicle: cost	20,000
Debit	Motor vehicle costs (additional extras)	3,350
Credit	Loan (to acquire vehicle)		2,350

Depreciation charge against the motor vehicle		
Debit	Depreciation (income statement)	154
Credit	Motor Vehicle: Accumulated depreciation (statement of financial position)		154

Interest on loan (unpaid) used to acquire the motor vehicle		
Debit	Finance costs	90
Credit	Interest accrual		90

Mobius (6): Period-end adjustments

Telephone line installation unpaid as at the end of the month

Debit	Operating expenses: Telephone line installation	100	
Credit	Accruals		100

Rent paid in advance (prepayment account required)

Debit	Prepayment (rent)	1,000	
Credit	Bank		1,000

Sales and related receivables account

Debit	Trade receivables	20,000	
Credit	Revenue		20,000
Debit	Bank	16,000	
Credit	Trade receivables		16,000

Adjustments for inventories, trade payables and cost of sales

Debit	Inventories (raw materials)	9,000	
Credit	Trade payables		9,000
Debit	Inventories (finished goods)	8,000	
Credit	Inventories (raw materials)		8,000
Debit	Cost of sales	6,000	
Credit	Inventories (finished goods)		6,000
Debit	Cost of sales	533	
Credit	Inventories (finished goods)		533
Debit	Trade payables	800	
Debit	Trade payables	7,000	
Credit	Bank		7,800

APPENDIX B
International Accounting/ Financial Reporting Standards (as at 02.04.2013)

NOTE: *This list excludes the work of the Interpretations Committee.*

International Financial Reporting Standards

#	Name	Issued
IFRS 1	First-time Adoption of International Financial Standards	2008*
IFRS 2	Share-based Payment	2004
IFRS 3	Business Combinations	2008*
IFRS 4	Insurance Contracts	2004
IFRS 5	Non-current Assets Held for Sale and Discontinued Operations	2004
IFRS 6	Exploration for and Evaluation of Mineral Assets	2004
IFRS 7	Financial Instruments: Disclosures	2005
IFRS 8	Operating Segments	2006
IFRS 9	Financial Instruments	2010*
IFRS 10	Consolidated Financial Statements	2011
IFRS 11	Joint Arrangements	2011
IFRS 12	Disclosure of Interests in Other Entities	2011
IFRS 13	Fair Value Measurement	2011

International Accounting Standards

#	Name	Issued
IAS 1	Presentation of Financial Statements	2007*
IAS 2	Inventories	2005*
IAS 3	Consolidated Financial Statements **Superseded in 1989 by IAS 27 and IAS 28**	1976
IAS 4	Depreciation Accounting **Withdrawn in 1999**	

#	Name	Issued
IAS 5	Information to Be Disclosed in Financial Statements **Superseded by IAS 1 effective 1 July 1998**	1976
IAS 6	Accounting Responses to Changing Prices **Superseded by IAS 15, which was withdrawn December 2003**	
IAS 7	Statement of Cash Flows	1992
IAS 8	Accounting Policies, Changes in Accounting Estimates and Errors	2003
IAS 9	Accounting for Research and Development Activities **Superseded by IAS 39 effective 1 July 1999**	
IAS 10	Events After the Reporting Period	2003
IAS 11	Construction Contracts	1993
IAS 12	Income Taxes	1996*
IAS 13	Presentation of Current Assets and Current Liabilities **Superseded by IAS 39 effective 1 July 1998**	
IAS 14	Segment Reporting **Superseded by IFRS 8 effective 1 January 2009**	1997
IAS 15	Information Reflecting the Effects of Changing Prices **Withdrawn December 2003**	2003
IAS 16	Property, Plant and Equipment	2003*
IAS 17	Leases	2003*
IAS 18	Revenue	1993*
IAS 19	Employee Benefits **Superseded by IAS 19 (2011) effective 1 January 2013**	1998
IAS 19	Employee Benefits (2011)	2011*
IAS 20	Accounting for Government Grants and Disclosure of Government Assistance	1983
IAS 21	The Effects of Changes in Foreign Exchange Rates	2003*
IAS 22	Business Combinations **Superseded by IFRS 3 effective 31 March 2004**	1998*
IAS 23	Borrowing Costs	2007*
IAS 24	Related Party Disclosures	2009*
IAS 25	Accounting for Investments **Superseded by IAS 39 and IAS 40 effective 2001**	
IAS 26	Accounting and Reporting by Retirement Benefit Plans	1987
IAS 27	Separate Financial Statements (2011)	2011
IAS 27	Consolidated and Separate Financial Statements **Superseded by IFRS 10, IFRS 12 and IAS 27 (2011) effective 1 January 2013**	2003
IAS 28	Investments in Associates and Joint Ventures (2011)	2011

#	Name	Issued
IAS 28	Investments in Associates	2003
	Superseded by IAS 28 (2011) and IFRS 12 effective 1 January 2013	
IAS 29	Financial Reporting in Hyperinflationary Economies	1989
IAS 30	Disclosures in the Financial Statements of Banks and Similar Financial Institutions	1990
	Superseded by IFRS 7 effective 1 January 2007	
IAS 31	Interests In Joint Ventures	2003*
	Superseded by IFRS 11 and IFRS 12 effective 1 January 2013	
IAS 32	Financial Instruments: Presentation	2003*
IAS 33	Earnings Per Share	2003*
IAS 34	Interim Financial Reporting	1998
IAS 35	Discontinuing Operations	1998
	Superseded by IFRS 5 effective 1 January 2005	
IAS 36	Impairment of Assets	2004*
IAS 37	Provisions, Contingent Liabilities and Contingent Assets	1998
IAS 38	Intangible Assets	2004*
IAS 39	Financial Instruments: Recognition and Measurement	2003*
	Superseded by IFRS 9 effective 1 January 2015	
IAS 40	Investment Property	2003*
IAS 41	Agriculture	2001

Other pronouncements

Name	Issued
Conceptual Framework for Financial Statements 2010	2010
Preface to International Financial Reporting Standards	2002
IFRS for Small and Medium Sized Entities	2009
IFRS Practice Statement Management Commentary	2010

APPENDIX C
Example earnings announcements

IBM plc 1Q13 Press Release

- Diluted EPS:
  - GAAP: $2.70, up 3 per cent;
  - Operating (non-GAAP): $3.00, up 8 per cent;
- Net income:
  - GAAP: $3.0 billion, down 1 per cent;
  - Operating (non-GAAP): $3.4 billion, up 3 per cent;
- Gross profit margin:
  - GAAP: 45.6 per cent, up 0.6 points;
  - Operating (non-GAAP): 46.7 per cent, up 1.0 points;
- Revenue: $23.4 billion, down 5 per cent, down 3 per cent adjusting for currency;
- Free cash flow of $1.7 billion, down $0.2 billion;
- Software revenue flat, up 1 per cent adjusting for currency;
  - Pre-tax: income up 4 per cent; margin up 1.2 points;
- Services revenue down 4 per cent, down 1 per cent adjusting for currency;
  - Pre-tax: income up 10 per cent; margin up 2.0 points;
- Services backlog of $141 billion, up 1 per cent, up 5 per cent adjusting for currency;
  - Closed 22 deals of more than $100 million in the quarter;
- Systems and Technology revenue down 17 per cent, down 16 per cent adjusting for currency;
- Growth markets revenue down 1 per cent, up 1 per cent adjusting for currency;
- Business analytics revenue up 7 per cent;
- Smarter Planet revenue up more than 25 per cent;
- Cloud revenue up more than 70 per cent;
- Reiterating full-year 2013 operating (non-GAAP) EPS expectation of at least $16.70.

ARMONK, N.Y., April 18, 2013 . . . IBM (NYSE: IBM) today announced first-quarter 2013 diluted earnings of $2.70 per share, a year-to-year increase of 3 per cent. Operating (non-GAAP) diluted earnings were $3.00 per share, compared with operating diluted earnings of $2.78 per share in the first quarter of 2012, an increase of 8 per cent.

First-quarter net income was $3.0 billion, down 1 per cent year-to-year. Operating (non-GAAP) net income was $3.4 billion compared with $3.3 billion in the first quarter of 2012, an increase of 3 per cent.

Total revenues for the first quarter of 2013 of $23.4 billion were down 5 per cent (down 3 per cent, adjusting for currency) from the first quarter of 2012.

"In the first quarter, we grew operating net income, earnings per share and expanded operating margins but we did not achieve all of our goals in the period. Despite a solid start and good client demand we did not close a number of software and mainframe transactions that have moved into the second quarter. The services business performed as expected with strong profit growth and significant new business in the quarter," said Ginni Rometty, IBM chairman, president and chief executive officer.

"Looking ahead, in addition to closing those transactions, we expect to benefit from investments we are making in our growth initiatives and from the actions we are taking to improve under-performing parts of the business. We remain confident in this model of continuous transformation and in our ability to deliver our full-year 2013 operating earnings per share expectation of at least $16.70."

First-Quarter GAAP – Operating (non-GAAP) Reconciliation

First-quarter operating (non-GAAP) diluted earnings exclude $0.30 per share of charges: $0.12 per share for the amortization of purchased intangible assets and other acquisition-related charges, and $0.18 per share for retirement-related charges.

Full-Year 2013 Expectations

IBM is reiterating its expectation for full-year 2013 GAAP diluted earnings per share of at least $15.53. Operating (non-GAAP) diluted earnings per share expectations remain at least $16.70. The 2013 operating (non-GAAP) earnings expectations exclude $1.17 per share of charges for amortization of purchased intangible assets, other acquisition-related charges, and retirement-related charges.

Geographic Regions

The Americas' first-quarter revenues were $10.0 billion, a decrease of 4 per cent (down 3 per cent, adjusting for currency) from the 2012 period. Revenues from Europe/Middle East/Africa were $7.3 billion, down 4 per cent (down 4 per cent, adjusting for currency). Asia-Pacific revenues decreased 7 per cent (down 1 per cent, adjusting for currency) to $5.7 billion. OEM revenues were $426 million, down 16 per cent compared with the 2012 first quarter.

Growth Markets

Revenues from the company's growth markets decreased 1 per cent (up 1 per cent, adjusting for currency). Revenues in the BRIC countries – Brazil, Russia, India and China – decreased 1 per cent (up 3 per cent, adjusting for currency).

Services

Global Technology Services segment revenues decreased 4 per cent (down 2 per cent, adjusting for currency) to $9.6 billion. Global Business Services segment revenues were down 3 per cent (flat, adjusting for currency) to $4.5 billion.

Pre-tax income from Global Technology Services was up 7 per cent and pre-tax margin increased to 16.1 per cent. Global Business Services pre-tax income increased 17 per cent and pre-tax margin increased to 15.1 per cent.

The estimated services backlog at March 31 was $141 billion, up 1 per cent year over year at actual rates (up 5 per cent, adjusting for currency). The company closed 22 service agreements of more than $100 million in the quarter.

Software

Revenues from the Software segment were flat at $5.6 billion (up 1 per cent, adjusting for currency) compared with the first quarter of 2012. Software pre-tax income increased 4 per cent and pre-tax margin increased to 31.5 per cent.

Revenues from IBM's key middleware products, which include WebSphere, Information Management, Tivoli, Social Workforce Solutions (formerly Lotus) and Rational products, were $3.5 billion, up 1 per cent (up 2 per cent, adjusting for currency) versus the first quarter of 2012. Operating systems revenues of $578 million were down 2 per cent (down 1 per cent, adjusting for currency) compared with the prior-year quarter.

Revenues from the WebSphere family of software products increased 6 per cent year over year. Information Management software revenues decreased 2 per cent. Revenues from Tivoli software increased 1 per cent. Revenues from Social Workforce Solutions (formerly Lotus) software increased 8 per cent, and Rational software decreased 2 per cent.

Hardware

Revenues from the Systems and Technology segment totalled $3.1 billion for the quarter, down 17 per cent (down 16 per cent, adjusting for currency) from the first quarter of 2012. Excluding Retail Store Solutions (RSS), revenues were down 14 per cent (down 13 per cent, adjusting for currency). Systems and Technology pre-tax loss increased $0.3 billion.

Total systems revenues, excluding RSS, decreased 13 per cent (down 13 per cent, adjusting for currency). Revenues from System z mainframe server products increased 7 per cent compared with the year-ago period. Total delivery of System z computing power, as measured in MIPS (millions of instructions per second), increased 27 per cent. Revenues from Power Systems were down 32 per cent compared with the 2012 period. Revenues from System x were down 9 per cent. Revenues from System Storage decreased 11 per cent. Revenues from Microelectronics OEM decreased 16 per cent.

Financing

Global Financing segment revenues were up 2 per cent (up 4 per cent, adjusting for currency) in the first quarter at $499 million. Pre-tax income for the segment increased 5 per cent to $538 million.

Gross Profit

The company's total gross profit margin was 45.6 per cent in the 2013 first quarter compared with 45.1 per cent in the 2012 first-quarter period. Total operating (non-GAAP) gross profit margin was 46.7 per cent in the 2013 first quarter compared with 45.7 per cent in the 2012 first-quarter period, with increases in Global Technology Services and Global Business Services.

Expense

Total expense and other income decreased 3 per cent to $7.1 billion, compared to the prior-year period. S,G&A expense of $5.6 billion decreased 5 per cent year over year. R,D&E expense of $1.6 billion increased 3 per cent, compared with the year-ago period. Intellectual property and custom development income decreased to $183 million compared with $255 million a year ago. Other (income) and expense was income of $60 million compared with prior-year income of $58 million. Interest expense decreased to $94 million compared with $110 million in the prior year.

Total operating (non-GAAP) expense and other income decreased 4 per cent to $6.9 billion compared with the prior-year period. Operating (non-GAAP) S,G&A expense of $5.4 billion decreased 7 per cent compared with prior-year expense. Operating (non-GAAP) R,D&E expense of $1.6 billion increased 1 per cent compared with the year-ago period.

* * *

Pre-tax income decreased 6 per cent to $3.6 billion. Pre-tax margin decreased 0.1 points to 15.4 per cent. Operating (non-GAAP) pre-tax income decreased 1 per cent to $4.1 billion and pre-tax margin was 17.4 per cent, up 0.8 points.

IBM's tax rate was 15.9 per cent, down 4.1 points year over year; operating (non-GAAP) tax rate was 17.3 per cent, down 3.2 points compared to the year-ago period. The lower tax rate is primarily due to benefits recorded to reflect changes in tax laws enacted during the quarter, including the reinstatement of the US Research and Development Tax Credit.

Net income margin increased 0.5 points to 13.0 per cent. Total operating (non-GAAP) net income margin increased 1.2 points to 14.4 per cent.

The weighted-average number of diluted common shares outstanding in the first-quarter 2013 was 1.12 billion compared with 1.17 billion shares in the same period of 2012. As of March 31, 2013, there were 1.11 billion basic common shares outstanding.

Debt, including Global Financing, totalled $33.4 billion, compared with $33.3 billion at year-end 2012. From a management segment view, Global Financing debt totalled $25.2 billion versus $24.5 billion at year-end 2012, resulting in a debt-to-equity ratio of 7.2 to 1. Non-global financing debt totalled $8.2 billion, a decrease of $0.6 billion since year-end 2012, resulting in a debt-to-capitalization ratio of 34.3 per cent from 36.1 per cent.

IBM ended the first-quarter 2013 with $12.0 billion of cash on hand and generated free cash flow of $1.7 billion, excluding Global Financing receivables, down approximately $0.2 billion year over year. The company returned $3.5 billion to shareholders through $0.9 billion in dividends and $2.6 billion of gross share repurchases. The balance sheet remains strong, and the company is well positioned to support the business over the long term.

Forward-Looking and Cautionary Statements

Except for the historical information and discussions contained herein, statements contained in this release may constitute forward-looking statements within the meaning of the Private Securities Litigation Reform Act of 1995. Forward-looking statements are based on the company's current assumptions regarding future business and financial performance. These statements involve a number of risks, uncertainties and other factors that could cause actual results to differ materially, including the following: a downturn in economic environment and corporate IT spending budgets; the company's failure to meet growth and productivity objectives, a failure of the company's innovation initiatives; risks from investing in growth opportunities; failure of the company's intellectual property portfolio to prevent competitive offerings and the failure of the company to obtain necessary licences; cybersecurity and data privacy considerations; fluctuations in financial results and purchases, impact of local legal, economic, political and health conditions; adverse effects from environmental matters, tax matters and the company's pension plans; ineffective internal controls; the company's use of accounting estimates; the company's ability to attract and retain key personnel and its reliance on critical skills; impacts of relationships with critical suppliers and business with government clients; currency fluctuations and customer financing risks; impact of changes in market liquidity conditions and customer credit risk on receivables; reliance on third party distribution channels; the company's ability to successfully manage acquisitions and alliances; risk factors related to IBM securities; and other risks, uncertainties and factors discussed in the company's Form 10-Q, Form 10-K and in the company's other filings with the US Securities and Exchange Commission (SEC) or in materials incorporated there in by reference. Any forward-looking statement in this release speaks only as of the date on which it is made. The company assumes no obligation to update or revise any forward-looking statements.

Presentation of Information in this Press Release

In an effort to provide investors with additional information regarding the company's results as determined by generally accepted accounting principles (GAAP), the company has also disclosed in this press release the following non-GAAP information which management believes provides useful information to investors:

IBM results and expectations –

- presenting operating (non-GAAP) earnings per share amounts and related income statement items;
- presenting non-global financing debt-to-capitalization ratio;
- adjusting for free cash flow;
- adjusting for currency (ie, at constant currency);
- adjusting for the divestiture of RSS.

The rationale for management's use of non-GAAP measures is included as part of the supplemental materials presented within the first-quarter earnings materials. These materials are available via a link on the IBM investor relations website at www.ibm.com/investor and are being included in Attachment II ("Non-GAAP Supplemental Materials") to the Form 8-K that includes this press release and is being submitted today to the SEC.

Conference Call and Webcast

IBM's regular quarterly earnings conference call is scheduled to begin at 4:30 pm EDT, today. The webcast may be accessed via a link at **http://www.ibm.com/investor/ events/1q13.phtml**. Presentation charts will be available shortly before the webcast.

Financial Results Below (certain amounts may not add due to use of rounded numbers; percentages presented are calculated from the underlying whole-dollar amounts).

Cal Chalco 2012

INTERNATIONAL BUSINESS MACHINES CORPORATION
COMPARATIVE FINANCIAL RESULTS
(Unaudited; Dollars in millions except per share amounts)

	Three Months Ended March 31,		Per cent Change
	2013	2012	
REVENUE			
Global Technology Services	$9,605	$10,035	−4.3%
Gross profit margin	36.7%	35.3%	
Global Business Services	4,484	4,637	−3.3%
Gross profit margin	28.6%	28.0%	
Software	5,572	5,600	−0.5%
Gross profit margin	87.2%	87.0%	
Systems and Technology	3,106	3,749	−17.2%
Gross profit margin	32.3%	34.2%	
Global Financing	499	490	1.9%
Gross profit margin	45.8%	50.7%	
Other	142	162	−12.4%
Gross profit margin	−158.5%	−74.8%	
TOTAL REVENUE	23,408	24,673	−5.1%
GROSS PROFIT	10,678	11,118	−4.0%
Gross profit margin	45.6%	45.1%	
EXPENSE AND OTHER INCOME			
S,G&A	5,577	5,886	−5.2%
Expense to revenue	23.8%	23.9%	
R,D&E	1,644	1,601	2.7%
Expense to revenue	7.0%	6.5%	
Intellectual property and custom development income	(183)	(255)	−28.4%
Other (income) and expense	(60)	(58)	3.8%
Interest expense	94	110	−14.4%
TOTAL EXPENSE AND OTHER INCOME	7,072	7,283	−2.9%
Expense to revenue	30.2%	29.5%	
INCOME BEFORE INCOME TAXES	3,606	3,836	−6.0%
Pre-tax margin	15.4%	15.5%	
Provision for income taxes	574	769	−25.4%
Effective tax rate	15.9%	20.1%	
NET INCOME	$3,032	$3,066	−1.1%
Net income margin	13.0%	12.4%	
EARNINGS PER SHARE OF COMMON STOCK:			
ASSUMING DILUTION	$2.70	$2.61	3.4%
BASIC	$2.72	$2.65	2.6%
WEIGHTED-AVERAGE NUMBER OF COMMON SHARES OUTSTANDING (M's):			
ASSUMING DILUTION	1,124.0	1,174.2	
BASIC	1,113.7	1,159.1	

INTERNATIONAL BUSINESS MACHINES CORPORATION CONSOLIDATED
STATEMENT OF FINANCIAL POSITION (Unaudited)

(Dollars in Millions)	At March 31, 2013	At December 31, 2012
ASSETS:		
Current Assets:		
Cash and cash equivalents	$10,585	$10,412
Marketable securities	1,407	717
Notes and accounts receivable - trade		
(net of allowances of $263 in 2013 and $255 in 2012)	10,084	10,667
Short-term financing receivables		
(net of allowances of $273 in 2013 and $288 in 2012)	16,141	18,038
Other accounts receivable		
(net of allowances of $20 in 2013 and $17 in 2012)	1,971	1,873
Inventories, at lower of average cost or market:		
Finished goods	519	475
Work in process and raw materials	1,902	1,812
Total inventories	2,421	2,287
Deferred taxes	1,592	1,415
Prepaid expenses and other current assets	4,747	4,024
Total Current Assets	**48,949**	**49,433**
Property, plant and equipment	40,056	40,501
Less: Accumulated depreciation	26,459	26,505
Property, plant and equipment – net	13,597	13,996
Long-term financing receivables	11,946	12,812
(net of allowances of $64 in 2013 and $66 in 2012)		
Prepaid pension assets	903	945
Deferred taxes	4,227	3,973
Goodwill	29,025	29,247
Intangible assets – net	3,601	3,787
Investments and sundry assets	5,011	5,021
Total Assets	**$117,258**	**$119,213**
LIABILITIES:		
Current Liabilities:		
Taxes	$4,678	$4,948
Short-term debt	8,725	9,181
Accounts payable	7,203	7,952
Compensation and benefits	3,964	4,745
Deferred income	12,971	11,952
Other accrued expenses and liabilities	4,583	4,847
Total Current Liabilities	**42,122**	**43,625**
Long-term debt	24,672	24,088
Retirement and non-pension post-retirement benefit obligations	19,069	20,418
Deferred income	4,409	4,491
Other liabilities	7,771	7,607
Total Liabilities	**98,044**	**100,229**

(Dollars in Millions)	At March 31, 2013	At December 31, 2012
EQUITY:		
IBM Stockholders' Equity:		
Common stock	50,522	50,110
Retained earnings	119,713	117,641
Treasury stock – at cost	(125,677)	(123,131)
Accumulated other comprehensive income/(loss)	(25,466)	(25,759)
Total IBM stockholders' equity	**19,092**	**18,860**
Non-controlling interests	122	124
Total Equity	**19,214**	**18,984**
Total Liabilities and Equity	**$117,258**	**$119,213**

INTERNATIONAL BUSINESS MACHINES CORPORATION
CASH FLOW ANALYSIS (Unaudited)

(Dollars in Millions)	Three Months Ended March 31,	
	2013	2012
Net Cash from Operating Activities per GAAP:	**$4,023**	**$4,291**
Less: the change in Global Financing (GF) Receivables	1,597	1,424
Net Cash from Operating Activities		
(Excluding GF Receivables)	**2,425**	**2,867**
Capital Expenditures, Net	(729)	(1,002)
Free Cash Flow		
(Excluding GF Receivables)	**1,696**	**1,865**
Acquisitions	(58)	(1,319)
Divestitures	10	0
Dividends	(948)	(870)
Share Repurchase	(2,593)	(3,015)
Non-GF Debt	(717)	657
Other (includes GF Receivables, and GF Debt)	3,473	3,094
Change in Cash, Cash Equivalents and Short-term Marketable Securities	**$863**	**$413**

INTERNATIONAL BUSINESS MACHINES CORPORATION
SEGMENT DATA (Unaudited)

(Dollars in Millions)	FIRST-QUARTER 2013				
	Revenue			Pre-tax Income/(Loss)	Pre-tax Margin
	External	Internal	Total		
SEGMENTS					
Global Technology Services	$9,605	$248	$9,852	$1,585	16.1%
Y-T-Y change	−4.3%	−15.4%	−4.6%	7.1%	
Global Business Services	4,484	180	4,664	703	15.1%
Y-T-Y change	−3.3%	−1.5%	−3.2%	17.0%	
Software	5,572	831	6, 403	2,014	31. 5%
Y-T-Y change	−0.5%	−1.1%	−0.6%	3.5%	
Systems and Technology	3,106	120	3,226	(405)	−12.5%
Y-T-Y change	−17.2	−20.5%	−17.3%	−286.7%	
Global Financing	499	541	1,040	538	51.8%
Y-T-Y change	1.9%	11.6%	6.7%	5.0%	
TOTAL REPORTABLE SEGMENTS	**$23,266**	**$1,919**	**$25,185**	**$4,435**	**17.6%**
Y-T-Y change	**−5.1%**	**−1.6%**	**−4.8%**	**0.0%**	
Eliminations/Other	142	(1,919)	(1,777)	(829)	
TOTAL IBM CONSOLIDATED	**$23,408**	**$0**	**$23,408**	**$3,606**	**15.4%**
Y-T-Y change	**−5.1%**		**−5.1%**	**−6.0%**	

(Dollars in Millions)	FIRST-QUARTER 2012				
	Revenue			Pre-tax Income/(Loss)	Pre-tax Margin
	External	Internal	Total		
SEGMENTS					
Global Technology Services	$10,035	$293	$10,328	$1,480	14.3%
Global Business Services	4,637	182	4,820	601	12.5%
Software	5,600	840	6, 439	1,945	30.2%
Systems and Technology	3,749	151	3,900	(105)	−2.7%
Global Financing	490	485	975	512	52.6%
TOTAL REPORTABLE SEGMENTS	**$24,511**	**$1,951**	**$26,462**	**$4,434**	**16.8%**
Eliminations / Other	162	(1,951)	(1,789)	(598)	
TOTAL IBM CONSOLIDATED	**$24,673**	**$0**	**$24,673**	**$3,836**	**15.5%**

INTERNATIONAL BUSINESS MACHINES CORPORATION US
GAAP TO OPERATING RESULTS RECONCILIATION
(Unaudited; Dollars in millions except per share amounts)

	FIRST-QUARTER 2013			
	GAAP	Acquisition-Related Adjustments*	Retirement-Related Adjustments**	Operating (Non-GAAP)
Gross Profit	$10,678	$95	$164	$10,937
Gross Profit Margin	45.6%	0.4Pts	0.7Pts	46.7%
S, G&A	5,577	(92)	(104)	5,381
R, D&E	1,644	0	(16)	1,628
Other (Income) & Expense	(60)	(7)	0	(67)
Total Expense & Other (Income)	7,072	(99)	(120)	6,853
Pre-Tax Income	3,606	194	283	4,084
Pre-Tax Income Margin	15.4%	0.8Pts	1.2Pts	17.4%
Provision for Income Taxes***	574	54	79	708
Effective Tax Rate	15.9%	0.6Pts	0.9Pts	17.3%
Net Income	3,032	140	204	3,376
Net Income Margin	13.0%	0.6Pts	0.9Pts	14.4%
Diluted Earnings Per Share	$2.70	$0.12	$0.18	$3.00

	FIRST-QUARTER 2012			
	GAAP	Acquisition-Related Adjustments*	Retirement-Related Adjustments**	Operating (Non-GAAP)
Gross Profit	$11,118	$89	$71	$11,278
Gross Profit Margin	45.1%	0.4Pts	0.3Pts	45.7%
S, G&A	5,886	(84)	(36)	5,766
R, D&E	1,601	0	4	1,605
Other (Income) & Expense	(58)	(1)	0	(59)
Total Expense & Other (Income)	7,283	(85)	(32)	7,166
Pre-Tax Income	3,836	173	102	4,111
Pre-Tax Income Margin	15.5%	0.7Pts	0.4Pts	16.7%
Provision for Income Taxes***	769	47	30	846
Effective Tax Rate	20.1%	0.3Pts	0.2Pts	20.6%
Net Income	3,066	126	73	3,265
Net Income Margin	12.4%	0.5Pts	0.3Pts	13.2%
Diluted Earnings Per Share	$2.61	$0.11	$0.06	$2.78

*   Includes amortization of acquired intangible assets and other acquisition-related charges.
**   Includes retirement-related items driven by changes to plan assets and liabilities primarily related to market performance.
*** Tax impact on operating (non-GAAP) pre-tax income is calculated under the same accounting principles applied to the GAAP pre-tax income which employs an annual effective tax rate method to the results.

Contact: IBM
            Mike Fay, 914-525-8476
            mikefay@us.ibm.com
            John Bukovinsky, 732-618-3531
            jbuko@us.ibm.com

CHALCO

中国铝业股份有限公司
ALUMINUM CORPORATION OF CHINA LIMITED*

(A joint stock limited company incorporated in the People's Republic of China with limited liability)

(Stock Code: 2600)

2013 First Quarterly Report

This announcement is made by Aluminum Corporation of China Limited* (the "**Company**" or, together with its subsidiaries, the "**Group**") pursuant to Part XIVA of the Securities and Futures Ordinance (Chapter 571 of the Laws of Hong Kong) and Rules 13.09 and 13.10B of the Rules Governing the Listing of Securities on The Stock Exchange of Hong Kong Limited.

1 Important Notice

1.1 The board of directors, the supervisory committee, the directors, supervisors and senior management of the Company guarantee that this report contains no false representation, misleading statement or material omission. All of them jointly and severally accept responsibility for the truthfulness, accuracy and completeness of the contents of this report.

1.2 All the directors of the Company attended the Board meeting.

1.3 The first quarterly financial report of the Company has not been audited.

1.4 Name of Person-in-charge of the Company   Xiong Weiping
Name of Person-in-charge of Accounting   Xie Weizhi
Name of Head of the Accounting Department   Lu Dongliang

Xiong Weiping, Person-in-charge of the Company, Xie Weizhi, Person-in-charge of Accounting, and Lu Dongliang, Head of the Accounting Department warrant the truthfulness and completeness of the financial statements in this quarterly report.

* For identification purpose only

2 Company Profile

2.1 Principal accounting information and financial indicators

Currency: RMB

	The end of the reporting period	The end of the previous year	Change from the end of the previous year (%)
Total assets *(Thousand RMB)*	**216,015,714**	175,016,882	23.43
Owner's equity *(or shareholders' equity) (Thousand RMB)*	**42,838,767**	43,835,118	−2.27
Net assets per share attributable to shareholders of the Company *(RMB per share)*	**3.17**	3.24	−2.16

		From the beginning of the year to the end of the reporting period	Change from the same period last year (%)
Net cash flow from operating activities *(Thousand RMB)*		−1,091,020	Net outflow decreased by 46.27%
Net cash flow per share generated from operating activities *(RMB per share)*		−0.08	Net outflow decreased by 46.27%

	The reporting period	From the beginning of the year to the end of the reporting period	Change from the same period last year (%)
Net profit attributable to shareholders of the Company *(Thousand RMB)*	**−975,040**	−975,040	Loss reduction of 10.42%
Basic earnings per share *(RMB per share)*	**−0.07**	−0.07	Loss reduction of 10.42%
Basic profit per share after extraordinary gains and losses *(RMB per share)*	**−0.13**	−0.13	N/A
Diluted earnings per share *(RMB per share)*	**−0.07**	−0.07	Loss reduction of 10.42%
Return on net assets (weighted average) *(%)*	**−2.28**	−2.28	Decreased by 0.14 percentage point
Return on net assets after extraordinary gains and losses (weighted average) *(%)*	**−4.09**	−4.09	Decreased by 1.82 percentage points

Deducting the gains and losses arising from extraordinary items and amount:

Unit: '000 Currency: RMB

Items	Amount
Gains and losses from disposal of non-current assets	−4,493
Government subsidies included in the gains and losses for the period (excluding government subsidies closely related to the ordinary business of the Company and are granted on an ongoing basis under the state's policies according to certain standard amount or quantity)	337,113
Profit arising from investment cost for acquisition of a subsidiary, an associate and a joint venture by the Company being less than its share of fair value of identifiable net assets of the investee on acquisition	578,218
Except for the hedging business that is related to the ordinary business of the Company, the fair value gains or losses arising from held-for-trading financial assets and liabilities and investment income from disposing held-for-trading financial assets and liabilities and available-for-sale financial assets	−34,853
Written back of the provision for impairment of accounts receivable that is individually tested for impairment	4,251
Other non-operating income and expenses other than above items	2,941
Income tax effect	−81,552
Minority interests effect (after tax)	−24,725
Total	776,900

2.2 Total number of shareholders and the top 10 shareholders not subject to trading moratorium as at the end of the reporting period

Unit: Share

Total number of shareholders as at the end of the reporting period 526,111

The top 10 shareholders of tradable shares not subject to trading moratorium

Name of shareholders (in full)	Number of tradable shares not subject to trading moratorium held as at the end of the period	Class
Aluminum Corporation of China	5,214,407,195	RMB denominated ordinary shares
HKSCC Nominees Limited	3,924,987,330	Overseas listed foreign shares
China Cinda Assets Management Corporation	800,759,074	RMB denominated ordinary shares
China Construction Bank Corporation Limited	609,146,645	RMB denominated ordinary shares
Guokai Financial Limited Company	415,168,145	RMB denominated ordinary shares
Baotou Aluminum (Group) Co., Ltd.	325,767,795	RMB denominated ordinary shares
Lanzhou Aluminum Factory	79,472,482	RMB denominated ordinary shares
Guizhou Provincial Materials Development and Investment Corporation	59,000,000	RMB denominated ordinary shares
Guangxi Investment Group Co., Ltd.	39,259,793	RMB denominated ordinary shares
Bank of China Limited — Harvest Shanghai Shenzhen 300 ETF Index Securities Investment Fund (嘉實滬深300交易型開放式指數證券投資基金)	19,187,944	RMB denominated ordinary shares

3 Significant Events

3.1 Material changes in major accounting items and financial indicators and the reasons thereof

☑ Applicable ☐ Not Applicable

1 Business tax and surcharges increased by 75 per cent, mainly attributable to the rising turnover tax deriving from the improved net income or expense from other operations of the Group.

2 Financial expenses increased by 41 per cent, mainly attributable to the larger size of interest-bearing debts from last year resulting from the new incorporation of the consolidated statements of China Aluminum Ningxia Energy Group Co., Ltd. into the Group.

3 Loss on asset impairment increased by 8,589 per cent, mainly attributable to the increase in the provision for inventory impairment following the lower price of major products of the Group at the end of the period.

4 Loss on fair value changes increased by 464 per cent, mainly attributable to the increasing floating loss on fair value changes arising from futures contracts held by the Group.

5 Investment income increased by 80 per cent, mainly attributable to the increase in gains from associated companies and joint ventures resulting from the new incorporation of the consolidated statements of China Aluminum Ningxia Energy Group Co., Ltd. into the Group.

6 Non-operating income increased by 1,289 per cent, mainly attributable to the higher fair value of the mining rights over the considerations engendered as a result of acquiring China Aluminum Ningxia Energy Group Co., Ltd. by the Group.

7 Non-operating expenses decreased by 43 per cent, mainly attributable to less donations made by the Group.

8 Total profit increased by 33 per cent, mainly attributable to the enhanced gross profit margin resulting from the strict control on costs, fees and expenses as well as the expansion of income sources.

9 Income tax expenses increased by 89 per cent, mainly attributable to the non-provision of deferred income tax assets for most of the losses occurred during the period.

10 Minority interests increased by 177 per cent, mainly attributable to the profit increase of subsidiaries controlled by the Group.

11 Held-for-trading financial assets decreased by 80 per cent, mainly attributable to less floating profit on the positions of the futures and forward foreign exchange contracts of the Group.

12 Notes receivables increased by 46 per cent, mainly attributable to the tightening national currency policy, which increased the use of bank's acceptance notes in settlement.

13 Accounts receivables increased by 219 per cent, mainly attributable to the extension of the credit period as a result of the tightening national currency policy, keen market competition and the increase in trade volume, as well as the new incorporation of the consolidated statements of China Aluminum Ningxia Energy Group Co., Ltd.

14 Prepayments increased by 65 per cent, mainly attributable to the prepayments for certain procurement with a view to expanding trading channels.

15 Interest receivable increased by 2,834 per cent, mainly attributable to the increasing accrued interests resulted from the entrusted loans to associates.

16 Other receivables increased by 40 per cent, mainly attributable to the additional entrusted loans to associates.

17 Other current assets increased by 52 per cent, mainly attributable to the new incorporation of the consolidated statements of China Aluminum Ningxia Energy Group Co., Ltd. into the Group, which increased deductible input tax under value-added tax.

18 Investment properties increased from nil at the beginning of the period, mainly attributable to the new incorporation of the consolidated statements of China Aluminum Ningxia Energy Group Co., Ltd. into the Group.

19 Construction materials increased by 119 per cent, mainly attributable to new incorporation of the consolidated statements of China Aluminum Ningxia Energy Group Co., Ltd.

20 Intangible assets increased by 156 per cent, mainly attributable to the new incorporation of the consolidated statements of China Aluminum Ningxia Energy Group Co., Ltd. into the Group, which increased raising the number of coal mining rights.

21 Financial liabilities held for trading increased by 288 per cent, mainly attributable to the increased floating loss on the positions of the futures and forward foreign exchange contracts of the Group.

22 Notes payable increased by 186 per cent, mainly attributable to the tightening of national currency policy, resulting in a proper increase of notes used in settling procurement.

23 Accounts payables increased by 46 per cent, mainly attributable to the tightening of national currency policy, resulting in the proper extension of credit period in procurement.

24 Advances from customers increased by 74 per cent, mainly attributable to the portion of payment received in advance based on clients' credibility.

25 Accrued interest increased by 77 per cent, mainly attributable to the larger size of interest-bearing debts of the Group.

26 Dividends payable increased by 71 per cent, mainly attributable to the cash dividends payable accounted by subsidiaries under the Group.

27 Long-term loans increased by 85 per cent, mainly attributable to the new incorporation of consolidated statements of China Aluminum Ningxia Energy Group Co., Ltd. into the Group, making additional long-term bank loans.

28 Special payables increased by 108 per cent, mainly attributable to the government subsidies added by the new incorporation of consolidated statements of China Aluminum Ningxia Energy Group Co., Ltd. into the Group.

29 Projected liabilities increased from nil at the beginning of the period, mainly attributable to the projected mining rights considerations payable upon acquisition of China Aluminum Ningxia Energy Group Co., Ltd.

30 Other non-current liabilities increased by 58 per cent, mainly attributable to the additional deferred income arising from the new incorporation of consolidated statements of China Aluminum Ningxia Energy Group Co., Ltd. into the Group.

31 Minority interests increased by 39 per cent, mainly attributable to minority interests added by the new incorporation of consolidated statements of China Aluminum Ningxia Energy Group Co., Ltd. into the Group.

32 For the first quarter of 2013, the Group recorded a revenue of RMB34.213 billion. Included in its total profit was a loss of RMB948 million, representing a reduction of loss of RMB466 million or 32.96 per cent from the loss of RMB1.414 billion for the corresponding period last year. Vested in the net profit attributable to owners of the parent company was a loss of RMB975 million, representing a reduction of loss of RMB113 million or 10.42 per cent from the loss of RMB1.088 billion for the corresponding period last year.

33 For the first quarter of 2013, the Group had increased its operating gross profit by 37 per cent compared to the corresponding period last year, of which, cost reduction of major products ranged between 6 per cent and 9 per cent, cutting the loss by approximately RMB1.4 billion. However, price reduction of major products ranged between 5 per cent and 7 per cent compared to the corresponding period last year, reducing the profit by approximately RMB1.3 billion.

34 For the first quarter of 2013, the Group continued to increase its effort in controlling the production and operating costs. During the period, selling expenses amounted to RMB458 million, representing an increase of RMB12 million from RMB446 million for the same period last year. Upon deduction of the additional RMB14 million resulting from the incorporation of China Aluminum Ningxia Energy Group Co., Ltd., such expenses decreased slightly as compared with the same period last year. Administrative expenses for the period amounted to RMB645 million, representing an increase of RMB23 million as compared with RMB622 million for the same period last year. Upon deduction of additional RMB80 million resulting from the incorporation of China Aluminum Ningxia Energy Group Co., Ltd., such expenses decreased by RMB57 million as compared with the same period last year. Finance expenses for the period amounted to RMB1.518 billion, representing an increase of RMB442 million as compared with RMB1.076 billion for the same period of last year. Upon deduction of additional RMB277 million resulting from the incorporation of China Aluminum Ningxia Energy Group Co., Ltd., such expenses increased by RMB165 million as compared with the same period last year, mainly attributable to the increase in the size of interest-bearing debts of the Group, offset by a decrease of 0.43 percentage point in the weighted average interest rate in the end of the first quarter of 2013 as compared with the end of the first quarter of last year.

3.2 Progress of significant events and effects thereof and analysis on solutions

☐ Applicable   ✓ Not Applicable

3.3 Implementation of undertakings by the Company, its shareholders and de facto controller

✓ Applicable   ☐ Not Applicable

1 During the A share issue of the Company in 2007, Aluminum Corporation of China ("Chinalco") undertook that Chinalco would arrange to dispose of its aluminum fabrication business, or the Company would acquire the aluminum fabrication business from Chinalco, and acquire the pseudo-boehmite business from Chinalco within a certain period of time following the listing of the Company's A shares.

In 2008, the Company successfully bid for the five aluminum fabrication enterprises under the control of Chinalco in an open tender process through the equity exchange. Since the market conditions for pseudo-boehmite are immature, Chinalco does not propose to inject its pseudo-boehmite business to the Company's portfolio. When conditions become mature, Chinalco will continue to duly complete the matters undertaken within the time limit.

2 On 22 August 2011, the Company issued a letter of undertaking of Aluminum Corporation of China Limited* to resolve the horizontal competition with Jiaozuo Wanfang Aluminum Company Limited in the aluminum business (中國鋁業股份有限公司關於解決與焦作萬方鋁業股份有限公司電解鋁業務同業競爭的承諾函), pursuant to which it undertook to make its best endeavours to eliminate by proper means the competition in aluminum business with Jiaozuo Wanfang within five years.

3.4 Warning on any potential loss in accumulated net profit for the period from the beginning of the year to the end of the next reporting period or any material change from the corresponding period last year and the reason thereof

☐ Applicable   ✓ Not Applicable

3.5 Implementation of cash dividend policy during the reporting period

The terms for the distribution of cash dividend were prescribed in the Articles of Association of the Company: 1) the Company takes full account of the returns to investors and distributes dividends to shareholders every year according to the pre-scribed ratio of distributable profit for the prevailing year; 2) the Company upkeeps a continuous and stable profit distribution policy whilst considering the long-term interest of the Company, the overall interest of its shareholders as a whole and the sustainable development of the Company; 3) cash dividends shall be considered first when the Company distributes dividends.

No final dividend was distributed during the reporting period.

Aluminum Corporation of China Limited*
Legal representative: **Xiong Weiping**
26 April 2013

4 Appendices

4.1 Consolidated Balance Sheet

As at 31 March 2013
Prepared by: Aluminum Corporation of China Limited*

Unit: Thousand RMB, Unaudited

Items	Closing balance	Opening balance
Current assets:		
Cash and cash equivalents	**12,260,366**	10,191,608
Settlement reserve		
Placements with banks and other financial institutions		
Held-for-trading financial assets	**1,754**	8,983
Bills receivable	**1,743,292**	1,190,643
Accounts receivable	**4,546,464**	1,425,219
Prepayments	**7,415,895**	4,481,005
Premiums receivable		
Receivables from reinsurers		
Deposits receivable from reinsurance agreements		
Interest receivable	**36,602**	1,248
Dividends receivable	**189,638**	189,638
Other receivables	**3,545,987**	2,530,189
Purchases of resold financial assets		
Inventories	**29,105,785**	25,596,476
Non-current assets due within one year	**28,000**	28,000
Other current assets	**5,141,209**	3,373,007
Total current assets	**64,014,992**	49,016,016

Items	Closing balance	Opening balance
Non-current assets:		
Entrusted loans and advances granted		
Financial assets available for sale		
Held-to-maturity investments		
Long-term receivables		
Long-term equity investments	18,207,573	19,213,415
Investment properties	7,443	0
Fixed assets	97,292,807	81,675,584
Construction in progress	18,464,278	14,382,407
Construction materials	415,572	190,100
Disposals of fixed assets		
Biological assets for production		
Oil and gas assets		
Intangible assets	11,519,148	4,491,491
Development expenses		
Goodwill	2,362,735	2,362,735
Long-term deferred expenditures	311,198	277,702
Deferred income tax assets	2,311,933	2,116,986
Other non-current assets	1,108,035	1,290,446
Total non-current assets	152,000,722	126,000,866
Total assets	216,015,714	175,016,882
Current liabilities:		
Short-term borrowings	46,660,575	40,313,218
Borrowings from central bank		
Deposit taking and deposit in inter-bank market		
Placements from banks and other financial institutions		
Held-for-trading financial liabilities	49,177	12,662
Bills payable	6,232,202	2,175,710
Accounts payable	7,144,644	4,883,484
Payments received in advance	2,231,083	1,278,746
Disposal of repurchased financial assets		
Handling charges and commissions payable		
Staff remuneration payable	475,639	400,807
Taxes payable	443,211	452,763
Interest payable	968,929	548,381
Dividends payable	211,905	123,707
Other payables	6,001,894	6,045,854
Reinsurance accounts payable		
Deposits for insurance contracts		
Agent brokerage fee		
Agent underwriting fee		
Non-current liabilities due within one year	10,475,637	10,946,325
Other current liabilities	17,681,830	16,671,754
Total current liabilities	98,576,726	83,853,411

Items	Closing balance	Opening balance
Non-current liabilities:		
Long-term borrowings	36,768,894	19,910,787
Debentures payable	20,708,269	16,724,865
Long-term payables		
Special payables	242,954	116,979
Projected liabilities	2,030,812	0
Deferred income tax liabilities		
Other non-current liabilities	1,008,005	639,690
Total non-current liabilities	60,758,934	37,392,321
Total liabilities	**159,335,660**	121,245,732
Owner's equity (or shareholders' equity):		
Paid-up capital (or share capital)	13,524,488	13,524,488
Capital reserve	13,987,858	13,987,858
Less: Treasury stock		
Special reserve	115,118	92,193
Surplus reserve	5,867,557	5,867,557
General risk provision		
Retained profit	9,405,364	10,380,404
Foreign currency translation differences	−61,618	−17,382
Total owner's equity attributable to the parent company	42,838,767	43,835,118
Minority interests	13,841,287	9,936,032
Total owner's equity	56,680,054	53,771,150
Total liabilities and owner's equity	**216,015,714**	175,016,882

Legal Representative of the Company: **Xiong Weiping**

Person-in-charge of Accounting: **Xie Weizhi**

Head of Accounting Department: **Lu Dongliang**

Balance Sheet of the Parent Company
As at 31 March 2013
Prepared by: Aluminum Corporation of China Limited*

Unit: Thousand RMB, Unaudited

Items	Closing balance	Opening balance
Current assets:		
Cash and cash equivalents	3,871,523	4,939,505
Held-for-trading financial assets		
Bills receivable	581,689	651,601
Accounts receivable	2,184,209	1,516,759
Prepayments	1,265,687	1,145,561
Interest receivable	32,608	5,814
Dividends receivable	240,348	240,348
Other receivables	9,510,099	7,812,881
Inventories	13,277,583	12,917,041
Non-current assets due within one year	28,000	28,000
Other current assets	918,524	992,623
Total current assets	31,910,270	30,250,133
Non-current assets:		
Financial assets available for sale		
Held-to-maturity investments		
Long-term receivables		
Long-term equity investments	29,815,764	26,096,514
Investment properties		
Fixed assets	51,767,755	52,636,716
Construction in progress	6,902,619	6,339,611
Construction materials	64,440	60,017
Disposal of fixed assets		
Biological assets for production		
Oil and gas assets		
Intangible assets	2,281,040	2,319,689
Development expenses		
Goodwill	2,330,945	2,330,945
Long-term deferred expenditures	69,168	70,829
Deferred income tax assets	1,511,195	1,525,206
Other non-current assets	322,430	322,430
Total non-current assets	95,065,356	91,701,957
Total assets	126,975,626	121,952,090

Items	Closing balance	Opening balance
Current liabilities:		
Short-term borrowings	**22,470,000**	19,370,000
Held-for-trading financial liabilities	**0**	11,222
Bills payable	**3,600**	0
Accounts payable	**3,030,797**	2,900,794
Payments received in advance	**392,059**	170,979
Staff remuneration payables	**258,610**	257,796
Taxes payable	**253,742**	230,190
Interests payable	**753,638**	421,281
Dividends payable		
Other payables	**2,380,397**	3,598,165
Non-current liabilities due within one year	**8,321,342**	8,321,342
Other current liabilities	**17,669,510**	16,669,968
Total current liabilities	**55,533,695**	51,951,737
Non-current liabilities:		
Long-term borrowings	**8,844,902**	9,147,902
Debentures payable	**18,910,491**	15,927,504
Long-term payables		0
Special payables	**96,880**	96,880
Projected liabilities		
Deferred income tax liabilities		
Other non-current liabilities	**479,205**	490,292
Total non-current liabilities	**28,331,478**	25,662,578
Total liabilities	**83,865,173**	77,614,315
Owner's equity (or shareholders' equity):		
Paid-up capital (or share capital)	**13,524,488**	13,524,488
Capital reserve	**14,401,214**	14,401,214
Less: Treasury stock		
Special reserve	**45,583**	25,686
Surplus reserve	**5,867,557**	5,867,557
General risk provision		
Retained profit	**9,271,611**	10,518,830
Total owner's equity **(or shareholders' equity)**	**43,110,453**	44,337,775
Total liabilities and owner's equity **(or shareholders' equity)**	**126,975,626**	121,952,090

Legal Representative of the Company:	Person-in-charge of Accounting:	Head of Accounting Department.
Xiong Weiping	**Xie Weizhi**	**Lu Dongliang**

4.2 Consolidated Income Statement

January to March 2013
Prepared by: Aluminum Corporation of China Limited*

Unit: Thousand RMB, Unaudited

Items		Amount for the period	Amount for the previous period
I.	**Total operating revenue**	**34,213,296**	33,589,657
	Including: Operating revenue	**34,213,296**	33,589,657
	Interest income		
	Premiums earned		
	Handling charges and commission income		
II.	**Total cost of operations**	**36,319,071**	35,187,086
	Including: Operating cost	**33,404,017**	32,997,696
	Interest expenses		
	Handling charges and commission expenses		
	Returned premium		
	Net expenditure for compensation payments		
	Net provision for insurance deposits		
	Policyholder dividend expenses		
	Reinsurance costs		
	Business tax and surcharges	**83,233**	47,485
	Selling expenses	**457,625**	446,125
	Administrative expenses	**645,200**	622,358
	Finance expenses	**1,517,509**	1,075,913
	Loss on assets impairment	**211,487**	–2,491
Add:	Gains on fair value changes (loss stated with "–")	**–28,543**	–5,058
	Investment income (loss stated with "–")	**234,330**	130,168
Including:	Investment income from associated companies and joint ventures	**198,861**	97,518
	Foreign currency exchange gains (loss stated with "–")		

Items	Amount for the period	Amount for the previous period
III. **Operating profit (loss stated with "–")**	**–1,899,988**	–1,472,319
Add: Non-operating income	**958,079**	68,956
Less: Non-operating expenses	**5,929**	10,440
Including: Loss from disposal of non-current assets	**41**	0
IV. **Total profit (total loss stated with "–")**	**–947,838**	–1,413,803
Less: Income tax expenses	**–28,995**	–252,717
V. **Net profit (net loss stated with "–")**	**–918,843**	–1,161,086
Net profit attributable to owners of the parent company	**–975,040**	–1,088,439
Minority interests	**56,197**	–72,647
VI. **Earnings per share:**		
(i) Basic earnings per share	**–0.07**	–0.08
(ii) Diluted earnings per share	**–0.07**	–0.08
VII. **Other comprehensive income**	**–44,237**	6,664
VIII. **Total comprehensive income**	**–963,080**	–1,154,422
Total comprehensive income attributable to owners of the parent company	**–1,019,277**	–1,081,775
Total comprehensive income attributable to minority shareholders	**56,197**	–72,647

Legal Representative of the Company: **Xiong Weiping**	*Person-in-charge of Accounting:* **Xie Weizhi**	*Head of Accounting Department:* **Lu Dongliang**

Income Statement of the Parent Company
January to March 2013
Prepared by: Aluminum Corporation of China Limited*

Unit: Thousand RMB, Unaudited

Items			Amount for the period	Amount for the previous period
I.	**Operating revenue**		**11,281,182**	11,644,680
	Less:	Operating costs	**11,178,820**	11,779,910
		Business tax and surcharges	**52,139**	30,485
		Selling expenses	**253,389**	257,492
		Administrative expenses	**319,102**	369,806
		Finance expenses	**773,650**	629,370
		Loss on assets impairment	**99,909**	–2,490
	Add:	Gains on fair value changes (loss stated with "–")	**11,222**	–2,461
		Investment income (loss stated with "–")	**844**	41,023
	Including:	Investment income from associated companies and joint ventures	**–21,465**	2,100
II.	**Operating profit (loss stated with "–")**		**–1,383,761**	–1,381,331
	Add:	Non-operating income	**154,440**	27,304
	Less:	Non-operating expenses	**3,888**	9,720
	Including:	Loss from disposal of non-current assets	**4**	4,381
III.	**Total profit (total loss stated with "–")**		**–1,233,209**	–1,363,747
	Less:	Income tax expenses	**14,011**	–270,925
IV.	**Net profit (net loss stated with "–")**		**–1,247,220**	–1,092,822
V.	**Earnings per share:**			
	(i) Basic earnings per share			
	(ii) Diluted earnings per share			
VI.	**Other comprehensive income**			
VII.	**Total comprehensive income**		**–1,247,220**	–1,092,822

| Legal Representative of the Company: **Xiong Weiping** | Person-in-charge of Accounting: **Xie Weizhi** | Head of Accounting Department: **Lu Dongliang** |

4.3 Consolidated Cash Flow Statement

January to March 2013
Prepared by: Aluminum Corporation of China Limited*

Unit: Thousand RMB, Unaudited

Items	Amount for the period	Amount for the previous period
I. Cash flow from operating activities:		
Cash received from product sales and rendering of services	**40,166,561**	41,509,164
Net increase in deposits from customers and placements from banks and other financial institutions		
Net increase in borrowings from central bank		
Net increase in placements from other financial institutions		
Cash received from premiums of original insurance contracts		
Net cash received from reinsurance business		
Net increase in deposits from policyholders and investments		
Net increase in disposal of held-for-trading financial assets		
Cash received from interest, handling charges and commissions		
Net increase in capital due to banks and other financial institutions		
Net increase in repurchases		
Refund of tax and levies received	**40,360**	6,133
Other cash received relating to operating activities	**384,116**	106,973
Sub-total of cash inflow from operating activities	**40,591,037**	41,622,270
Cash paid for purchase of goods and receipt of services	**36,719,807**	40,177,772
Net increase in loans and advances to customers		
Net increase in placements with central bank and other financial institutions		
Cash paid for claims on original insurance contracts		
Cash payment for interest, handling charges and commissions		
Cash payment for policyholder dividend		
Cash paid to and on behalf of employees	**1,904,542**	1,835,916
Taxes and surcharges paid	**583,207**	943,196
Other cash paid relating to operating activities	**2,474,501**	695,881
Sub-total of cash outflow from operating activities	**41,682,057**	43,652,765
Net cash flow from operating activities	**−1,091,020**	−2,030,495
II. Cash flows from investment activities:		
Cash received from disposal of investments	**16,806**	0
Cash received from returns on investments	**269,242**	85,540
Net cash received from disposal of fixed assets, intangible assets and other long-term assets	**203,388**	5,018

Items	Amount for the period	Amount for the previous period
Net cash received from disposal of subsidiaries and other operating entities		
Other cash received relating to investment activities	31,846	18,776
Sub-total of cash inflow from investment activities	521,282	109,334
Cash paid to acquire fixed assets, intangible assets and other long-term assets	2,420,930	2,241,422
Cash paid for investment	234,412	490,000
Net increase in pledged loans		
Net cash paid for acquisition of subsidiaries and other operating entities	403,187	0
Other cash paid relating to investment activities	1,099,874	127,728
Sub-total of cash outflow from investment activities	4,158,403	2,859,150
Net cash flows from investment activities	**−3,637,121**	−2,749,816
III. Cash flow from financing activities:		
Proceeds received from investments		
Including: Proceeds received by subsidiaries from minority shareholders' investment		
Cash received from borrowings	20,884,209	25,240,588
Cash received from issue of debentures	5,971,500	2,000,000
Other cash received relating to financing activities	365,400	0
Sub-total of cash inflow from financing activities	27,221,109	27,240,588
Cash paid for repayment	18,100,772	17,131,398
Cash paid for dividend and profit distribution or interest repayment	1,569,160	804,686
Including: Dividend and profit paid by subsidiaries to minority shareholders		
Other cash paid relating to financing activities	470,689	0
Sub-total of cash outflow from financing activities	20,140,621	17,936,084
Net cash flows from financing activities	**7,080,488**	9,304,504
IV. Effect on cash and cash equivalents due to change in foreign currency exchange rate	**−3,484**	7,863
V. Net increase in cash and cash equivalents	**2,348,863**	4,532,056
Add: Balance of cash and cash equivalents at the beginning of the period	**9,063,593**	11,644,741
VI. Balance of cash and cash equivalents at the end of the period	**11,412,456**	16,176,797

Legal Representative of the Company:	Person-in-charge of Accounting:	Head of Accounting Department:
Xiong Weiping	**Xie Weizhi**	**Lu Dongliang**

Cash Flow Statement of the Parent Company
January to March 2013
Prepared by: Aluminum Corporation of China Limited*

Unit: Thousand RMB, Unaudited

Items	Amount for the period	Amount for the previous period
I. Cash flow from operating activities:		
Cash received from product sales and rendering of services	**13,117,368**	13,978,147
Refund of tax and levies received	**14,431**	4,133
Other cash received relating to operating activities	**174,676**	43,432
Sub-total of cash inflow from operating activities	**13,306,475**	14,025,712
Cash paid for purchase of goods and receipt of services	**12,342,654**	12,668,162
Cash paid to and on behalf of employees	**1,130,131**	1,125,869
Taxes and surcharges paid	**653,589**	579,371
Other cash paid relating to operating activities	**666,418**	402,664
Sub-total of cash outflow from operating activities	**14,792,792**	14,776,066
Net cash flow from operating activities	**−1,486,317**	−750,354
II. Cash flows from investment activities:		
Cash received from disposal of investments		
Cash received from returns on investments	**12,160**	23,695
Net cash received from disposal of fixed assets, intangible assets and other long-term assets	**56,705**	15,811
Net cash received from disposal of subsidiaries and other operating entities		
Other cash received relating to investment activities	**0**	15,228
Sub-total of cash inflow from investment activities	**68,865**	54,734
Cash paid to acquire fixed assets, intangible assets and other long-term assets	**863,190**	999,540
Cash paid for investment	**583,000**	1,023,110
Net cash paid for acquisition of subsidiaries and other operating entities	**4,387,630**	0
Other cash paid relating to investment activities	**21,087**	78,183
Sub-total of cash outflow from investment activities	**5,854,907**	2,100,833
Net cash flows from investment activities	**−5,786,042**	−2,046,099

Items	Amount for the period	Amount for the previous period
III. **Cash flows from financing activities:**		
Proceeds received from investments		
Cash received from borrowings	**7,900,000**	14,508,000
Cash received from bond issue	**6,000,000**	2,000,000
Other cash received relating to financing activities	**365,400**	0
Sub-total of cash inflow from financing activities	**14,265,400**	16,508,000
Cash paid for repayment	**7,103,000**	8,820,400
Cash paid for dividend and profit distribution or interest repayment	**550,941**	573,149
Other cash paid relating to financing activities		
Sub-total of cash outflow from financing activities	**7,653,941**	9,393,549
Net cash flows from financing activities	**6,611,459**	7,114,451
IV. **Effect on cash and cash equivalents due to change in foreign currency exchange rate**	53	3,485
V. **Net increase in cash and cash equivalents**	**−660,847**	4,321,483
Add: Balance of cash and cash equivalents at the beginning of the period	**4,396,234**	4,081,999
VI. **Balance of cash and cash equivalents at the end of the period**	**3,735,387**	8,403,482

Legal Representative of the Company:	Person-in-charge of Accounting:	Head of Accounting Department:
Xiong Weiping	**Xie Weizhi**	**Lu Dongliang**

As at the date of this announcement, the members of the Board of Directors comprise Mr. Xiong Weiping, Mr. Luo Jianchuan and Mr. Liu Xiangmin (Executive Directors); Mr. Shi Chungui and Mr. Lv Youqing and Mr. Liu Caiming (Non-executive Directors); Mr. Zhang Zhuoyuan, Mr. Wang Mengkui and Mr. Zhu Demiao (Independent Non-executive Directors).

APPENDIX D
Discount tables

TABLE Appendix D.1

Years	1%	2%	3%	4%	5%	6%	7%	8%	9%	10%
1	0.990	0.980	0.971	0.962	0.952	0.943	0.935	0.926	0.917	0.909
2	0.980	0.961	0.943	0.925	0.907	0.890	0.873	0.857	0.842	0.826
3	0.971	0.942	0.915	0.889	0.864	0.840	0.816	0.794	0.772	0.751
4	0.961	0.924	0.888	0.855	0.823	0.792	0.763	0.735	0.708	0.683
5	0.951	0.906	0.863	0.822	0.784	0.747	0.713	0.681	0.650	0.621
6	0.942	0.888	0.837	0.790	0.746	0.705	0.666	0.630	0.596	0.564
7	0.933	0.871	0.813	0.760	0.711	0.665	0.623	0.583	0.547	0.513
8	0.923	0.853	0.789	0.731	0.677	0.627	0.582	0.540	0.502	0.467
9	0.914	0.837	0.766	0.703	0.645	0.592	0.544	0.500	0.460	0.424
10	0.905	0.820	0.744	0.676	0.614	0.558	0.508	0.463	0.422	0.386
11	0.896	0.804	0.722	0.650	0.585	0.527	0.475	0.429	0.388	0.350
12	0.887	0.788	0.701	0.625	0.557	0.497	0.444	0.397	0.356	0.319
13	0.879	0.773	0.681	0.601	0.530	0.469	0.415	0.368	0.326	0.290
14	0.870	0.758	0.661	0.577	0.505	0.442	0.388	0.340	0.299	0.263
15	0.861	0.743	0.642	0.555	0.481	0.417	0.362	0.315	0.275	0.239
16	0.853	0.728	0.623	0.534	0.458	0.394	0.339	0.292	0.252	0.218
17	0.844	0.714	0.605	0.513	0.436	0.371	0.317	0.270	0.231	0.198
18	0.836	0.700	0.587	0.494	0.416	0.350	0.296	0.250	0.212	0.180
19	0.828	0.686	0.570	0.475	0.396	0.331	0.277	0.232	0.194	0.164
20	0.820	0.673	0.554	0.456	0.377	0.312	0.258	0.215	0.178	0.149

TABLE Appendix D.1   *continued*

Years	11%	12%	13%	14%	15%	16%	17%	18%	19%	20%
1	0.901	0.893	0.885	0.877	0.870	0.862	0.855	0.847	0.840	0.833
2	0.812	0.797	0.783	0.769	0.756	0.743	0.731	0.718	0.706	0.694
3	0.731	0.712	0.693	0.675	0.658	0.641	0.624	0.609	0.593	0.579
4	0.659	0.636	0.613	0.592	0.572	0.552	0.534	0.516	0.499	0.482
5	0.593	0.567	0.543	0.519	0.497	0.476	0.456	0.437	0.419	0.402
6	0.535	0.507	0.480	0.456	0.432	0.410	0.390	0.370	0.352	0.335
7	0.482	0.452	0.425	0.400	0.376	0.354	0.333	0.314	0.296	0.279
8	0.434	0.404	0.376	0.351	0.327	0.305	0.285	0.266	0.249	0.233
9	0.391	0.361	0.333	0.308	0.284	0.263	0.243	0.225	0.209	0.194
10	0.352	0.322	0.295	0.270	0.247	0.227	0.208	0.191	0.176	0.162
11	0.317	0.287	0.261	0.237	0.215	0.195	0.178	0.162	0.148	0.135
12	0.286	0.257	0.231	0.208	0.187	0.168	0.152	0.137	0.124	0.112
13	0.258	0.229	0.204	0.182	0.163	0.145	0.130	0.116	0.104	0.093
14	0.232	0.205	0.181	0.160	0.141	0.125	0.111	0.099	0.088	0.078
15	0.209	0.183	0.160	0.140	0.123	0.108	0.095	0.084	0.074	0.065
16	0.188	0.163	0.141	0.123	0.107	0.093	0.081	0.071	0.062	0.054
17	0.170	0.146	0.125	0.108	0.093	0.080	0.069	0.060	0.052	0.045
18	0.153	0.130	0.111	0.095	0.081	0.069	0.059	0.051	0.044	0.038
19	0.138	0.116	0.098	0.083	0.070	0.060	0.051	0.043	0.037	0.031
20	0.124	0.104	0.087	0.073	0.061	0.051	0.043	0.037	0.031	0.026

APPENDIX E
Annuity factors

TABLE Appendix E.1

Years	1%	2%	3%	4%	5%	6%	7%	8%	9%	10%
1	0.990	0.980	0.971	0.962	0.952	0.943	0.935	0.926	0.917	0.909
2	1.970	1.942	1.913	1.886	1.859	1.833	1.808	1.783	1.759	1.736
3	2.941	2.884	2.829	2.775	2.723	2.673	2.624	2.577	2.531	2.487
4	3.902	3.808	3.717	3.630	3.546	3.465	3.387	3.312	3.240	3.170
5	4.853	4.713	4.580	4.452	4.329	4.212	4.100	3.993	3.890	3.791
6	5.795	5.601	5.417	5.242	5.076	4.917	4.767	4.623	4.486	4.355
7	6.728	6.472	6.230	6.002	5.786	5.582	5.389	5.206	5.033	4.868
8	7.652	7.325	7.020	6.733	6.463	6.210	5.971	5.747	5.535	5.335
9	8.566	8.162	7.786	7.435	7.108	6.802	6.515	6.247	5.995	5.759
10	9.471	8.983	8.530	8.111	7.722	7.360	7.024	6.710	6.418	6.145
11	10.368	9.787	9.253	8.760	8.306	7.887	7.499	7.139	6.805	6.495
12	11.255	10.575	9.954	9.385	8.863	8.384	7.943	7.536	7.161	6.814
13	12.134	11.348	10.635	9.986	9.394	8.853	8.358	7.904	7.487	7.103
14	13.004	12.106	11.296	10.563	9.899	9.295	8.745	8.244	7.786	7.367
15	13.865	12.849	11.938	11.118	10.380	9.712	9.108	8.559	8.061	7.606
16	14.718	13.578	12.561	11.652	10.838	10.106	9.447	8.851	8.313	7.824
17	15.562	14.292	13.166	12.166	11.274	10.477	9.763	9.122	8.544	8.022
18	16.398	14.992	13.754	12.659	11.690	10.828	10.059	9.372	8.756	8.201
19	17.226	15.678	14.324	13.134	12.085	11.158	10.336	9.604	8.950	8.365
20	18.046	16.351	14.877	13.590	12.462	11.470	10.594	9.818	9.129	8.514

TABLE Appendix E.1 *continued*

Years	11%	12%	13%	14%	15%	16%	17%	18%	19%	20%
1	0.901	0.893	0.885	0.877	0.870	0.862	0.855	0.847	0.840	0.833
2	1.713	1.690	1.668	1.647	1.626	1.605	1.585	1.566	1.547	1.528
3	2.444	2.402	2.361	2.322	2.283	2.246	2.210	2.174	2.140	2.106
4	3.102	3.037	2.974	2.914	2.855	2.798	2.743	2.690	2.639	2.589
5	3.696	3.605	3.517	3.433	3.352	3.274	3.199	3.127	3.058	2.991
6	4.231	4.111	3.998	3.889	3.784	3.685	3.589	3.498	3.410	3.326
7	4.712	4.564	4.423	4.288	4.160	4.039	3.922	3.812	3.706	3.605
8	5.146	4.968	4.799	4.639	4.487	4.344	4.207	4.078	3.954	3.837
9	5.537	5.328	5.132	4.946	4.772	4.607	4.451	4.303	4.163	4.031
10	5.889	5.650	5.426	5.216	5.019	4.833	4.659	4.494	4.339	4.192
11	6.207	5.938	5.687	5.453	5.234	5.029	4.836	4.656	4.486	4.327
12	6.492	6.194	5.918	5.660	5.421	5.197	4.988	4.793	4.611	4.439
13	6.750	6.424	6.122	5.842	5.583	5.342	5.118	4.910	4.715	4.533
14	6.982	6.628	6.302	6.002	5.724	5.468	5.229	5.008	4.802	4.611
15	7.191	6.811	6.462	6.142	5.847	5.575	5.324	5.092	4.876	4.675
16	7.379	6.974	6.604	6.265	5.954	5.668	5.405	5.162	4.938	4.730
17	7.549	7.120	6.729	6.373	6.047	5.749	5.475	5.222	4.990	4.775
18	7.702	7.250	6.840	6.467	6.128	5.818	5.534	5.273	5.033	4.812
19	7.839	7.366	6.938	6.550	6.198	5.877	5.584	5.316	5.070	4.843
20	7.963	7.469	7.025	6.623	6.259	5.929	5.628	5.353	5.101	4.870

REFERENCES

Chapter 1

International Federation of Accountants (2011) A Proposed Definition of 'Professional Accountant', Agenda Paper 7-B

Jones, M (2011) *Creative Accounting, Fraud and International Accounting Scandals*, John Wiley & Sons Ltd, Chichester, UK

Kaplan, R S (2011) Accounting scholarship that advances professional knowledge and practice, *The Accounting Review*, 86 (2), pp 367–83

Pacioli, L (1497) *Summa de arithmetica, geometria, proportioni et proportionalita*, Venice, Italy

Supplementary reading

Carnegie, G D and Napier, C J (2010) Traditional accountants and business professionals: portraying the accounting profession after Enron, *Accounting, Organizations and Society*, 35 (3), pp 360–76

DeCoster, D T and Rhode, J G (1971) The accountant's stereotype: real or imagined, deserved or unwarranted, *Accounting Review*, 46, pp 651–64

International Accounting Standards Board (2010) The Conceptual Framework for Financial Reporting 2010, IFRS Foundation Publications Department, London

Chapter 2

Gallagher, M and Paul, B (2012) Assessing Going Concern: Stakeholders would benefit from clarity in US disclosure requirements, *Point of view*, PricewaterhouseCooper LLP Publications, December

Supplementary reading

Bakar, N B A and Said, J M (2007) Historical cost versus current cost accounting, *Accountants Today*, January

Elliott, B and Elliott, J (2011) *Financial Accounting and Reporting*, 15th edn, Pearson Education, Harlow

Fahnestock, R T and Bostwick, E D (2011) An analysis of the fair value controversy, *Proceedings of The American Society of Business and Behavioral Sciences at Las Vegas*, 18 (1), pp 910–21

Hendriksen, E F and Van Breda, M F (1992) *Accounting Theory*, 5th edn, Irwin Professional Publishing, Burr Ridge, IL

Institute of Chartered Accountants in England and Wales (2009) Going concern: don't panic, *Accountancy*, January

Laux, C and Leuz, C (2009) The crisis of fair-value accounting: making sense of the recent debate, *Accounting, Organizations and Society*, 34 (6), pp 826–34

Power, M (2010) Fair value accounting, financial economics and the transformation of reliability, *Accounting and Business Research*, 40 (3), pp 197–220

Chapter 3

Chen, K H and Shimerda, T A (1981) An empirical analysis of useful financial ratios, *Financial Management*, pp 51–60

Ryanair Holdings plc (accessed 18 December 2013) Annual report 2012 [Online] http://www.ryanair.com/en/investor/download/

Chapter 4

Abraham, S, Marston, C and Darby, P (2012) Risk Reporting: Clarity, relevance and location, Institute of Chartered Accountants of Scotland, Research Report, ISBN 978-1-904574-87-3

Cyert, R M and March, J G (1963) *A Behavioral Theory of the Firm*, Prentice-Hall, Englewood Cliffs, NJ

Frankel, R, Johnson, M and Skinner, D J (1999) An empirical examination of conference calls as a voluntary disclosure medium, *Journal of Accounting Research*, 37 (1), pp 133–50

Mitchell, R K, Agle, B R and Wood, D J (1997) Toward a theory of stakeholder identification and salience: defining the principle of who and what really counts, *Academy of Management Review*, 22 (4), pp 853–86

Supplementary reading

Barker, R G (1998) The market for information – evidence from finance directors, analysts and fund managers, *Accounting and Business Research*, 29 (1), pp 3–20

Barker, R, Hendry, J, Roberts, J, *et al* (2012) Can company-fund manager meetings convey informational benefits? Exploring the rationalisation of equity investment decision making by UK fund managers, *Accounting, Organizations and Society*, 37 (4), pp 207–22

Brown, S, Hillegeist, S A and Lo, K (2004) Conference calls and information asymmetry, *Journal of Accounting and Economics*, 37 (3), pp 343–66

Cornelissen, J (2011) *Corporate Communication: A guide to theory and practice*, 3rd edn, Sage, London

Frankel, R, Johnson, M and Skinner, D J (1999) An empirical examination of conference calls as a voluntary disclosure medium, *Journal of Accounting Research*, 37 (1), pp 133–50

Mayew, W and Venkatachalam, M (2012) The power of voice: managerial affective states and future firm performance, *Journal of Finance*, 67 (1), pp 1–44

Mayew, W J, Sharp, N Y and Venkatachalam, M (2013) Using earnings conference calls to identify analysts with superior private information, *Review of Accounting Studies*, **18**, pp 386–413

Chapter 5

Comshare, Inc (2000) Comshare Survey of Top Financial Executives: Planning and budgeting today [Online] www.comshare.com

Libby, T and Lindsay, R M (2010) Beyond budgeting or budgeting reconsidered? A survey of North-American budgeting practice, *Management Accounting Research*, **21** (1), pp 56–75

Pyhrr, P (1973) *Zero-base Budgeting: A practical management tool for evaluating expenses*, John Wiley & Sons, Inc, New York

Supplementary reading

Hansen, S C (2004) *The Closed Loop: Implementing activity-based planning and budgeting*, Bookman, Indianapolis, IN

Hansen, S C, Otley, D T and Van der Stede, W A (2003) Practice developments in budgeting: an overview and research perspective, *Journal of Management Accounting Research*, **15**, pp 95–116

Chapter 6

Johnson, H T and Kaplan, R S (1987) *Relevance Lost: The rise and fall of management accounting*, Harvard Business School Press, Boston, MA

Kaplan, R S and Norton, D P (1992) The balanced scorecard – measures that drive performance, *Harvard Business Review*, **70** (1), pp 71–79

Kaplan, R S and Norton, D P (1996) *The Balanced Scorecard: Translating strategy into action*, Harvard Business School Press, Boston, MA

Kaplan, R S and Norton, D P (2008) *The Execution Premium: Linking strategy to operations for competitive advantage*, Harvard Business School Press, Boston, MA

Starovic, D (2003) *Performance Reporting to Boards: A guide to good practice*, CIMA, London

Chapter 7

Supplementary reading

Baumol, W J (1952) The transactions demand for cash: an inventory theoretic approach, *Quarterly Journal of Economics*, **66**, pp 545–56

Miller, M H and Orr, D (1966) A model of the demand for money by firms, *Quarterly Journal of Economics*, 80 (3), pp 413–35

Tobin, J (1956) The interest elasticity of the transactions demand for cash, *Review of Economics and Statistics*, 38 (3), pp 241–47

Chapter 8

McCarthy, J E (1960) *Basic Marketing: A managerial approach*, Richard D Irwin, Homewood, IL

Schulz, D E, Tannenbaum, S I and Lauterborn, R F (1993) *Integrated Marketing Communications*, NTC Publishing Group, Lincolnwood, IL

Shimizu, K (1973) *Advertising Theory and Strategies*, Souseisha Book Company, Japan

Chapter 9

Supplementary reading

Ogier, T, Rugman, J and Spicer, L (2004) *Real Cost of Capital: A business field guide to better financial decisions*, Financial Times/Prentice Hall, Harlow

Smit, H T J and Trigeorgis, L (2004) *Strategic Investment: Real options and games*, Princeton University Press, Princeton, NJ

Chapter 10

Peters, T J and Waterman, R H (1982) *In Search of Excellence: Lessons from America's best-run companies*, Profile Books, London

INDEX

NB: page numbers in *italic* indicate figures or tables

ABC inventory management 276, *276*
Abraham, Santhosh, Marston, Claire and Darby,
        Phil 160
absorption costing 294–99
accountancy, introduction to 3–49
    accounting research 10–11
    business, types of 23–26
        business purpose 26
        limited company 24–25, *25*
        partnership 24
        sole trader 23–24
    comprehension questions 38–39
        answers 41–44
    definitions
        accountant 8
        accounting 7
    exercises 39–41
        answers 44–49
    financial accountants 11, *11*, 12–16
        Big Four firms 13–14
        function on 14
        qualifications 12–13
        services provided by 15
        users of 15–16
    financial statements, overview 26–38
        fit together, how they 27, *37*
        problems, key 37–38
        required information 26–27
        terminology 28
        Tesco example 29–36, *30–31*, *32*, *33*, *34*,
            36
    information, useful 17–20, *19*
        enhancing characteristics 18
        fundamental characteristics 18
        materiality 20
    management accounting 11, *11*
    origins of 12
    regulation 16–17, 20–21, *22*
        Conceptual Framework (F) 15–17, 26–27
        IFRS Foundation *20*, 21
        IFRS Interpretations Committee 21
        International Accounting Standards Board
            (IASB) 21, *22*
        principles 17
accounting rate of return (ARR) 335–39

AccountingWEB UK 13
accounts payable, managing 269
accounts receivable, managing 264–68
    credit setting and control 264–67, *266*
    debt collection 267
    debt factoring 268
    invoice discounting 267–68
accruals concept 66
acid test ratio 123
activity-based budgets *200*, 200–01
activity-based costing (ABC) and pricing 300–02
alternative depreciation methods 77
Aluminium Corporation of China Limited
        (CHALCO) 167
Amazon 168–69, 318
Anglo American 115–16
annuities 352
Apple 169
    iPad 314
    stratified pricing 317
Asda 310
asset financing 278–79
    finance lease 279
    hire purchase (HP) 278–79
    operating lease 279
Association of Chartered Certified Accountants
        (ACCA) 12

balanced scorecard 227–30, *228*
Balanced Scorecard, The 227
Baumol–Tobin model 254–57, *255*, *256*
    worked example 256–57
Bernstein, Michelle 129
Beyond Budgeting Round Table (BBRT)
        194–95, 197
BHP Billiton 116
Big Four firms 13–14
BM plc 167
BMW Group plc 126
Bonderman, David 121
Bradford & Bingley 137
break-even point (BEP) 378, *379*
budgeting 175–208
    activity-based budgets *200*, 200–01
    'budget', definition of 176

comprehension questions   201–02
    answers   203–05
exercises   202–03
    answers   205–08
importance of   176
limitations of   194–98
    behaviour, influence on   196–97
    cost   195–96
    volatile environments   197
merchandizing businesses   194
not-for-profits   193
planning and control   176–78, 177
preparing   185–92
    sequence of events   185
    worked example   186–92
production businesses   192
public sector businesses   193
rolling budgets   198–99
service businesses   192–93
setting   178–84, 179, 181
    bottom-up   182–84
    financial budget   181
    incremental   184
    master budget   181
    operational budget   181
    top-down   182, 184
zero-based budgets   199–200
bundle pricing   318
business entity concept   65
business, types of   23–26
    business purpose   26
    limited company   24–25, 25
    partnership   24
    sole trader   23–24
'buy one get one free' (BOGOF)   318

Canadian Institute of Chartered Accountants
        (CICA)   12
capital asset pricing model (CAPM)   346
capital gearing ratio   135–36
capital rationing   352–54
capital turnover   224
Carstensen, Laura   13
cash budget   259–63, 263
cash conversion cycle   249, 249–50
    lead time   250
cash flow   247–91
    accounts payable, managing   269
    accounts receivable, managing   264–68
        credit setting and control   264–67, 266
        debt collection   267
        debt factoring   268
        invoice discounting   267–68
    asset financing   278–79
        finance lease   279
        hire purchase (HP)   278–79
        operating lease   279

Baumol–Tobin model   254–57, 255, 256
    worked example   256–57
cash budget   259–63, 263
cash conversion cycle   249, 249–50
    lead time   250
cash-flow forecast, interpreting a   279–83
compensating balances motive   254
comprehension questions   284
    answers   286–88
exercises   285–86
    answers   288–91
financing cash flow   249
importance of   248
inventory management   270–78
    ABC inventory management   276, 276
    economic order quantity (EOQ) model
        273–74
    inventory turnover ratio   271–72
    just-in-time (JIT)   277–78
    reorder levels   272–73, 273
investment cash flow   249
Miller–Orr model   257–59, 258
    worked example   259
operating cash flow   248
opportunity cost   251, 270
overtrading   251, 252
precautionary motive   252–53
speculative motive   253
transaction motive   252
worked examples   251, 260–63, 265, 269,
        272, 275, 280–83
Chartered Accountants Ireland (CAI)   12
Chartered Institute of Management Accountants
        (CIMA)   216, 223
Chartered Institute of Public Finance and
        Accountancy (CIPFA)   12
Chen, Kung and Shimerda, Thomas   97
Chiarello, Michael   129
Circle   183
Cisco Systems   362
Closed Loop, The   200
Coca-Cola   316
CompareNet   251
competitive advantage analysis   362
competitive pricing   317
concepts and systems   50–95
    accruals concept   66
    comprehension questions   85
        answers   89
    conservativism   68–69
    cost of sales working   62
    disaggregation   69
    double-entry bookkeeping   57–58
    exercises   85–88
        answers   90–95
    going concern   66–68
    materiality   70

measurement rules 65
neutrality 69
property, plant and equipment
    alternative depreciation methods 77
    non-current assets, disposal of 76–77
    recognition and subsequent measurement 76
    worked example 77–79, *78, 79*
prudence 68–69
purpose of 51
record keeping 79, *80*
statement of cash flows 55–57, 85
    estimates 56
    timing 56
    transactions 56
    working capital 56, 57
statement of comprehensive income
    51–53, *53*
    gross profit 52
    operating profit 52
    profit for the year 52
statement of financial position (balance sheet)
    54–55
    current assets 54
    current liabilities 54
    non-current assets 54
    non-current liabilities 54
    worked examples 58–62, 63–64, 70–76,
    80–84
Conceptual Framework for Financial Reporting (F)
    15–17, 26–27
conservativism 68–69
Consortium of Advanced Management,
    International (CAM–I) 200
Consultative Committee of Accountancy Bodies
    (CCAB) 12
consumer behaviour and perceptions 311–14
    ethics 313
    marketing mix, the 311
    perception of value, quality and difference
    313
    product positioning 312
controllability principle 212
Co-operative Bank 136–37
corporate social responsibility (CSR) reporting
    165–66
cost centres 211, 295
cost of sales working 62
cost pools 300
Costa 168
cost-driver analysis 361–62
cost-volume-profit analysis 375–88
    advertising 386
    break-even point (BEP) 378, *379*
    change in production systems 384–86
    change in selling price 383–84
    equation 379–80
    fixed costs 376–77, *377*

margin of safety 381–83, *382*
    revenue 375–76, *376*
    total costs 378, *379*
    variable costs 377–78, *378*
    worked examples 380–81, *382*, 383–84,
    385–86
Council Directive 78/660/EEC (Fourth EU
    Directive on Company Law) 68
Cruise, Tom 316
current assets 54
current cost accounting 65
current liabilities 54
current ratio 122
Cutifani, Mark 115–16

dangerous stakeholder *164*
debt collection 267
debt factoring 268
definitive stakeholder *165*
Dell 278
Deloitte 3, 13
Delta Airlines 128–30
demanding stakeholder *164*
dependent stakeholder *164*
depreciation 331
disaggregation 69
discounted cash flow (DCF) 339–46
    compounding 340
    discounting 340–42
    internal rate of return (IRR) 343–46
    net present value (NPV) *342*, 342–43
discretionary stakeholder *164*
Disney 335
dividend cover 138
dividend yield 140
dominant stakeholder *164*
dormant stakeholder *164*
double-entry bookkeeping 57–58
Dun and Bradstreet 248

earnings announcements 166–67
earnings per share (EPS) 141–42
economic order quantity (EOQ) model 273–74
economic value added (EVA) 225, 226
EDF Energy 345
efficiency ratios 124–32
    inventories holding period 127–28
    trade payables payment period 130–31
    trade receivables collection period 126–27
Emirates Airlines 253
Ernst and Young (EY) 13
European Financial Reporting Advisory Group
    (EFRAG) 68
Execution Premium, The 230

Facebook 170
finance lease 279

financial accountants   11, *11*, 12–16
  Big Four firms   13–14
  function on   14
  qualifications   12–13
  services provided by   15
  users of   15–16
financial analysis   96–174
  comprehension questions   147
    answers   151–53
  exercises   148–51
    answers   154–58
  financial ratios, overview   97
  horizontal analysis   101–04, *102–03*
  ratio analysis
    acid test ratio   123
    capital gearing ratio   135–36
    current ratio   122
    dividend cover   138
    dividend yield   140
    earnings per share (EPS)   141–42
    efficiency ratios   124–32
    gross profit margin   116–17
    interest cover   137–38
    introduction to   97, 107–08
    inventories holding period   127–28
    investor ratios   140–44
    liquidity ratios   121–24
    net profit margin   117–19
    price to earnings ratio (P/E ratio)   142–43
    profitability ratios   108–21
    return on capital employed (ROCE)   111–14
    solvency ratios   132–39
    trade payables payment period   130–31
    trade receivables collection period   126–27
    weaknesses and limitations   145–46
  reasons for and user needs   98–99, *99–100*
  trend analysis   101–04, *102–03*
  vertical analysis   104–07, *105, 106*
financial budget   181
Financial Services Authority (FSA)   137
financial statements, overview   26–38
  fit together, how they   27, *37*
  problems, key   37–38
  required information   26–27
  terminology   28
  Tesco example   29–36, *30–31, 32, 33, 34, 36*
Firefly   251
full-cost-plus pricing   294–99

Gallagher, Mike and Paul, Beth   67
going concern   66–68
Google   109, 168–69
Gordon, Ian   136–37
Graham's The Family Dairy   115
gross profit   52
gross profit margin   116–17
Guillon, Bruno   110

HBoS   137
hire purchase (HP)   278–79
historical cost accounting   65
Hotmail   251

IASplus.com   3
IBM   396
In Search of Excellence   390
InBev   200
inflation   349–51
  comprehension questions   171–72
    answers   172–74
  corporate social responsibility (CSR)
    reporting   165–66
  earnings announcements   166–67
  information, demand for   161–62
  investor presentation   166–67
  press coverage   167–70
  social media and internet bulletins   170–71
  stakeholder management   162–65, *163*
    dangerous stakeholder   *164*
    definitive stakeholder   *165*
    demanding stakeholder   *164*
    dependent stakeholder   *164*
    discretionary stakeholder   *164*
    dominant stakeholder   *164*
    dormant stakeholder   *164*
ING Direct   253
Institute of Chartered Accountants in
    Australia (ICAA)   12
Institute of Chartered Accountants in
    England and Wales (ICAEW)   12
Institute of Chartered Accountants in
    New Zealand (ICANZ)   12
Institute of Chartered Accountants in
    Scotland (ICAS)   12
Institute of Chartered Accountants in
    Zimbabwe (ICAZ)   12
interest cover   137–38
internal rate of return (IRR)   343–46
International Accounting Standards
  IAS 1 *Presentation of Financial Statements*   27
  IAS 16 *Property, Plant and Equipment*   70, 73
  IAS 33 *Earning per Share*   142
  IAS 7 *Statement of Cash Flows*   27
International Accounting Standards Board (IASB)
    2, 16, 17, 21, 22, 26, 28, 38, 69
International Federation of Accountants
    (IFAC)   8
International Financial Reporting Standards
    (IFRSs)   2, 21, 160
  IFRS Foundation   *20*, 21
  IFRS Interpretations Committee   21
inventories holding period   127–28
inventory management   270–78
  ABC inventory management   276, *276*
  economic order quantity (EOQ) model   273–74

inventory turnover ratio   271–72
just-in-time (JIT)   277–78
reorder levels   272–73, *273*
investment appraisal   327–72
    accounting rate of return (ARR)   335–39
    annuities   352
    capital asset pricing model (CAPM)   346
    capital rationing   352–54
    competitive advantage analysis   362
    comprehension questions   363
        answers   366–67
    cost-driver analysis   361–62
    depreciation   331
    discounted cash flow (DCF)   339–46
        compounding   340
        discounting   340–42
        internal rate of return (IRR)   343–46
        net present value (NPV)   342, 342–43
    exercises   363–66
        answers   368–72
    inflation   349–51
    money method   350
    Monte Carlo simulation method   360
    opportunity costs   347–48
    payback period (PP)   332–35
    probability analysis   359–60
    qualitative considerations   357–58
    real method   350
    real options   361
    replacement of assets   354–56
    risk, return, and timing   329
    scenario analysis   359
    sensitivity analysis   359
    taxation   349
    value chain analysis   361
    weighted average cost of capital (WACC)
        346
    worked examples   330–31, 333–35, 338,
        339, 348, 350–51, 352, 353–56, 360
investment cash flow   249
investment centre   212
investor ratios   140–44
    dividend yield   140
    earnings per share (EPS)   141–42
    price to earnings ratio (P/E ratio)   142–43
invoice discounting   267–68

Johnson, H Thomas and Kaplan, Robert   227
Jolie, Angelina   316
just-in-time (JIT)   237, 238, 277–78

Kaizen   321
Kaplan, Robert   10–11
    Johnson, H Thomas and Kaplan, Robert
        227
    Kaplan, Robert and Norton, David   227–30
KPMG   13, 223

lean manufacturing   277
Lehman Brothers   123
Libby, Theresa and Lindsay, Murray   178
life-cycle costing and pricing   237, 302–04, *303*
limited company   24–25, *25*
liquidity ratios   121–24
    acid test ratio   123
    current ratio   122
loss leaders   318
Lucasfilm   335

margin   298
margin of safety   381–83, *382*
marginal-cost-plus pricing   299
market skimming pricing   315–16
market types   308–10
    monopolistic competition   310
    monopoly   309–10
    oligopoly   310
    perfect competition   309
marketing mix, the   311
mark-up   298
master budget   181
materiality   20, 70
McCarthy, E Jerome   311
merchandizing businesses   194
MG Rover   123
Microsoft   251
    Xbox 360   304
Miller–Orr model   257–59, *258*
    worked example   259
Mitchell, Ronald, Agle, Bradley and Wood, Donna
        163
mixed measurement model   65
money measurement concept   65
money method   350
monopolistic competition   310
monopoly   309–10
Monte Carlo simulation method   360
Moody's   136
Morrison, Diane   108
Morrisons   310
Mulberry   110
MV Agusta   316

net present value (NPV)   342, 342–43
net profit margin   117–19
neutrality   69
Next   333
Nintendo   304
Nokia   397
non-current assets   54
non-current liabilities   54
Northern Rock   137
not-for-profits   193, 230–34, *231*
    3Es   232
    example balance scorecard   *233–34*

oligopoly 310
one-off pricing 319
operating cash flow 248
operating lease 279
operating profit 52
operational budget 181
operational decision making 373–408
   comprehension questions 401
      answers 403–05
   cost-volume-profit analysis 375–88
      advertising 386
      break-even point (BEP) 378, *379*
      change in production systems 384–86
      change in selling price 383–84
      equation 379–80
      fixed costs 376–77, *377*
      margin of safety 381–83, *382*
      revenue 375–76, *376*
      total costs 378, *379*
      variable costs 377–78, *378*
      worked examples 380–81, 382, 383–84,
         385–86
   exercises 401–03
      answers 405–08
   relevant costing *388*, 388–400
      opportunity costs 394–95
      outsourcing 390–93
      qualitative factors 395–96
      shutting down business segments 396–99
      sunk cost 389
      worked examples 391–93, 394–95,398–99
   steps in *374*, 374–75
operational performance management 210
opportunity cost 251, 270, 347–48, 394–95
optional pricing 316
outsourcing 390–93
overhead absorption rate (OAR) 297
overtrading 251, 252
Oxford Instruments plc 68

Pacioli, Luca 12
Page, Larry 109
Pareto Principle 276
Parsa, Ali 183
partnership 24
payback period (PP) 332–35
penetration pricing 318–19
perfect competition 309
performance management 209–46
   balanced scorecard 227–30, *228*
   behavioural risks of 235
   comprehension questions 239
      answers 242–43
   controllability principle 212
   exercises 239–41
      answers 244–46

just-in-time (JIT) 237, 238
life-cycle costing 237
   3Es 232
not-for-profits 230–34, *231*
   example balance scorecard *233–34*
operational performance management 210
performance indicators
   capital turnover 224
   economic value added (EVA) 225, 226
   non-financial 226–27
   residual income (RI) 225
   return on investment (ROI) 224, 226
performance reporting 216
PEST analysis *236*, 236–37
public sector businesses 232
responsibility centres
   cost centres 211
   investment centre 212
   profit centre 212
   revenue centre 211
standard costing 216–18
strategic performance management 210
target costing 237
throughput accounting 237
total quality management (TQM) 237, 238
variance analysis 218–23, *219*
   fixed overhead variance 222–23
   labour variance 222
   materials variance 221–22
   rate variance 218
   sales variance 221
   variable overhead variance 223
   volume variance 218
   worked examples 213–15, 220, 225–26
PEST analysis *236*, 236–37
Peters, Tom 390
Pitt, Brad 316
Porter, Michael 237
predatory pricing 318
premium pricing 316
price elasticity of demand (PED) 304–08, *306*
   factors determining 306–08
price to earnings ratio (P/E ratio) 142–43
PricewaterhouseCoopers 13, 125
pricing 292–326
   3Cs 293, *293*
   absorption costing 294–99
   activity-based costing (ABC) and
      pricing 300–02
   bundle pricing 318
   competitive pricing 317
   comprehension questions 322
      answers 324–25
   consumer behaviour and perceptions 311–14
      ethics 313
      marketing mix, the 311

perception of value, quality and difference
    313
  product positioning   312
cost centre   295
cost pools   300
exercises   322–23
  answers   325–26
full-cost-plus pricing   294–99
Kaizen   321
life-cycle costing and pricing   302–04, *303*
marginal-cost-plus pricing   299
market skimming pricing   315–16
market types   308–10
  monopolistic competition   310
  monopoly   309–10
  oligopoly   310
  perfect competition   309
mark-up vs margin   298
new vs existing market   314
new vs existing product   314
one-off pricing   319
optional pricing   316
overhead absorption rate (OAR)   297
penetration pricing   318–19
premium pricing   316
price elasticity of demand (PED)   304–08, *306*
  factors determining   306–08
stratified pricing   317
target pricing and costing   320, *320*
value engineering   321
value pricing   318
volume- vs price-driven strategy   315
worked examples   294–97, 299, 301–02, 319
probability analysis   359–60
product positioning   312
production businesses   192
profit centre   212
profitability ratios   108–21
  gross profit margin   116–17
  net profit margin   117–19
  return on capital employed (ROCE)   111–14
property, plant and equipment
  alternative depreciation methods   77
  non-current assets, disposal of   76–77
  recognition and subsequent measurement   76
  worked example   77–79, *78, 79*
prudence   68–69
psychological pricing   313
public sector businesses   193
Pyhrr, Peter   199

ratio analysis
  efficiency ratios   124–32
    inventories holding period   127–28
    trade payables payment period   130–31
    trade receivables collection period   126–27
  introduction to   97, 107–08

investor ratios   140–44
  dividend yield   140
  earnings per share (EPS)   141–42
  price to earnings ratio (P/E ratio)   142–43
liquidity ratios   121–24
  acid test ratio   123
  current ratio   122
profitability ratios   108–21
  gross profit margin   116–17
  net profit margin   117–19
  return on capital employed (ROCE)   111–14
solvency ratios   132–39
  capital gearing ratio   135–36
  dividend cover   138
  interest cover   137–38
weaknesses and limitations   145–46
real method   350
real options   361
regulation   16–17, 20–21, 22
  Conceptual Framework (F)   15–17, 26–27
  IFRS Foundation   *20*, 21
  IFRS Interpretations Committee   21
  International Accounting Standards Board
    (IASB)   21, *22*
  principles   17
Relevance Lost   227
relevant costing   *388*, 388–400
  opportunity costs   394–95
  outsourcing   390–93
  qualitative factors   395–96
  shutting down business segments   396–99
  sunk cost   389
  worked examples   391–93, 394–95, 398–99
residual income (RI)   225
responsibility centres
  cost centres   211
  investment centre   212
  profit centre   212
  revenue centre   211
return on capital employed (ROCE)   111–14
return on investment (ROI)   224, 226
revenue centre   211
Rio Tinto   116
rolling budgets   198–99
Ryanair   101, 112
  Chairman's report   120–21
  efficiency   *131–32*
    inventories holding period   128
    trade payables payment period   130–31
    trade receivables collection period   127
  horizontal analysis and trend analysis   *102–03*,
    107
  investment   *143–44*
    dividend yield   140
    earnings per share (EPS)   142
    price to earnings ratio (P/E ratio)   143

liquidity *123–24*
  acid test ratio 123
  current ratio 122
profitability *119*
  gross profit margin 117
  net profit margin 118
solvency *138–39*
  capital gearing ratio 136
  dividend cover 138
  interest cover 138
vertical analysis *105, 106,* 107

Sainsbury 310
Samsung 218, 317
scenario analysis 359
Schulz, Don, Tannenbaum, Stanley and Lauterbon, Robert 311
Schumacher, Michael 316
sensitivity analysis 359
service businesses 192–93
Shimizu, Koichi 311
Skype 251
sole trader 23–24
solvency ratios 132–39
  capital gearing ratio 135–36
  dividend cover 138
  interest cover 137–38
Sony 304
South African Institute of Chartered Accountants (SAICA) 12
Spanair 121
stakeholder management 162–65, *163*
  dangerous stakeholder *164*
  definitive stakeholder *165*
  demanding stakeholder *164*
  dependent stakeholder *164*
  discretionary stakeholder *164*
  dominant stakeholder *164*
  dormant stakeholder *164*
standard costing 216–18
Standard Life 333
Starbucks 168–69
statement of cash flows 55–57, 85
  estimates 56
  timing 56
  transactions 56
  working capital 56, 57
statement of comprehensive income 51–53, *53*
  gross profit 52
  operating profit 52
  profit for the year 52
statement of financial position (balance sheet) 54–55

current assets 54
current liabilities 54
non-current assets 54
non-current liabilities 54
Statoil 197
Stern Steward & Co 225
strategic performance management 210
stratified pricing 317
Summa de arithmetica, geometria, proportioni et proportionalita 12
sunk cost 389
Sutherland, Euan 137

TagHeuer 393
target pricing and costing 237, 320, *320*
taxation 349
Tesco plc 29, *30–36*, 51, 310
Texas Instruments 199
throughput accounting 237
Tootell, Barry 137
total quality management (TQM) 237, 238
Toyota 238, 277
trade payables payment period 130–31
trade receivables collection period 126–27
trend analysis 101–04, *102–03*
Twitter 170

UK Competition Commission (UKCC) 13–14
Underwood, Toby 125

value chain analysis 361
value engineering 321
value pricing 318
variance analysis 218–23, *219*
  fixed overhead variance 222–23
  labour variance 222
  materials variance 221–22
  rate variance 218
  sales variance 221
  variable overhead variance 223
  volume variance 218
vertical analysis 104–07, *105, 106*
Vodafone 169

Waterman, Robert 390
weighted average cost of capital (WACC) 346
Wet 'N' Wild 125
Whitbread plc 67
working capital 56, 57

Yammer 251
YouTube 170
zero-based budgets 199–200

CPSIA information can be obtained at www.ICGtesting.com
Printed in the USA
BVOW09s2315180714

359755BV00003B/5/P

9 780749 469139